£39.50

NAPOLEON AND THE
WORLD WAR OF 1813

NAPOLEON AND THE WORLD WAR OF 1813

Lessons in Coalition Warfighting

J. P. RILEY

FRANK CASS
LONDON • PORTLAND, OR

First published in 2000 in Great Britain by
FRANK CASS PUBLISHERS
Newbury House, 900 Eastern Avenue,
London IG2 7HH, England

and in the United States of America by
FRANK CASS PUBLISHERS
c/o ISBS, 5824 N.E. Hassalo Street,
Portland, Oregon 97213–3644

Website www.frankcass.com

British Library Cataloguing in Publication Data

Riley, J. P.
  Napoleon and the World War of 1813 : lessons in coalition
  warfighting
  1. Napoleon, I, Emperor of the French, 1769–1821
  2. Napoleonic Wars, 1800–1815 – Campaigns 3. Combined
  Operations (Military science) 4. Strategy 5. Tactics
  I. Title
  940.2'7

ISBN 0 7146 4893 0 (cloth)

Library of Congress Cataloging-in-Publication Data

Riley, Jonathon, 1955–
  Napoleon and the World War of 1813 : lessons in coalition
  warfighting / J.P. Riley.
      p.   cm.
  Includes bibliographical references and index.
  ISBN 0-7146-4893-0. – ISBN 0-7146-4444-7 (pbk)
  1. Napoleon I, Emperor of the French, 1769–1821– Military
  Leadership. 2. Napoleonic Wars, 1800–1815–Diplomatic history.
  3. Wars of Liberation, 1813–1814. 4. France–Foreign
  relations–1792–1815. 5. France –Colonies–North America.
  I. Title.
  DC236.R55 1999
  940.2'7–dc21   99–16266
                                                      CIP

Typeset by The Midlands Book Typesetting Company, Leicestershire
Printed in Great Britain by MPG Books Ltd, Bodmin, Cornwall

Contents

༄༅༅༅

PART THREE: SPAIN AND THE MEDITERRANEAN

PART FOUR: AMERICA

CONCLUSION

Illustrations

❦

Maps and Figures

PART TWO: CENTRAL EUROPE

PART THREE: SPAIN AND THE MEDITERRANEAN

PART FOUR: AMERICA

Foreword

❧❦❧

A CCORDING TO EUCLID (fl. 300 BC) ' . . . the whole is greater than the sum of its parts'. The dramatic events of 1813 were certainly complex, and several notable British and American military historians have been publishing useful materials on this period from 1993 to the present. Now we have J.P. Riley's fascinating and novel work on the whole of 1813.

Brigadier Riley's approach has, in many ways, 'cut the Gordian knot' of this difficult period by broadening the military and political events. The vast Napoleonic struggle of Central Europe is certainly well covered here, but the author has interestingly also considered the important Peninsular War of 1813 and the events – small but significant – in the United States and Canada. As a result we are therefore given accounts not only of the Battle of Leipzig, but also Vitoria and the significant but small Sackett's Harbor and Crysler's Farm engagements – and many others. Riley has indeed covered 'a Worldwide conflict', and historians, soldiers and serious readers will certainly be interested in his broad landscape.

The modern British soldier has many responsibilities and difficult challenges, both at home and abroad – and Jonathon Riley is certainly no exception. Joining Sandhurst in 1973, he was commissioned into The Queen's Regiment. After being appointed Brigade Major of the 6th Armoured Brigade in 1990, following training at the Staff College and command of a company on operations in Northern Ireland, he transferred in 1991 into The Royal Welch Fusiliers (RWF) where he was soon promoted to Lieutenant-Colonel. As his career successfully developed, he was posted for two tours in former Jugoslavia under the command of the United Nations.

There he received his DSO in 1995. No fewer than 21 members of his RWF battalion received gallant and distinguished service awards for serving in Goražde where they defended the enclave from attack by the Serbs. Subsequently he was appointed Chief-of-Staff of the 1st Armoured Division at Herford in Germany. In 1998–99 he commanded 1st Mechanized Brigade in England before returning to Bosnia as Deputy Commander of the NATO Multinational Division (South West).

Since being commissioned, Brigadier Riley has received two university degrees (one in geography, another in history), and has published four interesting books; the third being '*White Dragon*' (1995) – a fascinating description of his battalion seeing active service in Bosnia. *Napoleon and the World War of 1813* is his second major work.

As a personal comment, it is always interesting for me, as a former lecturer at RMA Sandhurst, to learn how my former Officer Cadets have developed in their careers as professional officers. I taught Jonathon Riley as a young man, and we have kept in touch occasionally, and of course I knew of his interests in the Napoleonic Wars *inter alia*. I was therefore delighted when he kindly invited me to visit the British Army of the Rhine in 1991 and to help him and his officers with a battlefield tour of Jena-Auerstädt (1806) – made all the more interesting by the Soviet Army's recent withdrawal from East Germany.

Subsequently Jonathon ran a second excellent battlefield tour of not only Leipzig, a battle which clearly fascinates him, but also Lützen and Bautzen and this interest has developed into this new book. It analyses not only 'the Struggle of Nations' in Germany but also Spain and North America during that year. I strongly recommend his latest enterprise. You will not be disappointed.

David G. Chandler
MA (Oxon), D. Litt, FRHist. S
March 2000

Legend to Maps

Battalion		Pontoon Bridging
Regiment		Gun line or position
Brigade		Redoubt
Division		Main Effort
Corps		Attack or advance
Army		Bridge unit
Group of Armies		Fortified position or entrenchment
Cavalry		
Infantry		Objective
Artillery		General line of deployment
Horse Artillery		Bridge
Engineers		Line of attack

PART ONE

COALITION AND WORLD WAR

Chapter I

Introduction

❧❧❧

I T IS AN undoubted fact that, since the Gulf War of 1991, there has been a considerable revival of interest in the mechanics of coalition war. This is probably because, despite the success of NATO over the past 50 years in deterring major war between existing states or alliances in Europe, the campaigns and small wars which have actually been fought outside Europe have been for the most part national affairs: one thinks of Vietnam, the Falklands War, Malaya and so on. The Gulf War reminded the world, after a long period of established alliance relationships, of the differences between established alliances and the essentially short term nature of coalitions. A successful alliance, like NATO, or like those which emerged in Europe during the nineteenth century, is often formed in peacetime against a readily identifiable, strategic threat, in order to provide long-term collective security for its members. Because of their long-term nature, alliances tend to produce political and military structures for consultation, liaison, command and control which over time become as well established as those of single nations. Military contributions tend to reflect the economic power of alliance members, but the mutual trust and co-operation which develops over time tends to overcome any tensions that differences in burden-sharing bring.

Coalitions, by contrast, are short-term, born for the moment: the individual members may be very diverse in political structure, economic power and culture, but are brought together in the face of a single unifying threat or common goal. Military contributions are inevitably based on more short-term considerations, and the resulting structures for consultation and decision-making are inevitably *ad hoc*. This is not to say that they do not work: the examples of Korea, and the Gulf, just as of the coalitions of 1813, prove that the achievement of a common purpose can be a powerful spur indeed.

It is always dangerous to try to draw direct parallels between the past and the present, and there are very great differences between the coalitions of 1813 and the great peace-time alliance of NATO, or indeed the Gulf War coalition. Even so, when reflecting on the tensions within NATO which the Balkan Wars of 1991–95 brought, for example, one can at least see that others have managed to deal with far greater stresses and strains, and yet remained effective partners. It is also apposite that the success of the 1991 Gulf coalition has since been further underscored by world-wide reductions in military power following the end of the Cold War, which have led most western European nations to the conclusion that if they are going to fight and win in the future, it will have to be in coalition. Even the mighty USA has come to this conclusion, if for a different reason – that of international legitimacy.

It seems therefore that the time is ripe for an examination of coalition war as an historical phenomenon: what conditions bring coalitions together, and what tend to pull them apart? What are the peculiar difficulties – both political and military – which distinguish it from the wars of nations or established alliances? Such an examination would be a dry beast indeed if taken in the abstract, and so the subject will be examined through an example. There are very many of these – since coalition war is in many ways the normal state of affairs and the conditions of the last 50 years an aberration – but the events of one year, the momentous Napoleonic year of 1813, are as good an example as can be found.

The grand alliance of 1813 in central Europe is particularly interesting because it is a prototype of all modern coalitions, with all their troubles. Indeed when one reviews the command relationships, and the fundamental disagreements of its members in terms of political ambition, it is hard to believe that it survived its first encounter with the enemy. It did so because of the existence of a threat greater than all considerations of mutual mistrust, a subject which will be explored more fully later.

The year 1813 holds an additional attraction because, long before 1914–18, it is also an example of *world* war. Simultaneous campaigns were under way in central Europe, Italy, Spain, and North America – where two campaigns were waged. The campaigns of Central Europe, Spain and North America are of especial significance since not only were they simultaneous, but also they were inter-related at the strategic level of war. In Europe, the 6th Coalition was formed in the aftermath of Napoleon's Russian disaster and it was this coalition which, by forcing

Napoleon to fight a war on two fronts, expelled French power from Germany, Italy and Spain. In doing so, it laid the foundations for the great power relationships in Europe which endured until 1878. The American war was a result of, and an influence on, the war in Europe: it arose from Napoleon's Continental System, it was connected to events in Spain through the Louisiana Purchase and trading interests, and it influenced British power both directly and indirectly.

Furthermore, 1813 is also illuminating in coalition war at the operational level. In each of the main theatres of war a different form of coalition was assembled. In Spain it was a British, Spanish, Hanoverian and Portuguese affair under British command. In central Europe it was a Russian, Prussian, Austrian and Swedish alliance, financed by Britain, and gradually joined by most of the smaller German states. In North America it was a combination of British, Canadian – including by a supreme irony French Canadian – and native American (Indian) interests. The political and diplomatic subtleties of the operational level therefore add to the picture of coalition war at the strategic level and this can be brought to life by an examination of war fighting, as an extension of the allied war aims, at the tactical level.

But Napoleon too was a coalition commander, a fact which is often forgotten and which is rarely addressed in any depth. It was Napoleon after all who created the Confederation of the Rhine, the Grand Duchy of Warsaw and the Kingdoms of Italy and Naples. In 1813 his armies contained formations of Poles, Danes, Saxons, Spaniards, Bavarians, Italians; a host of contingents from other smaller German states; and individuals from practically every nation in western Europe.

The difference between the Napoleonic model and the 6th Coalition was an important one: Napoleon retained sole command of his coalition, called no councils of war, consulted no allies and in doing so, exercised a power similar to that of the USSR in the Warsaw Pact, something which we today, in much watered-down form, would recognise as lead nation status. The 6th Coalition, by contrast, had to arrive at a common policy by the difficult processes of compromise, subordinating the separate interests of its members to the overriding common purpose of defeating Napoleon.

An additional reason for choosing 1813 is that it is a furrow which has not been much ploughed in this particular way. Most studies of the later Napoleonic period focus on the 1812 campaign in Russia or on 1815, neglecting the vital link which was made possible by the Russian disaster and which ended – a year to the day after Napoleon's departure

from Moscow – in his defeat at Leipzig by the assembled nations of
Europe. This defeat led directly to the allied invasion of France both
from east of the Rhine and from over the Pyrenees. Across the Atlantic,
after the British-Canadian-native American alliance spent 18 months
on the defensive, late 1813 saw the first real prospect of an end to the
war, following the frustration of the American invasion prospects and
the allied attack on Buffalo. It also showed that Napoleon was right,
that solidarity, or unity, is probably the centre of gravity in coalition
warfare, and military defeat can shatter that essential unity.

The book is structured in five parts. Part One is a general discourse
on coalition war, related directly to the situation of world war in 1813.
This addresses not only the formation and conduct of coalitions as
political expedients, but also the qualities required for coalition
command, and the particular difficulties faced by coalition commanders
at the operational level. The formation of the different coalitions
underpinned by British finance, as well as the Napoleonic coalition, are
traced and related as much to economic and political factors as to
military events. This part of the book is the cornerstone: the essential
glue which binds together the rest of the book. Parts Two, Three and
Four are campaign studies. These pick up and illustrate the strategic
concept outlined in Part One, at the operational level, through an
examination of each theatre of war, and also outlines the links between
each of the theatres.

Part Two considers Central Europe, excluding the peripheral Danish
theatre, for it was in Germany that 1813 brought the decisive act in
Napoleon's life-or-death struggle against the allies. It begins by
considering the rearmament of Europe and then traces the offensive
French campaign in the spring. The summer saw the transformation of
Austria from neutral to belligerent, a transformation brought about by
Napoleon's refusal to compromise. The accession of Austria to the allies
led into the autumn campaign, which began with Napoleon on the
defensive at Dresden; continued through the defeat of his lieutenants
at Dennewitz, Kulm and the Katzbach; and ended with the culmination
of the German War of Liberation, the great Battle of the Nations at
Leipzig, the greatest battle in Europe before 1914.

Linked directly to events in central Europe was the war in the Iberian
Peninsula and to a lesser extent in Italy, although this is only alluded to
in passing here because major operations occurred only in 1814. The
weakening of the French garrison there in order to shore up the position in central Europe, along with the growth of allied power, created

the conditions for an allied offensive. This offensive, after the decisive Battle of Vitoria, led directly to French expulsion from Spain and the allied invasion of France coinciding with that from Germany. Once Iberia was free from French domination, this invasion provided an example of the tendency of coalitions to pull apart once success is achieved, and the consciousness of separate interests overshadowing the mood of common purpose – in this case between Britain, Spain and Portugal.

The Canadian War of 1812 demonstrated links with French, Spanish and British policy as well as complex coalition aspects involving French Canadians and native Americans. In Upper Canada 1813 proved a mixed year for the allies. The Americans regained control of Lake Erie, allowing the American General Harrison to recapture Fort Detroit before defeating the allies at the Battle of Moraviantown (also called the Battle of the Thames). In the Niagara peninsula, between Lakes Erie and Ontario, however, the US invasion was thrown back, and the allies followed up their success by sacking and burning the town of Buffalo in New York State. This area of operations was significant for the demonstration of close naval and military co-operation shown by the Americans and for the collapse of Britain's allies, the Indian confederacy, after the death of Chief Tecumseh at Moraviantown. The US victory at Moraviantown could have negated the repulse on the Niagara, but the chance was thrown away when Congress ordered the abandonment of this area of operations in order to concentrate on Montreal.

In Lower Canada, a two-pronged American attack was planned into Canada, aimed at the capture of Montreal. Here too, operations began well for the Americans with successful amphibious operations leading to the sack of York, the capture of Fort George, and the repulse of the allied attack on Sackett's harbour. But the invasion was thwarted at Chateaugây and Crysler's Farm. Thus by the end of the year, the operational situation was transformed and as a by-product, the belligerents had begun the negotiations from which came the eventual Peace of Ghent on Christmas Eve 1814.

After Part Four, the whole work is brought together once more by the Conclusion which aims not only to draw the lessons of this specific time, but also to relate them as far as one safely can to the general business of coalition warfare.

Chapter II

A New Order – The 6th Coalition in Europe

∾༄☙

If two more states combine against each other, the result is still politically speaking a single war. But this political unity is a matter of degree.[1]

Clausewitz

I N DECEMBER 1812 it was clear that Napoleon had suffered a shattering defeat in Russia, but it was by no means clear either that this defeat would prove decisive, or that a new European coalition was about to be formed. Napoleon's military potential was still huge: he controlled most of Germany, including the Confederation of the Rhine and parts of Prussia; Poland; Italy, Illyria and Naples; the Low Countries and Denmark; Switzerland; and half of Spain. He was nominally allied with Prussia and Austria, his arch-enemies the British were now at war in America as well as Spain, and he controlled the mountain barriers of the Pyrenees and the Alps as well as the fortresses on most of Europe's major river lines. This great span of command certainly gave him the ability to raise new armies to replace the horrific losses of 1812 while his enemies were still far from united. Over the coming year it must have seemed as if the 6th Coalition came into being, if not by chance, at least by a gradual process of accumulation which was accelerated by public opinion and military events.

Who then were the enemies who could thwart Napoleon's ambitions? First of course was Britain, his implacable opponent, whose armies had fought in alliance with those of Portugal, Spain, Sicily and Hanover, waging constant war against his southern flank in the Mediterranean. But to Napoleon, although the allies had been successful at times, how did even the Battle of Salamanca compare to the enormity of the struggles on the Moskova or the Berezina? To both the French emperor and the Tsar, the 'Spanish Ulcer', even in December 1812, was still only an irritation. In the central European theatre, Napoleon's main – indeed only – opponent was Russia, but the Russian armies had suffered almost as severely as had the French during the terrible winter campaign. The Russian troops were exhausted, supplies were low, and the generals were unwilling to push on into the west. The British government had as incomplete a picture of Russian intentions at this point as did the French.[2] Time was needed to change all this and any delay would, in the short term at least, work to Napoleon's advantage.

Since April 1812, the Tsar Alexander I had had an agreement of mutual assistance with the Regent of Sweden, the former Napoleonic Marshal Bernadotte. This had followed Napoleon's refusal in February 1811 to back the proposed Swedish conquest of Norway from his ally Denmark, and had been considerably hastened by his insistence that Sweden should enforce the Continental System. The Swedes had more to lose than to gain by doing so and Bernadotte's reluctance to press matters against Britain led to the French occupation of Swedish Pomerania in January 1812, thus giving the Tsar his first ally. As early as January 1813, Lord Castlereagh, the British Foreign Secretary, had re-stated the principle which would guide the actions of his government:

> Whatever scheme of policy can most immediately combine the greatest number of powers and the greatest military force against France, so as to produce the utmost effect against her, before she can recruit her armies and recover her ascendancy, is what we must desire to promote.[3]

In March 1813, Britain took the first step in this long process of uniting all Europe against Napoleon, endorsing the Swedish-Russian pact through the Treaty of Stockholm. This treaty brought Sweden a considerable British subsidy, promises of territory in Norway and the West Indies at the expense of Napoleon and his client, Denmark, and an British garrison of six infantry battalions for the port city of Stralsund in Swedish Pomerania. Such a garrison had originally been put in place in 1807 when a force of 8,000 King's German Legion troops under Lord Cathcart had been dispatched as the advanced guard of a corps of 34,000 which was to link up with Swedish and Prussian troops and advance against the French. This scheme had come to nothing as a result of Napoleon's victory at Friedland on 14 June 1807, after which the troops had been withdrawn.[4]

In April 1813 Prussia too acceded to the Treaty of Stockholm, allying

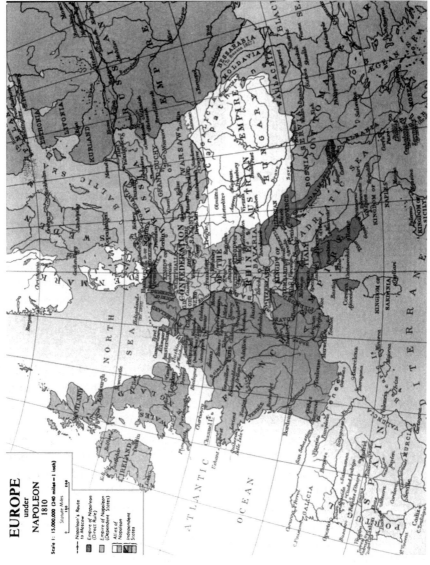

Napoleon's Empire before
his defeat in Russia.
France extended to the
Rhine, included the Low
Countries as well as much
of North Germany and
North Italy. Only Britain,
Portugal, Sardinia and
Sicily were his foes. Only
Sweden and the Ottoman
Empire outside of Russia
were not dependent on
him. [Muir's Historical
Atlas]

EUROPE
under
NAPOLEON
1810

Scale 1: 15,000,000 (240 miles = 1 inch)

Statute Miles

0   120   250

- - - - Napoleon's Route
         to Moscow

Empire of Napoleon
(Direct Rule)

Empire of Napoleon
(Dependent States)

Allies of
Napoleon

Independent
States

herself with Sweden, and in May 1813, Bernadotte's army landed at Stralsund. Although the army did not become fully engaged until after the Trachenberg-Reichenbach plan,[5] preferring to operate against the Danes, its presence considerably extended the potential of the allied military effort.

Britain had already further enhanced this military power by mediating in the Russo-Turkish War, achieving the Treaty of Bucharest on 28 May 1812.[6] The end of this war allowed troops to be released from Russia's southern front to confront Napoleon's invasion in the north.

But there was in early 1813 no indication that Austria meant to abandon the French alliance, nor did Prussia present as yet any semblance of threat: the movement which would soon burst out into the *Befreiungskrieg* (War of Liberation) was still buried. Thus the possibility that in 12 months' time, the armies of Austria, Prussia and Russia would cross the Rhine; while those of Britain, Portugal and Spain would march into Bordeaux, must have seemed unworthy of even the most casual speculation. The spark which ignited the collective will to fight against Napoleon was lit on 30 December 1812 by the Convention of Tauroggen between a Prussian army corps and the Russians.[7] It was this that would make two wars, one Franco-Russian and the other in the Peninsula, into a European, coalition war.

In the Russian camp it was Count Nesselrode who was the driving force behind the idea of coalition. At Alexander's headquarters during the winter of 1812/13, he had pushed forward the view that Russia alone would never force a settlement with France on any other basis but the status quo. Such a settlement would not provide stability, for it would leave Napoleon's power base intact. Thus the end of any war must be to restrict Napoleon to at least the so-called 'natural frontiers,' and the means to that end must be a coalition. The Convention of Tauroggen had therefore to be translated into a treaty which would be the basis of that coalition. As things fell out, not only would this coalition destroy Napoleon's empire, it would also be the basis of a general Russian-Prussian alignment which would last until 1878.

At first though, it seemed that the convention would lead into a blind alley, for King Frederick William III of Prussia would not accede to any alliance with Russia – at least while French troops remained on Prussian territory. But Tsar Alexander, who by the end of January 1813 had determined to press on into Europe, knew well that Frederick William was already ensnared by the convention, and in any case could not long resist the pressures which were growing in Prussia to throw off the

French alliance. Alexander dispatched Baron Stein, who was able to terrify Frederick William in a few hours into agreeing terms with Russia: on 28 February 1813, Prussia and Russia were formally allied by a treaty signed at Kalisch[8] on the Polish frontier.

It was followed three weeks later by Frederick William's proclamation *An Mein Volk* ('To My People') on 17 March 1813, and thus began what is still known in Germany as *Befreiungskrieg*, the War of Liberation, although with the Confederation of the Rhine still bound to Napoleon, it was more of a German civil war. Even at this early stage the seeds of future dissent were being sown. United by the common fear of Napoleon, the potential conflict over Poland – and those areas of Polish territory currently owned by Prussia and Austria which the Tsar coveted – remained under the surface. For the time being it seemed enough that Alexander wished to lead a European war of liberation, and Frederick William to free his own country and restore its lost territory.

The French disaster in Russia which filled Alexander with hope, filled Chancellor Count Metternich of Austria with alarm. Metternich was in favour of a European equilibrium that would restore monarchial rule as well as limit territorial ambitions. He was deeply concerned by the dangers unleashed by revolutionary sentiment following Napoleon's restructuring of Italy and Germany, and Stein's talk of resurrecting a united Germany under Prussian leadership was a further threat to Austrian dominance. In addition, Polish national feeling, which Napoleon had awakened, threatened instability in the east. In a multi-ethnic entity like the Habsburg Empire, nationalist sentiment was a truly dangerous thing – it was only natural, therefore, that Metternich should favour a policy of equilibrium.

This policy seemed in danger in late 1812, for to Metternich there was a sense of danger in the possibility of Napoleon and Alexander making a separate peace on terms favourable to Russia, ignoring Austria which was still in alliance with France. Metternich responded with characteristic skill. He sent General Count von Bubna to Napoleon, warning the Emperor not to take the Austrian alliance for granted, nor to assume that rivalry between Prussia and Austria was irreversible. At the same time he sent Count Stadion to the Tsar, warning him that Napoleon was still dangerous and likely to raise a new army. His third emissary was Baron Wessenberg, who was sent to London to suggest that a continental peace was now possible – a suggestion which was firmly rebuffed by a British government with no interest in making any peace with Napoleon which did not address maritime rights, the independence of the Low Countries, and the British pledges to Sweden, Sicily, Portugal and Spain. Lord Liverpool, the British Prime Minister, wrote in disgust that 'Nothing could be more abject than the Councils of Vienna at this time.'[9] So that Wessenberg, branded as the agent of submission, withdrew having made no entry into Whitehall's confidences.

No further real progress towards extending allied unity was made until the Armistice of Pleiswitz in June. Napoleon's victories at Lützen and Bautzen certainly provided the stimulus of fear, and at this point London again took a hand. After Wessenberg's embassy, Lord Liverpool was well aware of the dangers of a continental peace based on a compromise between Napoleon and the Tsar, and later between Napoleon and the allies through the mediation of Austria. Two British liaison officers, General Lord Cathcart and Major-General Sir Charles Stewart (Castlereagh's half-brother), had been attached to the Prussian and Russian headquarters, and these two made it very plain to the allies that Britain would never agree to any peace which disregarded her interests: financial subsidies, therefore, would only continue so long as Britain was in full knowledge of the allied councils, a position strengthened immeasurably by the news of the Battle of Vitoria, which came in while the Congress of Prague was in session. British accession to the coalition was never, therefore, in any doubt and even before any formal treaty was agreed, she acted in concert with Russia, Sweden and Prussia.

But there were at this stage of the war still four distinct allied policies which had to be reconciled before the coalition of 1813 could complete its work, leaving aside the particular policies of London in the Americas. These were those of Britain, Spain, Portugal and Sicily; those of Britain, Sweden and Russia; those of Russia and Prussia; and finally those of Austria, who had yet to be fully transformed from mediator to ally.[10] While the Congress of Prague was still in progress, the British ambassadors signed treaties with Prussia on 14 June and with Russia on 15 June, and agreed subsidies of £1,500,000 in return for a promise that no separate peace would be made with Napoleon. This was a powerful lever in obliging Austria to accede to the Treaty of Reichenbach 12 days later. The treaty was only to come into effect if Napoleon refused Austrian mediation but one must conclude that once Britain had compelled all the allies to fight for her war aims as well as their own, Napoleon was bound to refuse the mediation and thus force Austria into Britain's arms. The treaties signed at Reichenbach were, therefore, a masterpiece of diplomatic skill, and were moreover the first real step towards Castlereagh's aim of uniting all the allies in one unbreakable block.

The British diplomacy was all the more remarkable since Metternich's view of the desirability of European equilibrium had been, if anything, reinforced by Napoleon's spring victories at Lützen and Bautzen. It was this view which had first led him to conclude the Treaty of Reichenbach on 27 June 1813, and thereafter to press on with a policy of mediation between Napoleon and the allies. But mediation was also driven by Austria's military unpreparedness: not until May 1813 was it possible to begin the formation of the Army of Bohemia, so that Napoleon's rejection of mediation coincided with the Austrian military revival and with the changed situation in Spain which Wellington's victory at Vitoria had brought. And while British diplomacy worked to bring the allies together, Napoleon, apart from trying to inflict military defeat, made no serious effort to keep Russia, Prussia and Austria apart. So at last, on 12 August 1813, the central European alliance was confirmed at Teplitz and on 9 October, Austria and Britain were at last formally and diplomatically united in the same purpose.

At this stage, something of London's grand design emerges. Britain had, throughout the development of the central European alliance, continued to follow the precepts which had been laid down by Pitt: that any expansion of Russia should be balanced by the strengthening of Austria and Prussia; that Prussian influence should be extended in northern and western Germany; that Austrian interests should be diverted away from competition with Prussia by extending her interests in Italy and Illyria; and that the colonial territories which Britain had conquered should be used as bargaining chips to achieve the balance of power described by the first three precepts.

To implement this policy, Pitt's successor, Lord Liverpool, used chiefly the weapon which Napoleon sought to destroy through his Continental System: finance. Britain had, by means of its commercial wealth, been the paymaster of coalition war in Europe since 1793. In 1813, it again embarked on a programme of subsidies in money and equipment amounting to £10,400,000; thus the vast financial resources of the British Empire underpinned the allied will to continue the struggle which reached its climax at Leipzig. The power of subsidy cannot be understated. Without it the allies, even Austria, had almost no chance of continuing the war. These subsidies amounted to £700,000 to Austria; £666,000 to Prussia; £2,486,000 to Portugal; £1,000,000 to Russia including £500,000 worth of arms; £877,000 to Spain; £440,000 to Sicily; and £1,335,000 to Sweden.[11] Therefore 'It was to

Tsar Alexander I of
Russia (1777–1825:
reigned from 1801)

[Orig. painting in
Apsley House, London]

Emperor Francis I of Austria
(1768–1835: reigned from 1792)
in old age.

[Orig. painting in Apsley House,
London]

King Frederick William III of Prussia (1770–1840: reigned from 1797).
[Orig. painting in Apsley House, London]

Crown Prince John of Sweden formerly Marshal Bernadotte (1763–1844: reigned from 1810)

the banker of Europe, rather than to an equal fellow combatant, that Metternich might be forced to pay attention.'[12]

Lord Liverpool's foreign minister, Castlereagh, also knew well that Metternich, even in his role of mediator, preferred the discipline of the Napoleonic order to 'the liberalism of the British, the sentimental intrusions of Alexander, or the rabid German nationalism of the *Tugenbund* (the League of Virtue) and Stein.'[13] So his message to the allies *via* his liaison officers had been a very distinct warning on the dangers to the allies of excluding Britain. This message had to be, if anything, intensified as 1813 continued and the allies won at Leipzig. Only by sticking firmly to Pitt's principles could Castlereagh hope to remain in the centre of the allied councils, especially bearing in mind the enormous colonial empire captured from Napoleon and his clients, as well as the power conferred by subsidies.

From the French perspective, the campaigns of 1813 in central Europe and Spain were essentially defensive, fought to defend the barrier of territory which the Committee of Public Safety and then Napoleon had conquered. This barrier, built up to ensure the security of France herself within the natural frontiers had pushed French power ever onwards – until it encompassed the Oder, the Vistula, Warsaw, Moscow and Madrid. Thus Napoleon existed only through success and greater success, and war was the means to obtain a favourable peace – that is, one which forced the major powers of Europe to recognise the empire. His armies were the therefore the instruments of his diplomacy; Napoleon made few mistakes in this diplomacy before 1812, after 1812 he had very few successes. Through both success and failure, Britain remained the implacable foe against whom both arms and diplomacy failed.

In spite of the agency of Britain, the allies were still not agreed on a unified strategy until early 1814, even though unified plans had been formed. This was due to a difference of opinion as to the final objective of the coalition. No-one was certain whether the desired end-state was the total destruction of Napoleon and all his works; or whether the Emperor of the French would be allowed, under a strict system of controls, to retain his throne. The eventual decision to restore the Bourbons signalled an acceptance of the former, but the need to make the Bourbons generally acceptable left the allies in the difficult position of being unable to insist on the sort of humiliating surrender terms that Napoleon invited by his regular rejection of terms.[14]

Throughout the year, as the coalition had grown, the objective of the British government became one of co-ordinating the various separate treaties which existed between the different coalition partners, into a single partnership.[15] The first step had been the dispatch of liaison officers, and the achievement at Reichenbach; the second the dispatch of Lord Aberdeen as an emissary to win the full trust of Austria. Aberdeen had quickly succeeded in obtaining a treaty by which Austria agreed not to make a separate peace with Napoleon in return for a subsidy of £1,000,000. But for the rest of the year he had made no progress towards a more generally binding treaty.

Thus in the aftermath of Leipzig, when peace without British involvement seemed distinctly possible, an emissary of greater political weight was urgently required: it was for this that Castlereagh himself armed at allied headquarters on 28 December 1813. Clausewitz, an active participant in the campaign of 1813, wrote the key chapters of *On War* as a result of his experiences in 1812 and 1813. He might have had this very example in mind when he later wrote his famous, but much misquoted lines, that

> We maintain . . . that war is simply a continuation of political intercourse, with the addition of other means. We . . . want to make it clear that war in itself does not suspend political intercourse or change it into something entirely different. In essentials that intercourse continues, irrespective of the means it employs.[16]

NOTES

1. Clausewitz, p. 596.
2. Muir, p. 243.
3. Castlereagh to Cathcart, cited in Muir, p. 244.
4. Muir, pp. 22, 24.
5. See Chapter IV.
6. Muir, p. 164.
7. See Part Two.
8. Chandler, pp. 872–3; Lefebvre, pp. 326–7 and 331–3.
9. Nicolson, p. 40; Muir, p. 251.
10. Muir, pp. 247–50. For a more detailed examination see Part Two.
11. Emsley, p. 136.
12. Nicolson, p. 57.
13. Ibid. p. 56.
14. Wellington's difficulties are described in Part Three.
15. See especially Muir, pp. 243–59.
16. Clausewitz, p. 605.

Chapter III

Napoleon as Coalition Commander

What is the world, O soldiers?
It is I:
I, this incessant snow,
This northern sky;
Soldiers, this solitude
Through which we go
Is I.

Walter de la Mare
Napoleon

B ECAUSE OF his supreme position at the centre of French power, Napoleon is seldom regarded as a coalition general, and indeed he faced none of the difficulties with which Wellington, Schwarzenberg or Prevost were so familiar. Napoleon called no councils of war, consulted no peer, had no need to placate any opinion. But it cannot be denied that by 1813, his armies were more and more reliant on manpower supplied by allied or client states, or annexed territories. This situation is a classic illustration of the fact, which is more difficult to determine among the central European allies, that coalitions are rarely a partnership of equals: power tends to lie with the strongest member, which will inevitably determine the effectiveness – politically as well as militarily – of the coalition.

Napoleon's wars began in order to guarantee the frontiers which the Revolution had won: essentially the Rhine, the Alps and the Pyrenees, the so-called natural frontiers of France. It was soon apparent, however, that these frontiers did not in themselves guarantee security and so had to be extended through the creation of buffer states. These in turn had to be defended, especially against the enmity of the British and their coalition-forming activities, and thus was born the system of client

Napoleon in 1813. (painting by Pagrest)
He turned 44 at Dresden on 15 August.
Although health and drive were no
longer at their peak, he still displayed
awesome mental and physical energy.

states and allies. Clearly, neither France nor Britain was capable of defeating the other without the extensive help of allies, except perhaps by a long and ruinous war of attrition.[1]

Quite apart from the considerable territories physically annexed to France, these client states took two forms, first, the satellite kingdoms and second, the allies. The satellite kingdoms had usually begun as liberated territory under the Directory, and were transformed into kingdoms by the imposition of members of Napoleon's own family as crowned heads of Holland, Spain, Westphalia, Italy and Naples and from these, Napoleon both drew military manpower and issued subsidies.

Italy, the most successful of the kingdoms, supplied a total of 142,000 conscripts and 44,000 volunteers over the years[2] and its contribution in 1813 alone was 36,000 conscripts for an army which numbered 90,000 men, of whom 10,000 were in Spain and 28,000 in Central Europe.

Westphalia, the creation of which marked the consolidation of the inner Empire,[3] did even better. In 1813 the Westphalian Army was 27,000 strong and the country also supported 30,000 French troops, making it the largest *per capita* supplier of manpower of all the satellite kingdoms and probably the most effective, as its troops served with distinction in every theatre of operations.

By contrast Naples produced an army of only 11,000, of whom only 2,000 were Neapolitans and the rest Germans, Frenchmen, Corsicans, Italians and even Africans. Spain, the subject of Part Three, was almost completely a lost cause. Although Spanish brigades served in the Army of Spain and in the Baltic, the French army in the Peninsula was never less than 190,000 strong and remarkably homogenous: Spain probably cost France 300,000 casualties and around one billion francs during 1808–13.[4] The Kingdom of Holland will not be considered here, as it was to be annexed to France.

The method by which these vast armies were raised was conscription. This was imposed throughout the Empire and its client states during the entire period of Napoleonic rule. No other policy intruded the Napoleonic state so forcefully into the lives of the people or the fabric of states, and no other engendered so much hatred. Without doubt a central issue of the Napoleonic Empire,[5] it was a continuous administrative problem for the heads of *départements* and *maires* to enforce it. Conscription was however the price of territorial gain for the

La Fête des Innocents: A satirical French cartoon jibes at the wasted lives of young men resulting from Napoleon's ceaseless annual treadmill of conscription.

client states, and a spur to reform since without effective administrative structures and policing, the demands of the armies could not be satisfied, and some form of independence thereby guaranteed.

After the satellite kingdoms came the allies, of which the most numerous and military significant were in Germany. But there were others: Switzerland is worthy of mention since the act of mediation following the end of the French occupation of the Helvetic Republic in 1803 made it more a satellite than an ally. The act guaranteed Swiss integrity, in return for a contribution of 16,000 Swiss recruited directly into the French Army.[6] After the Battle of Leipzig, the Swiss declared themselves neutral, but did not withdraw their nationals from the French armies.[7]

Sweden, although its estates elected Bernadotte to the dignity of crown prince, never became a satellite kingdom. Its determined independence and its disregard of the Continental System following Napoleon's refusal to back Swedish claims on Norway led inevitably to the French occupation of Swedish Pomerania in January 1812. This in turn brought Sweden into Russia's arms in return for the promise of eventual Russian assistance with the conquest of Norway. The Danes, the then owners of Norway, were in alliance with Napoleon having been pressured into the Continental System by the Treaty of Tilsit, and driven more firmly into Napoleon's arms by the British seizure of the Danish fleet in 1807, which made the maintenance of control over Norway almost impossible in the face of Swedish ambition.

Traditional French policy in Germany had been to support the second-order German states like Baden, Württemberg, Saxony and Bavaria; as well as the electors and prince-bishops of Mainz, Cologne and Würzburg. The aim of this policy was to maintain French influence on both banks of the Rhine, but Bonaparte's early pursuit of an alliance with Prussia risked losing the support of the Catholic states, until the Treaty of Pressburg remodelled the political map of Germany. This 1805 treaty enlarged not only Prussia, but also Württemberg, Baden and Bavaria, consolidated many fragmentary land holdings, halved the number of smaller states, and as a result diminished the influence of Austria.

This process was completed by the creation of the Confederation of the Rhine in 1806. This confederation was wholly Napoleon's creature, which united the second order states of Germany in an alliance which was protected by, and was dependent on, the French empire. Thus not only was Austrian influence diminished, but so too was that of Prussia.

Napoleonic Germany, 1807. The settlement that would last until 1813 [Muir's Historical Atlas]

The first move towards the confederation was the Franco-Bavarian treaty of August 1805, by which Bavaria contracted to supply 20,000 troops in return for Napoleon's promise to 'seize all occasions which present themselves to augment the power and splendour of the House of Bavaria and to procure for its States the rounding ('*arrondissement*') and consistency of which they are capable'.[8]

This treaty was followed in September 1805 by an alliance with

Baden, from which 3,000 troops were secured, and in October with Württemberg for 8,000 or 10,000 troops in return for a guarantee of independence and integrity. This treaty also, interestingly, underwrote the position of the Elector against his own Estates should they object to the obligations of the treaty. In addition, Reizenstein, the Baden minister of state, proposed the creation of a security zone between Austria and France, in which Brixen, Trent and South Tyrol would be ceded to Italy; and North Tyrol, Swabia and Upper Austria to Bavaria, Würzburg and Württemberg. This scheme was partly implemented by Napoleon in the Treaty of Pressburg in December 1805 and this treaty, which also severed the ties between his client states and the Holy Roman Empire, created the conditions for the confederation to take shape.

The act of confederation was signed in July 1806, and the confederating states were Bavaria, Württemberg, Dalberg, Baden, Berg, Hesse-Darmstadt, Nassau-Usingen, Nassau-Weilburg, Hohenzollern-Hechingen, Hohenzollern-Sigmaringen, Salm-Salm, Salm-Kirburg, Isenburg-Birstein, Arenberg, Leichtenstein and Leyen. These were soon afterwards joined by Würzburg, Saxony and the five Saxon duchies; Lippe-Schaumberg and Lippe-Detmold; the three Anhalt duchies; Waldeck; Schwarzburg-Rodelstadt and Schwarzburg Sonderhausen; the four principalities of Reuss; Mecklenburg-Strelitz and Mecklenburg-Schwerin; the Grand Duchy of Oldenburg; and the Episcopal city of Frankfurt-Main. The Kingdom of Westphalia was also on its creation declared a member.[9]

The treaty of confederation brought the Holy Roman Empire of the German Nation to an end and established a new *diet* in Frankfurt-Main, with Napoleon appointed as Protector. The treaty also made a further re-allocation and consolidation of territory, and suppressed a large number of the smaller states: in fact, about half the total number of states in Germany disappeared. For Napoleon, article 12 of the treaty was crucial:

> There shall be between the French Empire and the Confederate States of the Rhine, collectively and separately, an alliance in virtue of which every Continental war which one of the Contracting Parties shall have to sustain shall immediately become common to all the others.[10]

Article 38 fixed the number of troops which the allies would supply: France would provide 200,000, Bavaria 30,000, Westphalia 12,500 and so on down to the smaller states which were bound to find 4,000 each.

Thus the confederation was partly a new bastion of the Rhine frontier, partly a source of manpower, and it made the *Befreiungskreig* of 1813 as much a German civil war as a war of liberation. Its creation ensured that Prussia would have to be broken, and also that the enmity of Britain would continue, since the British would never consent to French control of the great continental river estuaries and ports. Indirectly, the confederation led to continued confrontation with Britain and the extension of the Continental System into Spain and Portugal: because of this, the armies of Britain, Russia and Prussia would meet one day in Paris.

If Westphalia marked the consolidation of the inner Empire, the creation of the Grand Duchy of Warsaw marked the emergence of an outer Empire. This state, built on the fires of Polish nationalism and the reactionary Polish aristocracy rather than on the ideals of the *Code Napoléon*, was ruled *in absentia* by Napoleon's ally Frederick Augustus I, King of Saxony but in practice Napoleon himself retained control of the duchy.[11] The creation of the duchy in 1807 gave the appearance of a step towards the re-establishment of Poland, although it was in reality only a tool of Napoleon's diplomacy designed as a compromise with Russia – since its territory was formed mostly at the expense of Prussia – while at the same time drawing the Poles into Napoleon's orbit. Napoleon's ally the King of Saxony was named as titular Grand Duke.

But just as the creation of the confederation ensured the enmity of Prussia, so the creation of the Grand Duchy of Warsaw was bound to offend Russia. In 1809 the duchy was enlarged by the addition of the Galician provinces of Austria and at this point, the Tsar demanded a guarantee that an independent Poland would never be revived. This he never got, but Napoleon never went further in the opposite direction either, issuing only vague pronouncements to the Poles in 1812, to the effect that he was embarking on a second Polish war.

Not unnaturally, this prospect raised enormous expectations from the Poles, who contributed an army of 90,000 men to the Russian campaign, the remnants of which were still fighting in central Europe right up to the end of the campaign of 1813. The total Polish contribution to the *Grande Armée* over a six year period was some 200,000 out of a population of 2.5 million.[12]

No other satellite state gave its military or political support to the French cause so readily as the Grand Duchy of Warsaw . . . [but] The Grand Duchy was a living monument to the contradictions in the Napoleonic state system.[13]

Just as Britain financed and assembled the various European coalitions, so too Napoleon gathered his clients. As more and more territories were brought under direct control of the Empire after 1809 – Dalmatia, the Papal States, Holland, Hanover, Northern Westphalia and the Hanseatic cities – largely to strengthen the Continental System,[14] so this trend became more marked. So what, in coalition terms, did this system of alliances produce?

A detailed look at the composition of Napoleon's armies in 1812 and 1813 provides some startling answers. In both years, the French armies in Spain, including those in Catalonia, numbered about 200,000 men of whom approximately 20,000 – 10 per cent – were allies. As Part Three will show, these were Italians, Germans and Spanish. The real degree of reliance on the clients and allies comes with an examination of the Central European army.

In 1812, the *Grande Armée* assembled for the invasion of Russia numbered 611,000 of whom 213,000, or one-third, were French. The remaining two-thirds consisted of 30,000 Austrians, 20,000 Prussians, 27,000 Italians and Croats, 5,000 Neapolitans, 17,000 Westphalians, 9,000 Swiss, 90,000 Poles and Lithuanians, 100,000 other Germans, and finally 100,000 from the annexed territories.[15]

In 1813, the army numbered between 230,000 and 280,000 at any one time[16] of which between 75,000 and 125,000 were certainly French – but this figure includes large numbers of Dutch, Catalonians, Illyrians, Belgians and northern Germans from the annexed territories. The remainder consisted of 8,000 Westphalians, 28,000 Italians, 12,000 Danes, 9,000 Bavarians as well as a separate Bavarian army of over 20,000 under Wrede, 13,000 Neapolitans, 15,000 Poles, 15,000 Saxons, 10,500 Württembergers, 7,000 from Baden, and 4,300 other Germans.[17] Only one-third or less of the army can truly be said to have been French.

To support these figures, a comparison of the various sources cited shows the corps structure of the *Grande Armée* in 1813 to have contained subordinate formations of nationalities as follows:

I   French, Polish.
II   French.
III   French, Baden, German.
IV   French, Italian, Croat.
V   French.
VI   French.

VII	French, Würzburger, Saxon.
VIII	Polish.
IX	French, Bavarian.
X	French, Polish, German.
XI	French, Italian, Würzburger, Westphalian, Polish.
XII	French.
XIII	French, German, Italian.
XIV	French

In addition, the Dutch, Swiss, Belgian, Spanish, many Germans and Portuguese were spread out as individuals throughout the corps. The table does not include the Danish auxiliary corps under Prince Frederick William of Hesse which co-operated with Marshal Davout's XIII Corps, or the Bavarian Army.

These are such staggering figures that it is impossible to believe that Napoleon could have fought either campaign with a truly French army. They also dispel any doubts about the huge importance of the Spanish war in keeping such large numbers of wholly French troops tied down. In 1813, only the Bavarian Army under General Count Wrede was allotted an independent role, as no doubt Napoleon had in his mind the defection of the Austrians and Prussians when defeat loomed in 1812. He was right to do so given the example of the Saxon and other German contingents at Leipzig, and the Bavarians soon after: thus even in a coalition like Napoleon's, there is truth in the notion of allied unity as the centre of gravity of a coalition army.

This explains why the contingents of the client states, although formed into national brigades and divisions, were integrated with French troops in all corps except the fanatically loyal VIII Polish. This is an exact, if overlooked, parallel with Wellington's much-lauded process of integrating his Portuguese brigades into British infantry divisions. Where Wellington's practice and Napoleon's part company is in adversity. Wellington always used his best British troops to cover a withdrawal, but in central Europe, as the campaign of 1813 drew to its close, we find the French client contingents being used, cynically, as rearguards. Thus at Leipzig, the bulk of Marshal Macdonald's troops on the final day were Poles, Italians and Germans.

And in the north, the Danes were faced with conducting a delaying action against odds of five-to-one around Hamburg[18] until they separated themselves from Marshal Davout before the combat of Bornhoeven, and subsequently concluded the Treaty of Kiel in January

1814. The casualty figures for 1813–14 bear this out: 21,000 out of 28,000 Italians; 5,500 out of 9,000 Bavarians; 9,000 out of 15,000 Poles.[19]

For Napoleon, coalition war must be seen as a vicious circle of necessity. The extension of the Empire flowed first from the nationalism unleashed by the Revolution, which Napoleon tried to harness as a French-led pan-European superstate. On St Helena, he presented this in highly propagandist terms:

> There are in Europe more than thirty million French, fifteen million Spanish, fifteen million Italians, thirty million Germans. I would have wished to make each of these peoples a single united body . . . Europe thus divided into nationalities freely formed and free internally, peace between states would have become easier: the United States of Europe would have become a possibility.[20]

What Napoleon really aimed to create was not a free association of peoples, but an empire of *départements* directed from Paris. From 1809 onwards this looked increasingly fragile as resistance to the French state grew in Italy, Spain and Germany. In Westphalia, for example, revolts broke out in 1811 following the Spanish example.[21] The further the scheme was extended, fuelled by the need to make the Continental System watertight, the larger were the military forces required both to defend the existing territory and to extend it. This need, combined with the huge losses in Spain, in Central Europe, and later in Russia, bore so heavily on the ability of France herself to supply manpower for the armies that reliance on the annexed territories, clients and allies had to increase. The price of greater reliance was increased security guarantees, thus completing the circle. So if Napoleon had succeeded in sustaining his empire after 1813 it must be certain that, like his *Grande Armée*, it would before long have become an organisation two-thirds foreign.

NOTES

1. For a discussion of this aspect see Muir, p. 5.
2. Connelly, p. 51.
3. Broers, p. 92.
4. Connelly, p. 341.
5. Broers, pp. 75–6.

6. Mowatt, p. 116.
7. Ibid. p. 117. Swiss neutrality was declared on 15 Nov. 1813.
8. Ibid. p. 153.
9. *Correspondance*, no. 13362, dated 15.xi.1807.
10. Mowat, p. 159.
11. Nicolson, p. 27.
12. Broers, p. 92.
13. Ibid. p. 93.
14. Ibid. pp. 176–7.
15. See especially Connelly, p. xviii, and Lefebvre, pp. 373–4.
16. See Part Two.
17. Emsley, p. 146; Aubert, p. 17; Nafziger, pp. 308–24.
18. Aubert, pp. 17–22, 40–1, 44–5.
19. Emsley, p. 146.
20. Mowat, p. 245.
21. Broers, p. 177.

Chapter IV

World War – The Continental System and the Americas

I. THE LOUISIANA PURCHASE

I T WAS THE effect of Napoleon's Continental System on the trading relations of the world which turned European war into world war, but this war, which was in full flood in 1813, was some time in the making. In the late eighteenth century, Americans for the most part regarded France with affection for her support in the Revolutionary War, following the Franco-American alliance of February 1778. The beginning of the revolution in France therefore caused much satisfaction in many quarters of the United States, but the Terror showed such an unacceptable face to the USA that after the declaration of war by France against Britain in 1793, the USA continued to trade with both belligerent nations. Indeed on 19 November 1794, the USA and Britain went so far as to sign a treaty of friendship, commerce and navigation.

This caused so much friction between the USA and France that in July 1798, Congress passed an act declaring the US government free of all treaty obligations towards France,[1] and even began preparations for war. In France, the Directory rapidly realised that matters had got out of control and resolved to regain American goodwill, inviting the US to send commissioners to France to negotiate a new treaty. By the time the commissioners actually arrived in Paris, the *coup* of Brumaire had made Bonaparte first consul, although Talleyrand remained in control of foreign affairs. Napoleon at once demonstrated his personal interest in the treaty negotiations by appointing his brother Joseph as one of the French commissioners, and the result was a significant diplomatic success. The Convention of Paris, concluded in September 1800, declared friendship and peace between the two countries, while leaving the question of the Franco-American treaty of 1778 to a future round of negotiations.

The real significance of this convention lay in its provision for free trade and a lowering of tariff barriers, since even in 1800, Britain was piling up a large war debt which could only be serviced by exports of manufactured goods. Since nearly one-third of this export trade was to the USA,[2] any diminution of it must assist France. At the same time, Bonaparte was engaged in the negotiations with London which led to the Peace of Amiens, and in concluding the second, secret, Treaty of San Ildefonso with Spain. By this latter treaty, France agreed to obtain Tuscany for the Duke of Parma – brother-in-law to King Charles IV of Spain – in return for which the Spanish government agreed to cede the territory of Louisiana to France, an arrangement which was subsequently confirmed in the Treaty of Lunéville in February 1801.

Louisiana was costing Spain over $340 million per year to maintain,[3] and combined with some alarm at US territorial ambitions this proved a powerful spur on the Spanish to give up the territory. This vast territory had been French until 40 years previously, and it seems likely that Napoleon dreamed of replacing the lost Canadian New France of the eighteenth century with another, linking the islands of the Caribbean, Martinique, St Lucia, Guadaloupe, Haiti and Hispaniola to the Mississippi valley and thence into the centre of North America – a French-speaking new world which would overshadow Spain, Britain and the USA.

But France could hardly take possession of the territory while still at war with Britain, for to do so would only invite the British to seize it, and thus the Peace of Amiens provided the opportunity for Napoleon to form General Victor's expeditionary force to secure the territory. Clearly, however, the Spanish government had second thoughts soon after the agreement and tried to delay the actual handover until Napoleon had promised never to cede the territory to a third power. The Spanish governor remained in post and in October 1802, he abolished the right of US citizens to trade through New Orleans.

This move, coming on top of the news of the cession which in itself seemed to President Jefferson to renew the prospect of confrontation and conflict with France, pushed Jefferson to seek the purchase of the territory.[4] In January 1803 he sent James Monroe as Minister Extraordinary and Plenipotentiary to Paris, authorising him to open negotiations for the purchase of the east bank of the Mississippi River and the island of New Orleans, which would give the US a secure frontier and an outlet for trade. Negotiations had actually been initiated by Livingstone, the regular US minister in Paris, prior to Monroe's arrival: Talleyrand was unwilling to negotiate, but Napoleon when approached, probably prompted by the likely renewal of war with Britain and the need for money, was willing to sell the whole territory.

When Monroe arrived, the matter was soon arranged. A treaty of cession was signed on 30 April 1803 which transferred Louisiana to the USA, binding the US to pay 60 million francs (15 million dollars), with interest. Spain had at this point no choice but to agree, but the deal was certainly one of the many causes of bitterness between France and Spain which would later erupt into open war. As it was, in November 1803, the French commissioner, Laussat, at last received possession of Louisiana from the Spanish authorities, and immediately notified the American commissioners who were waiting at Fort Adams. On 20 December 1803, New Orleans became an American city, and the size of the USA doubled.

II. THE CONTINENTAL SYSTEM

The Continental System which came to its fullness under Napoleon had begun as early as 1793. That it developed as it did, however, was the result of Napoleon's inability to carry through the invasion and conquest of Britain. After this, the system was really the only method for him to attack the English directly. In the aftermath of the collapse of the Peace of Amiens, French client states and allies, like Spain and Naples, were obliged to adopt the embryo system, and so too was Prussia after the formation of the Franco-Prussian alliance of February 1806. The closure of the Prussian coast to British trade brought in a state of war with Britain and a blockade of Prussian ports by the Royal Navy in April and May 1806.[5] Furthermore the articles which established the Confederation of the Rhine in July 1806 forbade all states in the confederation from trading with Britain.

It was not until after alliance with Prussia had turned into war, and then war into conquest, that the Continental System was codified in the Berlin Decree.[6] In these decrees, which had monumental conse-quences for the Napoleonic state and its clients, Napoleon laid down the doctrine that it was the failure completely to exclude British influence which had led to the continuation of war, since 'a great number of the Cabinets of Europe are sooner or later influenced by England: and without a solid peace with that Power, our people cannot enjoy the benefits which are . . . the unique object of our life.' To bring about this solid peace, Napoleon proposed to put the British Isles in a state of exclusion. He was quite clear that in doing so, he was accepting war to the end: either Britain would be brought down or his empire would be destroyed – there was no possibility of compromise – and in this light, the attitudes of both the British government and Napoleon towards the Congress of Prague and the Frankfurt proposals are completely understandable. Napoleon knew well that the British national debt was enormous: in 1812 it had reached £500 million, and by comparison, it did not approach the same figure again until the First World War. Only the export trade could service this kind of debt and thus maintain Britain's ability to sustain war.[7]

The important articles of the Berlin Decrees were first, that the British isles were placed in a state of blockade; second, that all commerce and all correspondence were interdicted; and third, in the fifth article, that all merchandise belonging to Britain, or coming from its factories and from its colonies, was forbidden. Article 10 stated that the decree would be communicated to Spain, Naples, Holland, Etruria and the other French allies; and although this was not stated, they would be obliged to consent to it. To underscore this last message, Napoleon immediately ordered Marshal Mortier to occupy the Hanseatic ports of Hamburg, Bremen and Lübeck, and to impose a land blockade on the estuaries of the Elbe and Weser rivers.[8]

The years 1806 to 1812 were years of enormous economic strain for the belligerent powers, and all Napoleon's diplomatic and military efforts were directed towards perfecting the system. The client states and allies, which as well as those already mentioned included the Confederation of the Rhine, the Grand Duchy of Warsaw and Denmark had no choice but to accept the system; other states were coerced into it by military defeat: by the time of the invasion of Russia, only Turkey, Sicily and Portugal were *officially* outside it. Not that the client states or reluctant allies were at all in favour of the system – quite the reverse. Louis Bonaparte, King of Holland, for example, tried to gain exemption from it, but received the reply that 'it is the only way to strike at England, and to force her to make peace. Without doubt it will cause harm to Holland and France; but it is worth while to suffer for a time and to have an advantageous peace.'[9] But only two months later Napoleon was again writing to Louis that 'I am informed that commerce between Holland and England has never been more active.'[10]

Where the system worked, and Napoleon kept out British trade, Europe suffered, for

> The Continental System was not a blockade of Great Britain by France, for the French navy was incapable of attempting this. Nor was it a blockade of the French Empire by the English, for the British government freely issued licences for trading with Europe. The Continental System was a blockade of the French Empire by itself. [11]

The Milan Decrees in 1807 [12] further extended the system by increasing the pressure on neutral nations – but incidentally doing little harm to Britain. This decree stated that any ship of any nation which submitted to search by the Royal Navy, or which paid any British dues, would be seized on entering a French port. The decrees, followed by the further decrees of St Cloud and Trianon in 1810, created the commercial borders of the French Empire, keeping British goods out, but with the intention of letting French industry and commerce fill the gap. This completely Franco-centric system even went so far as to exclude manufactured goods from industrial areas within the Empire when they competed with France. Michael Broers cites the example of the Grand Duchy of Berg, in which the resulting job losses were dramatic: some 10,000 by 1810, a contributing factor to the revolts which broke out in the Confederation of the Rhine in January 1813. [13]

The Continental System really only worked where the French dominated all the coasts. France and Italy were relatively secure, but Spain, Portugal, Holland, Belgium and the Baltic were never properly committed. This state of affairs was largely behind the incorporation of Holland into France in 1810, followed by northern Hanover and part of Westphalia in 1811. Even so it almost worked, albeit indirectly, as America was more closely embroiled in the affairs of Europe. But the extension of the system by the annexation of the north German littoral was bound to offend the Tsar, who was already on bad terms with Napoleon over the matter of the proposed marriage of the Grand Duchess Anna. The annexed territory included the Baltic port of Lübeck, but also included the possessions of the Duke of Oldenburg, a cousin of the Tsar, which had been guaranteed by the Franco-Russian Treaty of Tilsit. Thus the annexations, aimed directly at control of the Baltic, directly threatened Russian interests and violated treaty obligations.

Tsar Alexander had, as a result of the Treaty of Tilsit, joined the Continental System but he had never excluded neutral shipping, which of course carried British trade. At Leipzig fair in 1810, for example, 700 wagon-loads of British goods were up for sale, all of which had come in through Russia, and in the same year, 1,200 ships under neutral flags discharged British goods in Russian ports.[14] Russia, in need of the money which customs dues provided, was not about to end this situation.

Tilsit had also bound the Tsar to force Sweden to join the system and the Tsar had done so, by war. In 1809, the Swedes had joined the system, and had forfeited Finland to the Tsar. But after this war, the Swedes had continued to trade freely with Britain and indeed, the more closely Napoleon controlled the north German coast and Denmark, the more the Swedes benefited from British trade both in Sweden proper and in Pomerania. This arrangement continued to prosper, despite a formal state of war between Sweden and Britain, and despite the election of Bernadotte as Crown Prince of Sweden in 1810. Indeed, Napoleon, by neither encouraging nor forbidding Bernadotte to accept the title seems to have accelerated Bernadotte's assimilation into Swedish life and the development of close relations between the Tsar and the Crown Prince.

Thus the Continental System, perhaps because it was never in operation for long, succeeded only in setting most of Europe against Napoleon. But given that only one-third of Britain's trade was with Europe, while two-thirds was with the rest of the world,[15] it was the indirect effect of the system which most nearly brought disaster to Britain and which was to bring her into conflict with America.

III. AMERICA

In response to the Continental System, the British tried to do two things: first, to keep open the seas so that any neutral nation, especially America, could trade with them. This, despite the best efforts of French privateers – French privateers took 500 British ships per year on average between 1793 and 1815, while by 1811, some 4,000 former French ships flew the British flag[16] – the Royal Navy generally succeeded in doing. Second, they aimed to penalise any neutral state which adhered to the system. The mechanism for achieving the latter was the Orders-in-Council, issued in response to the Berlin Decrees from January 1807.[17] The first order stated that

> No vessel shall be permitted to trade from one port to another, both of which ports shall belong to or be in the possession of France or her allies, or shall be so far under their control, as that British vessels may not freely trade thereat.

Subsequent orders and the system of licences increased the pressure on both neutrals and states within the Continental System to defy Napoleon, and thus British goods continued to reach Europe in neutral ships which were further encouraged by relaxation of the British navigation acts. As time went on, the licence system became a vital measure for keeping Wellington's Peninsular Army fed, chiefly on American grain.

In America, controls imposed by both France and Britain were bitterly resented, although it is doubtful if either President Jefferson, or his successor Madison, realised that the Berlin Decrees had brought in a total war. In 1807, Jefferson introduced an embargo act which prohibited US trade with all foreign nations. This act did far more harm than good, was widely ignored, and was replaced by the Non-Intercourse Act (1809), which prohibited trade with either France or Britain until each dropped their blockade decrees. This act was intended to force both belligerents to abandon their controls, but again it did more harm to the US than to France or Britain. Napoleon's response was the Decree of Rambouillet, by which all US shipping entering French ports or found on the high seas was subject to seizure.[18] In 1810, Congress repealed the act, but offered to either belligerent power which respected neutral rights the reward of refusing trade with the other.

Napoleon's response was that the Milan Decrees would be revoked on the understanding that so would the Orders-in-Council, and in November 1810, Madison gave London three months to repeal the orders and, receiving no satisfactory response, re-imposed the embargo act. Thus Napoleon, who had no intention whatsoever of weakening his system, hoodwinked the US and pushed her further towards war with Britain. Certainly, given the trade figures already described, the most dangerous situation for Britain was a successful Continental System and a disruption of US trade, and this is exactly what occurred in 1811.

The results for the British economy were dramatic. Lancashire was deprived of raw cotton, and goods began to pile up at ports. British exports to the US fell from £11 million per year to £2 million, and the government found itself forced to pay for the vital American grain in gold rather than in goods. Weekly wages for workers fell by two-thirds, and in industrial Lancashire, a fifth of the population was thrown onto the rates by unemployment as the mills were forced to close.[19] Worse still, food prices rose 87 per cent above their pre-war levels because of a bad harvest and the need to import grain from Italy, Poland, and even

France – which Napoleon permitted in order to accelerate the drain on his rival's exchequer.

By late 1811 there were riots in Nottinghamshire, Staffordshire, Lancashire and Yorkshire, which required the diversion of troops from the Peninsula:[20] the situation was critical, for a militant rebellion in Britain now would certainly have handed victory to Napoleon. But in fact, relief was already in sight. The embargo and non-intercourse acts had been hugely unpopular in America, especially in New England, and were widely ignored by the mercantile community who were happy to continue to use British licences. In this they were encouraged by the British, who after 1812 continued to trade with New England while blockading southern ports from the Gulf coast to Long Island, thus increasing national divisions and anti-war sentiment in New England.

But Britain's real saviour was the Tsar. His famous *Ukase* of December 1810,[21] which in effect gave preferential treatment to US shipping and thereby opened the door to British trade, effectively spelled the death of the Continental System. Napoleon's invasion of Russia in 1812 accelerated the process by opening the ports of Russia and Sweden to British ships as well: by the spring of 1813, British exports were at their highest level for years: total exports were valued at £118 million for the year 1812–13, while taxation yielded £68 million, or five times the pre-war figure.[22] Thus Britain, with a population of only 18 million, was in a position to subsidise the armies of the 6th Coalition which would at last bring Napoleon down.

Meanwhile matters went from bad to worse between Britain and America. The issue of impressment aside, the matter of the Orders-in-Council was one of the stated reasons for Madison's declaration of war in 1812. By the time of the declaration, the British government had revoked the orders – there seemed no need for them any longer – but this news did not reach Washington in time. But the other issues remained unanswered and the British seemed willing to fight to uphold them, especially impressment, and to use economic weapons to undermine Madison at home.

The issue of privateering is worthy of remark, for apart from the invasion of Canada, this was the only method by which America could attack Britain directly. This it did essentially through private enterprise – privateers – backed up by its small naval resources, with considerable success. The privateers interfered with the sea communications between Britain and the Peninsula, and Wellington's dispatches are full of complaints about the inability of the Royal Navy to check their activities. These charges are dealt with in Part Three. These both intercepted cargoes bound for Spain, and forced other ships to sail in convoy thus slowing down the supply rate. The system did, however, have disadvantages: it diverted the best men and resources from the US Navy; and because it was private enterprise, it was more likely to try and intercept the rich, profitable East Indiaman than the less glamorous, but vital, supply brig loaded with weapons, ammunition, or equipment.

The British blockade on American ports was however effective, for US shipping losses were close to those of Britain: The Royal Navy took 1,400 American ships and 20,000 seamen between 1812 and 1815.[23]

Certainly by late 1812, Madison was in a difficult position: both France and the US were at war with Britain, but for reasons which were only indirectly related, and each regarded the other as a neutral. Spain and Portugal were closely allied with Britain but Madison wished to make no hostile moves against either, since such a move might well have committed the US to a war in defence of Joseph Bonaparte's claim to the Spanish throne, a claim manifestly against the wishes of the Spanish people. Nor could he take sides against the Portuguese, who had also risen up against their French invaders. Thus even with an eye on the Spanish and Portuguese colonies in the Americas, Madison held his peace.

So trade continued with Spain and Portugal, and with Canada too.[24] Indeed US grain fed not only the Peninsular Army, but also the British army in Canada, and to a large extent the civilian populations of Spain and Portugal thanks to the British licences. It was a trade which had to be kept going, even when to pay for the grain in gold meant that allied troops fell six months in arrears of pay. So while American and British troops fought each other in Canada, and American privateers attacked British ships on the coast of Europe, the Americans sustained the allied war effort. This was the paradox of coalition and world war in 1813.

NOTES

1. Mowat, p. 88.
2. Markham, p. 143; Emsley, pp. 123–33.
3. Fregosi, p. 219.
4. ibid, p. 221.
5. *Hansard*, vi, pp. 806 and 891.

6. *Correspondance*, no. 11281 dated 19.xi.1806 and 11283 dated 21.xi.1806.
7. Broers, pp. 96, 223.
8. *Correspondance*, no. 11284 and 11285, dated 21.xi. 1806.
9. *Correspondance*, no. 11378 dated 3.xii.1806.
10. *Correspondance*, no. 11880 dated 25.ii.1807.
11. Mowat, p. 204.
12. *Correspondance*, no. 13391 dated 17.xii.1807.
13. Broers, pp. 224–5.
14. *Correspondance*, no. 17099 dated 4.xi.1810.
15. Markham, p. 143.
16. Chandler, *DNW*, p. 100.
17. The Orders are printed in *Hansard*, x, pp. 126–48.
18. Heidler, p. 13.
19. Bryant, p. 50.
20. *Hansard*, xi, p. 603.
21. Mowat, p. 206.
22. Bryant, p. 53.
23. The figures are a compilation drawn from Boers, Hitsman, Stanley, Wood, and Forester.
24. See Part Four.

PART TWO

CENTRAL EUROPE

Chapter V

After 1812 – Europe Rearms

❦

I. FRANCE: THE EMPIRE AT BAY

I N 1806, WHEN NAPOLEON had last conducted a campaign in Germany, he had been strategically and operationally on the offensive. Now he was on the defensive. For on 5 December 1812, the defeated Emperor had left his army at Smorgoni, leaving Marshal Murat, the King of Naples, to command the 60,000 or so men who represented all that was left of the *Grande Armée* after the *débâcle* in Russia. Many have criticised his decision to leave the army but from the Napoleonic standpoint, it was the only thing to do. The Russians were in pursuit, albeit cautiously; Prussia and Austria – and therefore much of the rest of Germany – were showing signs of unreliability; and his implacable foes the British continued their war against him both at sea and in Spain. Another army had to be raised, and quickly.

Not only was France itself under threat, but Bonaparte's reputation had also been seriously dented. The 29th *Bulletin* of the *Grande Armée*,[1] issued from Molodetchno on 3 December, reached Paris on 16 December. In it Napoleon confessed that an atrocious calamity had befallen the army, so that only his personal presence in Paris would forestall the consternation, perhaps even panic, that the *Bulletin* would cause. Moreover, in the longer term, his imperial ambitions still remained and he was already resolved to recover both his prestige and the territory which he had lost. No thought of any compromise peace settlement entered his mind; complete victory was his aim. And indeed, there would be times during the forthcoming year that this would look distinctly possible.

So a new army was to be raised from scratch, for the old army, which in its day had bludgeoned most of Europe into submission, had been to all intents and purposes destroyed in Russia. Little remained to form a

Boney Hatching a Bulletin — or Snug Winter Quarters !!!

Boney Hatching a Bulletin: George Cruickshank's Dec. 1812 cartoon on Napoleon's plight in Russia. [BM catalogue no. 11,920]

nucleus – only 500 fit men were left of the 50,000-strong Imperial Guard Corps;[2] I, II, III and IV Corps could muster a mere 6,400 men between them. In any case, such troops that remained of the old army were required to keep the Russians at bay and thus buy time for the formation of the new army. To restore the empire, therefore, Napoleon determined on a colossal force of 650,000 men distributed between Central Europe, Spain, Italy and the Low Countries. Of these some 200,000 – or to make him unbeatable, 300,000 – would be required for the Central European theatre, for it was here that the issue would be decided and here, therefore, that in terms of grand strategy, Napoleon placed his main effort.

Of course a relatively well-trained and battle hardened army of almost 200,000 men did exist – in Spain. But these men were needed on France's southern frontier to keep the allies out. Other sources must therefore be tapped, although in the end, Napoleon was forced to weaken his Peninsular army, with fatal consequences, by withdrawing the four remaining regiments of the Imperial Guard as well as cadres of experienced NCOs, many of whom had to be commissioned to make good the serious shortage of regimental officers. To these cadres were added the first available fresh troops, some 137,000 conscripts called up during the Russian campaign and who had now completed their training, who were from all over the annexed territories. In addition there were around 80,000 men of the National Guard, who were formed into 88 new battalions. This made good much of the shortfall in the infantry; the reconstitution of the cavalry however appeared impossible and indeed the numbers and quality of the cavalry would remain a serious weakness for the rest of the war. Even so, the foundations were laid by mobilising 3,000 gendarmes. A total of 12,000 naval gunners, idle because of the British domination of the seas, were formed into artillery units and a further 24 battalions of infantry were formed from surplus sailors.

But even these measures were not enough. The conscription class of 1814 was therefore called forward early at the age of 16 – some were as young as 15 – and it was these youths whom the wagsters named 'Marie-Louises' after the Emperor's second wife. There was also a stiff combing-out of sick men and of those who had evaded conscription in earlier years. Italy was required to produce 30,000 troops to supplement the considerable numbers of Danes, Bavarians, Saxons, Westphalians, Württembergers, Dutch, Swiss, Poles and Belgians already in the army; more foreigners, especially Germans, were hoped for. Last of all, the municipalities of France itself were required to produce 20,000 additional troops along with 5,000 municipal guards, old soldiers retired on pension. To equip this host there was frenzied activity across France:

> France was one vast workshop . . . the entire French nation overlooked [Bonaparte's] reverses and vied with each other in displaying zeal and devotion. It was as glorious an example of the French character as it was a personal triumph for the Emperor, who with amazing energy directed all the resources of which his genius was capable into organising and guiding the great national endeavour. Things seemed to come into existence as if by magic.[3]

By dint of these means it began to look as if Napoleon might after all meet his target. But his new army had severe limitations: the troops were inexperienced; they were from an enormous variety of nationalities; and the young boys and old men who now formed much of the army were less resilient than the veterans of previous campaigns, being especially unsuited to the sort of long distance marching which a Napoleonic campaign usually entailed. The Marquis de Caulaincourt, a general and Grand Master of the Horse, described the army as 'an organised mob'[4] – but it was a more formidable force than it first appeared, and one which would show surprisingly good morale:

> Certainly, the new troops were not the equals in value of the bands destroyed in Russia, and, moreover, their constitution exposed them to a rapid exhaustion: nevertheless, they were good . . . Anyhow, the army with which Napoleon opened the campaign was a good instrument of war; however, it had in itself serious germs of weakness.[5]

More serious than the deficiencies in men was the chronic lack of suitable, trained horses for the cavalry. The cavalry had almost ceased to exist in 1812 and was never rebuilt to Napoleon's entire satisfaction. Time after time in the coming campaign it would let him down and gradually, unable to gain intelligence or follow up tactical successes, Napoleon gradually surrendered the initiative to the more mobile allies. Suitable draught horses for the artillery and commissariat were also in short supply, although the artillery was 'very good and numerous, though the draught horses were rather young'.[6]

It was not all bad news. Even as late as 1813, Napoleon enjoyed a considerable advantage over his enemies in the organisation of his army and of his staff. The French Army had instituted an all-arms divisional organisation in 1793,[7] and in 1804, with his armies swollen by conscription, Napoleon created seven army corps of up to five divisions. Each corps was in effect a miniature army organised for the task and the assessed abilities of its commander, normally a marshal. A corps would contain varying proportions of infantry, cavalry, artillery, engineers and bridging, with integral supply and medical units. The size of the corps could vary enormously, sometimes amounting to between one third and one half of the army. Because they were so well balanced, the corps were capable of fighting a superior enemy for some time and, as a basic principle, Napoleon would insist on corps being able to support each other. This meant moving a maximum of one day's march apart – about 20 miles. Thus a corps could survive on its own for some time until other help arrived, as Ney's corps at Lützen would prove.

This organisation allowed the French to move on several routes simultaneously thereby easing the pressure on limited roads and providing each corps with a discreet area for foraging, a significant factor in the 1813 campaign where the commissariat was somewhat inadequate. 'Even the rats starve where the *Grand Armée* marches' was the popular cry of the time. General movement would also help confuse the enemy as to the exact location of the main effort. It thus enabled Napoleon to move faster than his opponents, essentially enabling him to get inside their decision making process, even though after nine years of campaigning it might be expected that his opponents would have learned something from their bitter previous experiences.

If the organisation was sound, the command and staff system was beginning to creak. At lower levels, the officer problem had been solved – at least in the short term – but the Marshalate was growing stale. Not that Napoleon intended delegating any responsibility to his marshals – he had never encouraged initiative nor trained his senior commanders; he required only that his marshals should carry out his instructions. In late 1813, both in Central Europe and in Spain, this would cost him dearly. As to the staff, Baron d'Odeleben, a Saxon officer, noted early in 1813 that

> it appears that in this campaign the officers of Berthier's headquarters staff were not so skilful nor experienced as those who had formerly surrounded him . . . As a whole, the army was too complex and imperfect a machine to permit true co-ordination during this campaign.[8]

Despite all the imperfections, Napoleon retained one major advantage – his own self-confidence. By late April he would be in the field with the prospect of meeting and defeating the armies of three, possibly five, major powers. This prospect would have crushed the spirit of other men and would have seemed hopeless to anyone who did not consider himself the mental superior to any combination of European monarchs. Here was his strength for, despite the Russian catastrophe, he not only retained his nerve but also the confidence of his youth.

Furthermore he derived enormous advantage in two factors in the forthcoming struggle: first his reputation, which although dented was still formidable; and second, his habit of attending to all but the most trivial tasks personally. The contrast was that the allies had to work as a team, not a situation which sits easily with autocrats. Napoleon alone, despite the presence of contingents from client states in his armies, was the co-ordinator of French policy and this to a great extent gave him the initiative.

II. A NEW ALLIANCE

In 1806, the Army of Prussia, which 20 years before under the great Frederick had been the embodiment of European military virtue, was comprehensively thrashed by Frederick's greatest pupil – Napoleon. The terms of the subsequent Treaty of Tilsit were designed by Bonaparte permanently to emasculate Prussian military power and to consolidate French ascendency in Germany. It had the opposite effect. Led covertly by the redoubtable Queen Louise until her death, and then by Baron Stein; fuelled by the influence of the poets Arndt and Körner; and permeated by the secret society of the *Tugenbund* – the League of Virtue – Prussian society had been regenerated. This is not to say that liberal ideas gained the ascendency, for this rejuvenation, led by the *junkers*, was not entirely what Stein had in mind.

Political rejuvenation was mirrored in the clandestine military reforms effected by Major Generals Scharnhorst and Gneisenau. The Treaty of Tilsit had limited the army to a maximum strength of 42,000 men, but over the years by the simple expedient of compelling a proportion of trained regulars to retire each year and replacing them with recruits, this strength had been almost doubled. By February 1813, Scharnhorst's *Krumpersystem*, begun in 1810, had produced a total available force of around 79,000 trained men.[9]

This was the nucleus around which the new Prussian army would be built. Almost all the existing regiments and battalions had been disbanded and new ones formed. Brigade, divisional and corps structures also rose from the chaos of 1806. Some 60,000 of the trained men were mustered into the infantry; the cavalry accounted for some 12,000 of the total and although the general shortage of horses after 20 years of war was felt here as in France, enough animals were available to ensure the efficiency of the cavalry, artillery and the supply services. The artillery had in fact required a major rebuilding programme, having lost over 800 guns in 1806. By 1813, 236 guns were available.

Ironically, the rebuilding of the army had been assisted by Napoleon himself. In 1812 he had demanded a contingent for the campaign in Russia and had authorised the raising of an additional 33,000 men, over and above the limits imposed at Tilsit. The contingent for Russia had been formed into a corps under the command of Major General Yorck but the regiments themselves had been based on companies of other regiments, which had then been replaced by recruits, so that the whole regiment would not be mobilised and perhaps lost.

Along with the reformation of the structure of the army, the old system of rigid discipline was replaced by 'a more enlightened attitude which stressed civic responsibilities rather than the former demand for feudal obedience; the lash had almost disappeared'.[10] By 1813, the military had risen as high in popular esteem as it had been low in 1806. Moreover, a fair standard of expertise was now available among the senior commanders. Below Scharnhorst came Clausewitz, at this time still in the Russian service; General of Cavalry Blücher, fired with hatred for Bonaparte; Yorck and Lieutenant General Bülow, who although less inspiring than Blücher, were at least competent as corps commanders and had benefited from serving under French command.

In 1812, the opinion-forming class of Prussia was seething with anti-French resentment and nationalist fervour, and was ripe for revolt. But again the scope of pan-German nationalism was weaker than has been at times portayed, especially in Germany. While Stein tried to incite a response to a nationalist message, the scope of revolt in Prussia, as later in Münster, Westphalia and elsewhere, was first anti-French; second anti-Napoleon; and third directed towards the restoration of the pre-Napoleonic state structures. It was, moreover, nobility led rather than an expression of mass dissent.[11] Tension between King Frederick William III and his people had existed since 1809 when the King had refused to join Austria in the war which ended at Wagram. Frederick William, after 1806, had more fear from Napoleon than his own people, and so had no will to oppose the Emperor.[12] Accordingly, he resisted the advice of Gneisenau. Tension turned to rage when Frederick William had given in to Napoleon's demands for troops in 1811 – Gneisenau wrote in disgust that 'The King stands ever by the throne on which he never sat.'[13]

The example of the Spanish guerrillas had filled Prussian youth with hope and shame; now the spectacle of the invincible French army limping back in rags from Russia was enough, in a single night, to bring underground resistance into open rebellion. Indeed, if the repercussions of the French defeat in Russia were profound in Prussia, they were immense throughout the whole of Germany. Although terror of the Emperor's name was enough to keep Saxony, Westphalia, Baden, Württemberg and Bavaria outwardly submissive, the flame of *Befreiungskrieg* – War of Liberation – was well and truly alight. The flame was fanned by the unlikely figure of Yorck, whom Clausewitz described as having

a fiery and passionate will, hidden by apparent coldness; a powerful ambition, suppressed by constant resignation. He was distinguished by strength

Lieutenant General Hans David Ludwig Yorck (1759–1830) painted as a field-marshal in or after 1821. He was made Count of Wartenburg after the place he crossed the Elbe in October 1813.

[Orig. painting in Apsley House, London]

Major General August Wilhelm Anton Gneisenau (1760–1831), Blücher's Chief of Staff in 1813–15. After Leipzig he was made a Count. Like Yorck, he wears the Iron Cross founded in 1813.
[Orig. painting in Apsley House, London]

Lieutenant General Gerhard Johann David von Scharnhorst (1755–1813), the leading Prussian military reformer. He died at Prague on 28 June of a leg wound received at the Battle of Lützen.
[Orig. painting in Apsley House, London]

and boldness of character . . . But he was gloomy, choleric and reserved, and a bad subordinate. He did not make friends easily. He was motivated by the desire for fame, and his natural abilities supplied the means for it . . . He was unquestionably one of the most distinguished men in our army.[14]

While the devastation of the French centre in Russia had been deliberately concealed from French commanders further afield, the Austrian corps under General of Cavalry Prince Karl von Schwarzenberg and Yorck's Prussians, forming part of the right and left wings respectively, had been secretly supplied with information by the Russians, who used Clausewitz as their medium for communicating with Yorck. Thus in December 1812 Yorck managed to separate his corps from Marshal Macdonald – the commander of the left wing of the army – and on 30 December he concluded the famous Convention of Tauroggen with the Russians. By this convention the Prussian corps became nominally neutral but in reality, although it took no part in operations against the French at this stage, it effectively changed sides.

In taking such a course, Yorck was walking a tightrope. The French would certainly have executed him for treason if they had laid hold of him, while King Frederick William, still in dread of Napoleon and conscious that French troops remained in Prussia, at first publicly disowned Yorck's action. In private, however, the King had already sent General von Knesebeck to the Tsar's headquarters with a draft treaty of alliance. This draft suggested that Prussia would join with the Russians in return not only for the restoration of Prussian territories lost in 1806 – which included much of western Poland and indeed Warsaw itself – but also territorial acquisitions in north Germany. The Tsar reacted unexpectedly to this proposal, knowing that, since opinion in Prussia was with Yorck, Frederick William was in no position to bargain. Stein was dispatched at once to Prussia where he so frightened the King with the spectre of losing his throne to the French on one hand and his own people on the other, that Frederick William was compelled to follow Yorck's lead. Thus Yorck, although by no means a major European military figure of the period, occupies a place of honour in the history of German nationalism as the initiator of overt revolt against Napoleon.

Certainly while French forces had remained in Prussia, Frederick William had feared Bonaparte more than the Russian alliance, but by early February 1813 Russian pressure and the rising spirit of revolt had compelled the French to retire. On 3 and 4 February Royal decrees augmented the regular forces by 110,000 *Landwehr*, or militia, a figure which was later increased by the addition of volunteers, *Freikorps*, garrison and depot battalions to 156,000 infantry and 18,500 cavalry – altogether, just over 6 per cent of the Prussian population was under arms, an astonishingly high figure by modern standards. On 27 February Frederick William secretly joined the Tsar at his headquarters on the Polish frontier: the Treaty of Kalisch was signed and ratified the following day and on 16 March Prussia openly declared war. Even so, the cautious Frederick William still had doubts, perhaps fearing another Jena. 'Well gentlemen' he remarked to his ministers, 'You force me to this course but remember, we must conquer or be annihilated.'[15] He was perhaps right to be cautious, for although the nucleus of the Prussian Army was in the field by February, it would clearly be some time before Prussian strength reached its peak. During the interval, therefore, the brunt of any fighting would be borne by the Russians.

But if the Prussians had not been idle between 1807 and 1812, neither had the Russians. They too had learned hard lessons: in their case the lessons of Austerlitz and the Polish campaign. In 1811, just prior to the French invasion, the Army had undergone significant reorganisation closely supervised by Tsar Alexander himself, who by his intervention (or interference) in military affairs often had direct results upon the tactical handling of troops. These were sometimes unfortunate, as Lützen would show, but at Leipzig his intervention undoubtedly saved the day. After 1812, having seen the French off the sacred soil of Russia, the Tsar clearly saw himself as the liberator of Europe – or as Chancellor Metternich called him, 'the conscience of Europe'.

This desire to intervene in European affairs was greeted with nothing short of disgust by Field Marshal Prince Kutusov, who remained in overall command of the Army, and so it was probably just as well that the structural reforms of the army were placed in the hands of General Barclay de Tolly. Barclay decided to abandon the existing concept of mixed divisions in favour of a corps structure similar to the French model. The Russian Army was an immense entity and it is by no means certain that the reforms of Barclay had reached all areas by the time of the war of 1812. Indeed many of the changes in uniform had not been activated by the close of the Napoleonic wars in 1815. To give an idea of the scale of the Russian Army, its size in 1812 was 14 grenadier battalions; 92 infantry regiments each of three or four battalions; 97 garrison battalions; 8 cuirassier regiments; 36 dragoon regiments;

Schlesische privilegirte Zeitung.

No. 34. Sonnabends den 20. März 1813.

Se. Majestät der König haben mit Sr. Majestät dem Kaiser aller Reußen ein Off= und Defensiv=Bündniß abgeschlossen.

An Mein Volk.

So wenig für Mein treues Volk als für Deutsche, bedarf es einer Rechenschaft, über die Ursachen des Kriegs welcher jetzt beginnt. Klar liegen sie dem unverblendeten Europa vor Augen.

Wir erlagen unter der Uebermacht Frankreichs. Der Frieden, der die Hälfte Meiner Unterthanen Mir entriß, gab uns seine Segnungen nicht; denn er schlug uns tiefere Wunden, als selbst der Krieg. Das Mark des Landes ward ausgesogen, die Hauptfestungen blieben vom Feinde besetzt, der Ackerbau ward gelähmt so wie der sonst so hoch gebrachte Kunstfleiß unserer Städte. Die Freiheit des Handels ward gehemmt, und dadurch die Quelle des Erwerbs und des Wohlstands verstopft. Das Land ward ein Raub der Verarmung.

Durch die strengste Erfüllung eingegangener Verbindlichkeiten hoffte Ich Meinem Volke Erleichterung zu bereiten und den französischen Kaiser endlich zu überzeugen, daß es sein eigener Vortheil sey, Preußen seine Unabhängigkeit zu lassen. Aber Meine reinsten Absichten wurden durch Uebermuth und Treulosigkeit vereitelt, und nur zu deutlich sahen wir, daß des Kaisers Verträge mehr noch wie seine Kriege uns langsam verderben mußten. Jetzt ist der Augenblick gekommen, wo alle Täuschung über unsern Zustand aufhört.

Brandenburger, Preußen, Schlesier, Pommern, Litthauer! Ihr wißt was Ihr seit fast sieben Jahren erduldet habt, Ihr wißt was euer trauriges Loos ist, wenn wir den beginnenden Kampf nicht ehrenvoll enden. Erinnert Euch an die Vorzeit, an den großen Kurfürsten, den großen Friedrich. Bleibt eingedenk der Güter, die unter

Faksimile einer von der Verlagsbuchhandlung W. G. Korn in Breslau zur Verfügung gestellten Nummer der „Schlesischen privilegirten Zeitung" vom 20. März 1813, die zuerst den Aufruf König Friedrich Wilhelms III. brachte.

King Frederick William III of Prussia's proclamation *An Mein Volk*, announcing mobilisation and the beginning of the War of Liberation. Published on 20 March 1813.

5 uhlan regiments; 11 hussar regiments; and an artillery train of 37 brigades.

Despite enormous losses in the 1812 campaign, which affected the victors as well as the vanquished, and a war in the southern provinces of the empire against the Turks, the Russian Army in 1813 had actually increased in the number of units. In addition to the regular forces, one should not forget that the Russians made excellent use of irregulars like the Bashkirs, Kalmachs and Cossacks, who gave a valuable superiority in mobile, mounted troops to the allies.

By no means all of this enormous army was committed to pursuing the French in Germany. In February 1813, at the time of the conclusion of the Treaty of Kalisch, the Russian forces in the Central European theatre of operations did not exceed 70,000 infantry, 30,000 cavalry and Cossacks, and 10,000 artillery and engineers – about 110,000 men in all.[16] There was also a command problem within the army precipitated by the increasing illness and frailty of Kutusov. By April he was so close to death that the Tsar was obliged to appoint a new Commander-in-Chief. The Tsar's choice was Lieutenant General Prince Wittgenstein, son of a German general in the Russian service, to whose appointment the Prussians agreed. However Lieutenant General Tormassov, the commander of the Guard Corps, and Lieutenant General Count Miloradovich both cited their seniority and refused to serve under Wittgenstein. A thoroughly unsatisfactory compromise was therefore reached by which Wittgenstein was given command of all allied formations except those of Tormassov and Miloradovich, which were held under the Tsar's personal control.[17]

These disagreements masked others, for the Tsar himself continued to interfere in matters of day-to-day command and surrounded himself with advisers whose counsel he seemed to prefer to that of Wittgenstein. These included Jean Moreau, the former French general and victor of Hohenlinden in 1800, who had lived in exile in America since being implicated in the royalist plot of 1804. The Tsar had summoned him back to Europe, and Moreau had agreed. As well as Moreau there was also Major General Count Karl von Toll, a German, and later still General Antoine Jomini, a Swiss. Last of all there was the British Major-General Sir Robert Wilson who after the French invasion had managed to get himself sent on a mission to the Russian Army. He had reached Smolensk in August 1812 by way of Constantinople, where he tried to mediate in the Russo-Turkish War. As the British government was already pursuing this policy, Wilson was advised to confine his activities purely to the military mission and his *Journal* is a fascinating description of the campaigns of 1812 and 1813 from the Russian perspective. Given the lack of any distinctive Russian doctrine the presence of so many advisers could only, and would eventually, lead to confusion. Confusion was something that the allies, faced with an opponent of the calibre of Bonaparte and looking as they did to the Tsar for inspiration, could ill afford.

While Prussia and Russia prepared for open war, the Austrians were still obliged to opt for guile. After the disastrous campaign of 1809, the strength of the Austrian Army had been fixed at 150,000 men, for such had been the demands of war against France, that the empire was practically bankrupt. The necessary economies had therefore been enforced largely at the expense of all aspects of the army. However when Napoleon invaded Russia, Chancellor Metternich made an uncharacteristic miscalculation. He did not believe that Napoleon would secure an overwhelming victory; still less did he believe that Tsar Alexander would emerge victorious. His estimate was that Napoleon would score a partial success and, with this in mind, he set out to insure himself and his country with both sides. With Napoleon he made a limited treaty, by which Austria would supply a contingent of 30,000 troops under Prince Schwarzenberg for the *Grande Armée*. But at the same time he assured the Tsar that 'Russia would find an active friend in the French camp without having to meet an enemy in war.'[18] And indeed the participation of the Austrian force in Russia can at best be described as half-hearted. This Austrian army corps, which comprised 23,000 infantry and 7,000 cavalry, represented almost the total effective force of the Austrian Army. Petre says that

> The corps of 1812 . . . appears to have been excellent, whilst reserves and recruits were perhaps not far behind the corresponding elements of the Prussian Army. The cavalry was generally good, the artillery less so . . .[19]

Like Yorck, Schwarzenberg had reached an agreement with the Russians, although as his Emperor was Napoleon's father-in-law and was bound to him in formal military alliance, Schwarzenberg would put nothing in writing. Under the terms of this agreement, the armistice of Zeyes,[20] Schwarzenberg retired on Cracow in late 1812, and from thence into Bohemia, leaving the Franco-Saxon corps of General Reynier to shift for itself while the Polish division of General Prince Poniatowski was left in Galicia. This division became so isolated from the retiring French army that, although it escaped the worst of the destruction, it was quite unable to take part in the opening of the campaign of 1813.

Austria itself, even with the return of Schwarzenberg, was in a similar position. Unable to put an army of any size into the field in central Europe and still maintain the security of her borders with Bavaria and in Italy, the Habsburg Empire was compelled to assume a position of armed neutrality, posing as mediator between Bonaparte and the allies. At the same time, however, furious covert moves were in hand to rebuild the army and to subvert Bavaria and Saxony from the French cause. It was not, therefore, until after the ten weeks' truce in August 1813 that Austria joined the allies, thereby adding a field army which had grown to 270,000 men and 290 guns,[21] and tipping the balance fatally against Napoleon.

The last prospective partner in the coalition of 1813 was Napoleon's former Marshal, Bernadotte – now Crown Prince and Regent of Sweden. Bernadotte's conduct as a Marshal of the Empire had, as at Auerstädt, been marked by crooked dealing. Now, having failed to gain French backing for his attempts to annexe Norway to the Swedish crown at the expense of France's ally Denmark, and having lost Swedish Pomerania to French occupation in January 1812, Bernadotte was out for revenge. Between April 1812 and March 1813, he had concluded treaties with the Tsar and with Britain, giving him substantial territorial gains in northern Europe and the West Indies as well as financial subsidies. Shortly afterwards he landed in Swedish Pomerania at the head of an army of 12,000 Swedes. To these were added 15,000 Germans recruited in Pomerania and the island of Rügen, and also a contingent of 6,000 Mecklenburgers. The Swedish Army was, at the time, generally reckoned to be first class, but Bernadotte clearly had no intention of risking it unless absolutely necessary. For him, membership of the coalition was purely a means by which he would gain territory and a seat at the councils of the mighty. To do this, it was enough merely to be present in the theatre of war. Small wonder, then, that the Swedish contingent took no part in active operations until after the ten weeks' truce and even then did very little actual fighting.

Thus as the campaigning season approached, both France and the allies needed time to complete their reorganisation and rearmament. Strategically, time would usually be on the side of the allies, for the longer the war lasted, the more their strength would increase. For Napoleon, on the other hand, an early tactical success might be

The Ornamental Embellishments Engraved by Topham the Portraits by Freeman.

From Portraits taken at Berlin, Vienna, Stockholm, St Petersburg & Paris.

Leeds, Pub.d by Edw.d Baines Aug.t 29 1814.

Five Commanders of the 6th Coalition. Interestingly, General Jean Moreau, the dead Frenchman, gets pride of place with Count Matvei Ivanovich Platov (1751–1818) Hetman of the Cossacks below him.

enough to shake coalition unity to an extent which would bring peace on his terms and guarantee his survival. His own dictum, that the essence of war consists of a careful and circumspect defence, followed by a rapid and audacious attack, seemed tailor-made for the occasion.

NOTES

1. *Bulletins de la Grande Armée*, pp.124–8.
2. Petre, p.9.
3. Caulaincourt, ii, p.345.
4. Ibid.
5. Lanrezac, pp.28–9.
6. Petre, p.19.
7. Chandler, p.159
8. D'Odeleben, ii, pp.363–4.
9. Broers, p.238; Paret p.139.
10. Chandler, p.873.
11. Broers, pp.239–42; Seeley, ii, p.519 and p.527.
12. Lehmann, p.295.
13. Ritter, p.104.
14. Parkinson, p.202.
15. Craig, p.59 and Lehmann, ii, p.514.
16. Petre, p.26; Lanrezac, p.39.
17. Chandler, p.880.
18. Beardsley, p.39.
19. Petre, p.28.
20. Cited in Martens, iii, p.67.
21. Petre, p.27.

Chapter VI

January to April 1813

I. ALLIED UNITY

T HE EMPEROR'S INSTINCTS were quite right, for unlike Napoleon, who
alone exercised the sole and unified command of the new *Grande
Armée* and the bodies of troops from his own allies and clients which
formed a part of it, the allies – at this stage only Russia and Prussia –
began even as early as February 1813 to suffer the difficulties of
prosecuting coalition warfare. The difficulties of divided command
within the Russian Army have already been mentioned, but between
the Russians and Prussians there were inevitable disagreements based
on national interest. The Russians, not unnaturally, were anxious to
preserve their lines of communication through Poland. The Prussians,
equally, were anxious to cover Berlin.

Such disagreements increased once Austria and Sweden joined the
coalition and although the Tsar generally took the lead, perpetual
councils of war and disagreements continued to be a characteristic of
allied operations right up until Leipzig. One practical method of
achieving unity of purpose was agreed, the creation of mixed formations: Bernadotte, Lieutenant General Count Kleist, Blücher and
Schwarzenberg would all command corps or armies composed of troops
of two or three nations. It was hoped that by mixing the troops in this
way, the temptation for any one nation to act on its own account would
be removed.

Allied moves in the early months were understandably cautious. The
Russians were suffering badly from sickness and straggling after the
rigours of the previous year, and the Prussians were far from achieving
full mobilisation. Nevertheless, after leaving considerable forces to watch
isolated French garrisons on the Vistula and Oder, and in Danzig, the
allies began to develop two distinct axes of advance. In the north,

Wittgenstein, reinforced by the Prussian corps of Blücher and Yorck to a strength of 50,000 men, was moving through northern Prussia in several well-separated columns. Further south the main Prussian line of advance lay from Warsaw to Kalisch and on into Saxony. The advance was led by the Russian corps of Lieutenant General Baron Winzingerode, joined in March by Blücher. The main body on this axis was, however, still inside Poland.

It was fortunate indeed for the allies that Napoleon himself was not yet in the field, for their forces were so far separated as to be unable to afford mutual support. In the event of a major engagement, the Emperor would undoubtedly have punished this error by adopting the strategy of the central position and destroying the allied armies piecemeal. As it was, a planned junction of the allied forces was forestalled by a much inferior force under General Eugène de Beauharnais, which gained for Napoleon the time he needed to prepare for what he believed would be his masterstroke.

II. EUGÈNE'S DELAYING OPERATION

When Napoleon had left Smorgoni, he had entrusted command of the remnant of his old army to Murat, King of Naples. This rump force was ordered to delay the advance of the Russians for as long as possible, in order to gain time for the rebuild of the *Grande Armée*. It was also ordered to hold the enemy as far to the east as possible. A glance at the map shows that this would be no easy task: there was little or no ground which seemed suitable for delaying operations between the Bohemian mountains and the Baltic and, although the area is crossed by a series of defensible river lines – the Vistula, Oder, Spree, Elbe and Saale – there were innumerable crossing places and too few French troops to cover the ground. Murat clearly hoped at first to defend the Vistula, but the news of Yorck's defection warned him to withdraw to the west of the river. Garrisoning the fortresses of Thorn and Danzig with the remnants of Marshal Macdonald's corps and a few fresh troops from East Prussia tied up his best men, and he then fell back in early January 1813 towards Posen. There Murat handed over his command to Eugène and himself returned to Naples, whence he returned during the ten weeks' truce.

Why Napoleon allowed the command to devolve on his stepson the inexperienced Eugène is not clear, especially as older and wiser heads were available in the shape of Marshals St Cyr and Davout. Moreover

MAP VI.i

CENTRAL EUROPEAN THEATRE, 1813
CAMPAIGN AREA

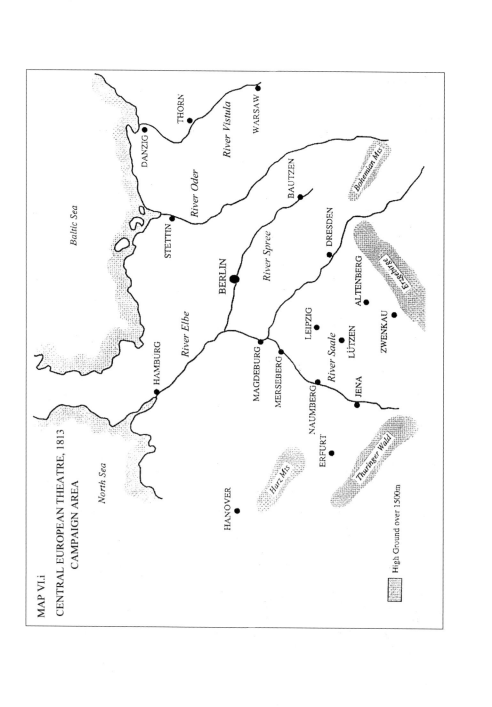

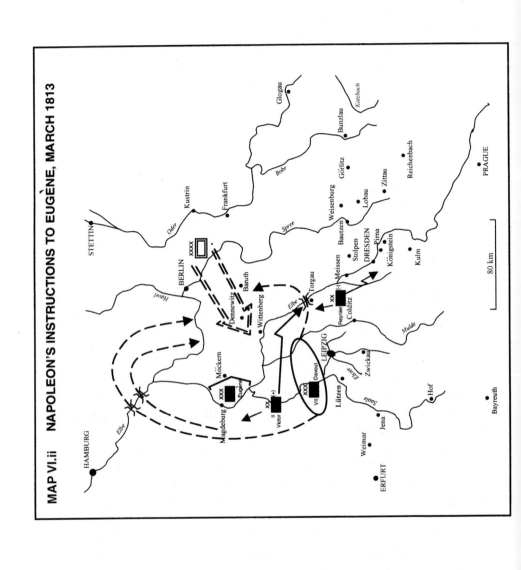

MAP VI.ii   NAPOLEON'S INSTRUCTIONS TO EUGÈNE, MARCH 1813

as the delaying action progressed, it became more and more obvious that Eugène had neither understood the Emperor's initial intentions, nor, as Napoleon's plans developed for a concentration of his new army around Erfurt, did Eugène grasp the need – if he was forced to withdraw – to draw the pursuing enemy towards the lower Rhine thus opening up an assailable southern flank for the main French army. For this, Napoleon himself must take the major blame: for appointing Eugène in the first place; for not ensuring that his intentions were clearly understood; and for seriously underestimating the relative strengths and force ratios between Eugène and the advancing allies.

Eugène took up his command on 16 January 1813 and after only two weeks' grace, Russian pressure – chiefly from Cossack troops whom Eugène, with his lack of cavalry, found impossible to counter effectively – forced him to withdraw to the Oder. Eugène himself commanded about 30,000 men in all, including the remnants of the Guard Corps and some 2,000 cavalry. This force he now concentrated around Frankfurt on Oder, where he was joined by Marshal St Cyr with two weak infantry divisons drawn from the 35th and 36th military districts. Another 13,000 men were tied down in garrisoning the Oder fortresses of Stettin, Krossen, Kustrin and Glogau. Finally at Glogau lay an additional 9,000 men commanded by General Reynier.

Behind Eugène's force, forming an operational second echelon, lay the garrisons of Berlin, about 6,000 men under Marshal Augereau; and Spandau, which was 3,000 strong. Further back still in a third echelon on the River Elbe was General Lauriston, who was concentrating his V Corps at the fortress of Magdeburg. Last of all, there were some 2,000 Saxon troops still in Swedish Pomerania, and also General Prince Poniatowski's Polish division in Galicia, but these troops were so far distant as to be unusable in the short term.

Napoleon's view of the correct course for the delay is stated in his *Correspondance*.[1] Here he lays down that Eugène should have defended the Oder from the eastern side in order to gain time for the move up of V Corps from Magdeburg. But Eugène's inexperience led him to retire west of the Oder and in this he was encouraged by Augereau, who feared an insurrection in Berlin – needlessly, for although the convention of Kalisch was signed on 28 February the nervous King Frederick William was, as we have seen, determined not to embark on military operations until the French garrison had left his capital. Napoleon was furious when news of this retreat west of the Oder reached Paris, but even as new instructions were being sent to Eugène, news of the

A Bashkir horse-archer, drawn from life by Wilhelm Schadow in 1813. The Bashkirs (from the Urals) were one of several Russian subject peoples who supplied irregular light cavalry for the allied armies in Central Europe.

Convention of Kalisch, and with it the Russian and Prussian advance westwards, decided Eugène on yet another withdrawal, to the west of Berlin. This withdrawal certainly encouraged the allies: as Napoleon himself wrote,

> Nothing could be less military than the course you have taken . . . it was quite clear that that was to call up the enemy. If on the contrary, you had

Cossacks, drawn from life in 1813, pawn some loot at the gate of German town.

Teenage ragged conscripts (the 'Marie-Louises') in the French Army drawn from life by Leopold Bayer in August 1813. Note the variety of footwear (or none) and headgear. They proved courageous in action but lacked the march stamina of their predecessors.

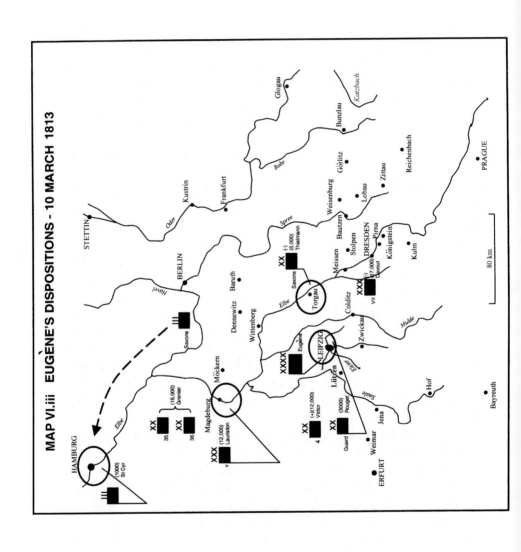

MAP VI.iii   EUGÈNE'S DISPOSITIONS - 10 MARCH 1813

taken up a position in front [to the east] of Berlin . . . the enemy would have had to believe you wished to fight a battle . . . You could have gained twenty days, which would have been very advantageous from a political, as well as a military point of view.[2]

The allied reaction was to dispatch a forward detachment of 7,000 cavalry and Cossacks and about 5,000 infantry ahead of their main army, hoping to rattle the French and keep them withdrawing. Sure enough, before this relatively puny and unsupported force Eugène, abandoning the garrisons of Frankfort-Oder and Krossen, obligingly withdrew. This time he did not stop until 10 March by which time his whole force was behind the Elbe.

From north to south, Eugène now disposed some 82,000 men, but his command was well dispersed over a frontage of 200 miles, and in various stages of readiness. This cordon of unconcentrated troops, with much of his combat power dissipated in isolated garrisons, and with no available reserves, demonstrates conclusively that Eugène had no grasp whatsoever of his master's intentions. On hearing news of these dispositions, Napoleon condemned them absolutely. Although he himself still underestimated the strength of the oncoming enemy, a series of letters[3] spelled out to Eugène what was required. Eugène himself must establish a blocking position east of Magdeburg. To his rear, Marshal Victor's reinforced division would guard the Elbe as far south as Torgau. From Torgau to the Bohemian mountains, Reynier's two weak divisions would screen the river, but were not to attempt to hold the city of Dresden if the enemy advanced against it in strength. Last, behind Victor, Davout's VII Corps would concentrate around the junction of the Elbe with the Plauen canal.

These dispositions had two purposes. First, and most immediately, both Victor and Davout, while denying the passage of the Elbe to the enemy, would also maintain bridgeheads at Torgau, Wittenberg and Dessau so as to be able to cross the river in support of Eugène if necessary. Second, the enemy would be forced by Eugène's position to attempt any crossing well above or well below Magdeburg, thus opening up a flank for Victor or Reynier to attack. In the longer term, although Eugéne's task was clearly still to delay the allies, his remit did not include fighting a major battle. If the allies came on in strength and forced him from the Elbe, he was to withdraw towards the lower Rhine, drawing the enemy after him. The last thing Napoleon wanted was for Eugène to fall back towards Erfurt, where his own developing plans required the concentration of the revitalised *Grande Armée*.

Napoleon made his intentions clear on 9 March but it was not until 18 March that Eugène decided to put these arrangements in train, and it was no easy task to reconcentrate his scattered army. More importantly it was not until 31 March that he himself moved east of the Elbe. By this time the allies, who for a week had been squabbling among themselves, had begun to move. Disagreeing with the ailing Kutusov, Wittgenstein decided to manoeuvre south-east of Magdeburg in order to pin Eugène's main body. Simultaneously he would throw a bridge across the Elbe at Rosslau so that, once he and Blücher had joined forces, he could cross the river in strength. Thus as Wittgenstein moved forward he encountered Eugène's force of about 50,000 men, including now 4,000 cavalry and 180 guns.[4] The result was the action around Möckern on 3, 4 and 5 April. This confused series of piecemeal battles ended at nightfall on 5 April with Eugène's withdrawal back over the Elbe precipitated by a false report that Wittgenstein was crossing the Elbe at Rosslau.

Eugène therefore took up a new, strong position on the lower Saale while at the same time on his flanks, St Cyr's troops had been forced out of Hamburg and Blücher occupied Dresden. Eugène had certainly gained some time on this occasion for his master, but had still not produced the Emperor's desired conditions, for he had drawn only a portion of the allied forces against him, rather than the main body. The allies, however, had inadvertently saved themselves in this respect, for they had still not concentrated. Moreover they were able to claim a victory at Möckern with the resulting morale effect in Germany. It was not until 19 March that the assembly of the allied armies began in earnest and by that time, Napoleon's own plans were already laid.

III. THE GRAND PLAN

As early as 11 March, in a letter to Eugène,[5] Napoleon had outlined a grand scheme for the reconquest of Germany and Poland. Circumstances were, however, to force him to modify this design, not least because the strength of his army was still insufficient for the task. By early April, the concentration of the new army, the Army of the Main, consisted of four corps: Marshal Ney's III Corps, 45,000 strong; Marshal Marmont's VI, 25,000; General Bertrand's IV, 30,000; and Marshal

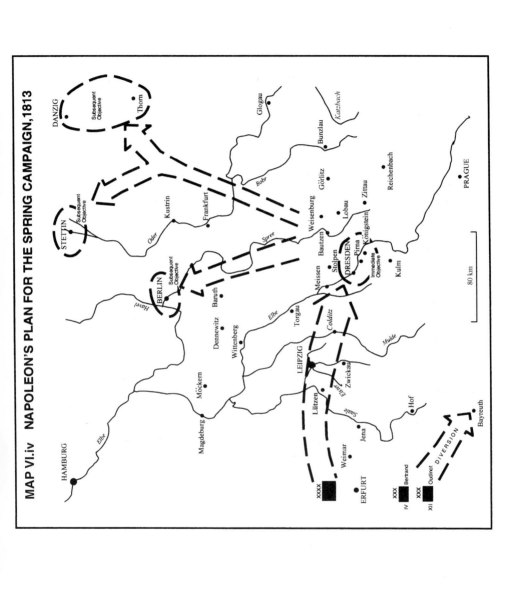

MAP VI.iv NAPOLEON'S PLAN FOR THE SPRING CAMPAIGN, 1813

Oudinot's XII, also 25,000. In addition there was the Guard Corps at a strength of only 15,000 and two weak cavalry corps. Further afield there were of course the troops on the Elbe: I Corps under Marshal St Cyr, with a strength of 20,000 along with General Sébastiani's II Cavalry Corps on the lower Elbe; with Eugène's Army of the Elbe remained General Rouget's division of the Guard, 3,500 strong, General Latour-Maubourg's I Cavalry Corps of 4,000 men, the V and XI Corps, each 22,000 strong, and parts of II and VII Corps.

This entire force numbered around 200,000 men,[6] and although it outnumbered the allies, who were still strung out on the line of march, it had several marked defects: it was itself dispersed; it was 100,000 men short of the strength which Bonaparte himself envisaged as being necessary for the task;[7] and it was chronically short of cavalry. Napoleon had already, in his correspondence with Eugène, shown his lack of detailed knowledge of the enemy which only cavalry reconnaissance could bring him; moreover he was more and more unable to keep the raiding Cossacks away from his lines of communication. Baron Marbot recorded a letter on this subject to his ally the King of Württemberg, in which Napoleon says that 'I would find myself in a position to finish matters very quickly if only I had 15,000 more cavalry; but I am rather weak in this arm.'[8]

Even so by 13 April Napoleon had enough information from Eugène to indicate a major allied advance across the Elbe towards Jena, and this gave him the opportunity he sought. His orders called for an immediate concentration of the army west of the Saale. From there he intended to detach the corps of Bertrand and Oudinot southwards in the direction of Bayreuth in order to distract the allies' attention. He himself would then advance on Leipzig and Dresden with the main body of the army, seizing the crossings over the Elbe in the allied rear and cutting their lines of communication.

Such a move would force one of two things: either a precipitate allied retreat over the Elbe with such a resulting loss of cohesion as might lead to the breakup of the coalition amid mutual acrimony and mistrust; or a major battle on terms favourable to the French: 'My intention is to refuse my right and allow the enemy to penetrate towards Bayreuth - the result will be my arrival at Dresden ahead of him, and his severance from Prussia.'[9]

From the destruction of the enemy army, either in battle or in retreat, would flow at least five important operational and strategic consequences. First, it would allow Napoleon to advance initially on

Berlin and subsequently on the Vistula, thus recovering his territory and the 50,000 or so experienced troops who still held out in isolated garrisons on the Vistula and Oder. Second, a quick victory would blood his new army and give it confidence. Third, his own wavering allies – Saxony, Bavaria and the rest – would be brought into line while the designs of Austria and Sweden would be thwarted. Fourth, the treachery of Frederick William and of Bernadotte would be punished – a lesson which would not be lost on others. Last, but by no means least, his own reputation and prestige would be restored.

NOTES

1. *Correspondance*, vol. xxv, no. 19688, dated 9.iii.1813 and no. 19721, dated 15.iii.1813.
2. *Correspondance*, vol. xxv, no 19688, dated 9.iii.1813.
3. Ibid no. 19721, dated 15.iii.1813.
4. Petre, p.45.
5. *Correspondance*, Vol xxv, no. 19857 dated 11.iii.1813.
6. The figures are drawn from a comparison of Montholon, ii, p.125; Chandler, pp.874–5; and Petre, pp.47–50, 55.
7. Chandler, p.875.
8. Marbot iii, p.250.
9. D'Odeleben i, p.34.

Chapter VII

The Spring Campaign

e⁄ᔕᕮᑎᐧ

I. THE APPROACH TO LÜTZEN

O N 1 MAY the French Army of the Main was ordered to complete its passage over the Saale and move on Leipzig in three columns, preceded by a strong advance guard. In the north, Lauriston's V Corps, Macdonald's XI Corps and the Guard would cross at Merseburg and move directly on Leipzig. In the centre, Ney's III Corps followed by Marmont's I Corps would cross at Weissenfels and head initially for Lützen. Further south, Bertrand's IV Corps and Oudinot's XII Corps would cross near Naumberg and head north-east.

Napoleon was aware of some kind of allied presence near Zwenkau but faulty reconnaissance, probably due to the inexperience of his cavalry, failed to reveal that at Zwenkau lay Wittgenstein's army of four Prussian corps, some 75,000 strong, supported by a further strong Russian corps in reserve. Napoleon therefore determined to retain the initiative by pushing on to occupy Leipzig, relying on Ney to protect his southern flank against this as yet unspecified threat.

The general advance was contested strongly in several places by the allies, especially at Poserna, just to the east of Weissenfels. Here Marshal Bessières, who had soldiered with Napoleon since 1796, was killed by a cannonball. Napoleon felt his loss sorely and

> regretted him more than did the army, which had never forgotten that it was the advice of this Marshal on the evening of the Battle of the Moskova, that had prevented Napoleon from completing his victory by sending in the Guard.[1]

Despite the opposition the French successfully crossed the river, but Napoleon clearly began to have second thoughts about his right flank. He therefore issued new orders for 2 May.[2] While Lauriston and Macdonald pressed on to Leipzig, Ney was to pause at Lützen in order

MAP VII.i
THE APPROACH TO LÜTZEN

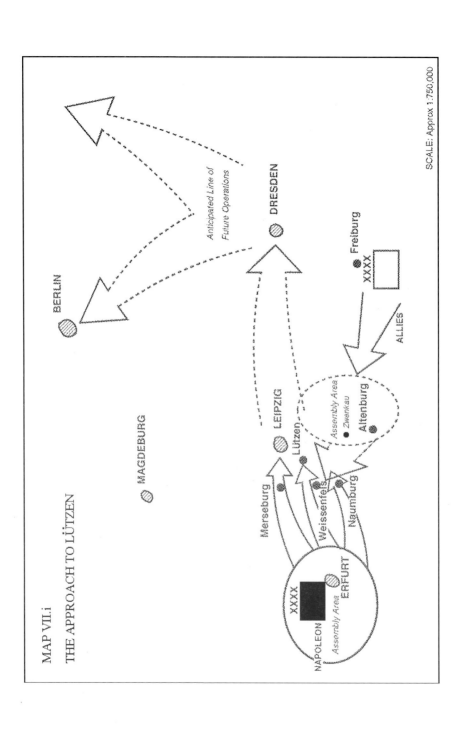

SCALE: Approx 1:750,000

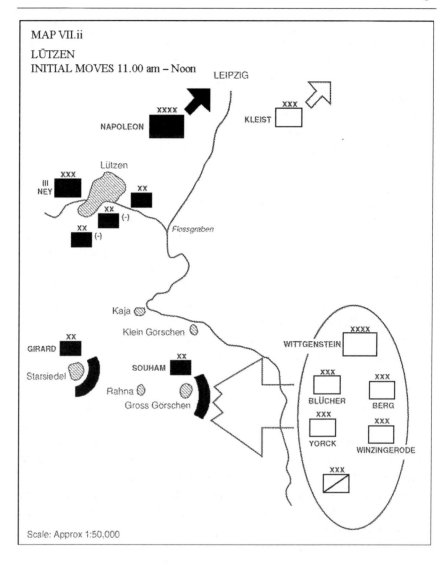

MAP VII.ii

LÜTZEN

INITIAL MOVES 11.00 am – Noon

LEIPZIG

NAPOLEON

Lützen

III
NEY

XX (-)

XX (-)

Flossgraben

Kaja

Klein Görschen

GIRARD

Starsiedel

SOUHAM

Rahna

Gross Görschen

KLEIST

WITTGENSTEIN

BLÜCHER

BERG

YORCK

WINZINGERODE

Scale: Approx 1:50,000

to allow Marmont to close up with him. Ney was further ordered to occupy the villages of Kaja, Rahna, Gross and Klein Görschen. Later he was also ordered to send strong reconnaissance forces forwards Zwenkau and Pegau. This last he neglected to do. Even Napoleon however still had little real expectation of a major enemy attack from Zwenkau. But should this happen, Ney would pin the enemy frontally with his own and Marmont's corps, while Napoleon manoeuvred the other corps from the north and south to attack the allied flanks.

Meanwhile patrols of allied cavalry were busy probing the Lützen area. In due course they reported to Wittgenstein that the main body of the French was pressing on towards Leipzig and that a weak flank guard was positioned in the area of Kaja. Another strong force was detected even further south, near Teuchern, which in fact was Bertrand's corps. The allied assessment was substantially correct, for not only had Ney failed to push out a strong screen as he had been ordered to do, but also he had retained three of his five divisions in Lützen itself, sending two out into the villages.

Wittgenstein decided therefore to annihilate this flank guard, being unaware of Ney's three reserve divisions. His orders were for General Kleist's corps to hold Leipzig in the north, while General Miloradovich's Russian corps was to move forward towards Zeitz to block Bertrand. Meanwhile the rest of the allied army, some 48,000 infantry, 24,000 cavalry and nearly 500 guns, was to press on towards Kaja, clear the French from the area, then cut the main Lützen –Weissenfels road before turning northwards to attack the flank and rear of the French main army. Thus after a sequence of events which provide a salutary lesson in the necessity for high quality reconnaissance forces, the scene was set for a classic meeting engagement.

II. LÜTZEN – THE MEETING BATTLE[3]

A meeting engagement occurs when two forces moving forward on the line of march, each with incomplete information on the other, collide. Victory goes to the side which is quickest to react to the situation and exploit the opportunity thus created to pin the enemy and destroy him. It was the sort of battle in which Napoleon, who welcomed the chaos of war as an ally, showed his genius.

On 2 May 1813, the allied army had been due to begin its move at 1.00 am. The army was to have been completely around the village of Kaja at 7.00 am that same morning. It proved a highly over-optimistic timetable, for in the manner of these things the move in darkness became very confused. It was not until 11.00 am that the leading corps reached their forward assembly areas south-east of Lützen.

The area around Lützen had changed little since Gustavus Adolphus had fought his last, and fatal, battle there in 1632. It has probably changed little today despite the impact of 40 years of collective agriculture. The open, arable land slopes gently from north-west to

FIG. VII.i

FRENCH ORDER OF BATTLE, LÜTZEN AND BAUTZEN

xxxx
Emperor Napoleon Bonaparte
Marshal Soult

Imperial Guard **xxx**	Bessières/Soult *19,000 Infantry* *5,000 Cavalry*	VII **xxx**	Reynier *12,000*
I **xxx**	Victor *15,000*	XI **xxx**	Macdonald *14,000*
III **xxx**	Ney *20,000*	XII **xxx**	Oudinot *14,000*
IV **xxx**	Bertrand *14,000*	I Cavalry **xxx**	Latour-Maubourg *6,000*
V **xxx**	Lauriston *10,000*	II Cavalry **xxx**	Sebastiani *5,000*
VI **xxx**	Marmont *20,000*	III Cavalry **xxx**	Kellermann *4,000*

south-east; the few villages are of stone houses with narrow, cobbled lanes and stone-walled gardens. A few hedges cross the area, notably along the Flossgraben stream which winds sluggishly past Klein and Gross Görschen. This stream would have been a hindrance to wheeled vehicles and guns, and would have disrupted infantry and cavalry formations, but it in no way constituted an obstacle. Some authorities speak of an escarpment to the east, and contemporary illustrations of the battle do depict a range of hills to the north. In reality there is neither escarpment nor hills, only a low crest about two kilometres south and east of Gross Görschen, which marks the course of the Flossgraben.

It was this low crest that Wittgenstein's scouts climbed just before midday. All that could be seen were around 2,000 French infantrymen

FIG. VII.ii

ALLIED ORDER OF BATTLE, LÜTZEN AND BAUTZEN

xxxx

Tsar Alexander I
King Frederick William III
Gen Wittgenstein (C-in-C)

PRUSSIANS	**RUSSIANS**

xxx

Lt Gen Berg (Prussian/Russian Corps)
7450   *31 Infantry Battalions*
3 Cavalry Squadrons
3 Artillery Batteries
Ataman Cossack Regiment

xxx

Lt Gen Barclay de Tolly (Russians)
13,5900   *10 Infantry Battalions*
18 Cavalry Squadrons
2 Artillery Batteries
2 Cossack Regiments

xxx

I   Lt Gen Kleist (Prussian/Russian Corps)
5480   *4 Infantry Battalions*
7 Cavalry Squadrons
5 Artillery Batteries
Cossack Regiment

xxx

II   Lt Gen Winzingerode (Russians)
10,525   *19 Infantry Battalions*
19 Cavalry Squadrons
7.5 Artillery Batteries
7 Cossack Regiments

xxx

II   Lt Gen Graf Yorck (Prussian Corps)
10,000   *12.5 Infantry Battalions*
12 Cavalry Squadrons
6.5 Artillery Batteries

xxx

III   Lt Gen Tomarssov
(Russian/Prussian Corps)
34,180   *14 Guards Battalions*
10 Grenadier Battalions
38 Cuirassier Squadrons
17 Guard Cavalry Sqns
18 Artillery Batteries

xxx

Gen Blücher (Prussian Corps)
23,500   *22 Infantry Battalions*
43 Cavalry Squadrons
10.5 Artillery Batteries

xxx

Lt Gen Miloradovich (Russians)
14,600   *10 Infantry Battalions*
34 Cavalry Squadrons
7 Artillery Batteries
4 Cossack Regiments

xxx

Lt Gen Prince Constantin
(Russian Reserve Corps)
20,000   *14 Infantry Battalions*
50 Cavalry Squadron
30.5 Artillery Batteries

xxx

Lt Gen Gorchakov (Russians)
13,700   *10 Infantry Battalions*
20 Cavalry Squadrons
8 Artillery Batteries
Cossack Regiment

busy cooking their lunch. There were no signs of sentries or supporting units, nor had the French placed pickets on the crest. Confident of a speedy victory, Wittgenstein ordered Blücher to send in his cavalry and sweep this paltry force aside. But as it moved forward into the attack, the Prussian cavalry suffered a severe shock. Instead of a bunch of frightened conscripts, the cavalrymen found themselves facing two complete French infantry divisions – which were themselves every bit as surprised as the Prussians. Just as at Auerstädt in 1806, Blücher had sent in his cavalry unsupported. To his credit, however, Blücher quickly realised that the tactical situation had changed, so he halted the cavalry and sent to the rear for his artillery. This delay gave just enough time for General Souham's French division to occupy Gross Görschen while General Girard's division occupied Starsiedel. Messengers were sent at once to bring up the rest of Ney's corps and the corps of Marmont.

By midday the action opened afresh. Allied cavalry moved in a wide arc to attack Starsiedel, where General Girard easily held his ground until at around 12.30 pm he was joined by elements of Marmont's corps. In Gross Görschen, however, Souham was forced out of the village by heavy Russian artillery fire. As he was evacuating the village, Ney arrived on the scene leading up the three reserve divisions in time to check Souham's retreat. With his typical impetuosity Ney at once ordered his whole corps to counter attack, and soon a desperate hand-to-hand battle was raging in the villages of Gross and Klein Görschen, and Rahna.

Napoleon, en route for Leipzig, was undoubtedly surprised by the volume of cannon fire he could hear from the south. The Emperor had reached Markranstädt some five and a half kilometres north-east of Lützen on the wake of Lauriston's V Corps before news reached him from Ney of the unexpected developments on his right flank. After a few moments' thought, he issued his orders. Ney and Marmont must at all costs continue to fix the enemy. The Guard was to march at once to Kaja. At the same time Marshal Macdonald would swing his corps south from the Leipzig road to attack the allied right flank while Bertrand moved up from the south to take the allied left. Finally, Lauriston would detach a single division to screen Kleist's corps in Leipzig before marching the rest of his corps to Markranstädt. Having issued his orders, the Emperor at once set out for the scene of battle.

Napoleon reached the battlefield at 2.30 pm and found the situation critical. Ney's corps, weary and badly mauled, was on the point of collapse and had been forced back from every village including Kaja. Moreover Bertrand had halted his advance from the south on

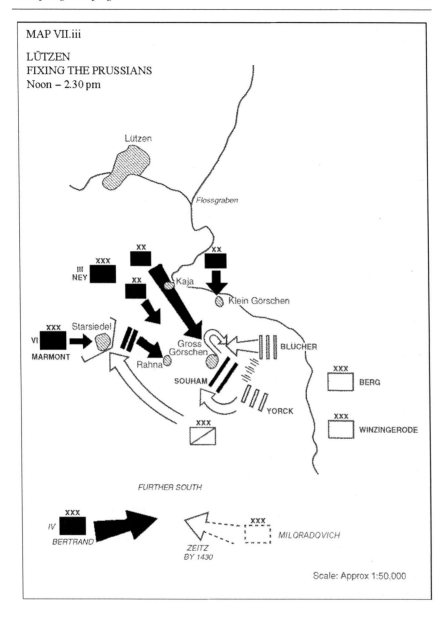

MAP VII.iii

LÜTZEN
FIXING THE PRUSSIANS
Noon – 2.30 pm

Lützen

Flossgraben

III
NEY

Kaja

Klein Görschen

Starsiedel

VI
MARMONT

Gross
Görschen

Rahna

BLÜCHER

SOUHAM

BERG

YORCK

WINZINGERODE

FURTHER SOUTH

IV
BERTRAND

*ZEITZ
BY 1430*

MILORADOVICH

Scale: Approx 1:50,000

discovering the approach of the corps of General Miloradovich towards
Zeitz. It was a moment when personal leadership was required, and
Napoleon responded to it. Riding among the uncertain conscripts he
exhorted them to stand firm and then himself repeatedly led them up
towards the enemy. His presence had a magical effect; confidence and

resolution flooded back into his troops. From all sides the cry of *'Vive L'Empereur!'* rose from wounded and unwounded alike.[4] Marmont later recorded that

> This was probably the day, of his whole career, on which Napoleon incurred the greatest personal danger on the field of battle. He exposed himself constantly, leading the defeated men of the IIIrd Corps back to the charge.[5]

In the desperate fighting which followed, General Scharnhorst was mortally wounded. The situation was grave: a desperate struggle still raged around the villages, and Ney and Marmont both appealed repeatedly for help. Napoleon refused to budge, even though the Guard Corps reached Kaja at 3.00 pm, for he knew that he could not commit his reserve until he could be sure of smashing the enemy. 'Tell your Marshal', he replied to Marmont's emissary, 'that he is mistaken; he has nothing against him; the battle turns about Kaja.'[6] But even as the struggle raged to and fro, every minute brought closer the approach of Macdonald and of Bertrand, who had now resumed his march.

A series of mistakes and mishaps on the part of the allies now came to Napoleon's aid. Blücher was wounded, and his command devolved on General Yorck, a much less inspiring leader. Worse still, Wittgenstein's reserves had not yet appeared. Wittgenstein had sent orders back for the III Reserve Corps of Tomarssov's Russian Guards and Grenadiers to move up to join the battle. Until they arrived, Wittgenstein was unwilling to risk a general attack. The delay seems to have been due to the personal intervention of Tsar Alexander who wished, apparently, to lead personally the final *coup de grâce*. So while Napoleon's strength grew and he husbanded his reserve for the right moment, the allies let their moment slip away. Wittgenstein was by now finding it increasingly difficult to control the battle: his leading corps were tiring and he was aware of the growing threat to his flanks – but he was too deeply embroiled to break off the action.

At last, at 4.00 pm, Tormassov's corps came up and Wittgenstein ordered a general attack. This almost succeeded: the French were driven out of Klein and Gross Görschen and the Prussians almost reached Kaja. Napoleon, knowing that he could not permit this degree of penetration at this time, unleashed a single division of the Young Guard which, in a spirited charge, drove the enemy back. The struggle for control of the village line once more raged on, but the allies were well and truly fixed, and by 5.30 pm the French outflanking forces were almost in position. Macdonald was just north of the village of Eisdorf on Ney's left, and Bertrand had made contact with Marmont's right.

But although the French had succeeded in re-occupying the villages after the Young Guard's charge, they now changed hands once again as a violent attack by the allies seized Klein and Gross Görschen and Rahna. But it was all too late, for Napoleon's concentration was now complete and his forces, although weary, outnumbered the enemy by around 110,000 to 80,000. At 6.00 pm, Napoleon judged that the time had come to settle the matter. General Drouot was ordered to mass the

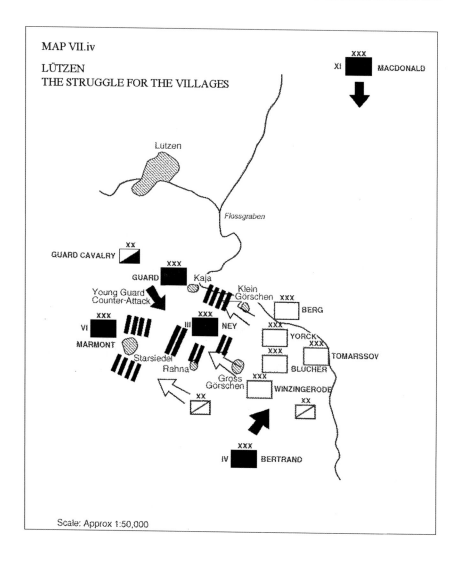

MAP VII.iv

LÜTZEN
THE STRUGGLE FOR THE VILLAGES

Lützen

Flossgraben

GUARD CAVALRY

GUARD   Kaja

Young Guard
Counter-Attack

Klein
Görschen

BERG

VI
MARMONT

NEY

YORCK

TOMARSSOV

Starsiedel
Rahna

Gross
Görschen

BLUCHER

WINZINGERODE

IV   BERTRAND

Scale: Approx 1:50,000

70 guns of the Guard Artillery into a great battery, protected by the Old Guard, to the south-west of Kaja. This he did at close range, so that very soon a devastating cannonade was raking the weary allied formations.[7]

The losses, on both sides, were horrific. Von Caemmerer says that 'The field between Klein and Gross Görschen resembled a bivouac where whole battalions had lain down.'[8] As the battery began its work, the Young Guard formed up in four columns each of four battalions and moved forward to the attack followed by the Old Guard, the Guard Cavalry and the remnants of Ney's III Corps. Within a short time, the

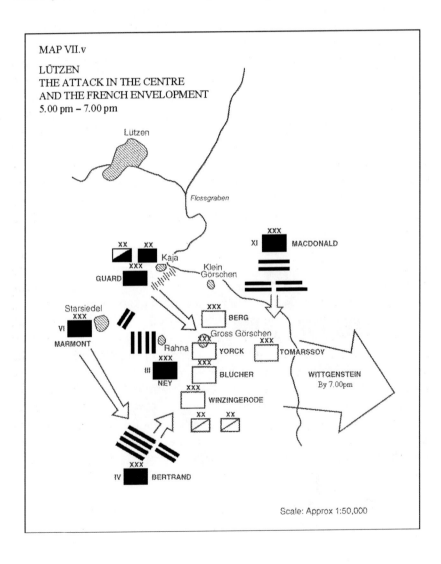

MAP VII.v

LÜTZEN
THE ATTACK IN THE CENTRE
AND THE FRENCH ENVELOPMENT
5.00 pm – 7.00 pm

Scale: Approx 1:50,000

allied centre was smashed, the villages retaken, and the entire Prussian and Russian line began to retire.

As the allies were thrown back by the attack of the Guard in the centre, so the French enveloping forces made their move. From the south came Bertrand, followed by Marmont from Starsiedel. Macdonald's corps formed up behind Eisdorf and crashed into the flank of the enemy. This was enough to settle the outcome, and the whole allied army began to retreat – but it did so in reasonable order. Two more hours of daylight would have clinched a shattering French victory, but the approach of night brought the battle to an end. The crippling shortage of French cavalry made pursuit almost impossible and the allied rearguard remained in good enough order to beat off Marmont's infantry.

Lützen undoubtedly ended in a victory for Napoleon, who had showed his old flair and skill of improvisation which had been absent for some time. Lützen not only gave Napoleon the initiative in 1813, but also, perhaps more importantly, it regained the reputation which he had lost in Russia. It had been dearly brought. The French lost 20,000 casualties; the allies lost 18,000[9] and in addition, they received a very severe shaking. Battles of manoeuvre, no less than battles of attrition, can be bloody affairs and the ferocity of the struggle at Lützen had shaken even Napoleon's equanimity, for it had been almost as dense a battlefield and as fierce a struggle as Borodino. 'These animals have been taught a lesson',[10] he remarked.

True, the allies had caught Napoleon by surprise but the customary flexibility of his dispositions – in three columns – had enabled him to react to the unexpected energetically and successfully; by applying the principles of concentration of force, speed and offensive action he had rapidly turned the tables on his enemies to seize back operational and tactical surprise. Speed was a key element, for Napoleon's insistence on rapid movement was entirely linked with concentration of force: the assembly of the greatest number of men at the correct time and place to achieve a favourable battle situation. Assembly is probably a better word than concentration, for in Napoleonic terms it usually meant, as here at Lützen, the placing of his major formations within marching distance of the place of battle. This he had achieved, after an approach march in which dispersion was the rule, since dispersion made use of more routes and was therefore quicker, increased security, and eased the forage problem.

At Lützen, just as at Jena, Napoleon achieved a phased concentration after a period of dispersion and thus managed to reconcile the

The Battle of Lützen, a contemporary wood cut part of a series depicting Napoleon's victories published at Épinal. It shows the decisive attack by the Young Guard with the French grand battery to the left.

principle of concentration of force with the sometimes contradictory requirements of security and deception. This is no easy matter, as Edward Luttwak points out in his description of the conscious use of paradox in war:

> As for secrecy and deception, the two classic agencies of surprise that often set the stage for manoeuvre, they too exact some cost of their own. Secrecy is often recommended to those who practise war as if it were costless, but an enemy can rarely be denied all knowledge of an impending action without some sacrifice of valuable preparations . . . every limit on the assembly and preliminary approach of the combat forces will leave them less well arrayed and less well positioned than they might have been.[11]

Therefore this reconciliation of the advantages and disadvantages of mass and dispersal, and the fusing of these two contradictory elements into a single operation of war, was as David Chandler points out,[12] Napoleon's greatest contribution to the art of war, and marked him as a true military genius. While his eighteenth century forebears – with the notable exception of Frederick the Great – distinguished rigidly between manoeuvring and giving battle, Napoleon, with his sights always fixed on the opportunity for a decisive battle, combined marching, fighting and pursuing into one process. Although the inadequacies of the pursuit robbed him of a complete success, Napoleon at Lützen had demonstrated the ability to achieve, even in 1813, the goal of manoeuvre – that is, he placed just enough forces to fix the enemy and, having fixed him, manoeuvred the rest of the army to destroy him.

Finally, the Napoleonic command system and his staff, weakened by losses as they were, were still clearly more than a match for the divided allies. Napoleon himself exercised undisputed command without any possibility of interference: Wittgenstein, on the other hand, faced the practical problems of a coalition commander at the tactical level: the need for consultation with the Prussians and the associated difficulties of language, different tactical doctrine and staff procedures, and interference from the Tsar all affected his ability to conduct battle with the speed and flexibility of his opponent.

On top of all that, Napoleon had once again shown that he could judge better than the allies the moment to launch reserves, and still understood better than they the vital necessity of supporting manoeuvre with firepower. His plan for battle, as worked out in the saddle and executed on the field, remains a classic blueprint for the conduct of a meeting engagement even today.

III. LÜTZEN TO BAUTZEN, 3–19 MAY 1813

Soon after the Battle of Lützen, Napoleon was already hard at work on plans to retain the initiative he had gained. Ney was allowed a day's rest and then with his own and Marmont's corps he was to move north to relieve the besieged French garrison in Wittenberg-Elbe. By 4 May it was becoming clear that the allied main body was retiring on Dresden, although the corps of Generals Kleist and Bülow remained undetected. Equally clearly, the allies were retiring in good order. One observer noted that 'The Prussian troops have covered themselves with glory, they have become once more the Prussians of Frederick.'[13] This view was perhaps stretching a point, but certainly the allies remained a formidable force.

Napoleon's limited cavalry was now fully occupied in trying to identify the exact locations of the allies. Napoleon himself felt it most likely that they would retire towards the city of Bautzen in order to preserve their line of communications through Warsaw, while detaching part of their force to screen Berlin. His plan now therefore called for a large detached force to be formed under Ney's command, consisting of II, III and VII Corps, reinforced by part of I Corps and II Cavalry Corps. This force was to cross the Elbe at Torgau and Wittenberg, take the Saxon Army into VII Corps, and threaten Berlin. While Ney moved north, Napoleon himself would follow the allies through Dresden, while Lauriston's V Corps would move on Grimma on the River Mulde to act as a link between the two forces. By this means Napoleon hoped to detach the Prussians from the Russians and then destroy the two armies piecemeal.

The focus on Berlin also reflects Napoleon's continuing preoccupation with his original intention of advancing to Danzig on the Prussian coast. Even allowing for Napoleon having a clear grasp of the difficulties of preserving allied unity, it is difficult to see why he was so obsessed with Berlin, unless it was to repay Frederick William's treachery. For it was a cardinal principle of Napoleon's to focus on the destruction of the enemy army in battle and not on the acquisition of territory. Either he had a very strong belief in the capture of Berlin as decisive point in his attack on allied unity, or else he had put aside his own belief, disregarding the probability that by beating the allied army in battle, he would inevitably capture Berlin. His orders to Ney undoubtedly led to Ney's command becoming spread out so, that in the forthcoming Battle of Bautzen, Ney was not strong enough to fulfil the Emperor's intention – even if he had understood what that intention was.

The allied withdrawal, meanwhile, was not unduly hasty and in fact, Napoleon's estimate had been quite correct. After some initial disagreements, it had been decided to leave Bülow's corps covering Berlin while the main army withdrew to Bautzen, where a strong new position was to be surveyed and prepared by the Russian engineers. As the allies withdrew, there was a sharp action at Colditz on 5 May when the French vanguard caught up with General Miloradovich's Russian corps, which was acting as rearguard. In spite of this the allies made good their withdrawal through Dresden on 7 and 8 May.

Napoleon followed up, throwing a bridge across the Elbe at Briesnitz just south of Dresden, covered by his artillery. Determined action in Dresden itself also succeeded in driving the allied rearguard from the city bridge before it could be demolished. Thus by the evening of 11 May Napoleon had 70,000 troops across the Elbe at Dresden, and another 45,000 at Torgau, while the allies offered no serious opposition at all to his crossing operations.

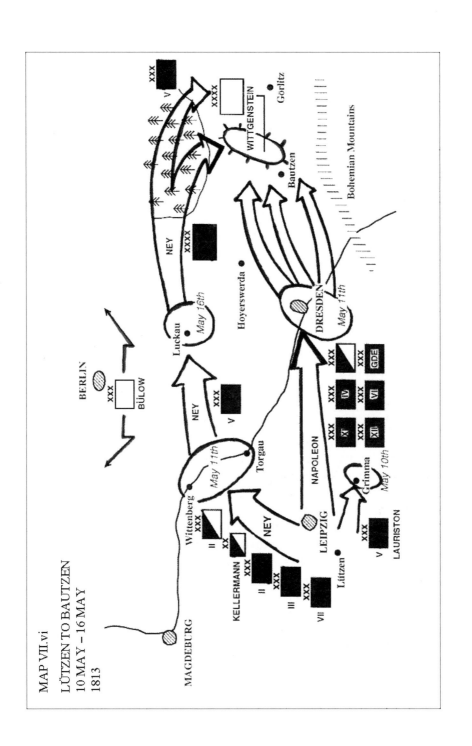

MAP VII.vi
LÜTZEN TO BAUTZEN
10 MAY – 16 MAY
1813

A short operational pause now followed, during which Napoleon decided to simplify his command arrangements to conform with his scheme for Ney's force. The Army of the Elbe under Eugène and the Army of the Main, Napoleon's main army, were merged. Eugène was removed from the scene and ordered to Italy,[14] where a strong corps of observation was being formed in order to tie down the Austrians, preventing their involvement in the Central European theatre.

Napoleon also used the pause to convert Dresden into his new centre of operations and to complete the assimilation of the Saxon Army into VII Corps. He then formalised the division of the army into two wings under Ney and himself, and reinforced Ney with Lauriston's V Corps, so that Ney's strength stood at 79,500 infantry and 4,800 cavalry. Napoleon himself retained command of 110,000 infantry and 12,000 cavalry.

On 12 May the IV, VI and XI Corps began a reconnaissance in force towards Bautzen in order to fix the allies, while Ney's army moved forward to concentrate at Luckau ready for a drive on Berlin. By 16 May, Macdonald, commanding the reconnaissance, had run the allies to ground at Bautzen. Napoleon therefore ordered the three corps concerned to fix the enemy while Oudinot's XII Corps worked around to the south of the allied position. Napoleon also sent word to Ney to be ready to march south with his own corps and Lauriston's V Corps, while detaching the II and VII Corps to continue the march on Berlin. But Ney failed completely to understand what was required of him, and in the end he marched south with his entire command. This was in many ways a sensible course and had he gathered his full strength, the outcome of Bautzen would have been substantially different. But as it was his two leading corps were separated by a full 24 hours' marching from the remainder.

On 18 May Napoleon sent further orders to clarify Ney's tasks and instructed him especially to cut the enemy's communications back through Lobau and Görlitz so that the allies would be forced onto the mountains along the Austrian frontier, where they would have to accept surrender or destruction, unless they violated Austrian neutrality. But still Ney did not grasp the Emperor's intention, and it must be said that Napoleon's instructions were far from clear. What the Emperor actually intended was very simple: to fix the allies frontally, and then roll up their position from the north and rear. Ney's slowness and Napoleon's divergence from his own principles were, however, to rob him of a decisive victory and ruin this brilliantly simple plan.

The allies, meanwhile, had reached Bautzen where Wittgenstein found a welcome reinforcement in the form of General Barclay de Tolly with 13,000 more Russian troops. Napoleon was not far behind them. By 10.00 am on 19 May he was close to Bautzen and he spent the day in a detailed observation and reconnaissance of the allied position. He saw that the allies had drawn up their forces in two lines along a series of shallow ridges, which they had fortified, with the River Spree to their front. The lines were some seven miles long, with the town of Bautzen as an occupied outwork slightly in advance of their centre. He also appreciated that the village of Hochkirch, where Frederick the Great had fought a bloody battle during the Seven Years War, was the key to the rear area since it commanded the main road eastwards towards Görlitz.

The Battle of Bautzen would provide a strong contrast with Lützen in three ways. First, Lützen was fought on a confined battlefield, while Bautzen took place on an extended frontage of seven miles. Second,

Russian General Mikhail Bogdanovich Barclay de Tolly (1761–1818) arrived in time to play a crucial role at Bautzen and was temporarily appointed allied C-in-C on 31 May 1813.

Lützen was a meeting engagement where ground was nothing; Bautzen was a setpiece battle fought on a selected position where ground was everything. Third, Lützen was won by manoeuvre, while Bautzen was – deliberately – to contain a strong element of attrition.

IV. BAUTZEN[15]

The area in which the Battle of Bautzen was fought is dominated by a series of rivers and intervening low ridges. The most significant of these rivers is the Spree. From the area below Bautzen the river flows in a steep sided valley some 50 metres deep, which is practically a gorge in places and is certainly a considerable obstacle. However it is of some significance that the command of the river valley varies from bank to bank. Also of significance is the number of large ponds in the river valley higher up, where the Spree becomes inconsiderable and is fordable in many places. Unlike the large reservoir which now exists just north of the town, many of these ponds were of great antiquity and were used for fish farming. These ponds, although not deep, and the marshy ground between, them were a serious obstacle to infantry and wheeled vehicles. Roughly parallel with the Spree and approximately two miles to the east of it is the Blossauer Wasser. In itself this is relatively unimportant, but its valley was also marshy and this afforded protection to any formation placing a position to the east of it. No doubt the allies first favoured holding the line of the Spree, but the varying command of the stream, the fordable nature of much of the river, and the attractiveness of the natural protection afforded by the Blossauer Wasser swung the argument in favour of a rear line with only an advanced guard action in Bautzen and along the Spree.

As well as the rivers, there is some higher ground of significance. In the extreme south are the densely wooded hills and the villages of Drohmberg and the Schmortzberg, which provided a strong flank. Just north of Bautzen and north-west of Kreckwitz is a confused mass of low, lumpy hills generally known as the Kreckwitz heights. On these heights the villages were fortified by the allies and abattis were set up in the woods. North of this area the ground is again generally flat with a few knolls, the most notable being between Malschwitz and Gleina and known as the Windmill Hill. All over this area the ground is still dotted with carp ponds.

Bautzen town in 1813 had between 7,000 and 8,000 inhabitants, living within the medieval defences, much of which were still intact. The deep, narrow gorge of the Spree to the west of the city was difficult for a frontal assault but the position could be turned via a stone bridge higher up or by fording the river lower down. The old walls had been modified by the construction of loopholes for artillery in order to produce interlocking fields of fire covering the Spree crossing and the main approach road to the town. There is no mention in any account of the battle of earthworks being constructed on the western bank of the river. This could have been due to the fact that the allies assumed that Bautzen itself was so naturally strong that it needed little improvement and any more work would detract from the main effort of construction behind the Blossauer Wasser. To that end it was relatively lightly held by only one regiment of Russian troops from the corps of General Miloradovich.

Having determined on the Blossauer Wasser as their main effort, the allies carried out numerous fortification works along the line, which generally afforded them excellent fields of fire. On the left, the line rested on the wooded hills of the Drohmberg and Schmortzberg. The centre ran from these hills to Kreckwitz, where the heights projected like a bastion on the allied right, and was covered by artillery redoubts whose fire swept the exposed slope. From here the line extended north and east towards Klix and Guttau. The scale of the effort expended on this position can be judged from the fact that the French engineers who later dismantled the position found 78 redoubts, batteries and emplacements throughout the allied defensive system. There were, however, two problems with the position. Despite being naturally very strong it was probably over extended; also its right, or northern, flank was not fixed on any particular feature and was vulnerable to an enveloping movement from the north.

Bautzen was a two-day battle, savagely fought. It will be recalled that Napoleon's plan called for his leading corps to pin the enemy frontally, a deliberately attritional attack designed to wear the allies down, which would be undertaken by the corps of Marmont, Oudinot and Macdonald. Ney and his own III Corps would then advance on the northern flank forcing the allies to weaken the centre and then commit their reserves in order to block this move. Concurrent with Ney's move, the corps of Lauriston would move from the north deep into the allied rear, seize the village of Hochkirch, and block the withdrawal route. Then at the critical moment, the Guard and the corps of Bertrand, under Soult's command, would smash the allied centre north of Bautzen. Although the allies were well entrenched, and Napoleon's formations were tired,

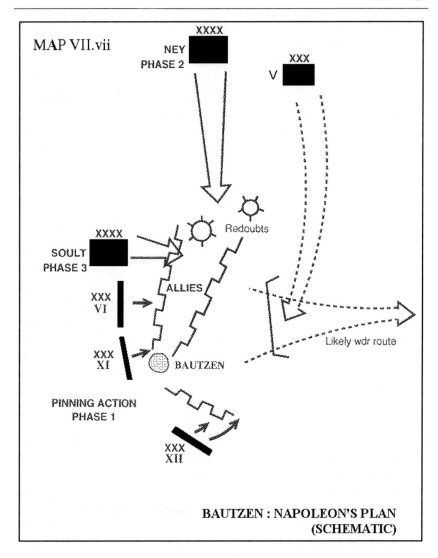

MAP VII.vii

NEY
PHASE 2

XXXX

XXX
V

Redoubts

SOULT
PHASE 3

XXXX

XXX
VI

ALLIES

XXX
XI

BAUTZEN

Likely wdr route

PINNING ACTION
PHASE 1

XXX
XII

**BAUTZEN : NAPOLEON'S PLAN
(SCHEMATIC)**

the French were at a numerical advantage throughout and Napoleon was confident that if all went well, Bautzen would be a second Jena.

Throughout 19 May the various French corps made their appearance and were drawn up as the map shows. The allies, aware of the approach of forces from the north, believed this to be a reinforcement to the frontal attack and tried to launch a spoiling attack using the corps of Barclay de Tolly and Yorck in order to cut off and destroy this reinforcement. This rash expedition achieved nothing but the loss of

2,000 men and by the early hours of 20 May Barclay had returned to the main position, followed at noon by Yorck. By the evening of that same day, Ney and Lauriston were both within striking distance of the allied right, although the corps of Victor and Reynier were spread out some distance behind. The enveloping manoeuvre was thus proceeding to plan – or so it seemed. The Emperor therefore decided, to ensure that Ney and Lauriston would be in position, that the whole of 20 May should be given over to the battle of attrition. The actual envelopment and final attack would be held over until 21 May.

For their part, the allies had also been making contingency plans. The orders for the battle which were issued on 19 May were extremely detailed and tried to provide for all contingencies, although they failed, notably, to produce any coherent defence against the very situation that Napoleon envisaged and which later occurred. In essence the allies planned to contain and exhaust any French attack, before themselves launching a counter attack around the French left – northern – flank with the idea of rolling the French up onto the mountains to the south. No provision was made for what was to happen if Napoleon did not attempt to seize the position immediately, nor for the likelihood of attack from the north. This rather blinkered attitude could, to a large degree, be attributed to the Tsar who had completely misread Napoleon's operational and tactical plans. The Tsar was convinced that it was Napoleon's aim to separate the allied armies from the Austrians and therefore the main effort of his attack would come against the allied left.

Napoleon had of course the opposite view, as, to his credit, did Wittgenstein, for by forcing the defeated allied army into Bohemia, Austria being neutral would either have to disarm the allies or declare for them. Being still unready for war, Austria would face the possibility of a French follow-up operation to Vienna which she could not prevent, and thus the collapse of the 6th Coalition would be the inevitable result. With the idea firmly fixed in the Tsar's mind that the only real danger could come from the south and west, the main effort was formed there by placing the bulk of the allied forces, including the reserve corps of the Grand Duke Constantin. Thus the inherent weakness of the position if attacked from the north was being reinforced by the dispositions of the defenders.

From early morning until noon on 20 May the French held back, but shortly after noon the bombardment of the allied line began. The first attacks began three hours later as Oudinot's troops crossed the Spree at the village of Singwitz. The river was very low at the time and the corps

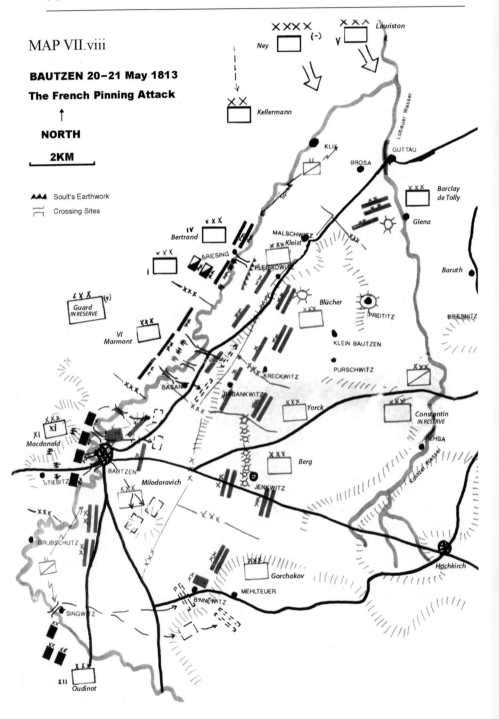

MAP VII.viii

BAUTZEN 20–21 May 1813

The French Pinning Attack

↑

NORTH

2KM

▲▲▲ Soult's Earthwork

〓 Crossing Sites

Ney

Lauriston

Kellermann

Löbauer Wasser

KLIX

BROSA

GUTTAU

Barclay
de Tolly

Glena

IV
Bertrand

BRIESING

MALSCHWITZ
Kleist

PLEISKOWITZ

Blücher

PREITITZ

Baruth

BRIESNITZ

Guard
IN RESERVE

VI
Marmont

KLEIN BAUTZEN

BASAN

KRECKWITZ

PURSCHWITZ

XI
Macdonald

BASANKWITZ

Yorck

Constantin
IN RESERVE

REHSA

STIEBITZ

BAUTZEN

Milodoravich

Berg

JENKWITZ

Kotitzer Wasser

GRUBSCHUTZ

Hochkirch

SINGWITZ

Gorchakov

MEHLTEUER

BINNEWITZ

XII
Oudinot

crossed easily by a mixture of fording and pontoon bridging. Having crossed, Oudinot reformed the corps and was able to outflank the corps of Miloradovich. He therefore came up against the southern flank of the corps of Gorchakov in the area of the village of Mehlteuer. By 6.00 pm Oudinot's artillery was pulverising the allied southern flank, fuelling the Tsar's obsession, so that although the allies were by now well aware of Ney's approach in the north, they miscalculated his strength and intentions – this after 21 years of war, during which the workings of the Napoleonic battle system must have become well known to them.

Oudinot continued his attack early on 21 May but by this time Gorchakov and Miloradovich had pulled back to oppose his advance directly. Oudinot's corps remained in action, under great pressure, all day and its commander not unnaturally appealed to the Emperor for assistance. He should have known better. His first appeal received no answer at all. The second received the response 'Tell your Marshal that the battle will be won at 3 o'clock and that until then he must do the best he can!'[16] That was all. It must have been small comfort to Oudinot to know that he was fulfilling exactly the role intended by the Emperor.

To Oudinot's north in Bautzen town it was Macdonald's XI Corps which forced the passage of the Spree under heavy fire from the defenders. Four crossings were established around the town – two at the southern end around the existing stone bridge, one at the northern end near the schloss, and the fourth about a quarter of a mile further north. By 6.00 pm on 20 May Macdonald had taken the town and his regiments had pushed up to half a mile beyond it, forcing back Miloradovich's troops. He renewed the attack on the morning of 21 May but fared little better than Oudinot – but he too was achieving the desired effect.

Further north still, Marmont's VI Corps, the final element in the pinning action, crossed the Spree at the same time as Macdonald and Oudinot using two bridging sites, which are now obliterated by the modern reservoir, and by fording. The division of General Compans managed to assist Macdonald by getting into the north-western suburbs of Bautzen soon after 3.00 pm, thus forcing the Russians to evacuate before they were enveloped. The remainder of Marmont's corps assaulted the Prussian lines on the east bank of the Spree held by the corps of Kleist and, after a hard fight, he was able to secure the high ground between Burk (then called Basan) and Basankwitz.

So much for the pinning attack, for by 6.00 pm on 20 May much of the allied advance guard position in the south was in French hands.

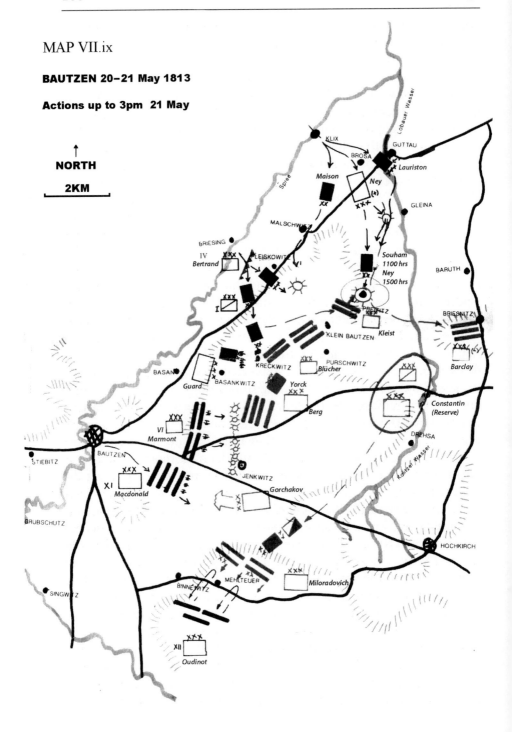

MAP VII.ix

BAUTZEN 20–21 May 1813

Actions up to 3pm 21 May

NORTH

2KM

Napoleon was therefore content to continue the attritional action of 21 May in this area, while the main effort now shifted to the envelopment and main attack in the centre and north.

At 4.00 am on 21 May new orders reached Marshal Ney. These instructed him to drive the allies from the area of Drehsa and then march on Weissenberg in the allied rear in order to complete the enveloping movement. These orders were, however, extremely confusing in two respects. First, Ney believed that he should march not on Weissenberg but on Hochkirch, since this was what Lauriston had originally been ordered to do. Second and more important, there were two villages of Drehsa. The first is now called Brosa, and is near Klix. The second is north of Hochkirch. Napoleon's order does not specify which he meant and there has been controversy ever since. Ney at once sent for further guidance and Napoleon explained the allied dispositions to the messenger. He also stated that Ney should be at Preititz by 11.00 am and that once he, Napoleon, had word of Ney's arrival there, and provided that the enemy reserves had been drawn off, then the final attack would be pressed home in the centre. Ney was further exhorted that the corps of Lauriston should move on his left so as to block the enemy withdrawal route. This direction should have been sufficient.

Ney's movement began soon after 5.00 am with Lauriston's corps leading. This corps was at a strength of only two divisions, as Ney had removed one division, and Lauriston was soon heavily involved with Yorck's advanced guard around Brosa. The 18,000-strong III Corps followed, led by Ney, who decided that to comply with the Emperor's instructions he should attack the corps of Barclay de Tolly and the Gleina redoubt, a feature which can still be traced on the ground. As Barclay had only 5,000 men available he was rapidly pushed back from Gleina onto the fortified village of Preititz, from where he called on Blücher for reinforcements. On arrival in Preititz, Barclay soon became aware of the advance of Lauriston on Ney's left and became seriously alarmed at the prospect of the allied army's right flank being completely turned. He therefore left two battalions only to help garrison Preititz and moved the main body of his corps to the south-east of some high ground around Baruth. There he faced his corps to the north to cover the vital withdrawal route from Bautzen towards Würschen.

By 10.00 am Ney had stormed and taken Gleina redoubt, and the division of General Maison, which Ney had detached from Lauriston's corps, was preparing to storm Malschwitz. Ney should now have pressed on to Preititz but he stuck rigidly to the Emperor's instruction to arrive at 11.00 am, even though with his strength had risen to 23,000 with the arrival of straggling divisions, and he could have secured Preititz with ease. Worse still, at this point Ney had a new idea. He had become aware of the Kreckwitz heights, which although not high, certainly dominate the area and draw the eye, and he became completely carried away with the idea that here lay the key to the allied position. At 11.00 am therefore he sent only one division to take Preititz, while the rest of the corps moved against Blücher. This was a fundamental error, for Ney had focused on the ground first, and the enemy second. Had he continued against Preititz with his whole force then he would have manoeuvred Blücher's force off the heights anyway and at the same time, removed pressure from Marshal Soult, who was having a decidedly difficult time. In fairness to Ney, when one sees the ground today it is easy to see how, despite the prominence of Hochkirch spire as a landmark for navigation in the distance, his attention would have been drawn by the heights – especially as his grasp of the essentials of Napoleon's plan was unsound.

Despite all the warning signs and the activity thus far, Tsar Alexander remained totally convinced that the danger still lay on the southern flank. Wittgenstein was, however, only too well aware of the danger in the north. 'I will wager my head' he said 'that this is only a demonstration; Napoleon's idea is to outflank our right and drive us into Bohemia.' In that one short sentence he had correctly summed up Napoleon's intention, but the Tsar refused to listen. Blücher meanwhile had received Barclay's request for assistance. Ney's delay before Preititz was just enough to give him time for action. He dispatched four battalions to the area above Klein Bautzen, and three more into Preititz. As these latter were advancing they met the leading elements of the French, who had disposed of Barclay's two battalions. The French leading elements were just leaving Preititz when the three Prussian battalions counter-attacked so vigorously that the French were pushed right back to Gleina. It was bitter hand-to-hand fighting, but it gained time on this flank for the allies.

Ney could now see the majority of the allied centre and knew that Napoleon had not yet attacked it. He sent word to Lauriston to abandon his task and join him. Lauriston was clearly unhappy, but he could not disobey. Leaving one division and half his cavalry to contain Barclay at Baruth he moved with his remaining troops – about 10,000 all told – to Preititz. His third division was still moving up and his fourth, detached by Ney, was still engaged in the villages of Malschutz and Pleiskowitz where it remained fully occupied until 3.00 pm. The attack on Preititz was renewed at 2.00 pm and for an hour the fighting swayed this way and that until at 3.00 pm, Ney gained the village. He had done so at great cost in casualties and in time. Urged now by Jomini, his chief of staff, to push on to Hochkirch, Ney still hesitated, attracted by the Kreckwitz heights. The outcome of this hesitation was that the allied line of retreat remained unclosed, with significant consequences. Worse still, Ney had failed to draw off the allied reserves or weaken the centre, making Soult's task a great deal harder.

So far there has been little mention of Soult, who it will be remembered was in command of the Guard and Bertrand's IV Corps, and who was to effect the master stroke which would win the battle in the centre. On 20 May Soult's troops had made an unopposed crossing of the Spree by a mixture of fording and pontoon bridging in an area where the river is an inconsiderable obstacle. Having secured the crossings, IV Corps appears to have spent the rest of the day on 20 May constructing a large earthwork or rampart parallel to the east bank of the Spree, in order to protect his sappers and the build-up of the two corps. The earthwork was probably two metres high and half a mile long and, since the passage of 178 years has done its work, a low bank is all that can still, just, be traced along some of its length.

Early on 21 May under cover of this earthwork, Soult moved up 20,000 infantry, 1,000 cavalry and 30 guns of IV Corps. Soult's intention, while the allies' attention was distracted by Ney, was to capture the area of Kreckwitz and Pleiskowitz, including the Pleiskowitz redoubt. At the same time, the Emperor ordered part of the Guard forward into the gap between the corps of Marmont and Bertrand, along with a sizeable proportion of the artillery of the Guard Corps. This, with the artillery of IV Corps, formed the favoured Napoleonic grand battery and from 1.30 pm onwards it began to fire on the allied centre. At 2.30 pm Napoleon, who had spent much of the morning sleeping, heard the sounds of Ney's attack and ordered Bertrand to attack. Under a murderous fire from the allied positions, the divisions of IV Corps began to advance and, despite heavy losses, by 3.00 pm they had compelled the corps of Blücher and Yorck to retire to the eastern edge of the high ground.

After 3.00 pm most of the action in the north centred around Blücher's position on the Kreckwitz heights. His position was becoming more and more perilous in that he was in great danger of being encircled, for Bertrand's attack had penetrated as far as the villages of

MAP VII.x

**BAUTZEN 20–21 May 1813
The Allied Withdrawal**

↑
NORTH

|— **2KM** —|

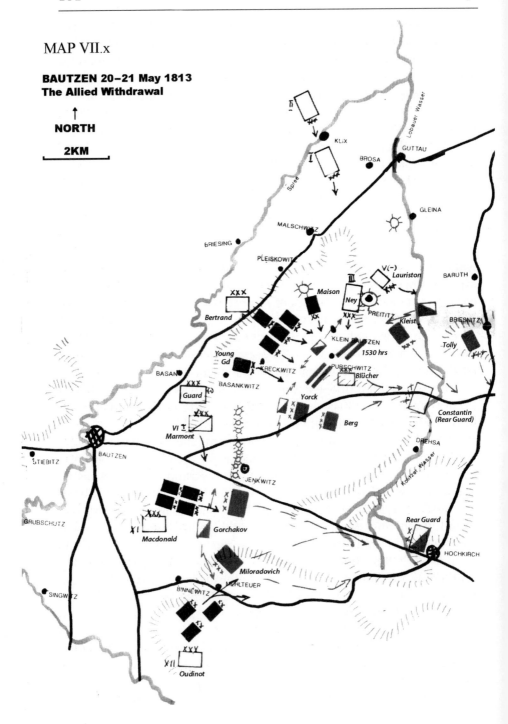

Doberschutz, Weinberg and Kreckwitz. At the same time Maison's division was advancing from Pleiskowitz, and Lauriston was still moving from the north-east. Worse still, he could see the Napoleon's Guard apparently advancing from Basankwitz towards Litten. Blücher's first reaction was to call for assistance from Yorck, and indeed he had good reason to be alarmed, for the high ground from which he had just retired, and on which the Imperial Guard was now developing its attack, was vital to the cohesion of the defence. In short, Blücher's position was untenable and he ordered a further withdrawal – just in time: Baron Muffling estimated that he had only 15 minutes to spare before being completely surrounded. Fifteen minutes, though, was enough. The Prussian retirement was carried out in perfect order covered by the cavalry. On reaching Kreckwitz Blücher's troops conducted a successful rearward passage of lines through part of Yorck's command, then continued the withdrawal for about half a mile to a new position south of Purschwitz. This limited movement was absolutely crucial for the allies' salvation, for as the Prussians left the high ground, the French rose to the attack. Ney's men from the north and Bertrand's from the west and south rushed onto the plateau to find the enemy gone. These two corps became hopelessly entangled and it was an hour before they could be reformed and realigned. Ney, realising to his disgust that the allies had given him the slip, realised also that it was his diversion towards the heights and his drawing in of Lauriston which had created the gap through which they had slipped. He at once sent orders to Lauriston to block the allied retirement, but it was too late – the allies had been forced to withdraw, but the attacks which should have destroyed them had missed the mark.

Wittgenstein, meanwhile, had not been idle. He had redeployed Yorck's corps to cover Blücher's movement and had committed part of the Russian Guards Division in support. Even so it was not until Ney recaptured Preititz that the Tsar finally realised the danger to the allied northern flank. Even he concurred at once that the only course of action was an immediate general retirement, for which orders were given at 4.00 pm. The retirement would be conducted in three columns: in the north, Barclay was to hold his position until the Prussian and Russian Guards had withdrawn to Würschen, after which he was to follow, covered by his cavalry. In the centre, the two Prussian corps would retire through the Russian reserve corps, which would act as rearguard to the army. In the south, Gorchakov and Miloradovich were to retire on Lobau.

In the centre, Napoleon still hoped that Marmont, the Guard, and the cavalry reserve would be able to push the Russian formations on the allied left onto Bohemia. However the rearguards retired in such steadfast order that the whole allied army got away. In particular, the inferior French cavalry could do nothing against the vastly superior numbers of the allies. Napoleon watched in fury as the allies marched off the field. 'What!' he cried 'after such a slaughter no trophies? These people will leave me no claws!' And so indeed the Battle of Bautzen ended. Like Lützen it was a bloody affair: the allies lost 11,000 killed and wounded, but few prisoners, and no trophies other than 19 spiked and disabled guns which had been abandoned. The French lost at least twice this figure, so although Napoleon was left in possession of the field, it was a Pyrrhic victory.

Bautzen should have been the perfect Napoleonic battle – why was it not? Its failings have as much to say on this as did the successes of Lützen. First, the declining quality of the *Grande Armée* was becoming obvious. At both Lützen and Bautzen, Napoleon had been obliged to commit the Guard, something rarely done in the past. On the allied side, the Russians and Prussians had shown determination and the desire for revenge and their troops were gaining in experience all the time. Second, Napoleon's command and staff system were still good, but they had declined. Napoleon had aimed to concentrate actually on the battlefield rather than short of it, and the event showed that the system was no longer capable of executing his intentions. Ney is often held responsible for the failure of the plan, but part of the failure must lie in an over-centralised command system which did nothing to educate subordinates or allow then initiative. The choice of Ney was equally flawed, as with a man so impetuous and so little given to analytical thought, there was every chance of a disaster. Possibly Napoleon hoped that Jomini would keep things on the rails, but as von Caemmerer has remarked, the cases in which a chief of staff can make up for the deficiencies of his commander are few. Third the shortage of cavalry made it very difficult to form a reserve capable of conducting a pursuit.

By contrast the allied superiority in quality and numbers of mobile troops allowed them to form an effective rearguard, and thus break clean. Last, in conducting coalition warfare, the allies continued to suffer from a divided command with particular disagreements between Wittgenstein and the Tsar. After Bautzen, Wittgenstein resigned in protest over the Tsar's interference and was replaced by Barclay de Tolly. The lesson for coalition war is a telling one.

V. AFTER BAUTZEN

It was as well for the allies that when Napoleon was able to pick up the pursuit eastwards on 22 May, he could do so only slowly. In the immediate aftermath of Bautzen, allied morale at all levels was far from high and there were more disagreements within the high command as to the future conduct of the war. As well as Wittgenstein's resignation, there were differences between the allies. Blücher and Gneisenau were prepared to offer battle again, while Barclay de Tolly proposed a retirement into Poland. Eventually a compromise, proposed by the Tsar, was adopted whereby the allies prepared to fall back in two columns on Schweidnitz in Silesia. From here, communications could be maintained both with Poland and with Austria while at least some defence of Prussian territory could be undertaken.

Meanwhile Napoleon had given orders to follow up the retreating allies. Reynier's VII Corps, with Latour-Maubourg's cavalry, set off for Reichenbach followed by the Guard Corps and Marmont's VI Corps. To the north marched Lauriston's V Corps. Further north again Macdonald's XI and Bertrand's IV Corps marched towards Lobau. The left flank was protected by III Corps at Weissenberg. Finally Oudinot's shattered XII Corps was left to rest at Bautzen and recover its strength.

By 10.00 am on 22 May the VII Corps had reached Reichenbach where a stiff action was fought against the allied rearguard under Prince Eugen of Württemberg. By 3.00 pm, Reynier had forced Eugen to withdraw to a position short of Gorlitz, but Eugen had achieved his mission of delaying the French advance. Reynier now asked the Emperor, who was close by, for permission to break off the action as his troops were close to exhaustion. The reply was a peremptory order to press on! As VII Corps began to move once more, a Russian cannon shot passed close to the Emperor and killed Grand Marshal Duroc. Napoleon had a great affection for Duroc and took his death, following close on that of Bessières, very badly. At Reichenbach, Duroc was joined in death by General of Engineers Kirgener and General Bruyère. The result was that, most uncharacteristically, Napoleon ordered the action to be broken off. Even so, the VII Corps had marched 17 miles and fought a five-hour action only a short time after the battle at Bautzen.

Throughout the next three days the allied withdrawal continued, followed up by the French. Despite the defeat of Bautzen and the process of retreat, the fighting spirit of the allied rearguard held up remarkably well so that, what with bad roads, frequent river crossings and delaying

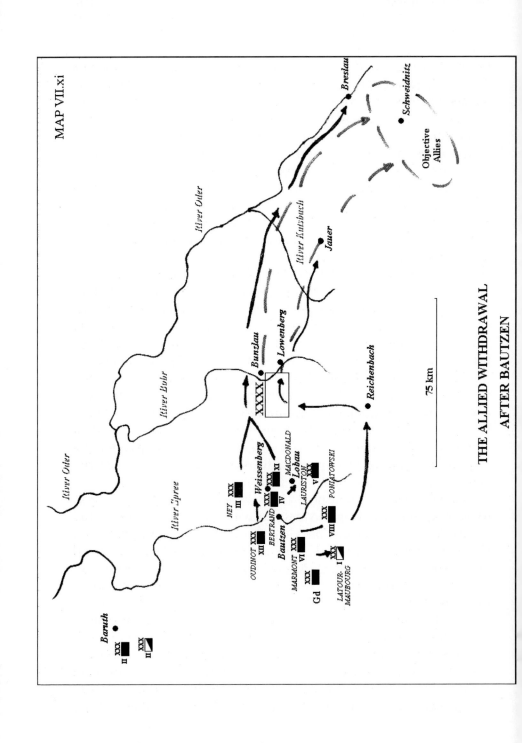

MAP VII.xi

THE ALLIED WITHDRAWAL
AFTER BAUTZEN

75 km

actions, the French advance began to slow. The XI Corps in particular fought a bitter 12-hour battle with the Russians on 25 May and on the following day the leading division of V Corps was heavily attacked by 3,000 Prussian cavalry supported by artillery near the village of Michelsdorf. The surprised French lost 1,000 men, a quarter of their strength, in less than 15 minutes. The remainder were only saved by the prompt arrival of the second division of the corps.

By 26 May the allied main body had passed over the Katzbach stream and on the following day swung south-east towards Schweidnitz, which was reached on 29 May. On arrival, the allies found that the fortifications of the place, demolished in 1807, had not been repaired so that its potential as a defensive position was nowhere near what had been hoped. Napoleon's main body was about two days' march behind the allies and on 1 June he occupied Breslau on the Oder. Here he was well situated west and north of the allies, able to cut off their withdrawal, and in an excellent position to inflict another, this time fatal, Bautzen.

News from elsewhere was good, too, for only three days earlier, Davout's corps had succeeded in retaking Hamburg. Only Oudinot had suffered a reverse. Sent northwards to threaten Berlin once his corps had recovered, he had been caught and defeated by Blücher at Luckau on 28 May. But all was not what it seemed. There were as many disagreements between the marshals as there were between the allied commanders;[17] the lines of communication were being constantly harassed by Cossacks, who had even attacked Leipzig itself and indeed entered the city in strength. And finally, Napoleon's conscript army was showing signs of exhaustion as battle, sickness, and straggling took their toll.

Both sides seemed therefore to have lost the chance of any quick, decisive victory. When the Austrians therefore proposed a ceasefire and the possibility, with their mediation, of a negotiated settlement, both sides were willing to accept. On 2 June a 36-hour truce began, extended on 4 June after a short conference to 20 July. This was again later extended to 10 August, with six days' notice to be given before hostilities recommenced.

A strip of neutral territory was designated between the armies in which neither side would position troops. Beyond this strip, the French accepted a ceasefire line roughly along the Katzbach to its confluence with the Oder, their northern limit would be the frontier of Saxony from the Oder to Wittenberg on the Elbe. From Wittenberg southwards they were confined to the west of the Elbe, inclusive of the islands in the river, and as much of the territory of the 32nd Military Division as they held on 8 June – in the event, most of it. The garrisons of Danzig, Mödlin, Zamosc, Stettin, Kustrin and Hamburg, if besieged, were to be supplied every five days. Thus the spring campaign came to an abrupt and somewhat unexpected close.

NOTES

1. Marbot, iii, p.250.
2. *Correspondance* vol. xxv, no. 19942, dated 1.v.1813.
3. This account is based on the descriptions of Baron Marbot, J.F.C. Fuller, and the author's personal reconnaissance of the ground.
4. D'Odeleben, p.51.
5. Marbot, v, p.15.
6. Petre, p.78.
7. Elting states that up to one-third of the French artillery ammunition was defective. Altogether 39,000 rounds were fired.
8. von Caemmerer, p.65.
9. Chandler, p.1120. Petre gives the French figure as 18,000 against 12,000 allies.
10. *Correspondance* vol xxv, no. 20031, dated 2.v.1813.
11. Luttwak, p.9.
12. Chandler, p.167.
13. Friederich, i, p.244.
14. *Correspondance,* vol. xxv, no. 20031, dated 12.v.1813.
15. The account of the battle is based on Marbot, Petre, Chandler and the author's personal reconnaissance of the ground.
16. Chandler, p.894.
17. See especially Petre, pp.146–7, 149.

Chapter VIII

The Ten Weeks' Truce

൞

I. WHY THE TRUCE?

S ECRET NEGOTIATIONS BETWEEN Napoleon and the allies for an armistice, or even a settlement, had been in progress since before the Battle of Bautzen, both with and without the mediation of Austria. The Austrian 'good offices' had been offered by Lieutenant General Count Bubna on behalf of the Emperor of Austria as early as 20 December 1812.[1] Napoleon had accepted the principle, although he no wish for an *armed* mediation. In the immediate aftermath of Bautzen, both Metternich and his own ministers Maret and Caulaincourt urged him to make a favourable settlement, but to no avail. By late May it seems with the benefit of hindsight that Napoleon had the possibility of peace on his own terms within his grasp: he had inflicted two sharp reverses on his enemies and was now poised to inflict at least another Bautzen – and maybe another Jena. Jomini later spoke of Napoleon's hesitation as the greatest mistake of his career,[2] so why did he not finish the war at Schweidnitz?

The answer is clear both from Napoleon's correspondence and from his situation. In two letters dated 29 May [3] and 2 June [4] he states that 'Two considerations have made up my mind: my shortage of cavalry, which prevents me from striking great blows, and the hostile attitude of Austria.' The weakness of the cavalry had been a recurring theme thus far both in reconnaissance and pursuit, but what of Austria? True, there were now close to 150,000 Austrian and Hungarian troops concentrating around Prague, from where they could certainly threaten Napoleon's southern flank. However on 1 June, with the allies at Schweidnitz, Napoleon was positioned in such a way that within 36 hours he could have interposed his army between the allies and their communications, forcing them either to accept battle with their backs to the Bohemian mountains or else make a forced march to the south-east.

For the allies, the first course risked being driven into Austria as Wittgenstein had foreseen, in which case it is hard to imagine Austria espousing the allied cause in the wake of a third defeat; the second would certainly separate the Russians and Prussians, perhaps permanently. At best, the allies would have been forced to a humiliating peace. At worst, their military power would have been destroyed.

But by 4 June the allies had moved out of the trap and the chance had passed: that Napoleon allowed it to pass without acting with the remorseless vigour which had characterised his earlier campaigns points to other factors influencing his decision. These factors were significant, and were essentially to do with the condition of his army. By 1 June, counting battle casualties, sick, and stragglers, the *Grande Armée* had almost halved in size since April. Modern estimates have concluded that a Napoleonic corps could lose 80 per cent of its strength over a period of eight months through sickness, disease, desertion, and straggling without firing a shot.[5] Some troops in both armies had now been marching and fighting steadily for five months. Reinforcements were on the way from France, but time was needed for their arrival.

Moreover there was a shortage of ammunition and food, partly as a result of the lengthy lines of communication, partly the result of an imperfect commissariat system, and partly because of Cossack raiding. Last, the army was very close to exhaustion. The campaign had, therefore, reached a culminating point in that the present level of operations could just about be maintained, but could not be developed any further. An operational pause was therefore an absolute necessity.

The allies too were in dire need of a pause. They had suffered two defeats and were, like Napoleon, losing men rapidly. Again, reinforcements were on their way from Prussia, Russia and Sweden but time was needed to allow them to come up. There was, too, a need to rethink allied strategic and operational plans given the disagreements within the high command. Austria was also in need of more time. The general direction of Austrian foreign policy had been clear since Schwarzenberg's defection in Russia, and moreover there was a score to settle with Napoleon, but the army was not yet ready for war. All in all the situation of the allies was extremely dangerous.

II. THE AUSTRIAN MEDIATION

The truce, which is known to history as the Armistice of Pleiswitz or Poischwitz, was therefore a matter of convenience rather than a genuine attempt to reach a negotiated peace. It was Metternich who had, as far back as March 1813, proposed the Austrian mediation to the allies after Bubna's mission to Napoleon. The Tsar had accepted at the time only because Metternich had assured him that it would fail. Certainly this position had not changed and the allies were more concerned to gain time to induce Austria to throw in her lot with the coalition. For his part, Metternich thought that in the wake of the spring campaign it might be possible to reach a continental peace, but not a maritime peace which would include British demands. Nor did he especially wish to see the total downfall of the Napoleonic system, which stood for the order and discipline he so much admired. All this led him to the conclusion that a compromise peace in Europe, which would force the British to a separate settlement, was most desirable. He therefore aimed to exclude Britain from the negotiations and thereby isolate her from the coalition.

This was not easy, especially given the presence of British plenipotentiaries; moreover the British signed treaties on 14 and 15 June with Russia and Prussia, and had already concluded an agreement with Sweden. This *fait accompli* did much to oblige Metternich to accede to the Reichenbach treaty with the allies on 27 June and to concede that once Britain was a full party to the treaty, her interests must also be recognised. By the terms of the Reichenbach treaty, Metternich agreed to present agreed allied demands to Napoleon as the basis for a settlement, which would be negotiated at a congress in Prague, and that if the Austrian mediation failed, Austria would join the allies.

Metternich met Napoleon on 26 June in the Marcolini Palace in Dresden. After a stormy meeting, Napoleon had agreed to the mediation and to the congress, which would commence on 5 July. Only four days later came news which had a profound bearing on the position of both Napoleon and the allies. This news was that of Wellington's decisive victory at Vitoria on 21 June (see Chapter XIV). This had a marked effect on flagging allied morale, while British prestige rose to new heights in Prussia and Hanover. In Russia the one and only *Te Deum* of gratitude for a foreign victory was sung. In Prague, Count Stadion rushed into Prince Metternich's bedroom to break the news, news which certainly undid Metternich's early intentions in regard to Britain and assisted the Austrian moves towards open membership of the coalition.

For Napoleon it was evil news indeed. Having milked Spain of its best troops in the spring he now faced the prospect of having the British at his back, a prospect of war on two fronts he could ill afford. His agreement to the prolongation of the armistice was given on the day following the arrival of the news of Vitoria, but he also needed time to influence the Spanish theatre more directly, and it was an indication of the gravity of the situation that Soult, who had only left Spain in the spring, and who was Napoleon's ablest lieutenant, was dispatched to take up the command.

The victory of the allied army in Spain also reinforced the conviction of Caulaincourt and Maret that peace must be secured now before all was lost. When Caulaincourt arrived at the Congress of Prague on 28 July Metternich warned him that unless Napoleon signed a peace treaty on 10 August, Austria would declare war on 11 August. Caulaincourt in answer gave the first hint of a rift in the French government and nation, which must have encouraged Metternich:

> You do not see in me the representative of the whims of the Emperor, but of his true interest and that of France. I am quite as European in these present questions as you can be. Bring us back to France by peace or war, and you will be blessed by thirty million Frenchmen and by all the clear-sighted servants and friends of the Emperor.[6]

Not that Napoleon was in any way gulled by the Austrian attitude. He regarded the position which the Austrians had adopted as mediator between himself and the allies, to say nothing of England and Sweden, as an act of barely concealed hostility, especially in the light of Schwarzenberg's defection in 1812. This he had made absolutely clear to Metternich at the Dresden meeting, kicking his hat to and fro across the room in his rage as he did so. Besides, he was well aware that the allies – and as far as he was concerned, probably Austria too, were receiving financial assistance from Britain.

Even so, Napoleon was confident of final victory but was prepared, if the terms were right – that is, if they restored him and his empire to their full extent and glory – to settle. Compromise was not on the cards, he saw no reason to do so: he had not been defeated; his prestige at home would certainly suffer badly if he gave in now; and who could say what future demands the allies might make? The whole direction of his foreign policy over the years had been geared to the acquisition of territory, and he was not about to change this without a fight. He therefore saw the allied proposals as a trap[7] and by so doing, although militarily he gained much from the truce, diplomatically his failure to compromise was an error which drove Austria and Britain together.

III. THE ALLIES

The conditions demanded by the allies at Prague were certainly more than Napoleon was prepared to concede after his relatively successful spring campaign, despite Caulaincourt's words, which were underlined by Berthier, as Metternich had noted during the negotiations on 26 June: 'The Prince of Neuchâtel [Berthier] said to me in a whisper "Do not forget that Europe needs peace – France above all else wants nothing but peace."'[8]

They were also rather more, as a whole, than Metternich himself wished to fight for. The allies were demanding no less than the restoration of Austria to her pre-1805 boundaries and of Prussia to her pre-1806 boundaries; the dissolution of the Confederation of the Rhine and the end of French influence in Germany; freedom for the Hanseatic ports; the dissolution of the Grand Duchy of Warsaw including the evacuation of the Pomeranian garrisons; independence for the Netherlands; and entire freedom from French influence in Italy. The influence of Britain was also apparent in the demand for the restoration of the ancient dynasty in Spain – Portugal was already free. No wonder then that, although he had agreed to the prolongation of the armistice, Napoleon eventually rejected the terms. No wonder too that Metternich, having been forced by Napoleon's intransigence into a position he did not much relish, is reported to have told Napoleon at their final meeting, 'Sire, you are a lost man.'[9]

Diplomatically then, the prolongation of the armistice had worked to the benefit of the allies. Militarily too it had allowed them some much needed time in two respects. First, the Russians and Prussians had completed their reinforcement; second, Austria had completed her mobilisation. By the middle of August the allied field armies numbered over half a million men, including 572 squadrons of cavalry, 68 regiments of Cossacks, and around 1,400 guns. Another 250,000 men were disposed in garrisons, sieges of isolated French fortresses, and in the reserves. For the Russians, the existing field army was to be supplemented by large numbers of reinforcements to make good losses and by the new 3rd Reserve Army, 60,000 strong, which had formed in Poland under General Bennigsen. Prussia, in addition to making good her losses with drafts of recruits, was raising a force of *Landwehr*, ill equipped and trained it is true, but 160,000 strong and capable of relieving other troops for limited operations. In addition, Bernadotte's Swedish corps north-east of Berlin numbered 40,000 although only 18,000 were actually committed to battle. Finally, the Austrians had about 123,000 men available for operations in the Central European theatre after taking account of the need to watch Italy and Bavaria. With time, these forces had the potential to grow even larger.

Seen in this light, is not surprising that the eventual allied plan relied heavily on attrition. For this reason it was deprecated by German theorists until Delbrück's interpretation of Clausewitz,[10] on the assumption that attrition was an inferior form of war, rather than a necessary strategy whose aim, having worn Napoleon down, was 'to strike the final blow with assurance'.[11] But the plan took much effort to form for the simple reason that as the coalition expanded, so did the consultation processes which coalition warfare demands. In outline, the allied plan was hammered out by the Tsar, King Frederick William, Prince Bernadotte and their advisers at Trachenberg Castle, north of Breslau, even while the Congress of Prague was in session. It was subsequently modified by Austria at Reichenbach on 19 July after her formal accession to the coalition.

Scharnhorst's view of the future direction of the war before his death in June had been that the allies should opt for a dispersed advance followed by a vigorous concentration when the opportunity arose for a decisive battle.[12] Austrian doctrine on the other hand was based on the writings of the Archduke Charles – the much-respected soldier who had been the first opponent to defeat Napoleon in the field, at Aspern-Essling. This doctrine advocated cautious manoeuvre and security of the base of operations, much after the manner of eighteenth century military thought. It was a philosophy based on the prudence which had so far effectively maintained the Hapsburg empire rather than risking it on a single battle.[13] Thus Lieutenant General Count Radetzky, the Austrian chief of staff, wrote operational memoranda in May and June, which although claiming the destruction of the enemy army as the proper object of the allies, in fact relied entirely on attrition of Napoleon's strength through campaign wastage rather than large-scale fighting. It was Schwarzenberg who proposed that the Army of Bohemia

King Frederick William III, Emperor Francis II and Tsar Alexander i show allied coalition solidarity at Prague. Behind the Tsar, Prince Schwarzenberg in the Austrian white uniform heads the assembled allied generals.

should advance on the French communications and that 'battle with a superior enemy force should be avoided until the Allied armies have united with us'.[14]

Toll, the Tsar's adviser, proposed several audacious plans but it was he who, by proposing a compromise between the Prussian and Austrian ideas, was father to the plan eventually developed. In this he was assisted by Bernadotte who, although thwarted in his plans to secure the overall command for himself, proposed that 'the centre of the Austrian Monarchy will become the grave of the great Napoleon'.[15]

The Trachenberg-Reichenbach plan therefore laid down allied operational objectives. First, it would be an offensive campaign, with the enemy's centre of operations, Dresden, as the first objective. A most important qualification was that a general action against Napoleon himself was to be avoided unless under highly advantageous circumstances. French forces were only to be attacked when divided and when the allies were superior in numbers. If any allied army was itself attacked by strong French formations, it would retire, while other formations fell on the French flanks and rear. Any fortresses encountered would be masked, but not besieged. This process would be accompanied by attacks on the French lines of communication by Cossacks, in the absence of any widespread partisan movement like that in Spain. Such attacks would, it was hoped, tie down French troops in isolated rear-area security detachments, which could then be destroyed piecemeal. This process of attrition would, it was felt, be a safer road to eventual victory than risking another large-scale battle just yet.

To put these plans into effect, the allies formed four armies, all multinational in composition, as a demonstration of solidarity. The main effort was placed with the Army of Bohemia under the command of Field Marshal Prince von Schwarzenberg, since the allies believed that Napoleon was most likely to attack southwards towards Prague. This army consisted of 220,000 Austrian and Prussian troops, the latter from Silesia. Schwarzenberg was to move, according to circumstances, towards either Hof, or Eger, or Silesia, or if ultimately necessary to retire on the Danube if Napoleon attacked. In the last case, Bernadotte's army would then attack the exposed French left flank and rear. To make this possible, Bernadotte's Army of the North was reinforced by Russian formations to a strength of 100,000. He was to leave 20,000 Swedes to mask Davout in Hamburg and then be prepared to advance either in support of Schwarzenberg, or preferably towards Leipzig. If he was attacked he was to retire, while the remaining allied

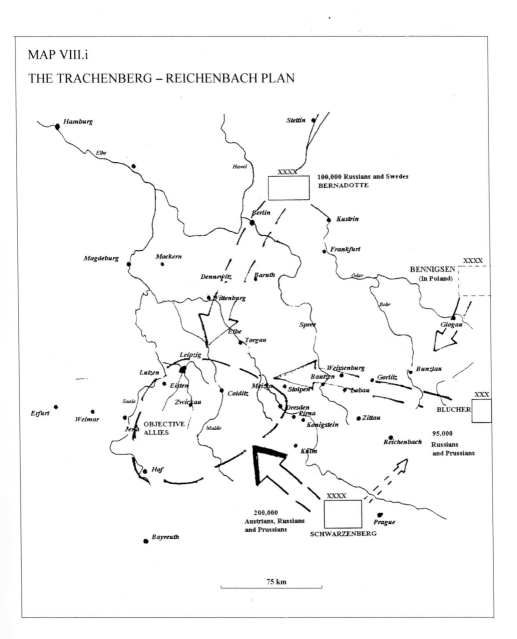

MAP VIII.i

THE TRACHENBERG – REICHENBACH PLAN

Hamburg

Stettin

Elbe

Havel

XXXX
100,000 Russians and Swedes
BERNADOTTE

Berlin

Kustrin

Magdeburg

Mockern

Frankfurt

Oder

XXXX
BENNIGSEN
(In Poland)

Dennewitz

Baruth

Wittenburg

Bobr

Spree

Glogau

Elbe

Torgau

Leipzig

Lutzen

Weissenburg

Bunzlau

Bautzen

Gorlitz

Eisten

Mrizen

Stolpen

Lobau

Colditz

XXX
BLUCHER

Saale

Zwickau

Dresden

Erfurt

Weimar

Pirna

Zittau

Jena

OBJECTIVE
ALLIES

Mulde

Konigstein

Reichenbach

95,000
Russians
and Prussians

Hof

Kulm

200,000
Austrians, Russians
and Prussians

XXXX

Prague

Bayreuth

SCHWARZENBERG

75 km

armies closed in on the French from the flanks and rear as before. The third army, the Army of Silesia under Blücher, was some 95,000 strong and composed of Russian and Prussian formations. Blücher was ordered to follow any French retirement towards the Elbe, cross the river, and unite with Bernadotte – but not risk a general engagement unless he was sure of success. Fourth, the Russian Reserve Army in Poland under Bennigsen was to advance towards Glogau ready either to attack the French main army in co-operation with the other allied armies, or else block any French advance into Poland.

Although no written Trachenberg plan survives it was a concept which suited the Austrian ends very well. In their eyes it left little to chance, would probably ensure success, and should preserve the Austrian Army for future moves. The plan also clearly shows signs that Napoleon's opponents had at last learned something from him, in particular the need to focus on the enemy army rather than on territory. But their deliberate avoidance of Napoleon's favourite device, the decisive battle, gave the plan – as originally conceived – little chance of achieving victory except by long drawn-out attritional processes. It can best be summarised as a strategy to 'avoid any unequal battle and so wear down the enemy, in order to fall on his weakened elements with superior forces and defeat them in detail'.[16]

Supreme command was vested in Schwarzenberg, who in the absence of the Archduke Charles was Austria's senior commander – and who enjoyed Metternich's confidence. In the strategic and operational direction of the campaign, his chief lieutenants were Count Radetzky, the Austrian chief of staff; and General Freiherr von Langenau, a Saxon defector. The question of the supreme command is worthy of consideration, given the interest it has aroused in recent times. Once Austria had joined the allies, Metternich was determined that her preponderance in terms of troops should be recognised: 'The important thing is to have the decisive voice in the determination of the military dispositions, and to maintain . . . the principle that the power that puts 300,000 men into the field is the first power . . .'[17]

The Tsar conceded the point, but still wished to influence the choice. The logical man in his view was the Archduke Charles, with the newly-defected Jomini as his chief of staff. This was, and is, an interesting proposal, although both were devotees of the methods of the *ancien régime* in warfare – and both were mistrusted by the Prussians who were scornful of Bernadotte, Moreau and Jomini, whom they regarded as renegades.[18] Not that Metternich considered such a combination as desirable, since he was aware of the personal connections between Charles and the Tsar; and in any case, Charles was out of favour with the Emperor of Austria and his ministers.[19] Metternich expected enough difficulties with his allies, without adding to them from within his own camp: 'We want a *Feldherr* who will make war, not one who wants to be a politician. The Archduke wants to be minister for foreign affairs too . . .'[20]

Schwarzenberg may have held the command, but the allied sovereigns all surrounded themselves with their own advisers: the Emperor Francis with General Duka; Frederick William with Knesebeck; the Tsar with Jomini, Moreau, Wolkonsky, General Count Arakchaiev, and Major General Count von Diebitsch. The turmoil which this crowd produced soon drove Schwarzenberg to complain bitterly that 'It really is inhuman what I must tolerate, surrounded as I am by feeble-minded people, fools of every description, eccentric project makers, intriguers, asses, babblers . . .'[21]

Orders were often transmitted from headquarters to the armies by the monarchs, who were also prone to issuing threats to withdraw or redirect their contingents when it suited them. Everyone, too, was suspicious of Bernadotte, accusing him of secret negotiations with the French, and (with some justice), of saving his own troops while sacrificing theirs.[22] But with all that said, the presence of the Emperors of Russia and Austria and the King of Prussia at allied headquarters did help to maintain allied unity and mitigate the independent spirit of Prussian, Russian and Austrian generals. Given Schwarzenberg's tactical incompetence at times in the forthcoming campaign, the Tsar in particular was also of real practical value in restraining him.

IV. NAPOLEON

While the allies consulted, Napoleon had been making good his losses as fast as only he could. By August he had formed Eugène's army in Italy, along with Count Wrede's Bavarians, to a strength of almost 200,000 men. This force would, he hoped, tie down the bulk of the Austrian armies if and when she entered the war. In addition, the Elbe fortresses and isolated garrisons accounted for another 50,000 men. In the central European theatre his main field army was reinforced to almost 400,000 men with an excellent artillery arm of 1,300 guns, but only 40,000 cavalry. This army, like that of the allies, was becoming

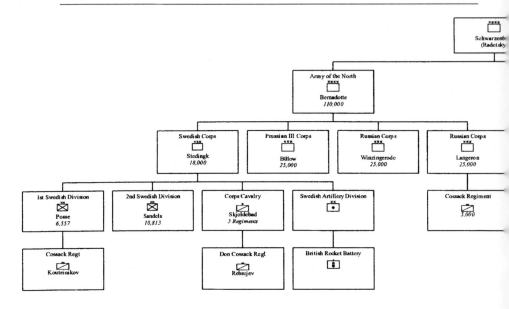

more and more multinational and now included formations of Danes, Poles, Italians, Saxons and other Germans, as well as a host of individuals from all corners of the empire. The difference was that Napoleon remained in complete command, with no requirement to consult his allies, was thus able to leave the formulation of his plans to a relatively late date – and it was 12 August before he completed them. He then took, for him, the unprecedented step of asking the opinions of his marshals. This may have been inspired by the loss of Ney's chief of staff, Jomini, who had defected to the allies after a quarrel with Berthier. More likely it was due to the circumstances, which were like no others which Napoleon had ever faced.

Clearly, Napoleon had no intention of retiring behind the Rhine to await the attack of a united Europe. Nor could he, given the force ratios, launch an all-out offensive operation. Then there was still the treachery of Sweden and Prussia which remained unpunished. It seems that Napoleon expected the allied main effort to be with the Army of Silesia,[23] possibly reinforced from Austria. Alternatively, he felt that the Austrian Army might move generally north or north-west to unite with the Army of Silesia. What he did not expect was what the allies actually did – that is, reinforce the Army of Bohemia from that of Silesia. His intentions, in the light of these expectations,

**ALLIED COMMAND STRUCTURE IN CENTRAL EUROPE
SEPTEMBER 1813**

FIGURE VIII.i

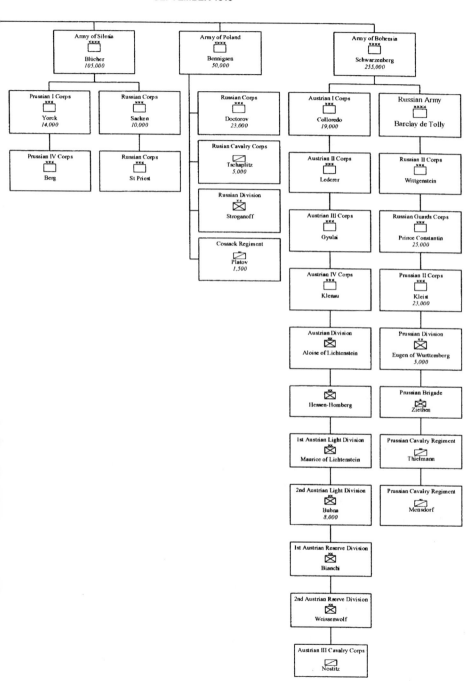

were set out in letters on the same day to Ney and Marmont[24] and to Oudinot[25] in which he states that

> It seems to me that the present campaign can only lead us to a good result if, to begin upon, there is a great battle . . . However, it appears to me that, in order to have a decisive and brilliant affair, there are more favourable chances in holding ourselves in a more concentrated position and awaiting the arrival of the enemy.

For the first time in his career, therefore, Napoleon was contemplating an operational, if not a tactical, defensive movement. But it was a movement which would contain and, he hoped, be the precursor to further offensive action: 'I need not say that, whilst disposing yourself in echelons, it is indispensable to threaten to take the offensive.'[26]

Napoleon's plan required a division of his forces – again this is most unusual for Napoleon who generally sought concentration – and given the strength of the allies this was a risky course. In the north, Oudinot was given an independent command consisting of IV, VII, XII and III Cavalry Corps; Davout's XIII Corps; Girard's division; and Dombrowski's Polish division. This was a total of 120,000 men. Oudinot's task was offensive: his forces were to advance on Berlin, subsequently to destroy Bernadotte's army, and then to advance on Stettin. In this scheme can be detected not only the desire to punish Frederick William and Bernadotte, but also traces of his original plan to recover his forces and territories in the east.

The choice of Oudinot was a strange one. Soult would have been the obvious choice, but Soult had left for Spain. Even so there remained St Cyr, Marmont, Davout, Augereau, or Mortier whom Napoleon had left behind in Moscow in 1812. All were proven all-arms commanders, and Mortier certainly knew Germany as well as any French general. Although Napoleon owed Oudinot a debt after the crossing of the Beresina, his choice for this command is difficult to understand and was ultimately to prove disastrous since the command was too large for his abilities. What the plan seems to show is that by 1813, and probably since the Danube campaign against Austria in 1809, Napoleonic armies had become too large and unwieldy for even Napoleon's genius to command. The staff work involved in controlling so many subordinate formations and the systems for issuing orders in a timely manner stretched the technology of the time to an unbelievable degree. It is arguable that this was one reason for

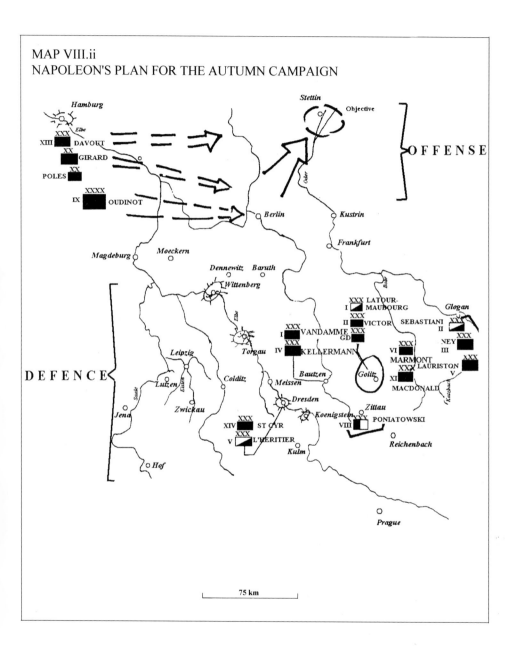

MAP VIII.ii
NAPOLEON'S PLAN FOR THE AUTUMN CAMPAIGN

Napoleon's far more competent performance in 1814, with more modest resources.

However in Napoleon's plan, while Oudinot carried out this offensive movement, the main effort would be placed in an operational defensive between Görlitz and Dresden. With his left flank and his rear firmly anchored on the mighty Elbe river, on which he held every crossing and every fortress, Napoleon felt that he could rest secure[27] and from this line, he could exploit any allied mistakes with the 300,000 men of I, II, III, V, VI, XI and XIV Corps; the Guard Corps; and the I, II, IV and V Cavalry Corps – not counting the garrisons of his fortresses. Thus the Elbe was not to be simply a line of defence: it was, with the city of Dresden which was fortified and developed as the centre of operations, a base for subsequent offensive movements: 'What is important to me is not to be cut off from Dresden and the Elbe; I care little for being cut off from France.'[28]

Leaving aside the choice of Oudinot, the plan had much to recommend it. The position of Austria remained uncertain until 12 August and had Napoleon determined on an offensive movement straight away in the south he would probably have had to deal with an allied withdrawal deep into Poland, whence he would have had to follow while the other allied armies closed in behind him. Given already the length of his communications, the state of his army, and the threat to his southern flank, such a prospect was not one to relish. Even so, Marmont was worried that Napoleon had divided his forces and had greatly underestimated the power of the reinforced Army of the North. In answer to Napoleon's request for advice he wrote some prophetic words: 'I greatly fear lest on the day on which Your Majesty gains a great victory, and believes you have won a decisive battle, you may learn that you have lost two.'[29]

NOTES

1. See especially Oncken, I, pp.390–3 and 395.
2. Petre, p.156.
3. *Correspondance*, vol. xxvi, no. 20398 dated 29.v.1813.
4. Petre, p.157.
5. Dunnigan, *Leipzig*.
6. Mowat, p.279.
7. Lefebvre, p.330.
8. Metternich, *Memoirs*, p.142.

9. Ibid.
10. Craig, pp.272–5.
11. Regele, p.121.
12. von Holleben, p.332.
13. *Wars of Napoleon*, p.132.
14. Kerchnawe, p.139; Regele, pp.121 and 126.
15. Pflugk-Hartung, pp.229–31.
16. Regele, p.124.
17. Ibid. pp.108 and 118.
18. See especially Müffling, p.82.
19. For a discussion, see Craig.
20. Regele, p.118.
21. Scott, p.99; Janson, p.80.
22. Petre, p.161.
23. *Correspondance*, vol. xxvi, no. 20360 and 20365 both dated 12.viii.1813.
24. Ibid. no. 20360 dated 12.viii.1813.
25. Ibid. no. 20365 dated 12.viii.1813.
26. Ibid. no. 20360 dated 12.viii.1813.
27. Ibid.
28. *Correspondance*, vol. xxvi, no. 20398.
29. Marmont, *Mémoires*, v, pp.14 and 207.

Chapter IX

Dresden

⌘

I. MARCH AND COUNTER-MARCH

O N 7 AUGUST, in accordance with their agreed plan, Russian troops began marching from Silesia to join the Army of Bohemia. Five days later, bonfires on the hills around Prague proclaimed that the peace conference was disbanded, and that the armies of Austria would march with their Russian and Prussian allies. That same day, Blücher, with the Prussian corps of Kleist and the Russian corps of Sacken, St Priest and Langeron, moved into the strip of neutral territory. By 15 August he was in contact with the French outposts.

Napoleon's reaction was immediate. He at once put his operational defensive scheme in the south in train by ordering the corps of Vandamme and Victor, and the Guard cavalry, to reinforce Poniatowski around Zittau. This force would protect his southern flank and be in a position to threaten Prague in future offensive operations if needed. Of his forces forward, Macdonald was to take post at Lowenberg on the Bobr river with V and XI Corps and II Cavalry Corps, while Ney with III and VI Corps moved to Bunzlau. The Guard Corps would move to Lauben. Thus disposed, Napoleon felt that 'when I am certain that Blücher . . . is advancing on Bunzlau and that Wittgenstein and Barclay de Tolly are in Bohemia, en route for Zwickau or Dresden, I shall march in force to carry away Blücher.'[1] This scheme was based on the assumption that Blücher had only 50,000 men, although his actual strength was nearer 90,000, which Napoleon did not realise for some time.

By 18 August Napoleon himself had reached Görlitz. Here he learned that the Russians had reached Bohemia and that the Austrians had crossed the Elbe. Uncharacteristically Napoleon decided on a change of plan – 'It is possible I might enter Bohemia at once and fall upon the Russians and catch them *en flagrant délit.*'[2] he wrote. He himself moved on to Zittau, but after a reconnaissance found that the Austrians, followed by the Russians, were marching westwards. There would be no allied attack northwards towards Zittau and even if there was, he was confident that the forces he had placed there, with time to fortify a position, could hold the enemy until he arrived with help. Discounting the possibility of an allied attack towards his centre of operations at Dresden, Napoleon decided to revert to his original scheme of destroying Blücher. By 2.00 pm on 20 August he was back at Görlitz issuing orders for an attack next day. This attack, towards Lowenberg, duly took place but it failed, for Blücher, in accordance with the allies' agreed plan, retired in the face of the attack. Napoleon, ignorant that this was the case, began to follow up what he saw as a retreat.

But on 22 August an urgent dispatch reached Napoleon from St Cyr in Dresden. The Marshal stated plainly that the reinforced Army of Bohemia was advancing towards Dresden on the west bank of the Elbe. His position was perilous and he needed help. Napoleon, although not fully accepting St Cyr's fears, realised that the situation was serious and decided to return to Dresden in person with the bulk of the army. The task of containing Blücher and securing the army's rear was left to Macdonald with III, V and XI Corps. The situation at Dresden was indeed serious. Schwarzenberg's first objective had been Leipzig, but as he crossed the high ground of the Erzgebirge, he had changed his axis of advance towards Dresden.

With only one French corps, the XIV, in front of them, the allies made excellent progress and by 25 August the leading Russian divisions had reached the outlying villages immediately south of the city. A strong counter-attack by XIV Corps recovered the high ground around the village of Strehlen but St Cyr was hopelessly outnumbered. The Tsar and Wittgenstein both wished to storm the city at once, a move which would almost certainly have succeeded, but Schwarzenberg refused. Having no inkling that Napoleon himself was now nearby, Schwarzenberg insisted on delaying the attack until the Austrian army had arrived. A golden opportunity was thus squandered.

But what of Napoleon? By the evening of 25 August he was at Stolpen, from whence he intended, with a force of 100,000 men, to cross the Elbe at Königstein and fall on the allies' rear, while St Cyr continued to hold Dresden. But at Stolpen he received two disquieting pieces of news. First, Oudinot's army in the north, marching on Berlin, had met a sharp defeat at the hands of General Bülow, so that Oudinot had ordered a withdrawal to Wittenberg-Elbe. With a gap opening up

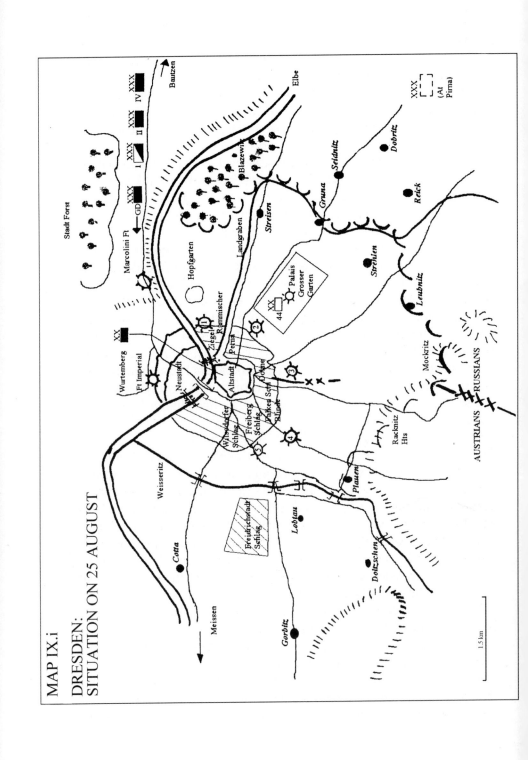

MAP IX.i

DRESDEN:
SITUATION ON 25 AUGUST

1.5 km

on his northern flank, Napoleon ordered V Cavalry Corps of General l'Héritier from the hard-pressed Dresden garrison to cover the exposed flank. Second, General Gourgaud had been dispatched to Dresden to report on the ability of the garrison to hold off the allies. His report, late at night on 25 August, was so gloomy that Napoleon realised that he must yet again change his plan or risk losing Dresden. He issued orders at once. Macdonald was to continue to hold Blücher at bay; the Zittau position was to be held by Poniatowski's VIII Corps alone. The corps of Marmont, Victor, Latour-Maubourg and the Guard would march at once for Dresden. However, the temptation of the blow on the allied rear was still strong and so the corps of Vandamme was ordered to cross the Elbe at Königstein and attack Pirna.

This compromise was to rob Napoleon of what should have been the decisive battle of the war: had Vandamme reinforced Dresden, the rest of the army could have struck a devastating blow on the allied rear, knowing that the Dresden garrison was strong enough to fix the allies frontally. While the allies certainly made a tactical error in not storming Dresden at once, Napoleon made a greater error still. His decision to switch the bulk of the army to Dresden and confront the allies head-on, although it gained a stunning tactical success, would ultimately cost him the campaign.

II. AT DRESDEN.

The great city of Dresden, the capital of Napoleon's ally, Frederick Augustus I, the King of Saxony, had been a fortress until it was dismantled in 1811. In 1813 it was a city of 30,000 people lying on both banks of the River Elbe. The river valley at this point is broad and open and is overlooked by high ground to the north-east and south-west. To the north, the Dresden forest came down almost to the Elbe while south of the river, two streams, the Landgraben and the Weisseritz, flanked the city. Of these, the Landgraben was an inconsiderable obstacle, but the Weisseritz was and is a fair sized stream with deeply entrenched clay banks. It was crossed by some six bridges and although in dry weather it could be forded in several places, in spate it was – as in August 1813 – an obstacle capable of dividing an advancing army.

The city itself has now spread far and wide, completely covering the old battlefield, although some landmarks can be discerned. In 1813 the majority of the built-up area of the city lay south of the Elbe in the walled *Altstadt*. Stretching away from this to a distance of one to one-and-a-half miles were suburbs or *schlags*, beyond which lay farmland and a network of villages. The last major feature south of the Elbe was the *Grosser Garten*, which is still there, a walled park almost a mile long and half a mile wide, whose tactical importance lay in the fact that if held by a defender, it enfiladed the approaches to the city from the south-east. North of the Elbe lay the *Neustadt*, surrounded by a ditch and rampart, connected to the *Altstadt* by a stone bridge, and two pontoons which Napoleon had caused to be built either side.

When Napoleon had decided to make the city his centre of operations he had garrisoned it with St Cyr's XIV Corps. The city had become a storehouse of ammunition, food and supplies of all kinds, as well as home to field bakeries and hospitals. Napoleon had also ordered the repair and improvement of the fortifications, along with those of the outlying fortresses of Königstein and Meissen, and although the building programme was not complete, the fortifications were now in reasonable order and capable of withstanding an assault. The *Altstadt* itself was protected by three lines of defence. Furthest out the French had constructed a ring of five redoubts around the city (marked I – V on the maps), a redoubt in the *Grosser Garten*, and two forts north of the river. Of these, redoubts I, II and III were not mutually supporting and redoubt IV was defective in that it was overlooked by buildings and had a good deal of dead ground around it. Next came the fortifications of the suburbs which St Cyr had undertaken. Here houses and garden walls had been prepared for musketry, and barricades and palisades erected. With a sufficient force of infantry and cannon, considerable delay could be inflicted on any attacker in this area. Finally came the ancient city wall of the city which St Cyr had strengthened and armed with cannon.

St Cyr's garrison consisted of about 20,000 troops. Of these, his own corps of three divisions (the fourth was at Königstein) held the outer defences. A Württemberg infantry division held the city itself, supplemented by some Dutch, Polish, Saxon and Baden battalions. St Cyr's reserve consisted of one French and one Italian cavalry regiment and two squadrons of Polish lancers. Truly this was a coalition force, probably more heterogeneous than the attacking allies. St Cyr was certainly under pressure as the allies moved in, but in fact, the French position was improving all the time. Between 22 and 26 August the main army marched 120 miles – an amazing achievement – so that by the evening of 26 August Napoleon would be able to confront the allies with 70,000 men, and on 27 August with 120,000.

Schwarzenberg had at last made up his mind to storm the city on 26 August and had he done so early in the day, he could still have pre-empted Napoleon's arrival and retrieved the lost opportunity of the day before. But his plan called for a preparatory reconnaissance in force during the morning of 26 August followed by a general attack to begin at 4.00 pm. The allied assault force was divided into five columns. On the right, Wittgenstein with 10,000 Russians was to attack towards redoubt I in order to draw as much as possible of the defenders' attention. On Wittgenstein's left, Kleist with 35,000 Prussians would attack the *Grosser Garten*. On his left, General Count von Colloredo's Austrian corps, minus one division, would demonstrate towards redoubt III in order to screen the batteries there. Next, General Marquis de Chasteler's Austrian corps would occupy Plauen and secure the left flank of the fifth column, 35,000 Austrians under General Count Ignatius Gyulai who would attack the village of Lobtau and then push on north of the Weisseritz, via the suburb of Friederichstadt, to the Elbe. In reserve would be one division of Chasteler's corps at Coschütz and two cavalry divisions, and also the Prussian Guards. Thus 100,000 allies prepared to confront 20,000 French; but just as at Lützen, the allies had left significant numbers of troops uncommitted: Prince Eugen of Württemberg with his division of 12,500 men secured the right flank of the army near Pirna, but the 50,000 men of the corps of Barclay de Tolly and Miloradovich remained unallocated, while Napoleon marched at full speed with all available forces.

III. THE BATTLE OF 26 AUGUST

Kleist's Prussians on the right were the first allied troops to advance. At 5.00 am they attacked the *Grosser Garten* and after three hours' fighting they had cleared the garden as far as the Palace redoubt. Supported by the Russians on their right they had cleared almost three-quarters of the garden by 9.00 am when they were ordered to pause. The Russians themselves had suffered badly from French artillery fire from the Marcolini redoubt but, keeping in close touch with Kleist's men, they too had made progress. In the allied centre, the Austrians made steady progress and by noon they were fighting to take redoubts IV and V, although they had not succeeded in gaining entry to either. Out on the left, good progress had also been made and here the Austrians had succeeded in reaching the Elbe.

The Battle of Dresden. The allies attack the city suburbs on 26 August accompanied by masses of artillery infantry caissons (four-wheel vehicles) for ammunition resupply.

But the allied commanders, watching the early moves from the Racknitz heights, were far from encouraged by the apparent progress of the attack. At 9.00 am, Napoleon himself had entered the city, followed by his Guard, which had marched 90 miles in 72 hours on rough roads and across country. After this prodigious feat of marching, the Guard was immediately committed to reinforce the defenders. Napoleon himself at once set out on a tour of the defences and soon the dreaded cries of '*Vive l'Empereur!*' began to reach the ears of the allied leaders. Clearly, the *Grande Armée* would not be far behind. Jomini realised that the capture of Dresden was now beyond the ability of the allies and he advised that the attack should be broken off at once. The Tsar agreed, but surprisingly, the King of Prussia thought otherwise. Hours of argument followed, at the end of which it was decided to cancel the planned general attack. But either Schwarzenberg failed to issue the cancellation, or else there was

confusion, for the signal guns for the attack were fired as planned and the attack went in.

On the allied right, the Russians advanced between the Landgraben and redoubt II, supported by the Prussians. Kleist's troops reached within ten yards of the suburb of Dohna[3] but the terrific fire from the defenders, followed by a vigorous counter-attack, halted the Austrians on Kleist's left and compelled a withdrawal. In the centre, between Kleist and the Weisseritz, the Austrians had at first made steady progress in spite of the enemy fire. Redoubt III and its supporting artillery broke the attack of the first two Austrian lines until suddenly, the guns fell silent – the ammunition was exhausted! Seizing the opportunity, the Austrians charged again, stormed the redoubt and after vicious hand-to-hand fighting threw the defenders out. The attacks on redoubts IV and V were less successful, for steady fire from the defenders and strong counter-attacks held all attacks. Beyond the Weisseritz too only limited further progress had been made by the Austrians towards Friederichstadt.

Napoleon, meanwhile, had been active. On its arrival the Guard Corps had been committed to bolster the defenders. Murat was sent to take command of the existing French troops in Friederichstadt who were now supplemented with eight infantry battalions, later reinforced to a full division, and, when it arrived at 2.00 pm, the whole of I Cavalry Corps, two divisions of the Young Guard and a regiment of the Old Guard under Mortier were sent to the suburb of Dohnesee; while another two Young Guard divisions and an Old Guard regiment under Ney went into Dippoliswalde and Falken, left and right of redoubt IV. The rest of the Old Guard was held in reserve in the *Altstadt*. By the time the allied main attack had been in progress for an hour, therefore, Napoleon's strength was around 70,000 and he was confident that his position was strong enough to keep the allies out. Moreover he now had enough cavalry, supporting infantry and artillery for some offensive counter moves.

French morale, too, was high. Despite the strength of the allied attack and the supporting cannonade there was only eagerness to confront the enemy. After Lützen and Bautzen, Napoleon's standing with his army was high and the troops expected nothing short of another crushing success by the commander they believed unbeatable. Between 5.00 and 6.00 pm therefore, Napoleon issued orders for a limited counter-attack: by 6.00 pm he was certain that the allied attack would have run out of steam and the conditions for a successful counter-attack created. So it was.

At 6.00 pm, Mortier's Young Guard divisions on the extreme left began their move from the Ziegel suburb. After an hour's desperate struggle, the Russians had been driven back to Windmill Hill and by 8.00 pm, to Blasewitz Woods and Striesen. Wittgenstein was so hard pressed that he personally rode to Barclay to ask for reinforcements, and a Prussian brigade took post behind Striesen until the village was evacuated at midnight. As the Young Guard had moved out of Ziegel, so the rest of Mortier's command attacked from behind redoubt II, driving back the Russians, and Kleist's Prussians from the northern half of the *Grosser Garten*. By 8.00 pm the antagonists were separated only by the width of the central avenue of the garden, where nightfall brought an end to the struggle.

In the centre, the Austrians had only just consolidated their hold on redoubt III when Ney's counter-attack began. The Young Guard's first attempt failed, but a group of 50 men managed to gain a lodgement, from which two regiments stormed the redoubt, taking 400

Austrian prisoners. So fierce had the fighting been that at the end of the day, 180 French and 344 Austrian dead were counted in the narrow area around the redoubt. Outside redoubts IV and V the Austrians were also forced back as Ney's infantry drove them across the Weisseritz and as far as Plauen. On the French right, beyond the Weisseritz, the Austrians fought a desperate defence but were eventually driven out of the suburbs.

Further south, Vandamme's corps had crossed the Königstein bridges at about the same time as Napoleon had begun his counter-attack, and had himself attacked the division of Eugen of Württemberg. Although Eugen's men fought well, they were forced by superior numbers to evacuate Pirna and fall back to a blocking position around Zehista. By the end of the day, therefore, the French had regained practically all the ground lost earlier to the allies. The French troops were jubilant at their success, gained in the face of superior numbers, and were further encouraged by the knowledge that the corps of Marmont and Victor were on their way; they were, too, well supplied with food and ammunition.

Not so the allies. The troops had fought bravely and well, they still fielded a force of 150,000 men, and they expected a reinforcement from the Prussian corps of Klenau. But indecision, confusion in the orders and the failure to commit enough troops early to the all-out storming of the city had resulted in the loss of all their hard-gained ground. The troops were now short of food, they knew that Vandamme was threatening their rear, they had lost confidence in their commanders, and to cap it all, it began to pour with rain.

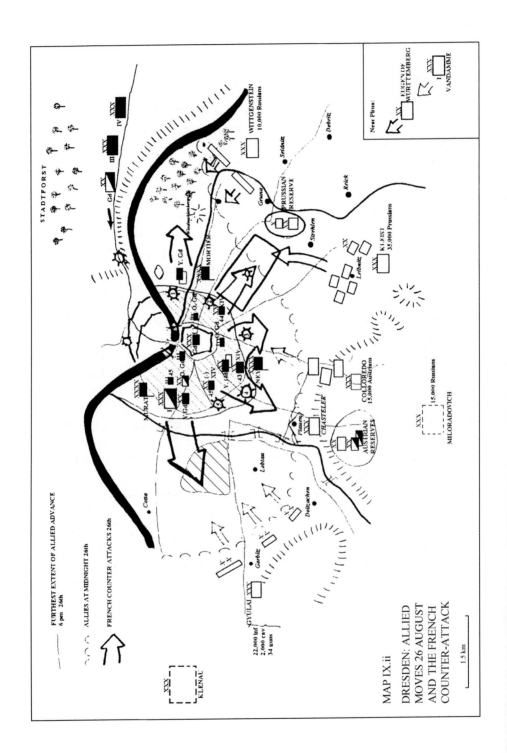

MAP IX.ii

DRESDEN: ALLIED
MOVES 26 AUGUST
AND THE FRENCH
COUNTER-ATTACK

- - - - - FURTHEST EXTENT OF ALLIED ADVANCE
6 pm 26th

ALLIES AT MIDNIGHT 26th

FRENCH COUNTER ATTACKS 26th

1.5 km

WITTGENSTEIN
10,000 Russians

PRUSSIAN
RESERVE

KLEIST
35,000 Prussians

COLLOREDO
15,000 Austrians

AUSTRIAN
RESERVES

15,000 Russians

MILORADOVICH

KLENAU

GYULAI

22,000 Inf
2,000 cav
34 uns

STADTFORST

Near Pirna:

EUGEN OF
WÜRTTEMBERG

VANDAMME

IV

III

Gd

V. Gd

MORTIER

O. Gd

O. Gd

MURAT

45

NEY

CHASTELER

Cotta

Lobtau

Dolitschen

Gorbitz

Plauen

Leubnitz

Strehlen

Gruna

Seidnitz

Debritz

Reick

Räcknitz

IV. THE BATTLE OF 27 AUGUST

As the corps of Victor and Marmont, and the Guard cavalry, arrived at Dresden, the two corps were assigned to the French right and centre respectively. Napoleon was inclined to believe that the allies would withdraw under cover of darkness and its torrential rain, but should they remain, he planned an offensive battle for the next day to build on the gains of 26 August. His intention was to hold in the centre and attack on both flanks, with his main effort on his right beyond the Weisseritz. He chose this course of action for two reasons. First, he hoped to cut the allies off from the two roads which offered the best withdrawal routes back into Bohemia. Second, because of the heavy rain, the Weisseritz was now in spate. If the French could secure the crossings as far south as Plauen, then the allied left could be isolated and destroyed, thus dealing the Austrians in particular a heavy blow and placing strain on allied unity.

On his right under Murat, Napoleon therefore massed the corps of Victor, a division of the Young Guard, and the whole of I Cavalry Corps reinforced with an additional division – a total of 23,000 infantry, 12,000 cavalry, and 106 guns to confront Gyulai's 22,000 infantry, 2,000 cavalry and 34 guns. On the French left, Ney with most of the Guard Corps mustered 40,000 infantry and 10,000 cavalry against the 24,000 of Wittgenstein and Kleist. In the centre the two holding corps of Marmont and St Cyr mustered 41,000, but with only two brigades of cavalry, against almost 100,000 allies including the bulk of their cavalry and guns. Thus Napoleon deliberately avoided the allies' invitation to an attritional slogging match by massing his strength on his flanks for an enveloping manoeuvre on terms of local, if not overall, superiority.

At 6.00 am on 27 August Napoleon rode to a position just behind redoubt IV where a tent had been pitched and a great fire lit. Here he stayed until 10.00 am when reports indicated that the attack beyond the Weisseritz was going well, and he then moved on to view events on his left and centre. On the left, Mortier had also moved at 6.00 am and an hour later had taken the village of Blasewitz. Moving north of the *Grosser Garten*, from which the Prussians had withdrawn at daybreak, his troops pushed on to Siednitz where they began to meet serious opposition from Wittgenstein's Russians. After another hour's fighting and several repulses, the French managed to take the village. Mortier then ordered his cavalry to by-pass Leubnitz and, wheeling northwards, threaten the Russian withdrawal down the Pirna road. In driving rain, this manoeuvre failed to accomplish its objectives and the Russians were able to pull back steadily.

Napoleon himself arrived in front of Reick at 11.00 am. The Russians in this village were well protected by the Landgraben and were supported by cavalry. Even so, Napoleon ordered the village to be taken. Two French assaults ended in bloody failure until the village, despite the rain, was set on fire by artillery. In the smoke, the Russians did not see that they were being surrounded and they thus failed to withdraw. None escaped. By noon, the French held the village. Napoleon next turned his attention to the centre, where St Cyr's corps was attacking Leubnitz from Strehlen. Here, all French attacks were driven off by the Prussians with heavy loss.

The Tsar meanwhile, seeing that the action between Leubnitz and the Elbe was going badly, and on the advice of his two counsellors Jomini and Moreau, ordered Barclay and Wittgenstein to counter-attack Mortier's front, while Miloradovich and Kleist counter-attacked towards Strehlen and Gruna. The order was queried by Barclay and before a decision could be reached, fate intervened. Disgusted by his failure at Leubnitz, Napoleon was on his way towards the right centre and on route, ordered a battery of guns to engage a group of horsemen on the Racknitz heights. The first round passed close to the Tsar, for the group was the allied commanders, and hit Moreau. The ball tore through his right leg, passed through his horse, and shattered his left leg as well. In agony, he was attended by the Tsar's surgeon, who amputated both his legs – but to no avail. Five days later, still in great pain, Moreau died at Tann in Bohemia. This incident so diverted the Tsar that the counter-attack on the allied right never took place and the French remained in possession of the field.

Away on the French centre right, meanwhile, Marmont's corps had pushed the Austrians back to Plauen, but otherwise had maintained only a holding action. The heaviest fighting of the whole day was further right still, beyond the Weisseritz. Murat began his attack between 6.00 and 7.00 am: Victor's corps, supported by the artillery, crossed the Weisseritz by the Freiburg bridge and divided into four columns. The first column moved south-west towards Dölzschen. By 2.00 pm the village was on fire and the Austrian troops penned hard against the rain swollen Weisseritz, which in this area flowed through a deep cutting. Here they had no choice but destruction or surrender, while across the river the Austrian reserves could do nothing but look on helplessly.

Victor's second and third columns, supported by his corps cavalry,

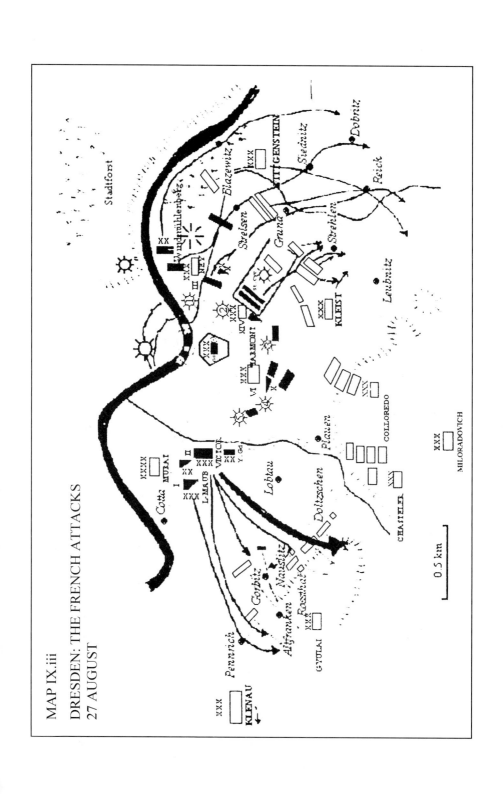

MAP IX.iii
DRESDEN: THE FRENCH ATTACKS
27 AUGUST

headed towards Rossthal and Wolfnitz respectively. By noon, the Austrians had been forced out of Wolfnitz and Ober Gorbitz and were in some disorder. Victor's cavalry could be seen preparing to charge, and the Austrians formed square. But the drenching rain had made the Austrians' flints and powder useless. Unable to fire their pieces, they were ridden down or compelled to surrender.

Victor's fourth column and, on its right, the bulk of Murat's cavalry, advanced along the Freiburg road pushing the Austrian troops back towards Pennrich, while the Young Guard infantry, moving south of the road, cut the withdrawal route. Threatened by infantry and cavalry, and unable to use their weapons, a large body of Austrian troops surrendered. Of Klenau's reinforcements there was no sign, for he had marched by a roundabout route and never reached the battlefield in time. Thus by 2.00 pm the entire Austrian left beyond the Weisseritz had been smashed. Almost 15,000 of the original 24,000 were prisoners, many others were dead or wounded, and only a fragment of the corps managed to escape towards Freiburg.

By 3.00 pm the Battle of Dresden was over. Napoleon, soaked to the skin, his famous cocked hat plastered round his ears, rode into the city followed by 1,000 prisoners. Another 12,000 followed, along with 3 generals, 64 officers of field rank, 15 captured standards, 26 guns and 130 ammunition wagons. Indeed, Napoleon had gained a most remarkable, if almost his last, victory of 1813.

The allies had made many mistakes, but Napoleon had once again shown a flash of his old genius. He had at once realised the advantages which the terrain and his interior lines offered, and he had boldly denuded his centre in order to create local superiority on the flanks on what was the first occasion in his career when he had not managed to assemble an equivalent or numerically superior force to his opponents.[4] For Napoleon this was indeed an innovation. As von Caemmerer said,

> When an army of 120,000 men, in the presence of 180,000 enemies, deploys from a bridgehead, then surrounds the enemy on both wings, and seriously damages both; when it compels a whole division to lay down its arms in the open field, when it brings in immediately from the battlefield 1,300 prisoners, fifteen standards and twenty-six guns, that is a quite undeniable victory.[5]

V. AFTER DRESDEN.

At the end of the day's fighting on 27 August Napoleon was sure that another day of combat would follow. Accordingly, he issued orders for the action to be renewed.[6] It was not until daybreak on 28 August that Marmont and St Cyr found the allies gone, their retreat covered by the darkness, rain and mist. An uncharacteristic delay of several hours followed – probably caused by the Emperor's vomiting illness – until the issue of Napoleon's orders for the pursuit of the allies. St Cyr was to march on Dohna, keeping in touch with Mortier who was ordered to Pirna. Vandamme was at the same time to move north of Hellendorf, cutting the road there. Marmont's corps was ordered towards Dippoldiswalde and Murat's two corps towards Freiburg. If Vandamme, Mortier or St Cyr could close up to the allies and stop them crossing into Bohemia, it was in Napoleon's mind that Murat and Marmont could wheel south-east, thus effecting an envelopment.

Napoleon himself set off for Pirna. On the way, he received dispatches from Vandamme, indicating that he had no great force in front of him. Napoleon therefore decided to halt the Young Guard at Pirna, return the Old Guard to Dresden, and order Vandamme to push on to Peterswalde. For the time being, the pursuit could, it seemed, be left to his lieutenants, especially as Napoleon was clearly far from well.

After the fatal wounding of Moreau, the allied commanders had held a council of war. Frederick William was for continuing the fight; Jomini advised withdrawing south-west towards Dippoldiswalde; the Tsar, the Emperor of Austria and Schwarzenberg were all for withdrawing into Bohemia and it was their view which prevailed. The orders called for three withdrawal routes to be used: the Russians and Prussians would march *via* Dohna and Peterswalde; Klenau *via* Freiburg; and the remaining Austrians through Dippoldiswalde. With some modifications in their route, Klenau reached Marienberg on 30 August and the Austrians got to Dux in Bohemia on the same date. The Russians and Prussians too had to modify their route. Covered by their rearguard, they marched south on two routes through Dippoldiswalde and Maxen, the main body having reached Fürstenwalde on 29 August.

Meanwhile the division of Eugen of Württemberg, now commanded by Lieutenant General Count Ostermann-Tolstoy, was also ordered to march *via* Maxen. Eugen himself urged that to do so would leave the Peterswalde road open to Vandamme and allow him to block the allies'

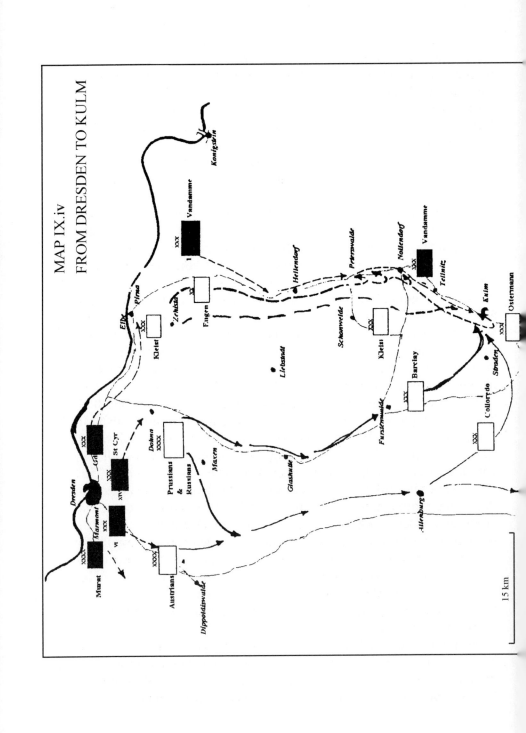

MAP IX.iv
FROM DRESDEN TO KULM

15 km

route across the Erzgebirge into Bohemia. Fortunately for the allies, he managed to persuade Ostermann to this view. The division had to fight its way to Hellendorf so that when Eugen assembled the command there late on 28 August, it was seriously depleted and hotly pursued by Vandamme. Throughout the day of 29 August the withdrawal continued with the Prussians turning at bay three times to face Vandamme. By 10.00 am the division, with a strength of 14,700, had reached Kulm.

Ostermann fortunately had the foresight to send an envoy to the allied sovereigns warning of his situation and the result was a message from the Tsar ordering Eugen and Ostermann to hold their position between Kulm and Priesten in order to cover the move of the rest of the army – for Eugen's analysis had been quite correct. But the Tsar, the King of Prussia and the Emperor also sent orders to all available troops to march to support Ostermann. By the end of the day, about 6,000 of these had reached Priesten.

Throughout the 29th the two formations, one Prussian and one French, battled around Priesten. The battle swung first one way and then the other as reinforcements arrived to bolster both sides. At 5.00 pm Vandamme made what he felt must be a decisive attack, but it was checked by the Prussian infantry and a charge by three regiments of cavalry. Vandamme broke off the action, meaning to wait until the rest of his corps, which was straggling badly, arrived during the night.

The remainder of the allied army continued to withdraw in good order and the French pursuit, hampered as ever by a lack of cavalry, was not pressed. The allied commanders themselves converged on Priesten during the evening of 29 August and by dawn on 30 August, their strength had risen to 44,000, while Vandamme had about 32,000. With their superiority in numbers, the allies planned to force Vandamme onto the defensive and destroy him. By 11.00 am, this plan had been pressed home so effectively that Vandamme's position was extremely perilous, and cannon fire was heard in his rear. At first, he believed it to be St Cyr or Mortier coming to his aid – but his hopes were soon dashed, for it was the corps of Kleist.

Kleist had originally been ordered to support Ostermann, but the routes were hopelessly blocked – all save one, the Peterswalde road. Kleist decided that boldness was his only possible course. He would force his way down the route, and fall on Vandamme's rear. After a forced march of eight hours, this is exactly what his bold move achieved. Vandamme's corps was destroyed: 10,000 prisoners, including

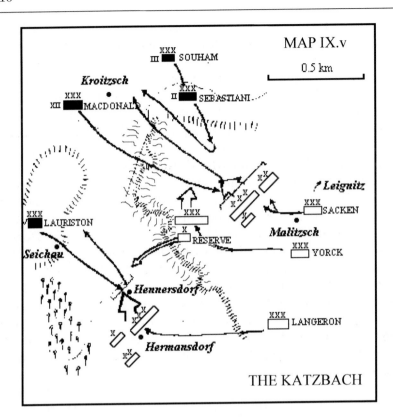

THE KATZBACH

Vandamme himself, were taken; another 5,000 were killed or wounded. The allies also took 82 guns, 200 wagons, 2 eagles and 5 colours. The foresight of Eugen in blocking Vandamme, the exertions of the allied sovereigns in reinforcing him, and the boldness of Kleist had produced the victory which had eluded the allies for so long.

> The Battle of Kulm changed into a cry of joy the despair which was spreading through the valleys of Bohemia.[7]

> The defeat of a corps may be made up for by the victory of an army, and even the defeat of one army may be balanced or even turned into a victory by the successes of a larger army, as happened . . . at Kulm.[8]

There was more to come. The news of Oudinot's defeat by Bülow at Grossbeeren was followed by the news of another allied success in the east. On 26 August, Macdonald, who had been left to prevent Blücher's army from advancing westwards, decided to cross the Katzbach and take the offensive. Unknown to him, Blücher had decided on a similar course. Macdonald crossed the Katzbach on the following day and thus while the main armies were engaged at Dresden, he and Blücher had fought a wholly unexpected meeting engagement in pouring rain. Macdonald had advanced in three well separated columns and the result was that Blücher, with the corps of Sacken and Yorck, was able to generate sufficient local superiority to smash Macdonald. The French had lost 14,000 prisoners, 36 guns, and 110 wagons.

It seemed that the allied plan of defeating Napoleon's lieutenants was vindicated. Marmont's gloomy prophecy too seemed fulfilled and it was hardly surprising that Napoleon took the news badly – for the situation at the operational level had been transformed. Mortier and St Cyr were censured for not supporting Vandamme, but Mortier certainly had only received his orders on 30 August, too late to affect the action. So now, far from having lost the initiative at Dresden, the allied Army of Bohemia was intact and its morale revitalised; the Army of Silesia and the Army of the North were threatening from the north and east; and the Reserve Army of Poland would soon be hastening westward. For all its success at the tactical level, Dresden had become, at the operational level, a wasted victory.

NOTES

1. *Correspondance*, vol. xxvi, no. 21390, dated 16.viii.1813.
2. *Correspondance*, vol. xxvi, no. 20408, dated 18.viii.1813.
3. Petre, p.204.
4. Clausewitz, p.283.
5. von Caemmerer, p.56.
6. *Correspondance*, vol. xxvi, no. 20479, dated 27.viii.1813.
7. Chandler, p.912.
8. Clausewitz, p.211.

Chapter X

Closing in

. . . did not Bonaparte, who used to rush at his enemies like a wild boar, twist and turn like a caged animal when the ratio of forces was no longer in his favour in August and September 1813, without attempting a reckless attack on any one of his enemies?[1]

I. THE DEFEAT OF NEY

ALTHOUGH HE HAD the benefit of hindsight, Clausewitz's description of Napoleon's frenetic period of activity is remarkably apt. In the aftermath of Grossbeeren, Kulm and the Katzbach, the Emperor conducted a thorough-going review of his operational plan and the courses open. These courses he reduced to two. First, he could block the allies in the north and east and concentrate the bulk of his army for a march south in order to destroy the Army of Bohemia and seize Prague. Second, he could block to the east and south while directing the bulk of his forces against the Army of the North and Berlin. His deliberations seem to show that he was prejudiced in favour of attacking northwards, for this course offered the chance of returning to the original campaign plan with the bonus of dealing a hard blow against Bernadotte. It also offered new sources of forage, which was becoming scarce in the south. Last, but perhaps most important, it offered the advantages of a central position.

Operating on interior lines, Napoleon felt he could take Berlin in three or four days and then be in a position to move against any developing allied threat, defeating the allied armies piecemeal before they could unite. The remarkable thing about both possible courses, is that Napoleon, uncharacteristically, still continued to fix his eyes on territory as much as on his enemy,[2] so that his belief in Berlin as a decisive point in the attack on allied unity was clearly still strong. At this particular time, such a belief was wrong, for by ignoring his greatest threat, the Army of Bohemia, he allowed it valuable time to recover from its rough handling at Dresden.

This northward option could not, however, be implemented, for Vandamme's defeat deprived Napoleon of much of the force he had planned to use to hold the southern flank. Then came the realisation that Macdonald had been comprehensively beaten on the Katzbach, so that Blücher was now a threat which could not be ignored. The drive on Berlin would go ahead, but in much reduced strength and without the Emperor. Furious at Oudinot's incompetence, Napoleon placed Ney in command, a move which provoked deep resentment in Oudinot. Moreover Ney, deprived of the influence of Jomini, was by no means a trustworthy lieutenant. Ney received his orders on 2 September.[3] These orders directed him to march first on Baruth and then on to Berlin, which he was to reach by 10 September.

Ney found his new 58,000-strong command, the Army of Berlin, north of Wittenberg-Elbe, with Bertrand's IV Corps on the right, Oudinot's XII Corps in the centre and Reynier's VII Franco-Saxon Corps on the left. Originally Napoleon had planned to support these troops with an additional corps positioned at Luckau, but events elsewhere, especially the need to reconstitute I Corps, prevented this. Ney's orders for 5 September directed XII Corps, followed by IV, to march towards the small town of Juterbog. The VII Corps was to march north and then east towards Baruth in order to form a strong flank guard.

Opposing Ney, the 150,000-strong Army of the North was well dispersed with a Prussian forward detachment under General Tauenzien, a veteran of Jena, on its southern flank; Bülow's Prussians in the centre; and to the north, the Swedish corps of Field Marshal Count von Stedingk and Winzingerode's Russians. Fully expecting a French offensive movement, Bernadotte's intention was that Tauenzien would occupy a blocking position around Dennewitz, 40 miles south-west of Berlin, with part of his force deployed forward at Zahna in order to delay any French advance. Once the French had closed up to Dennewitz, the rest of the army would fall on the enemy flanks and rear from the north.

During 5 September both armies proceeded according to plan. Tauenzien's advanced guard duly encountered the French at Zahna, and was driven out. Ney at once ordered the advance to continue on the 6th, except that while IV and VII Corps continued to march on Oehna, Oudinot was to wait for IV Corps to get clear of the town before

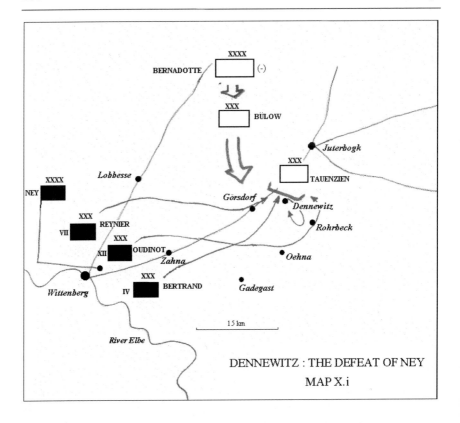

DENNEWITZ : THE DEFEAT OF NEY

MAP X.i

himself marching on its left flank. It was about 2.00 pm therefore before
XII Corps began to move, so that the three French corps became well
separated during the day. The IV Corps had marched at 8.00 am and at
11.00 am it reached Dennewitz to find Tauenzien's 10,000 Prussians
on rising ground north of Dennewitz, well supported by cavalry and
artillery, although much of the Prussian infantry was *Landwehr*.

Bertrand decided to attack at once, which he did with some success,
driving in both Prussian flanks. But Tauenzien's men, with great
courage and determination, held their ground long enough for Bülow's
38,000-strong corps to come up and put in a vigorous counter-attack.
Although this attack was repulsed by the French, Bertrand was forced
to retire two miles south-east towards the village of Rohrbeck.

A lull in the fighting followed until 2.30 pm when the leading division of Reynier's corps arrived. Ney, who had also arrived, ordered a
further attack which retook some of the lost ground and at one point
threatened to pierce the Prussian position. Moreover Oudinot's corps

was by now at Oehna while Bernadotte's Swedes and Russians were still several miles away – Ney had a perfect opportunity to reinforce his success in the centre and smash the Prussians. He threw it away.[4] Oudinot, instead of being ordered to the village of Görsdorf, was ordered to march up on Bertrand's right flank. Still piqued at having Ney placed over him, Oudinot obeyed this order to the letter. By the time he had closed up to the battlefield by a roundabout route, Bernadotte himself appeared at 5.30 pm at the head of his main body, 70 battalions of Russians, Swedes and Mecklenburgers, and a fierce allied counter-attack smashed into the depleted corps of Reynier and Bertrand.

The whole French force, Oudinot's unmarked corps included, broke and fled in the wildest confusion – nor did the French stop until they were safely back on the Elbe. Although the allied losses were consider-able, around 10,500 killed and wounded, Ney had lost 22,000 killed, wounded and prisoners along with 53 guns, 412 wagons and 3 colours. The remnant of his force was so disorganised that it could scarcely any longer be called an army.

II. LOST OPPORTUNITIES

If Napoleon had been angry with Oudinot, his rage with Macdonald after the Katzbach knew no bounds. While Ney's army had moved north, the Emperor had set off for Bautzen with his Guard, Marmont's VI Corps and Latour-Maubourg's I Cavalry Corps. By 4 September he was at Hochkirch meeting the stragglers and fugitives from Macdonald's demolished army. These were being pursued closely by the 10,000 men of Blücher's advanced guard so, true to form, the Emperor at once went over to the attack. Murat with III Corps and Latour-Maubourg's cavalry was ordered to move on Wurschen; Macdonald with V and XI Corps and Sébastiani's cavalry was to move on Murat's right; while the Franco-Polish VIII Corps under Prince Poniatowski acted as flank guard to the south at Lobau. The Emperor himself moved with Macdonald while the Guard and VI Corps remained in reserve.

But the wily Blücher soon realised who was opposing him. Who else could have turned Macdonald's defeated rabble around in such a near-miraculous way? In accordance with the agreed allied plan, Blücher at once ordered a retirement. The French followed as far as Görlitz, by which time Napoleon had guessed the Prussian intention. Declining to accept the bait and be drawn into Silesia, Napoleon left Macdonald to

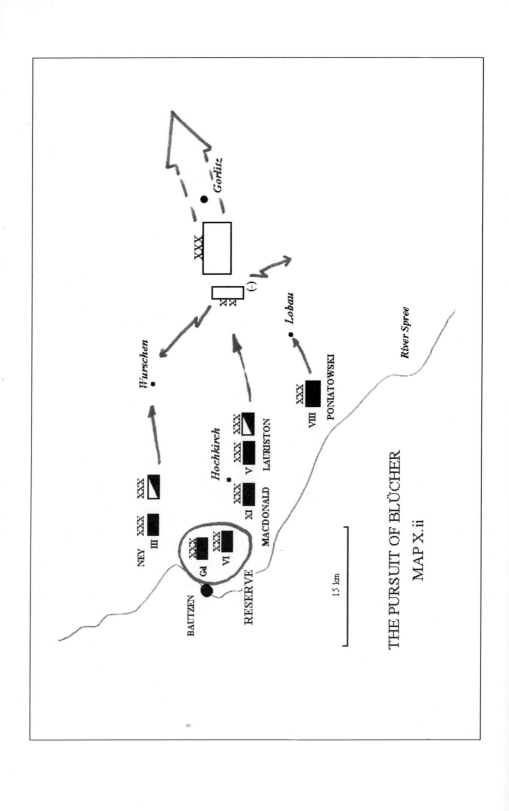

THE PURSUIT OF BLÜCHER
MAP X.ii

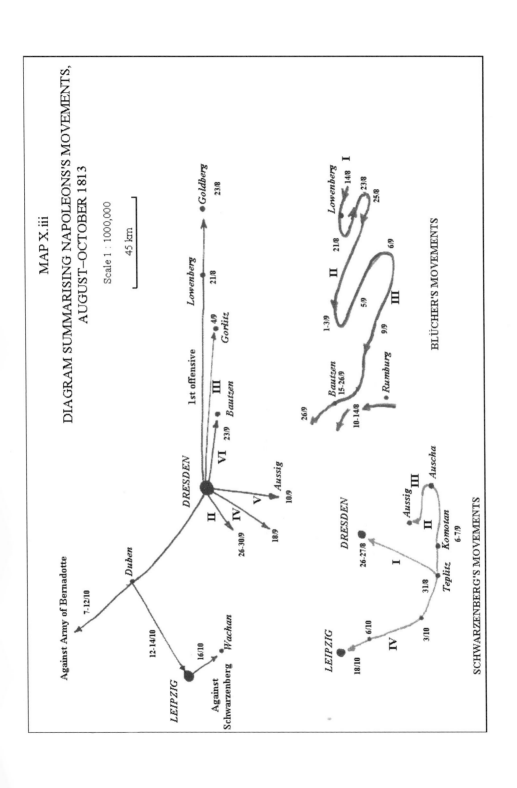

MAP X.iii

DIAGRAM SUMMARISING NAPOLEON'S MOVEMENTS,
AUGUST–OCTOBER 1813

Scale 1 : 1000,000

45 km

BLÜCHER'S MOVEMENTS

SCHWARZENBERG'S MOVEMENTS

shadow Blücher once more while he returned to Bautzen with the Guard and VI Corps.

On returning to Bautzen, Napoleon's initial intention was to resume his drive northwards, but again events thwarted him. On 6 September he received word from St Cyr that the Army of Bohemia was advancing once more against Dresden. This was partly true for a body of 60,000 Austrian troops was advancing on the east bank of the Elbe against Macdonald's southern flank – Schwarzenberg clearly hoped that, in combination with Blücher, he could force a battle on terms favourable to the allies which would complete the destruction of Macdonald's army. At the same time, Barclay de Tolly was moving with the combined Russian and Prussian contingents of the Army of Bohemia on the west bank of the Elbe. Barclay's move was essentially a deception designed to tie up French forces which might otherwise be sent to tip the balance against Schwarzenberg and Blücher and to reinforce this, Barclay was ordered to retire if Napoleon himself appeared. It was this deception movement which had attracted St Cyr's attention.

Napoleon reacted speedily, meaning to bring the allies to battle if he could. He set out at once with his Guard to join St Cyr, who on 7 September had placed his own corps in a blocking position around Pirna. Here Napoleon joined him on the following day and at supper that evening he received news of Ney's defeat. In contrast with his anger at Oudinot and Macdonald, he took the news well enough,[5] ordering Berthier to instruct Ney to take up a blocking position on the east bank of the Elbe at Torgau.[6] He then conferred with St Cyr and, accepting his advice, decided to march towards Teplitz and so cut the allied communications back into Bohemia. This movement began early the next day, But like Blücher, Schwarzenberg soon guessed who was behind this aggressive move and ordered a hasty countermarch.

By 10 September his Russian and Prussian corps were assembling near the scene of Vandamme's destruction, although the Austrians were still far off. At 11.00 am that day, Napoleon himself arrived. St Cyr advocated an attack at once in order to destroy this portion of the allied army but surprisingly, Napoleon, the man who had taken such risks at Jena and the crossing of the Alps, hesitated. Perhaps he feared to descend into Bohemia while Bernadotte followed up the defeated Ney towards Dresden, or perhaps he considered the force ratios unfavourable, for certainly the French had had difficulty with their artillery on the rough roads. Whatever the reason, he seemed to lose interest, and left St Cyr to continue to press the allies while he himself returned north.

On the 17th he was back again, for despite being pushed northwards initially, St Cyr had launched a counter attack which took the French once more to Kulm. By now, however, the Austrians had been able to concentrate a formidable force, his troops were growing desperately weary, and the French had still not resolved their difficulties with the artillery: Napoleon hesitated again, and the opportunity for battle slipped by.

If Napoleon appeared somewhat *distrait*, it was because there were worrying distractions further afield. Throughout the autumn campaign, French communications had been harried mercilessly by German partisans and flying columns of Cossacks and Bashkirs, whose activities were almost out of control. At Weissenfels on 12 September, for example, a column under Lieutenant General Baron von Thielmann, a Saxon who had changed sides early in 1813, had taken 1,000 prisoners and 26 guns. Six days later, the same column took 200 prisoners in Mersebeck. At Altenburg on 28 September Thielmann again, with seven Cossack regiments and some *Freikorps* drove out the French garrison and took another 1,000 prisoners. This pattern was being repeated throughout Germany and the result, combined with battle losses, sickness and straggling was alarming. Since the end of the armistice the French had lost 150,000 men killed, wounded and taken prisoner, and another 50,000 sick and straggling. The supply situation was also bad, and raiding was being exacerbated by deteriorating roads and bad weather, so that his troops were reduced to only eight ounces of bread per day instead of 28, and had almost no meat.[7]

There was more bad news from Napoleon's allies. After the Battle of Kulm, the Tyrol had broken out in revolt and declared for Austria. After Dennewitz, the Danes had abandoned Davout in Hamburg and retired on Lübeck. In Westphalia, General Chernikov's Cossacks had driven King Jerome Bonaparte from his capital and declared the end of the puppet kingdom. Even worse, although he did not know it, the Bavarians had concluded an armistice with the allies on 17 September. On 8 October, having received promises of territory from the allies, Napoleon's oldest ally in Germany formally changed sides. Thus only Saxony, Baden-Baden and Württemberg were left and all were shaky. The Saxon troops of VII Corps in particular, sullen that their country was bearing the brunt of the war, were only kept in place by the exhortations of their king, Frederick Augustus.

Napoleon was forced to turn his attention to this drastic situation. First, he ordered the move of large quantities of flour and other stores to Dresden by barge,[8] the transfer of which was to be covered by the move of Marmont and Murat with their entire corps.[9] Next, he set about pacifying the rear areas. General Lefebvre-Desnouëttes' division was reinforced to a strength of 4,000 cavalry at Freiburg and 2,000 at Lorge – a diversion of resources that Napoleon with his chronic lack of cavalry could ill afford. This force was ordered to clear the Cossacks from the west side of the Elbe,[10] while a division of Victor's corps was also ordered to Freiburg and the newly-formed IX Corps of Marshal Augereau was ordered to march to Jena from Würzburg in order to keep open the crossings over the Saale.

Next, a partial reorganisation of the army took place. Oudinot was called away from the north to command a small corps of two divisions of the Young Guard, while I Corps, destroyed at Kulm, was partly reformed by drafts of divisions from other corps, especially from XII Corps which Napoleon disbanded and redistributed to make good losses elsewhere. With these precautions in hand, Napoleon hoped to be able to join Ney at Torgau, but again, the allies forestalled him: Napoleon for the first time must have had the distinct impression that he had lost the initiative.

In the midst of all the French reorganisation, Blücher had begun to move again and quickly drove in Macdonald's outposts. Two divisions of the Young Guard were ordered forward at once and Napoleon indicated that as soon as the weather improved, he would go himself. On 22 September he wrote to Macdonald,[11] ordering him to carry out a preliminary reconnaissance in force. On 23 September he himself joined Macdonald as promised and, advancing towards Bischofswerda, met and drove back Blücher's force. But yet again, Napoleon hesitated to deliver a decisive blow: to be sure, Bernadotte was again threatening Ney around Wartenburg, but Napoleon seemed to have lost his old drive. As Yorck put it,

> The fact is, that that equilibrium between insight and promptitude, which he himself pointed out as most desirable in a general, was no longer present, and we thus understand why irresolution, with wavering, inconsequent, illogical action, and therefore failure, were the result.[12]

III. BEHIND THE ELBE

Reviewing the state of his army and the events of the past three weeks, the unpalatable facts must have become clear to Napoleon: he was

Gebhard Lebrecht von Blücher (1742–1819), drawn from life in his July 1814 visit to England. He was an inveterate pipe-smoker even in the quieter moments of battle. Blücher was promoted Field Marshal for his outstanding service on 16 Oct. 1813.

exhausting his own dwindling troops and achieving nothing. The allies' refusal to offer battle to the Emperor himself, but wear down his subordinates was succeeding remarkably well – so much so that Napoleon was being kept off-balance, and was compelled to dash hither and thither to assist one or other of his marshals to react to an allied move, but then usually arriving too late and with too little force to achieve any decisive result. Faced with this situation, the Emperor came to a decision – not, as Yorck suggests,[13] at his own initiative, but in response to the allied moves. His decision was to abandon all territory including the distant garrisons on the Oder and Vistula and to pull his army back behind the Elbe, maintaining strong bridgeheads at Königstein, Pilnitz, Dresden, Meissen, Wittenberg-Elbe, Torgau and Magdeburg. Husbanding his remaining 260,000 men and 784 guns he would watch the allies, and, if they took the offensive, he would concentrate and compel them to fight.

The allies too had recast their ideas and were about to embark on the series of moves which would lead them to victory. The Army of Poland was now on the move, and Bennigsen was ordered to unite with the Army of Bohemia. This combined army would then operate through

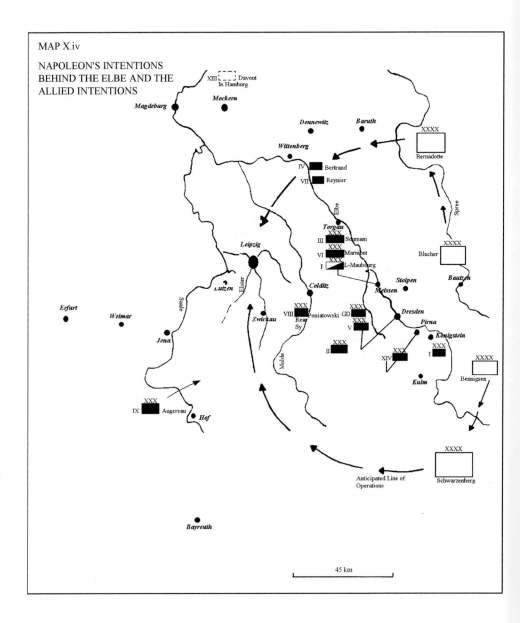

MAP X.iv

NAPOLEON'S INTENTIONS
BEHIND THE ELBE AND THE
ALLIED INTENTIONS

45 km

the Erzgebirge mountains towards Leipzig, thus cutting the French communications. Blücher was ordered to cover the flank of Bennigsen's march after which he was to march north and unite with Bernadotte. This second army would then force the line of the Elbe and drive back the French.

Napoleon began his moves on 24 September and by the end of the month his army was disposed according to plan. Coincidentally, Blücher too began his move on 25 September. Moving rapidly, his army crossed the Elbe on 3 October and drove Bertrand's corps from its positions at Wartenberg, while Bernadotte's army crossed between Wittenberg and Dessau. To Napoleon, it seemed that the allies had divided their forces and delivered him the opportunity for knock-out blows successively against each main army. After some deliberation, Napoleon decided to leave Murat with II, V and VIII Corps and some cavalry to fix the Army of Bohemia south of Chemnitz;[14] the defence of Dresden against the *Freikorps* and the threat of Bennigsen was entrusted to St Cyr[15] with his own XIV Corps and I Corps. Napoleon was clearly in two minds about Dresden but in the end, its possible future potential as a centre of operations against Schwarzenberg justified tying up two corps.

This decision arguably cost Napoleon the Battle of Leipzig. By disregarding his own principles of concentrating every available man and gun for his main effort against the enemy army and ignoring considerations of ground or internal politics, Napoleon fatally compromised his chance of a decisive success. Thus on 6 October when he moved north against Bernadotte and Blücher, he went with a strength of 150,000 men, a force ratio of one to one.

Napoleon believed that Blücher was positioned around Duben, with Bernadotte further north, a belief which was basically correct. His intention was to interpose his force between the two allied armies, create a local superiority against each one, and defeat them sequentially before they could unite. But Blücher, with his superior cavalry, quickly divined Napoleon's intention so that, although Napoleon's troops accomplished the astonishing feat of marching nearly 80 miles in two days, the move towards Düben found only Blücher's rearguard division on 9 October. Disgusted, Napoleon considered pressing on towards Berlin, but news from the south, where Murat was engaged against Schwarzenberg, caused him to hold back.

Blücher meanwhile had made good his escape not eastwards towards Berlin, but *westwards*, so that by 12 October he had reached Halle on the Saale. Bernadotte had initially fallen back towards the Elbe and

Tsar Alexander in Germany, meeting civic leaders and clergymen in liberated territory during the campaign of 1813. He was easily the most charismatic of the allied sovereigns.

would have gone further still had not Blücher, who disliked, despised and mistrusted Bernadotte personally, insisted that both their armies continue to march towards Leipzig to effect a junction with Schwarzenberg. But Bernadotte, who it will be remembered had almost lost his head on the *guillotine* after his 1806 prevarication at Auerstädt, hesitated. In the end, Blücher marched alone, followed at a distance of several days' march, by a doubtful and rather disgruntled Bernadotte.

South of Dresden, Schwarzenberg was making heavy going through the Erzgebirge. With 240,000 men at his disposal he was being roughly handled by Murat, who conducted a highly skilful delaying operation with his three corps totalling 42,200 troops. Leaving the Austrian corps of Chasteler, 10,000 strong, to guard Bohemia, the allied advance had begun on 7 October; on the 10th an opportunity to attack and destroy Murat's force at Borna was missed.[16] Slowly the army moved north-west, while Murat retired before them, maintaining contact with his cavalry. By 14 October the allies had reached Lieberwolkwitz and Maarkleeberg close to Leipzig and there, for a whole day, the cavalry of both sides fought the largest cavalry contest of the year. Murat's 9,800 cavalry were so closely massed and the allies' so dispersed that neither side was able to achieve a decision and the action, which was in essence the opening action of the Battle of Leipzig, was inconclusive.

By this time, the possibility of the allies uniting at Leipzig was very real, if not imminent, and Murat's dispatches had woken Napoleon to the fact that he had to act very quickly indeed. Napoleon also realised that the strength of the allies was such that he had no choice but to adopt an operational, and possibly a tactical, defensive. On 12 October Marmont had been sent with VI Corps and the Guard to Taucha near Leipzig with orders to support Murat. At 3.00 am on 14 October Napoleon followed this with orders to all corps for a general concentration of the army at Leipzig,[17] and specific orders to Macdonald to move with all speed:

> I hope you will arrive here [Düben] in good time today. It is necessary to cross the river at once. There can be no doubt that during tomorrow – the 15th – we shall be attacked by the Army of Bohemia and the Army of Silesia. March with all haste . . .[18]

Napoleon also believed that Bernadotte was some distance away and given that, he might be able to destroy the Army of Bohemia before the arrival of the Army of the North.

Napoleon entered Leipzig at noon on 14 October and immediately rode to join Murat, whose clever delay battle had succeeded in retaining control of much of the ground of tactical importance in the vicinity of the city. Napoleon's reconnaissance soon convinced him that an allied assault was imminent: his concentration was not a moment too soon. By nightfall on 14 October, 157,000 French troops, including allies, were already in the vicinity while a further 18,000 under Reynier were expected within 48 hours. But Davout was still in Hamburg with 25,000 men; and St Cyr in Dresden along with the other Elbe garrisons deployed at least another 30,000 who were being effectively masked by 20,000 men of the corps of General Ostermann whom Bennigsen had detached for just this purpose.

The Army of Bohemia, immediately south of Leipzig, now numbered 203,000 Austrians, Russians and Prussians. Blücher was approaching from Halle with 54,000 Russians and Prussians, while Bernadotte's 85,000 Russians, Swedes and Mecklenburgers moved in from the north east. Bennigsen too was within striking distance. Schwarzenberg, King Frederick William, and Bernadotte remained uneasy about fighting Napoleon in person, but the fiery spirit of Blücher and the determination of the Tsar were equal to the occasion. It was clear that a major and probably decisive engagement would be fought on terms highly advantageous to the converging allies.

NOTES

1. Clausewitz, p.389.
2. Yorck, ii, p.308.
3. *Correspondance*, vol.xxvi, no.20502, dated 2.ix.1813.
4. Some authorities (such as Chandler) state that Ney could not see the situation at Görsdorf due to dust and smoke.
5. St Cyr, iv, p.148.
6. *Correspondance*, vol.xxvi, no.20537, dated 8.ix.1813.
7. Lefebvre, p.336.
8. *Correspondance*, vol.xxvi, no.20619.
9. Ibid.
10. Ibid. no. 20562.
11. *Correspondance*, vol.xxvi, no.20609, dated 22.ix.1813.
12. Yorck, ii, p.322.
13. Ibid, p.324.
14. *Correspondance*, vol.xxvi, no.20698.
15. Ibid. no.20719. See also St Cyr, iv, p.433.
16. von Caemmerer, p.73.
17. *Correspondance*, vol.xxvi, no.20799, dated 14.x.1813.
18. Ibid. no.20801, dated 14.x.1813.

Chapter XI

Leipzig

❧❦❧

I. THE NATIONS ASSEMBLE

IN NAPOLEON'S ARMY at Leipzig there were Frenchmen, Italians, Neapolitans, Spaniards, Portuguese, Dutch, Belgians, Swiss, Poles, Saxons, Württembergers, Westphalians, Bavarians – and a host of contingents from smaller German states – Croats and Illyrians. Against him fought Prussians, Russians, Hungarians, Austrians, Czechs, Slovacks, Slovenes, Mecklenburgers, Swedes, British, Cossacks, Bashkirs and Kalmachs. In all, well over half a million men contended for a period of six days. It was the largest engagement of the Revolutionary and Napoleonic wars and the greatest – and bloodiest – battle in Europe before the First World War. History knows it as the Battle of the Nations. It could have no other name.

Like Dresden, the city of Leipzig has spread out so far in modern times that the site of the battle is totally obscured. Even fewer features remain at Leipzig than at Dresden, other than the road pattern and some traces of the old city. In 1813, Leipzig had a population of about 30,000. Like Dresden, Leipzig too had been a fortress in former years and the old wall still stood around the *Altstadt*, which was about half a mile square. Five gates opened into the wall and beyond them, the suburbs had begun to spread. Some of these suburbs were areas of substantial stone houses and garden walls, although those to the north and west were poorer quarters with narrow, winding streets and poor, crowded dwellings.

The most noteworthy feature of the city's location was the various water obstacles. Chiefly these were the Elster, Pleisse and Parthe rivers, which conveniently divided the ground around the city. To the east and south, between the Parthe and Pleisse, lay a series of low ridges which were eminently suitable for the defence. Here country the was generally open, so that cavalry and guns could move freely, although some ponds and marshes did exist in low-lying areas. The highest feature in this area was the Galgenberg, although the Kolmberg was conspicuously crowned by an old Swedish redoubt, a relic of the Thirty Years war. Most of the villages outside the suburbs lay in this area. These were solidly built agricultural settlements of which the most important were Markkleeberg, Sommerfeld, Liebertwolkwitz and Stötteritz. The Parthe river flowed by this area in a generally north-westerly direction and was a sluggish, tortuous stream with steep and in places marshy banks, making it an obstacle to troops.

South and south-east of the city, between the Pleisse and Elster, lay an area of marshy ground protecting the defences of the city. The two streams flowed generally south to north and were interconnected by a mass of marshy channels, with some woods and gardens in between, making this a very difficult area indeed for troops in rigid formations and virtually impassable for the movement of wheeled vehicles and guns. As the Elster flowed north-west of the city, it made a right-angled turn towards the west and was joined by the Luppe, a small stream also flowing from the south, and the combined stream then flowed through an area very similar to that between the Elster and the Pleisse. Further west, towards Lindenau, the country became almost a level plain while to the north, between the Rivers Elster and Parthe, the land was also relatively flat and well drained except along the banks of the Elster, which were marshy.

As well as the water obstacles, another significant feature of Leipzig was the convergence of routes from all directions. Of most significance was the road west through Lindenau, since this afforded the only real withdrawal route for the French army. Over the marshy ground this route was carried on a causeway which had five stone and several wooden bridges in a space of one-and-a-half miles. The largest bridge, over the Pleisse, lay just outside the Rannstadt gate of the city. There were other bridges too, further south, but in order to make the ground between the Elster and the Pleisse even more of an obstacle, these had been demolished, which had the additional effect of cutting the only alternative withdrawal route towards Lützen. Napoleon had ordered the existing defences of the city and those in the suburbs to be improved by loopholing and palisading, and some earthworks and small redoubts had been constructed around Lindenau. Altogether the position did provide the French with the opportunity to fight on interior lines with a strong defensive position at their backs, while the allies would have to approach over some very difficult ground.

Even with his back to the wall, Napoleon had no intention of fighting a purely defensive action. On 16 October he would have about 159,000 men available, including 27,000 cavalry and 690 guns.[1] His plan, as shown in the diagram, was to hold off the expected advance of Blücher, and possibly Bernadotte, in the north with III, IV, VI Corps, and the VII Franco-Saxon Corps, all under Ney's command, while the garrison of Leipzig, about 7,000 Germans and Italians under General Arrighi, would hold open the line of communication – possibly the line of withdrawal – through Lindenau. His main effort, however, would be placed between the Pleisse and Parthe, where almost 120,000 men would be assembled for an attack on Schwarzenberg's main army. The II and V Corps and VIII Franco-Polish Corps, supported by III Cavalry Corps, would pin the allied army frontally, while XI Corps and II Cavalry Corps under Marshal Macdonald would turn the allied right and draw off the reserves. The *coup de grâce*, a smashing blow in the centre, would be delivered by the Guard Corps, IX Corps, either the IV or VI Corps drawn from Ney's command at the appropriate moment, and the I and V Cavalry Corps, all supported by as many guns as could be assembled. In short, this would be a classic example of the decisive Napoleonic battle.

The allies too planned to go onto the offensive. Schwarzenberg's initial proposal placed the allied main effort in the constricted and marshy ground between the Elster and the Pleisse. This plan met with violent opposition and eventually the Tsar told Schwarzenberg that he could do as he pleased with the Austrians, but that the Russians must come east of the Pleisse. The modified plan, again shown in the diagram, called for the reinforced corps of General Gyulai (19,000) to assault west of the Elster and seize the Lindenau position, thus cutting the French communications. The corps of General Meerfeld (28,000) would attack towards Leipzig between the Elster and the Pleisse, while Blücher's army attacked from the direction of Halle. The main effort was placed against the line of villages Markkleeberg–Wachau–Liebertwolkwitz which would be the objective of four columns under General Barclay. The Russian and Prussian Guards (24,000) were held in reserve at Rotha, but the Austrian reserves under General Baron Bianchi were placed west of the Pleisse.

This plan was, however, significantly flawed in several key aspects. First, as the armies of Bernadotte and Bennigsen, and indeed several Austrian formations as well, had not yet come up, the total allied strength was only just over 200,000 including 40,000 cavalry, a force

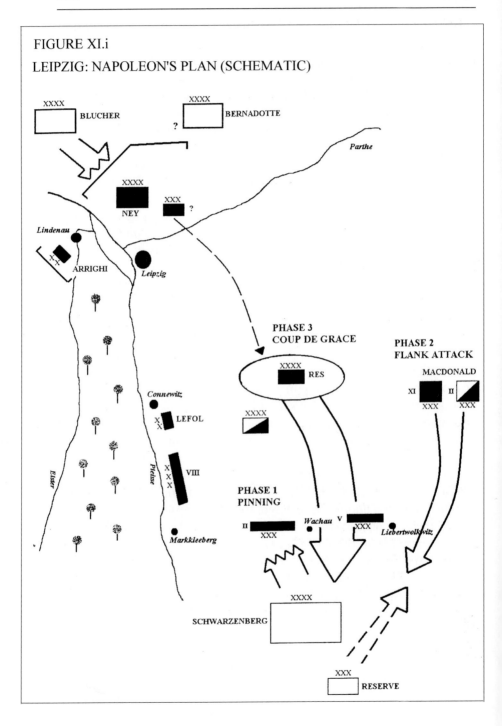

FIGURE XI.i

LEIPZIG: NAPOLEON'S PLAN (SCHEMATIC)

FRENCH ORDER OF BATTLE - LEIPZIG. *Total 150,000 men, 700 guns rising to 170,000 men by 17 October.*

xxxx Ney	xxxx Napoleon	
xxx **III, Souham** *20,000 French*	xxx **Young Guard, Mortier,** *15,000 French*	xxxx **I Cavalry, Latour-** **Maubourg,** *6,000 French*
xxx **IV, Bertrand** *14,000 French*	xxx **Old Guard, Curial** **Friant** *4,000 French*	xxxx **III Cavalry,** **Kellermann,** *3,000* *French and Poles*
xxx **VI, Marmont** *20,000 French,* *poles, Germans*	xxx **Guard Cavalry** *5,000 French*	xxx **IV Cavalry,** **L'Héritier** *4,000 French*
	xxxx **II, Victor** *15,000 French*	xxxx **V Cavalry, Milhaud** *4,000 French*
	xxxx **V, Lauriston** *10,000 French*	**Guard Cavalry**
xx ⊠ **Arrighi** *7,000 Germans,* *Italians*	xxxx **VII Reynier** *14,000 French and* *Germans (expected 16 Oct.)*	xxxx **Macdonald** *(Expected 16 Oct.)*
⊠	xxxx **VIII, Poniatowski** *10,000 Poles*	xxxx **XI, Macdonald** *14,000 French and* *Germans*
⊠	xxxx **IX, Augereau** *10,000 French*	xxxx **II Cavalry,** **Sébastiani,** *5,000 French*
⊠	xx ⊠ **Lefol**	

ratio of only 1.25:1 over the French, although the allies deployed nearly twice as many guns. Second, a considerable number of these allied troops were held in reserve, in positions from which they would be unable to influence the main effort. Third, while two-thirds of Napoleon's forces would be massed for his main effort, the allies committed only one-third, about 77,000. Finally, the bitter lesson of the Weisseritz at Dresden had not been learned, for the Elster cut off Meerfeld's corps from contact with the rest of the army.

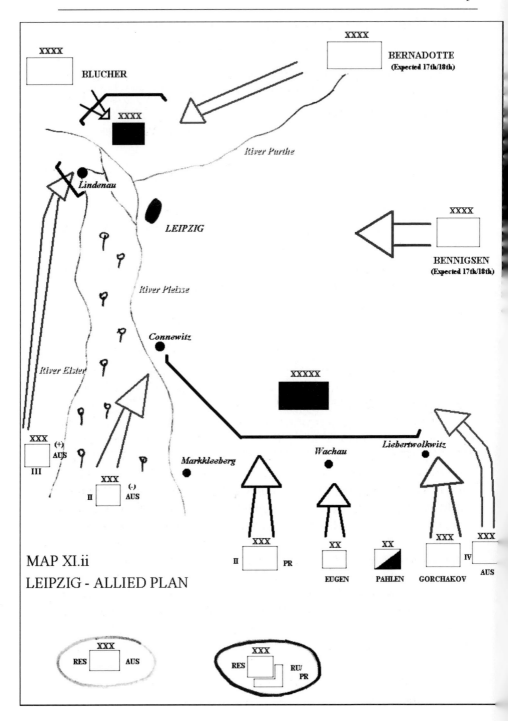

MAP XI.ii

LEIPZIG - ALLIED PLAN

II. THE BATTLES OF 16 OCTOBER – WACHAU, LINDENAU AND MÖCKERN

If anyone doubted that the decisive moment of the War of Liberation had arrived, their doubts must have been set aside by Schwarzenberg's general order to the army – an unmistakeable cry for allied unity:

Brave Soldiers!

We come to the vital moment of our sacred war; the hour of decision beckons, prepare for combat. The bond that unites our warlike nations in a single cause will bring us success on the field of battle. Russians! Prussians! Austrians! You all fight in a righteous cause, for the freedom of your country, for the immortality of your name!

All for one, one for all! It is with this great and potent cry that we must open the sacred struggle; keep faith with this and victory will be yours.

Charles, Field Marshal
Prince of Schwarzenberg.[2]

The planned deployments occupied the energies of both sides for the whole of 15 October. That night, the French troops witnessed the sky illuminated by a blaze of rockets fired by the allies – a signal announcing the imminent union of all the armies and the beginning of battle. The next day dawned cold and wet with a thick mist so that the allied attack was put off until 8.00 am. At 9.00 am Napoleon arrived at the Galgenberg and saw that the allies had pre-empted his attack. He therefore reinforced the threatened areas of his line at Wachau, Markkleeberg and Liebertwolkwitz with additional artillery and most of the infantry of the Guard, and waited for the allied attack to spend itself.

For the conduct of the main allied attack, Barclay had delegated responsibility to Wittgenstein. Hoping to turn the left flank of the French position, Wittgenstein had spread the five formations available for his attack over a frontage of six miles: this dispersion, combined with the weather, meant that visual contact – and therefore the cohesion of the attack – was immediately lost. The Tsar, arriving on the high ground south of Güldengossa at 9.00 am, at once appreciated the weakness of the attack and he ordered up the Russian and Prussian reserves to the area of Gräbern and Güldengossa. He also sent word to Schwarzenberg,

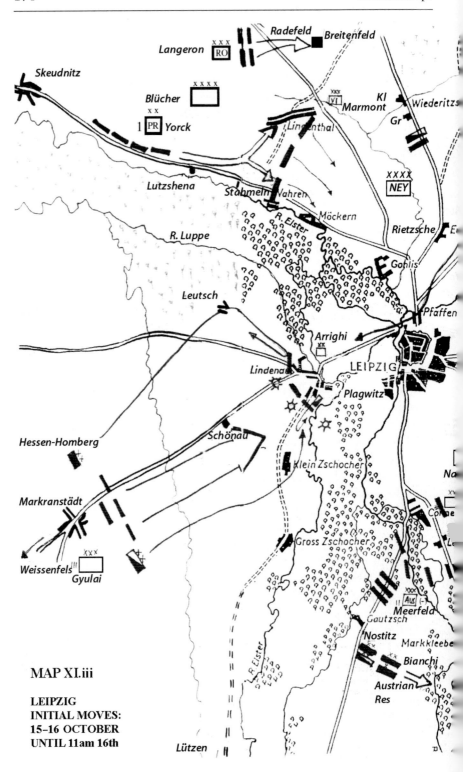

Langeron [x x x | RO]
Radefeld   Breitenfeld
Skeudnitz
Blücher [x x x x]
[x x]
1 [PR] Yorck
KI
Marmont   [x x x | VI]   Wiederitz
Gr
Lindenthal
Lutzshena
Stahmeln Wahren
[x x x x | NEY]
R. Elster   Möckern
Rietzsche   E
R. Luppe
Gohlis
Leutsch
Pfaffen
Arrighi [x x]
Lindenau   LEIPZIG
Plagwitz
Hessen-Homberg
Schönau
Klein Zschocher
Na
Markranstädt
Co...e
L...
Gross Zschocher
Weissenfels [x x x | III]
Gyulai
[x x x | Aus (-)]
Meerfeld
Gautzsch
Nostitz   Markkleebe...
R. Elster
Bianchi [x x]
MAP XI.iii
Austrian
Res

**LEIPZIG
INITIAL MOVES:
15–16 OCTOBER
UNTIL 11am 16th**

Lützen

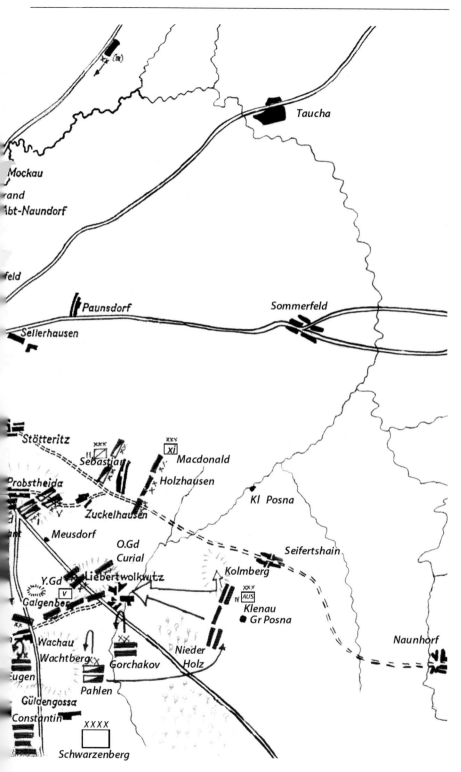

Taucha

Mockau

rand

bt-Naundorf

feld

Paunsdorf

Sommerfeld

Sellerhausen

Stötteritz

Sebastian

Macdonald

Probstheida

Holzhausen

Zuckelhausen

Kl Posna

Meusdorf

O.Gd
Curial

Seifertshain

Y.Gd

Liebertwolkwitz

Kolmberg

Galgenberg

Klenau

Gr Posna

Naunhof

Wachau

Wachtberg

Gorchakov

Nieder
Holz

Eugen

Pahlen

Güldengossa

Constantin

XXXX

Schwarzenberg

who was west of the Pleisse and therefore not present at the main effort, to send the Austrian reserves to support the attack.

Eugen of Württemberg's division was the first allied formation to advance. By 9.30 am Eugen was in Wachau, but was effectively prevented from getting beyond the village by heavy French artillery fire. The French II Corps also immediately counter-attacked Wachau, and for the next one-and-a-half hours a furious hand-to-hand struggle raged in the village. Wachau changed hands several times, for Eugen was determined to hold his position, but by 11.00 am he was forced to withdraw just south of the village.

On Eugen's left, Kleist's Prussian corps stormed and took Markkleeberg but again, French artillery fire stopped him from exploiting northwards. His attempts to support Eugen by attacking on the west side of Wachau were also repulsed with heavy loss. At 11.00 am, Kleist still held Markkleeberg, but his corps was badly mauled.

Over on Eugen's right, Gorchakov's Russians had advanced on the south side of Liebertwolkwitz without waiting for Klenau's Austrians to support them from the east. Neither the Russian infantry, nor General Count von Pahlen's cavalry division, could make any progress in the face of the French artillery and both fell back. Eugen therefore, under pressure as he was, extended one of his brigades to try to maintain contact with the Russians.

Klenau, meanwhile, had not begun his attack on the east of Liebertwolkwitz until 10.00 am. By 11.00 am his left was in the village and his main body had succeeded in occupying the high feature of the Kolmberg. From there he could see the ominous signs of a French advance developing around Holzhausen. He therefore asked for help from Pahlen, and received 14 cavalry squadrons in support.

Napoleon had every reason to feel satisfied with events so far. The main allied attack had been held, while west of the Pleisse, Meerfeld had been repulsed from the Dölitz-Lössnig area by vigorous counter-attacks. Macdonald and II Cavalry Corps were marching into position for the planned attack on the allied right, and it was these troops that Klenau had seen from the Kolmberg. Napoleon also expected the arrival of the corps of Souham and Marmont from the north to reinforce his main effort, so he now prepared to pass from the defensive to the offensive. Macdonald was ordered to storm the Kolmberg and then turn the allied right. Once this movement was complete, Napoleon intended to let lose a general attack. Oudinot with one Young Guard corps was to advance on Auenhain, Lauriston on Güldengossa, Mortier and the other Young Guard corps towards the Nieder Holz.

This attack would be supported by the fire of a great battery of 150 guns, positioned between Wachau and Liebertwolkwitz, which would shatter the allied centre. Having thus penetrated his enemies' position, Napoleon planned to commit the corps of Souham and Marmont, when they arrived, to drive the allied left into the Pleisse and their right off their communications with Dresden, thus winning the battle.

Shortly before noon, Macdonald began his attack on the Kolmberg. Despite a gallant charge by some Austrian cavalry, this attack was completely successful, and Klenau himself narrowly escaped capture when his horse was shot from under him. The repulse of Klenau's corps compelled the retirement of Gorchakov and Pahlen and consequently, Lauriston's troops were able to clear Liebertwolkwitz. Kleist too was forced out of Markkleeberg by the Young Guard, was reinforced from the allied reserves, counter-attacked, but was forced back again. By 2.00 pm he retained only a precarious hold on the southern edge of the village. Only Eugen of Württemberg, with two-thirds of his division dead or wounded around him, still held his ground.

Thus by 2.00 pm, the allies had been to all intents and purposes driven back to their starting points. It was Dresden all over again, and it seemed that all that was needed now was for Napoleon to complete another stunning victory. The I Cavalry Corps and the Guard cavalry were massed around Meusdorf, Oudinot and Lauriston formed attack columns between Wachau and Markkleeberg, and south of Liebertwolkwitz Victor formed up with Mortier's Young Guard behind him. Although there was still no sign of Bertrand, or Marmont, or Souham, Napoleon was nevertheless so confident of success, that he sent word for the bells of Leipzig to ring for a victory.

At 4.00 pm Macdonald's troops resumed their advance towards Siefertshain, Klein Pössna and University Wood in order to complete the turning movement on the allied right. Some progress was made and by dark, the French held the Nieder Holz. But an unexpectedly stiff fight had been put up by Klenau's Austrians in Siefertshain and Gross Pössna so that by the end of the day the French advance had been effectively stopped.

On the allied left, too, the fortune of battle began to change. Poniatowski's VIII Corps and Augereau's IX Corps advanced against Kleist who, in desperate straits, retired on Cröbern. As he did so, the Austrian cavalry reserve arrived from over the Pleisse and at the same

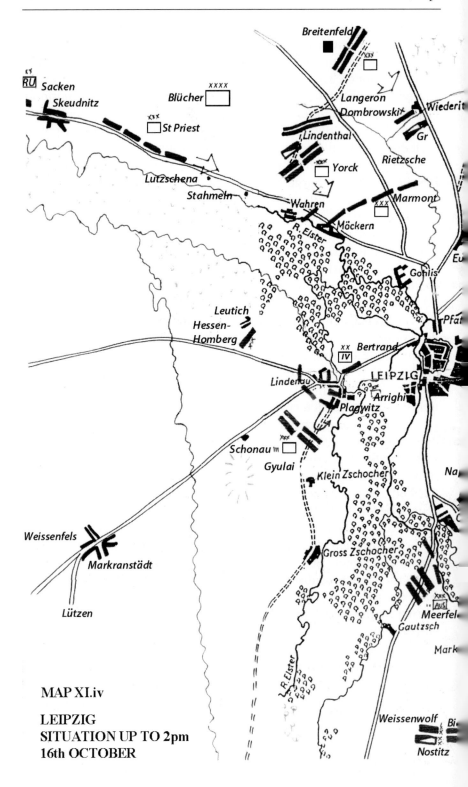

RU Sacken
Skeudnitz
Blücher XXXX
St Priest
Breitenfeld
Langeron
Dombrowski
Wiederit
Gr
Lindenthal
Rietzsche
Yorck
Lutzschena
Stahmeln
Wahren
Marmont
Möckern
R. Elster
Gohlis
Eu
Leutich
Hessen-
Homberg
Pfa
XX IV Bertrand
LEIPZIG
Lindenau
Arrighi
Plagwitz
Na
Schonau
Gyulai
Klein Zschocher
Weissenfels
Markranstädt
Gross Zschocher
AUS
Meerfel
Lützen
Gautzsch
Mark
R. Elster
Weissenwolf Bi
Nostitz

MAP XI.iv

LEIPZIG
SITUATION UP TO 2pm
16th OCTOBER

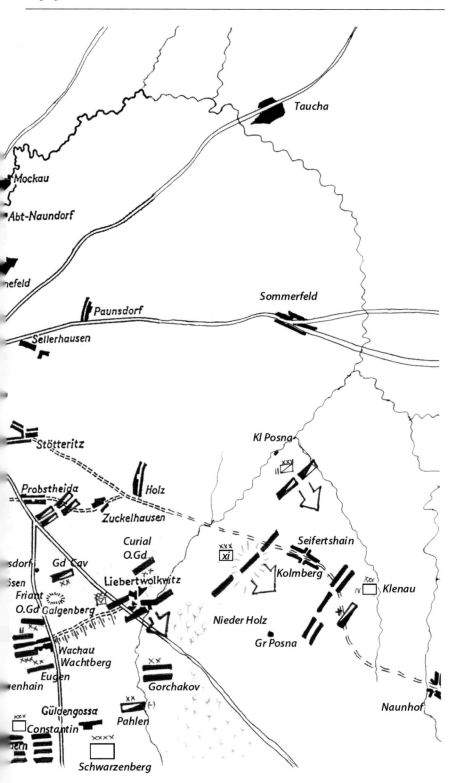

Taucha

Mockau

Abt-Naundorf

nefeld

Sommerfeld

Paunsdorf

Sellerhausen

Stötteritz

Kl Posna

Probstheida

Holz

Zuckelhausen

Curial
O.Gd

Seifertshain

Kolmberg

Klenau

sdorf

Gd Cav

ssen

Liebertwolkwitz

Friant

O.Gd Galgenberg

Nieder Holz

Gr Posna

ii

Wachau
Wachtberg

Eugen

enhain

Gorchakov

Naunhof

Güldengossa

Pahlen

(-)

Constantin

ern

Schwarzenberg

time, the French Guard cavalry and part of III Cavalry Corps appeared on the plain just north of the village. The Austrians at once charged, driving the French back, but themselves suffered heavy loss and were in turn driven back on Cröbern. The French infantry pressed forward again but fortunately for Kleist, the Austrian reserve infantry under Bianchi, following up the cavalry from over the Pleisse, debouched from Cröbern just at the right moment to check the French advance. This move had the additional effect of relieving pressure on Meerfeld, so that he at last managed to cross the Pleisse, and it had the further effect of checking the advance of Oudinot and Victor towards Auenhain.

By 5.30 pm it was clear that the French right was in dire straits, so much so that Napoleon committed a division of the Old Guard and one division of Souham's corps which had at last come up, to stabilise the situation. By dark, Bianchi's advance with Kleist advancing on his right had almost reached Dölitz, but here it was halted. Meerfeld too, whose troops had actually entered Dölitz, was halted and then thrown back. Meerfeld himself, being rather short-sighted, rode into some Poles of VIII Corps whom he mistook for Hungarians, and was captured.

While the French left had made limited progress and the right was being repulsed, Drouot's great battery continued to fire on the allied centre. Behind the battery I Cavalry Corps was massed, waiting its moment. At 2.30 pm, while the cavalry action on the French right was in full swing, the corps commander, General Doumerc, who was standing in for the wounded Latour-Maubourg, ordered a division of 2,500 French and Saxon cuirassiers to charge from the western end of the great battery. This charge carried away one of Eugen of Württemberg's depleted battalions and captured 26 guns – but it did not stop there. Cutting through Eugen's men, the 18 cavalry squadrons arrived in front of the high feature of the Wachtberg, where Tsar Alexander and the King of Prussia were watching the progress of the battle. For a moment it seemed that the allied monarchs might be captured, but the impetus of the French charge was spent. As the cuirassiers struggled through the ponds at the foot of the Wachtberg, they were themselves charged by the Cossacks of the Tsar's bodyguard, followed by 13 squadrons of cuirassiers from the Russian reserve. Those French and Saxons who managed to escape fled back behind the battery, pursued by the Russians, who were halted only by the fire of Drouot's guns.

Despite the counter-charge, Eugen's division was in tatters, and it had now been forced right back to a line between Auenhain and Güldengossa. But at Güldengossa the Tsar ordered the assembly of a battery of

94 Russian guns, and there too the Russian and Prussian Guards from Prince Constantin's Reserve Corps were marching in support. This was more than enough to stabilise the allies' situation so that, despite Macdonald's gains, the majority of the allied position had been salvaged. The result of the day's fighting on the southern front was, therefore, a bloody draw – thanks to the determination of the allies. Had Napoleon been reinforced as he had expected, it would have been a different story, and so it is now necessary to look further afield in order to understand why the additional French forces had not appeared.

West of the Pleisse, Gyulai's task was to attack Lindenau, linking the corps of Meerfeld with Blücher's attack from the north-west and if possible drawing French troops away from the allied main effort. Gyulai did not expect to be able to take the fortified position of Lindenau and so decided to mount a demonstration only. At about 8.00 am his scouts reported fighting south of Leipzig and so the Austrians began to advance. By 10.30 am they had closed up to Klein Zschocher, which was taken after a fierce struggle with a French forward detachment. The Austrians pressed on again to where the French garrison troops of Lindenau under General Arrighi were drawn up across the Lützen road between Lindenau and Plagwitz, with their artillery in redoubts and a small body of cavalry holding their left. Gyulai's artillery at once began to bombard the French infantry, while his superior cavalry drove the French horsemen, who attempted to attack, back behind their guns. The main body of the Austrian infantry now advanced on Plagwitz, but repeated attacks on the place failed in the face of the well-placed French artillery.

On Gyulai's left, however, General Prince Hesse-Homburg's division was able to capture the village of Leutsch. Beyond lay a mass of ditches and streams covered by the fire of French batteries in Lindenau. Slowly, patiently, the Hessians worked their way through this morass and succeeded in storming the defences of the causeway, only to be ejected by a counter-attack. A second attack was mounted; it too succeeded briefly but was then thrown out by Arrighi's counter-attack.

At 10.00 am Ney had dispatched Bertrand's corps south to support Napoleon as he had been ordered. The corps was on its way when Bertrand received an urgent message from Arrighi, asking for assistance at Lindenau. Since Arrighi was clearly extremely worried about the possibility of losing the only line of communication, Bertrand accordingly turned from his route and moved with his whole corps to Lindenau – a position which was so strong that an additional brigade

A view of the field of Leipzig, the allied sovereigns are on the small hill in the middle ground. The wounded, and French prisoners, proceed to the rear.

would probably have sufficed. It was Bertrand's arrival which ensured the repulse of Hesse-Homburg's division, which retired on Leutsch. Bertrand, hearing the bells of Leipzig ringing to announce an apparent victory south of the city, then attempted to advance towards Klein Zschocher, only to be twice repulsed by Austrian fire.

After this, the action about Lindenau was confined to artillery fire until night when Gyulai, maintaining small forward detachments in Klein Zschocher, Schönau and Leutsch, withdrew his corps to Markranstädt. He had not captured Lindenau, but he had drawn Bertrand away from Wachau, so that his attack had been more successful than he could have hoped.

While Lindenau was being successfully defended, the bloodiest of the three engagements of the day was being fought out north of Leipzig, between the forces of Marmont and Blücher. Marmont had been ordered by Ney to find a position which would block the northern approaches to Leipzig city. Accordingly, he selected a defensive line between Lindenthal and Breitenbach, on the very ground where in 1631 Gustavus Adolphus had defeated Tilly. Marmont insisted, however, that this position required 30,000 troops to hold it, as against the 14,000 that his own corps actually contained. His corps, VI, was, next to the Guard, probably the best in the *Grande Armée*, being composed for the most part of experienced soldiers; it also, like VII Corps, contained several regiments of Saxon and other German infantry, as well as General Dombrowski's Polish division. Saxon cavalry regiments made up the entire corps cavalry. Napoleon promised Marmont that, if he was attacked, Bertrand's and Souham's corps would assist him – although he had no intention of keeping this promise. As most of these formations lay around Eutritzsch, Marmont was satisfied, so he set about fortifying his main position and dispatched an advanced guard to occupy the village of Radefeld.

On the evening of the 15th, Marmont received a report that Blücher was about to march from Halle. At 10.00 pm that night, from the church tower in Lindenthal, he watched the sky lit up by the glow from the camp fires of the Army of Silesia: he at once sent word to Napoleon, and again received assurances of support.[3] All, therefore, seemed well. But early next morning, 16 October, a thunderbolt struck. Napoleon's instructions[4] insisted that, as no significant enemy force opposed him, Marmont was to march south to join the main army and his place was to be taken by Bertrand. Despite knowing his master to be in error,

Marmont had no choice but to obey. No sooner had he begun to move, than Blücher's advanced guard occupied Radefeld.

Blücher's main body had spent the night of 15/16 October at Skeuditz. Blücher knew very well that he could expect no support from Bernadotte for at least another full day, for the British liaison officer, Colonel Stewart, had arrived in his camp to warn him. Nevertheless, old General *Vorwärts* decided to press on. His intention was to seize the high ground around Radefeld and then decide on subsequent moves once he had identified the French position. He was particularly concerned about the possibility of a French defence on the Düben road, and he therefore placed the main effort of his army on the left. His orders called for the Russian corps of General Count Langeron to advance on Radefeld. General Baron Sacken's Russian corps would follow, with General Count St Priest's Russians following up. Yorck's Prussian corps was to advance down the main road from Halle as far as Lützschena, and then swing north to Lindenthal.

Blücher's main body did not begin to move until 10.00 am, but Langeron had no difficulty in occupying Radefeld, since Marmont had withdrawn his advanced guard. Still worried about the Düben road, Blücher then ordered Langeron to press on so as to be able to dominate that approach from Breitenfeld. Yorck, meanwhile, advanced as he had been ordered. His main body forced the Saxon cavalry to evacuate Lindenthal, while his advanced guard pressed on down the main road, pushing the French out of Stahmeln and Wahren. These moves soon made Marmont aware that continued withdrawal by his corps would be disastrous, and he therefore took up a new blocking position between the village of Möckern and the Rietzsche stream, with Dombrowski's Poles and the Saxon cavalry occupying Gross and Klein Wiederitzsch. He still hoped for support from Souham's III Corps, although he knew that Bertrand had been committed southwards.

It was 2.00 pm before Blücher realised the true extent of the French position. He ordered Langeron to clear Wiederitzsch at once, but still preoccupied with the Düben road, he moved Sacken's corps forward to screen the approach. Langeron sent his advanced guard regiment and his leading division against Wiederitzsch, where a desperate fight soon raged between the Russians and their hereditary enemies, the Poles. By 3.00 pm, the Poles had been driven from the village in disorder and had fallen back on Euritzsch, when Marmont's Saxon cavalry charged the Russians. Seeing this, the Poles rallied, turned back, and an unstoppable counter-attack threw the Russians out of the village.

Once again the Russians attacked and once again the Poles were driven back on Eutritzsch, when General Delmas' division of III Corps appeared, escorting a baggage train. Although the division was less than 5,000 strong, the size of the baggage train gave it the appearance of a corps. The Russians, seriously alarmed, withdrew north-east of Wiedertitzsch until Langeron realised the true size of the new force and resumed the attack, supported now by the leading division of St Priest's corps which Blücher had ordered forward. This time, there was no counter-attack. Delmas' division and the Poles were thrown back over the Parthe with heavy losses.

Yorck, too, had realised the true extent of the French position and had wheeled his main body south-east from Lindenthal. Once Langeron had moved on Wiederitzsch, Yorck moved on Möckern. His first two assaults on the village failed, and there ensued one of the bloodiest struggles of the entire war for possession of Möckern, surpassing even that of Lützen. The village changed hands time and again as both sides sent in reinforcements.

At the same time, Yorck determined to attack the centre of the French line as well as the village. Here too the initial Prussian attacks were repulsed with great slaughter. But as the French prepared to follow up the repulse with a counter-attack, several ammunition wagons blew up with tremendous force, spreading panic and confusion. Seeing this and gaining heart, the Prussians returned to the attack but again the French rallied and drove their enemies back. An attempt by one brigade to assist the fight in Möckern met with repulse and near disaster – it could have been worse still: Marmont ordered the Saxon cavalry to charge but its commander refused, probably treacherously in the light of subsequent actions by the Saxons.

Back in Möckern, Yorck's men had at last succeeded in gaining control of the village after 5 pm, and now the climax of the battle arrived. Marmont personally led his infantry forward to destroy the remnants of the Prussian attack on his centre, but Yorck, realising his peril just in time, brought up his corps cavalry. Charging furiously forwards, the Prussian horsemen swept away Marmont's leading battalions and their supporting Saxon cavalry, and crashed into the midst of Marmont's guns. The *mêlée* which ensued was merciless with cavalry, infantry and gunners fighting hand-to-hand with any and every weapon within reach until at last, the French broke and fell back. With Möckern gone, Marmont could do nothing but retire as best he could as the whole of Yorck's corps pressed forward.

As the fall of night brought an end to the fighting, and Marmont's shattered men bivouacked where they stood between Gohlis and Eutritzsch, the victorious Prussians broke into a vast, solemn chorus of the great Lutheran hymn 'Nun danket alle Gott'. Well they might: Yorck's corps had lost nearly 8,000 men, or one-third of its strength, and Langeron had lost 1,500. But they had inflicted at least 7,000 casualties on their enemies and had taken 2,500 prisoners, 53 guns, an eagle and two colours. Marmont's corps had lost well over half its strength and was almost ineffective.

What then was the result of the fighting on 16 October? South of Leipzig it was on the face of it a drawn battle. The allied attack early on had achieved some tactical surprise and the Tsar's intervention had ensured that Napoleon's main attack had been held. At Lindenau, the French had held open their communications, but Gyulai had successfully prevented Bertrand from decisively reinforcing Napoleon's main effort, while at Möckern, Blücher had shut Napoleon in from the north.

Nothing less than complete victory would have served Napoleon in his situation. As it was, he had scarcely held his own. He could expect little further help – only Reynier's 18,000 men and this, taking into account his losses, would only raise his strength to around 170,000. The allies, on the other hand, could expect the arrival of Colloredo, Bernadotte and Bennigsen, bringing their strength to over 320,000 men.

III. THE BATTLE LOST

The night of 16/17 October should have found Napoleon hard at work planning a withdrawal. The route through Markranstädt could easily have been forced given the relative strengths of Napoleon's main army and Gyulai's corps; an escape to the Rhine would have left Napoleon with an army over 50,000 stronger for the campaign of 1814 than was to be the case. Instead, the night found the *Grande Armée* in a wet, miserable and hungry bivouac on the battlefield. Napoleon's tent was pitched in the bed of a dried-up pond at Stötteritz, and here the captured Meerfeld was brought before him. Napoleon, who knew Meerfeld, spoke to him briefly then, and recalled him later that evening. Napoleon asked how strong the allied army was. Meerfeld replied that it was more than 350,000 men. Napoleon then asked whether the allies realised that he was there, and whether they would attack again. Meerfeld replied that they did, and they would.

Napoleon is reputed to have asked 'Shall this war last forever? It is surely time to put an end to it. Austria should speak the word of peace, and not listen to Russia, because Russia is under the influence of England, and England wishes for war. I am ready to make great sacrifices.'[5] Meerfeld replied that the Emperor of Austria would not separate himself from his allies, and that England wished only for a Europe free from the domination of one power. Napoleon said 'Let England give me back my islands [i.e. in the West Indies] and I will restore Hanover, Holland and the Hanseatic cities.'[6] But he would not agree to the suppression of the Confederation of the Rhine nor the loss of his territories in Italy and Illyria.

Meerfeld then told him that Bavaria had gone over to the allies. Napoleon replied that she would repent it. He then proposed another armistice and negotiations for peace, during which he would retire behind the Saale while the Russians retired behind the Elbe and the Austrians into Bohemia. Saxony would stay neutral. Meerfeld told him flatly that the allies would never agree to such terms now and would not leave Germany even if they could not drive the French over the Rhine. Napoleon replied that to be driven back thus, he would have to lose another battle, and this one was not yet lost.

Napoleon then concluded the interview and sent Meerfeld back to the Emperor Francis with a letter. Francis was delighted to see Meerfeld again, as he had feared him dead, but said that he could speak to him only in the presence of his allies; the Tsar and Frederick William, having come this far, would have none of Napoleon's proposals.

During the night the bad news from Möckern came in. With his losses and his low ammunition stocks, Napoleon now knew that he could not last out a repetition of the battles of 16 October and, torn as he was between military necessity and holding on to his empire in Germany, he made up his mind to withdraw. Even so, probably for domestic political reasons, he determined to keep the field for one more day. For the same reason there was no large-scale bridge building to supplement the single withdrawal route over the Lindenau causeway. Napoleon's orders were not issued until 7.00 pm on 17 October after a day of skirmishing, for the allies had decided to postpone their attack until 18 October in order to ensure that their entire force would be present.

Napoleon ordered Bertrand to leave Lindenau late on 17 October and secure the passages over the Saale and the Unstrut rivers at Freiberg, Weissenfels, Merseberg and Bad Kösen. The rest of the army left its

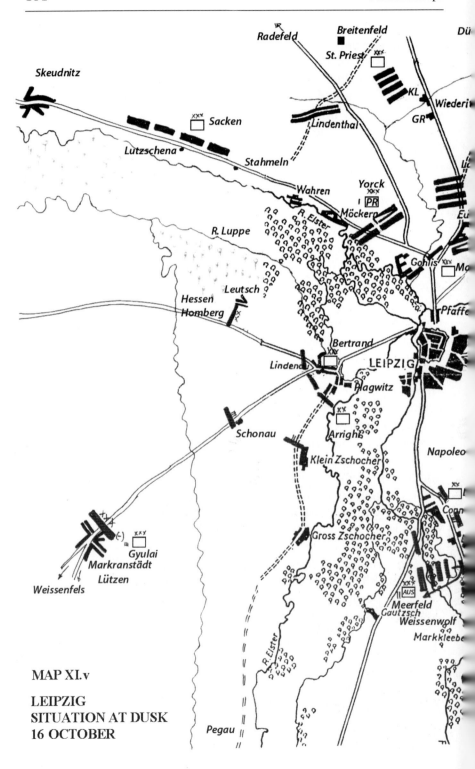

Radefeld

Breitenfeld

Dü

St. Priest

Skeudnitz

KL

Wiederi

Sacken

GR

Lindenthal

Lutzschena

Stahmeln

Wahren

Yorck

PR

Möckern

Eu

R. Luppe

R. Elster

Gohlis

Mo

Leutsch

Pfaffe

Hessen
Homberg

Bertrand

LEIPZIG

Linden

Plagwitz

Schonau

Arright

Napoleo

Klein Zschocher

Gross Zschocher

Conn

Gyulai

Markranstädt

Lützen

AUS

Weissenfels

Meerfeld

Gautzsch

Weissenwolf

Markkleebe

MAP XI.v

**LEIPZIG
SITUATION AT DUSK
16 OCTOBER**

Pegau

bivouacs at 2.00 am on 18 October in pouring rain for new positions, for the Emperor planned to hold a line much closer in towards Leipzig: but he had no thoughts of further offensive action. The right wing of the army was placed under Murat's command and consisted of II, VIII and IX Corps; the Old Guard; and I, IV and V Cavalry Corps. This wing was to defend between Connewitz and Probstheida. The centre was placed under Macdonald's command. With his own XI Corps, V Corps and the Guard cavalry, he was to defend between Zuckelshausen and Holzhausen. Ney continued to command the left wing with Reynier's VII Corps newly arrived, III and IV Corps and two cavalry divisions. His task was to defend between Paunsdorf and Schönefeld. Dombrowski's Polish division with two cavalry divisions was ordered to block the approach from Gohlis into the north of Leipzig, while Mortier with the Young Guard and Arrighi's division held open the causeway at Lindenau.

The allied plan for 18 October called for an attack in six great columns. The main effort would be with the attack from the south on Markkleeberg, Lössnig, Wachau, Liebertwolkwitz. Bennigsen would turn the French left by attacking towards Probstheida and Holzhausen. Blücher would continue to advance on the north-east side of the city, with Bernadotte between Blücher and Bennigsen. Gyulai would once again attack Lindenau from the south.

The allied attack began at 7.00 am. After a night of rain, the day had broken dull and cheerless, but by 8.00 am, with the attack well under way, the sun broke through. The allied first column had to fight hard to push the French forward detachments out of Dölitz, Dösen, and Lössnig but by 2.00 pm the column, commanded by General Colloredo in the absence of the wounded Prince of Hesse-Homburg, had closed up to the main French position in front of Connewitz. On its right, Barclay had closed up to Probstheida where he paused to allow Bennigsen to complete his turning movement.

Bennigsen's column advanced on four axes: Klein Posna, Siefertshain, the Kolmberg and the Nieder Holz. By 2.00 pm, after some stiff fighting and two cavalry actions, he too had driven the French back onto their main position between Zuckelshausen and Paunsdorf. Bennigsen's right around Paunsdorf engaged VII Franco-Saxon Corps and it was here that the celebrated desertion of the Saxon cavalry and two divisions of Saxon and Westphalian infantry took place. In the long run this action did no good to its commanders: General Normann and several other

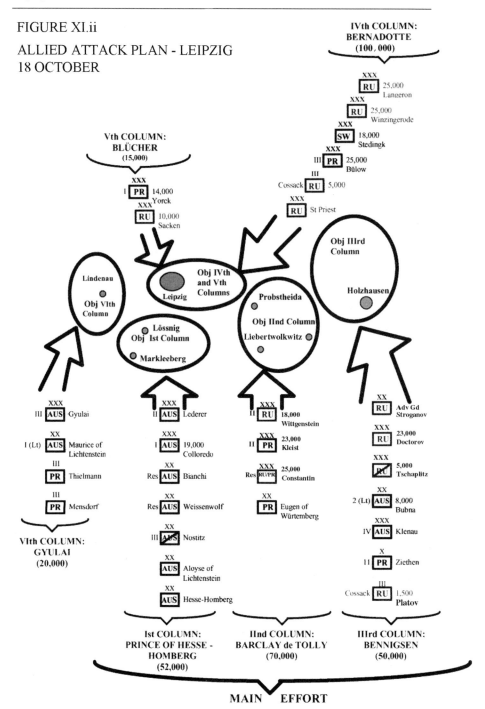

FIGURE XI.ii

ALLIED ATTACK PLAN - LEIPZIG
18 OCTOBER

IVth COLUMN:
BERNADOTTE
(100,000)

XXX RU 25,000 Langeron
XXX RU 25,000 Winzingerode
XXX SW 18,000 Stedingk
III PR 25,000 Bülow
III Cossack RU 5,000
XXX RU St Priest

Vth COLUMN:
BLÜCHER
(15,000)

XXX I PR 14,000 Yorck
XXX RU 10,000 Sacken

Obj IIIrd Column

Lindenau
Obj VIth Column

Obj IVth and Vth Columns
Leipzig

Lössnig
Obj Ist Column
Markleeberg

Probstheida
Obj IInd Column
Liebertwolkwitz

Holzhausen

XXX III AUS Gyulai
XX I (Lt) AUS Maurice of Lichtenstein
III PR Thielmann
III PR Mensdorf

VIth COLUMN:
GYULAI
(20,000)

XXX II AUS Lederer
XXX I AUS 19,000 Colloredo
XX Res AUS Bianchi
XX Res AUS Weissenwolf
XX III AUS Nostitz
XX AUS Aloyse of Lichtenstein
XX AUS Hesse-Homberg

Ist COLUMN:
PRINCE OF HESSE -
HOMBERG
(52,000)

XXX II RU 18,000 Wittgenstein
XXX II PR 23,000 Kleist
XXX Res RU/PR 25,000 Constantin
XX PR Eugen of Würtemberg

IInd COLUMN:
BARCLAY de TOLLY
(70,000)

XX RU Adv Gd Stroganov
XXX RU 23,000 Doctorov
XXX RU 5,000 Tschaplitz
XX 2 (Lt) AUS 8,000 Bubna
XXX IV AUS Klenau
X 11 PR Ziethen
III Cossack RU 1,500 Platov

IIIrd COLUMN:
BENNIGSEN
(50,000)

MAIN ▼ EFFORT

senior officers were subsequently cashiered and banished, while the regiments concerned were disbanded.[7]

Away east of Leipzig, Bertrand's corps had burst out of Lindenau, throwing Gyulai's attack back over the Elster and the Luppe. By 2.00 pm, Bertrand had opened up the route towards Weissenfels and was marching hard for the Saale. At the same time, north of the city, Blücher's men were heavily engaged against Ney at Gohlis, while the corps of Langeron and St Priest, having pushed Marmont's corps back on Schönefeld, awaited the arrival of Bernadotte around Möckern and Breitenfeld respectively, where they had been ordered to support his forward move. All around Leipzig, therefore, the engagement was general, except that between Bennigsen and Blücher there was still no sign of Bernadotte. In fact, by 2.00 pm the leading corps of the Army of the North, the Prussian corps of Bülow, had almost closed up to the battlefield although the rest of the army was some two hours' march behind it and did not cross the Parthe until 4.00 pm.

It was thus between 2.00 pm and 5.00 pm that, having closed up to the main French line, the main allied attack developed. Colloredo's column was itself counter-attacked by Augereau's corps and by Poniatowski. Lössnig changed hands several times and the allies held on with great difficulty. Resuming the attack, Colloredo was unable to take Connewitz, although by nightfall Poniatowski's corps had been reduced to 2,500 effectives. Barclay's column attacked Probstheida, which was the vital ground in the French defensive position. Barclay himself wanted to wait for support on his flanks, but the Tsar insisted on an immediate attack. Three attempts were made and all were repulsed with dreadful losses on both sides. The struggle was truly heroic, but at 5.00 pm, the allied monarchs, who were receiving better news from their right, forbade any further attack here.

The news was that Bennigsen's troops, supported by the famous British rocket troop of the Royal Horse Artillery, had closed up and had captured the villages of Zweiaundorf and Molkau. Here two other Saxon infantry brigades and a battery of 22 guns deserted to the allies. Napoleon afterwards attributed his defeat to this desertion[8], but as the total strength of these Saxons was only 4,000 men, this is hardly a loss which could have influenced so widespread a battle as Leipzig. A strong French counter-attack was mounted towards Bennigsen, which he repulsed, but was himself unable to make any further progress before nightfall.

It was the arrival of Bernadotte which had allowed Bennigsen to go

Leipzig, evening 18 October 1813. Field Marshal Prince Schwarzenberg (mounted left) reports victory to the allied sovereigns on a hillock astride the road between Liebertwolkwitz and Probstheida. Two captured Napoleonic eagles flutter over Schwarzenberg's staff. This P. Krafft painting is in the Austrian Army Museum, Vienna.

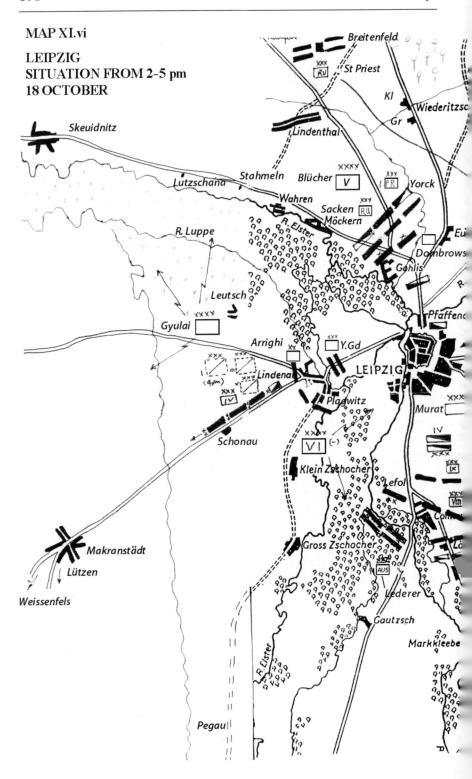

MAP XI.vi

LEIPZIG
SITUATION FROM 2-5 pm
18 OCTOBER

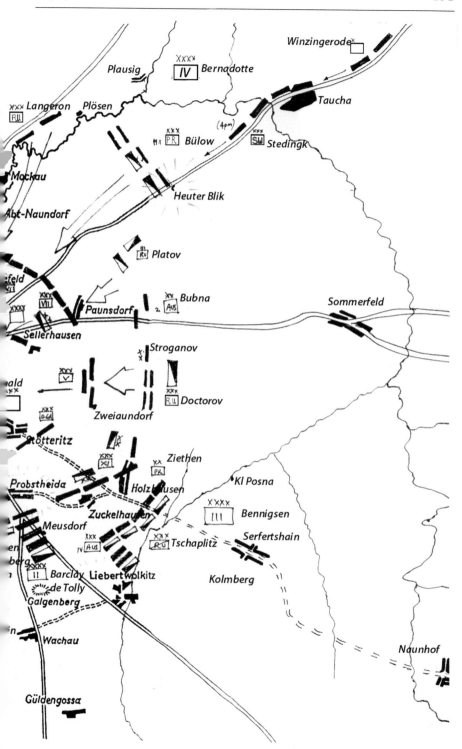

as far as he did. Bernadotte committed only his artillery, saying 'Provided the French are beaten, it is indifferent to me whether I or my army take a part, and of the two, I had much rather we did not.'[9] Even so, Bernadotte's arrival had important consequences in the north. Langeron's attack on Schönefeld from the north was supported by St Priest on his right and by attacks by Bernadotte's Russians and Prussians from the north-east, towards Sellershausen. Sellershausen was taken, but Schönefeld was strongly fortified, protected by marshes and well garrisoned. When Langeron's men eventually took the place the artillery ammunition of his corps was exhausted and the troops were forced out by a counter-attack. The arrival of Russian and Swedish guns sent by Bernadotte saved the day: Ney, his last reserves spent, was forced back on Leipzig itself with the disorganised remnants of his command.

By dusk then, the French, although still holding their positions in many areas, had received a very severe mauling indeed. Their ammunition was almost completely exhausted (16,000 artillery rounds were left on the 19th, 200,000 having been fired), food and water were scarce, and casualties were heavy: all in all, they were scarcely in any condition to continue the fight, and it was fortunate for them that there was on the allied side no commander capable of exploiting the situation to full advantage. The allied attack, as on the 16th, had been general with the main effort directed towards the strongest, rather than the weakest, French positions. The army of Bernadotte, strong enough to have achieved decisive action, had arrived too late and when it did it acted only in a supporting role.

> Night fell; the sky glowed red, Stötteritz, Schönefeld, Dölitz, and one of the suburbs of Leipzig were in flames. Whilst with us [i.e. the allies] all were intoxicated with joy . . . indescribable confusion reigned in the enemy's army. Their baggage, their artillery, their broken regiments, the soldiers who had been for days without food, were stopped for want of bridges over the streams around Leipzig. In the narrow streets resounded the cries of woe of innumerable wounded, as our shot and shell fell upon them. Over the battlefield, so recently filled with the thunder of 2,000 guns, there reigned the silence of the grave.[10]

IV. THE STORMING OF LEIPZIG.

Even while the battle of 18 October was in full swing, the French retreat had begun. Gyulai had reported Bertrand's break-out during the afternoon, and the small Austrian detachment at Weissenfels had been warned to throw down the bridge there. In fact, the Emperor had ordered the retreat to begin at 11.00 am and from that time, a stream of traffic began to move down the Lindenau causeway. Everything not immediately needed for the fight was dispatched: baggage, artillery parks, camp stores, wagons; and at 4.00 pm I, III and V Cavalry Corps were ordered west of Lindenau.

By evening, news of the retreat reached Blücher and so while the rest of the army bivouacked, Yorck's weary corps was dispatched to occupy the passages of the Saale at Halle and Merseberg. Marching all night, the Prussians gained their objective early on 19 October – but there was no concerted attempt by the allied high command to forestall the French retreat by occupying Freiburg, Kösen or Naumberg, or by destroying bridges using the allies' very considerable advantage in cavalry and Cossacks. The only formation sent in pursuit, apart from Yorck's corps, was Count Bubna's Austrian light division. Possibly the allies were only too glad to offer Napoleon the chance to disappear, so as not to have to face him in person when the attack on Leipzig was resumed. For the attack was to be resumed. Schwarzenberg's orders for 19 October were simple:

> All parts of the Army must be ready in battle order at daybreak to renew the battle. In case of the enemy's retreat, the army will advance, as on the 18th, in five columns concentrically on Leipzig . . .[11]

Napoleon, meanwhile, had issued orders for the retreat of the rest of his army. The city of Leipzig itself would continue to be defended by two Baden battalions, an Italian battalion, and about 1,200 Saxon troops – the only remnant of the Saxon Army. Macdonald with the remnant of VII and VIII Corps, which of course contained large numbers of Poles and Germans, and his own XI Corps was ordered to act as rearguard and if possible hold off the allied attack for another day. The causeway at Lindenau was to be mined, and was to be blown once the rearguard had broken contact and withdrawn. The rest of the army began thinning out from its forward positions at 2.00 am on 19 October; by 5.00 am the allied patrols began to bring news of their departure. It was a year to the very day since Napoleon had marched out of Moscow.

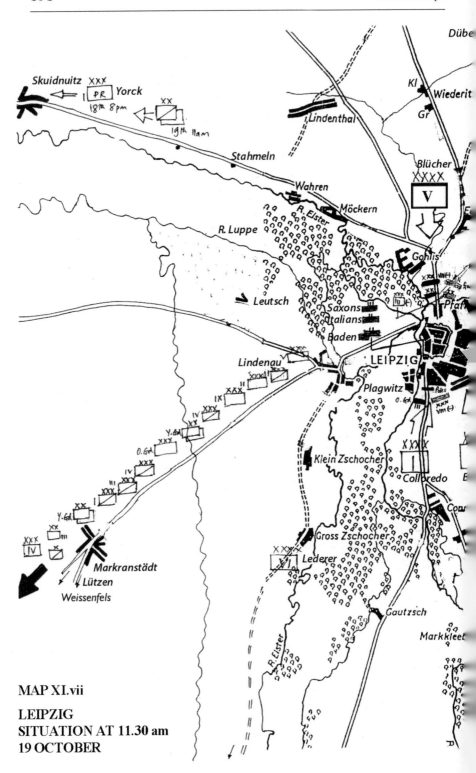

Dübe

Skuidnuitz XXX
                PR Yorck
           18th 8pm
                        XX
                    19th 11am

Stahmeln

Wahren

R. Elster   Möckern

R. Luppe

Leutsch

Lindenthal

Kl Wiederit
Gr

Blücher
XXXX

V

Gohlis

Saxons
Italians

Baden

Pfaf

Lindenau

LEIPZIG

Plagwitz

IX XXX

IV XXX

Y.Gd
XX

O.Gd XXX

IV XXX

I XXX

Y.Gd XX

XXX XX
IV

Markranstädt
Lützen
Weissenfels

Klein Zschocher

Colbredo

Cour

Gross Zschocher

Lederer
XXX

Gautzsch

Markkleet

R. Elster

MAP XI.vii

**LEIPZIG
SITUATION AT 11.30 am
19 OCTOBER**

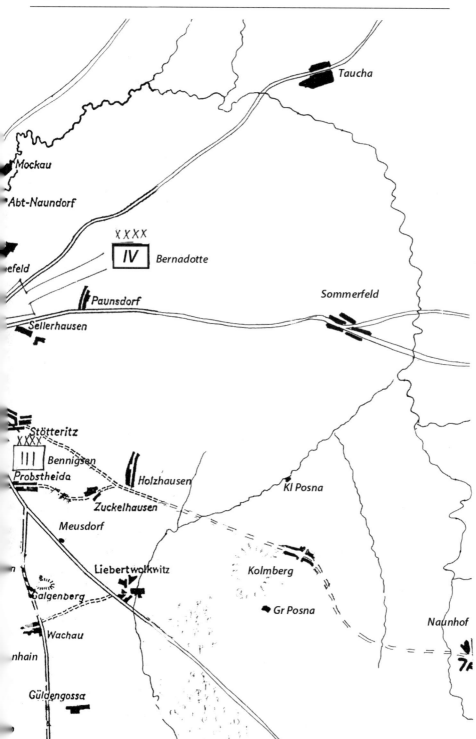

At 7.00 am the allies began to advance once more on the city and by 10.00 am they stood outside suburbs. By 11.30 am the French had been everywhere driven in to the *Altstadt* and although they had stood their ground valiantly until now, with Napoleon himself gone, the troops' thoughts turned towards flight. As the allies advanced from the north and south, the one escape route looked in danger. Fighting was desperate at the northern and eastern gates of the city and around the Parthe bridge, with fearful losses on both sides, but by 12.30 pm the allies were in the city and all hope for the French rearguard had gone.

Shortly before 1.00 pm Napoleon, who was sleeping at Lindenau, was awakened by the roar of a huge explosion: the causeway had been blown. The demolition had been in the charge of a Colonel Montfort of the engineers who, going to Lindenau to try to discover which corps was to be the last to retire, had delegated control of the demolition to a corporal, along with strict orders not to blow the charge unless the allies were about to capture the causeway intact. But with the roads crammed with troops, Montfort had been unable to get back to the site and the wretched corporal, seeing Russian skirmishers approaching, panicked and lit the mine. It blew up with appalling effect and as the smoke cleared, the troops left on the far side realised that they must either fight to the death, swim for the far side, or surrender. Thousands surrendered, others tried to swim of whom many drowned. Macdonald managed to swim the Elster on his horse, but Poniatowski, who had only received his Marshal's baton from the Emperor's hands on 15 October, was drowned in the attempt.

Just after 1.00 pm the Tsar and the King of Prussia, with Schwarzenberg and their staffs, rode into Leipzig marketplace. Cheering troops lined the streets, bands played, swarms of ecstatic civilians came out from sheltering in cellars to crowd windows and roofs. In the market square, the sovereigns met Bernadotte and Bennigsen; Blücher and Gneisenau arrived a little later, followed by the Emperor of Austria. The only other monarch present was the hapless King of Saxony – who was also titular Grand Duke of Warsaw – Frederick Augustus. The unfortunate king had refused to accompany Napoleon and had remained in the city to meet his fate. He was arrested in the Tsar's name and later sent to Berlin as a prisoner of war.

The Battle of the Nations was over. The allies had lost by most estimates something like 50,000 killed and wounded.[12] Napoleon's losses were more severe still: the allies had taken 15,000 prisoners and 5,000 deserters, many of whom were Poles and Germans. At least another 15,000 were sick in the hospitals, but at least 40,000 had been killed and wounded – most estimates make the total around 75,000. These losses included 6 general officers killed, including Prince Poniatowski; 11 generals and marshals wounded, including Ney, Macdonald, Marmont, Souham, Latour-Maubourg and Sébastiani; and 36 generals captured, including Lauriston, Reynier and Prince Emilien of Hesse. French materiel losses included 28 colours and eagles; 325 guns – half the French artillery – 900 ammunition wagons, 720 tons of powder, and 40,000 muskets and rifles.

V. AFTERMATH.

Napoleon crossed the Rhine with an army of 80,000 men, of whom perhaps 60,000 were fit to fight. There can be no doubt, despite Napoleon's own attempts to disguise the fact, that the French army was comprehensively defeated at Leipzig; only the inadequacies of the allied pursuit allowed the campaign, and the war, to go on into 1814. There were complex political as well as military reasons for this, which will be discussed in the next chapter.

But even in defeat, Napoleon was already looking further afield. There was a sense of defeat permeating the *Grande Armée*, especially among the Poles and other allies, which had to be overcome. In the wake of the death of Poniatowski, many Poles especially wished to return to Poland, their homeland now in Russian hands. However, as General Henryk Dembinski later recounted,

> We resolved to accompany the French Army to the Rhine, and share its dangers until the last moment, and then return home. The Emperor welcomed our deputation favourably. He appreciated our chivalrous devotion . . . He told the deputation 'Assure your compatriots that when they arrive at the Rhine they will be absolutely free to do as they wish.'
>
> Several days later, when we reached the Fulda, our corps approached the main route at the same time as the Emperor was passing . . . He addressed us for a long time, urging us not to abandon him.
>
> 'Read the *Moniteur* . . . you will see that Poland existed in my thoughts . . .' The conversation continued for over three-quarters of an hour, always in a tone of confidence and reproach.[13]

Meanwhile, Bertrand had reached Weissenfels late on 18 October and word was sent to him to occupy all the country between Kösen and

Leipzig marketplace, afternoon 19 October. The Tsar and King of Prussia greet the Crown Prince of Sweden (Bernadotte).

Cossacks strip a body in the battle-scarred village of Möckern after Leipzig.

Merseberg, as well as Freiburg, and watch the passages over the Saale. He was also to collect all available stores and position these in depots along the army's withdrawal route. At the same time Marshal Kellermann, in Mainz (which was then a French city, called Mayence), was ordered to collect all available troops, including recruits, at Erfurt and Würzburg, and to provision the latter city. Kellermann was also ordered to call out the National Guard for the defence of France itself, for Napoleon was sure that an invasion was imminent. Last, orders were sent to St Cyr at Dresden to escape as best he could. Torgau and Wittenberg could also be given up, provided that the garrison troops could escape and not be made prisoners.

The main army retreated slowly on Weissenfels. Napoleon, not unnaturally, was apprehensive of attack but he need not have been. At Erfurt he rested two days before resuming the march westwards. At Hanau on 30 October he was intercepted by a force of 27,000 Bavarians and 25,000 Austrians, who until recently had faced each other as enemies across the River Inn. The Bavarian commander, General Wrede, posted his men on open ground on the east bank of the River Kinzig, prompting Napoleon to remark that he had made Wrede a count, but he could not make him a general! In a remarkable feat of arms, getting a beaten army to win only 11 days after a colossal defeat, Napoleon pushed the opposition aside. The army then marched on and reached Frankfurt am Main late on 31 October, and Mainz on 2 November. The allies reached Frankfurt two weeks later, and there they halted. Clausewitz had this to say of the halt:

> The feigned defence of the Rhine, then, sufficed to bring the Allies to a halt and make them decide to postpone the crossing until the arrival of reinforcements – a period of six weeks. These six weeks must have been of incalculable benefit to Bonaparte. Without the show of resistance on the Rhine, the battle of Leipzig would have led the Allies straight to Paris.[14]

But matters were rather more complex than Clausewitz's analysis suggested, although Blücher was clearly of the same opinion at the time.[15] In this context, although the War of Liberation was over, the important lessons for coalition warfare from the end of 1813 are as much political and diplomatic as they are military.

NOTES

1. Petre, p.329.
2. The original is in French, cited in Plotho, p.18.
3. *Correspondance,* vol.xxvi, no.20805, dated 15.x.1813.
4. Ibid, no.20814, dated 16.x.1813.
5. Quoted in Beardsley, p.69.
6. Ibid.
7. Petre, p.361.
8. *Correspondance,* vol.xxvi, no.20830 dated 20.x.1813.
9. Scott, p.114.
10. Danilewski, pp.259–60.
11. Plotho, p.70.
12. See Petre, pp.382–3, who gives French casualties as 54,000; Plotho, p.87.
13. Byrd and Dunn, pp.195–7.
14. Clausewitz, p.444.
15. Henderson, p.197.

Chapter XII

Across the Rhine

❧

THE WAR OF Liberation may have been over, but the war against Napoleon was not. On 9 September Russia, Prussia and Austria had signed the Treaty of Teplitz; Britain had concluded agreements at Reichenbach, and at Teplitz on 30 October. Bavaria had also acceded to the coalition by the Treaty of Ried on 8 October and therefore the 6th Coalition, although not yet bound as Castlereagh wished by one single agreement, was now a very effective diplomatic unit. Under these treaties, the allies had essentially agreed to fight for the dissolution of the Confederation of the Rhine and the freedom of the independent nations of Europe from French influence. Significantly, they had also agreed not to make any separate negotiations for peace.[1] Now that the allied armies had reached the Rhine, the first major objective had been achieved: the confederation was utterly ruined; Prussia was restored to her old boundaries; and the independent states of Germany were restored – although there was no general agreement on Napoleon's strength or capability.

This being so, it was Metternich's view that new negotiations must be undertaken, and he was determined to take up the proposals which Napoleon had offered through Meerfeld in the middle of the Battle of Leipzig. Lord Aberdeen, the British ambassador to the Austrian court, agreed: Britain, having expended huge sums on subsidising the coalition and funding the Peninsular War, was by no means averse to peace if the terms were right. The Tsar too agreed in principle. Frederick William was in agreement with Yorck's view, that the army needed time to recover. Bernadotte had by this time diverted his attention to a campaign in Denmark, in order to secure Norway. His view (perhaps not surprisingly) was that a campaign in France might lose all that had been won thus far, a view which Count Bubna shared.[2]

A meeting between the Tsar, Aberdeen, and Metternich took place in Meiningen on 29 October. Here it was agreed to lay down as a basis of peace the so-called natural frontiers of France – the Rhine, the Alps and the Pyrenees – while at the same time issuing a proclamation to the people of France stating the allies' war aims. It was further agreed that the publication of this proclamation, as well as the sending of envoys to state terms to Napoleon, should take place before the allies entered France. Therefore, although the Rhine fortresses were to be besieged and plans laid, no further offensive movements would be undertaken until an answer was received from Napoleon. If he rejected peace, or tried to undermine allied unity by making separate treaties, this would be publicly announced and it would be war to the end.[3] Thus the French people would, it was hoped, blame Napoleon for any continuation of a ruinous and probably hopeless war.

In early November a fuller consideration of the allied proposals took place in Frankfurt am Main. This council of war was attended by the Emperor of Austria, Tsar Alexander, Metternich, Stadion, Nesselrode, Duka, Wolkonski, von Hardenberg, Humbolt, and Knesebeck; also Lord Cathcart, Lord Aberdeen and General Stewart; Pozzo di Borgo, the Corsican with a *vendetta* against Napoleon, who was now in the pay of the Tsar; and Stein, now in Russian service and chief administrator of all conquered territories. The council agreed that Baron St Aignan, brother-in-law to Caulaincourt and ambassador at the court of Saxe-Weimar, should be sent to the Emperor to propose the confinement of France within the natural frontiers. If Napoleon would accept such a condition as a preliminary to a general peace, then Britain would compromise over free trade and shipping. It was further proposed that, while not stopping the prosecution of the war, a neutral area on the west bank of the Rhine would be declared as the venue for negotiation. The latter point was considered to be important, especially by Metternich, who did not believe that Napoleon would ever accept terms unless forced to do so by military defeat. He wrote as much to Caulaincourt on 20 November: 'Napoleon will make no peace, of that I am convinced, though nothing would make me happier than to find I am mistaken.'[4]

Metternich would have been happy to be mistaken, chiefly because he still feared that the destruction of France would tilt the European balance of power too far in favour of Russia. So far, Russia had done well out of the war: Alexander had gained territory from Prussia in 1807, from Austria in 1809, Swedish Finland in 1809, and Turkish Bessarabia in 1811. The Tsar had now also re-conquered Poland, and Metternich clearly feared that Alexander might wish for more still, perhaps at the expense of Austria. But all the signs were that Bonaparte would fight, thus continued allied unity was the overriding consideration.

In parallel with diplomatic activity, therefore, an allied campaign plan for the invasion of France had to be drawn up. This was undertaken principally at the Tsar's insistence,[5] although Metternich remained highly suspicious of the Tsar's ambitions: the Russian armies were now larger, stronger, and fresher than those of their allies, and Russian losses at Leipzig had been comparatively light. If the Tsar decided to push on without the rest of the allies, the consequences for a general restitution of the old order would be grave. Metternich therefore only wanted such military activities as would hold the coalition together, and support his own objective.

After much discussion, the plan agreed on was for Blücher's army, 107,000 strong, to cross the Rhine and fix the French field army, while the main allied army of 155,000 men under Schwarzenberg marched into Switzerland – then neutral but pro-French – crossed the Rhine and attempted to link up with Wellington's Anglo-Portuguese army. This force would be reinforced as soon as possible by an additional 68,000 troops from the Austrian Army of Italy. The conquest of the Netherlands would be undertaken by Bernadotte's army. The Austro-Bavarian Army, 100,000 men including the Prussian corps of Bülow, under Wrede, was to link Blücher and Schwarzenberg, protect Germany, and guard the middle Rhine; while Bennigsen's Army of Poland continued to reduce the remaining French fortresses east of the Rhine. Once this was accomplished, Bennigsen was to reinforce Bernadotte. It was a strategy designed to avoid a major engagement, while pressuring Napoleon into negotiating seriously.[6]

On 9 November the main Austrian army began its move towards Switzerland, but on 13 November King Frederick William arrived at Frankfurt. He at once declared himself opposed to crossing the Rhine unless all else failed, although Radetzky, Schwarzenberg, and the majority of his own commanders – especially Blücher – were in favour of an invasion. Frederick William also continued to hold to the view, perhaps rightly, that a period of rest was needed, for the armies were certainly near exhaustion after the rigours of the autumn campaign. From this position he refused to budge and so operations were suspended pending an answer from the allied envoy St Aignan.

Metternich's next duty was to draw up the manifesto to the French people, which was distributed by the thousand on the west bank of the

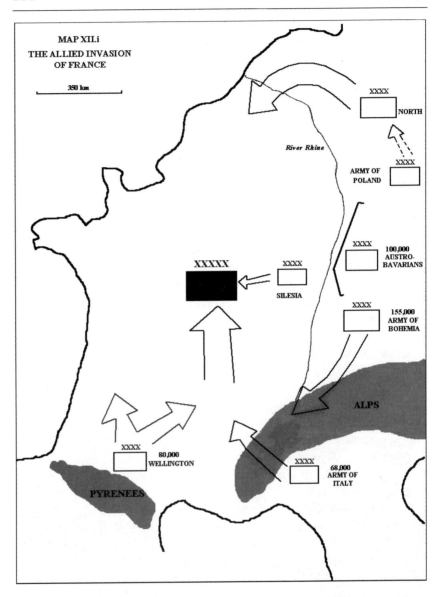

MAP XII.i
THE ALLIED INVASION
OF FRANCE

350 km

River Rhine

XXXX
NORTH

XXXX
ARMY OF
POLAND

XXXX
100,000
AUSTRO-
BAVARIANS

XXXX
155,000
ARMY OF
BOHEMIA

XXXXX

XXXX
SILESIA

ALPS

XXXX
80,000
WELLINGTON

XXXX
68,000
ARMY OF
ITALY

PYRENEES

Rhine. It was generally reckoned to be a masterpiece – even Napoleon praised it as appealing to the French character. The manifesto stated that the allies were united in the belief that French power must be confined within the natural frontiers; the allies did not make war on France herself, but against the preponderance which, unfortunately for France and for Europe, Napoleon had long exercised outside these frontiers. The manifesto went on to say that the allied sovereigns wished to see France great, strong and happy, and enjoying an extent of territory which she had not known under her Kings.[7] Thus the first use which the allies made of the victory of Leipzig was to offer peace, not war.

Napoleon was certainly in a difficult position. St Aignan had warned him that the allies could not be divided and he was well aware of the psychological dimension of war which lay behind the manifesto. His position was not made any easier by divisions in the nation and the government. He himself still clung to the idea of making peace after a victory, thus keeping as much as possible of his empire. On the other hand his chief ministers, Maret and Caulaincourt, believed that no victory was possible, and were intent on peace as soon as possible. Next there was an influential group of men with fortunes founded on Napoleon's success: Talleyrand, de Pradt, Dalberg and others. These men knew quite well that Napoleon was doomed but believed that France, and they themselves, could be saved by making terms with the allies which laid all responsibility for Europe's woes on Napoleon alone.

A *Long Pull*, an English cartoon by Thomas Rowlandson published on 25 November 1813 welcomes Holland's revolt against Napoleon from the 15th that month, after allied cavalry crossed the frontier, and reflects the general belief that the end was in sight. The French Emperor and his brother Joseph despair on the far right. [BM Catalogue no. 12,102]

Last came the mass of the French people, willing to give up the empire but attached to the natural frontiers and the civic freedoms gained in the revolution. It was at the last two groups in particular that the manifesto was aimed.

Napoleon himself accepted nothing from the allies at once, but the allies' terms became so well known that 'there formed in the palace, in the city, in the council a sort of league to push Napoleon into that way of safety. M. le Duc de Vicence [i.e. Caulaincourt] was the soul of it, and M. de Talleyrand was not a stranger to it.'[8]

Eventually Napoleon sent a letter from Paris to Metternich,[9] in which he suggested Châtillon-sur-Seine as a place of negotiation and that he would accept the Frankfurt proposals if England would make it possible to conclude a peace founded on what he termed 'the balance of power in Europe, on the integrity of Nations within their natural boundaries, and on the absolute independence of all states, without any form of supremacy by sea or land'. If he thought this letter would succeed, he was wrong. His first mistake was to try to end his difficulties with Spain by releasing Ferdinand VII from prison and recognising him as King of Spain in place of Joseph Bonaparte. The accompanying Treaty of Valençay on 11 December was not, however, ratified by the Spanish regency as being contrary to Spain's agreements with Britain,[10] and the suspicion was aroused that Napoleon did not mean business at all, but was still attempting to divide the allies.

He was wrong too because he misjudged the effect of the letter on Metternich. Metternich had already sent Pozzo di Borgo to London to ask that either Wellington, or Canning, or Castlereagh should join the allied headquarters. It was Castlereagh, the secretary of state, who came. Second, Metternich believed that Napoleon's letter showed him to be close to collapse: only a little more pressure might be required to finish the war on the allies' terms. Thus on 21 December 1813, the allied armies began to march. The crossing of the Rhine, and the arrival of Castlereagh, thus marked the end of the campaign of 1813 and the beginning of the last days of Napoleon, both as military commander and as statesman.

* * *

One hundred and thirty-one years later another successful coalition war in Europe had just been concluded, following a similarly spectacular *débâcle* in Russia. Josef Stalin was being congratulated on the success of his troops in Germany. 'How proud you must be', one of the allied officers present remarked, 'that Russian troops have entered Berlin.' The Communist Generalissimo fixed his questioner with a beady glare, and replied – 'Tsar Alexander I reached Paris.'

NOTES

1. Martens, i, p.610 and iv, p.70.
2. Müffling, p.90.
3. See especially Mowat, pp.282–3.
4. Browning, p.77.
5. Sorel, viii, p.185.
6. Kissinger, p.112.
7. Cited in Mowat, p.285.
8. Pasquier, ii, p.107.
9. *Correspondance*, vol.xxvi, no.21460, dated 2.xii.1813.
10. Martens, i, p.654.

PART THREE

SPAIN AND THE MEDITERRANEAN

Chapter XIII

In Fortune's Way

⁂

I. THE SPANISH ULCER

T HE INFAMOUS 29th *Bulletin* did not reach King Joseph Bonaparte in Madrid until 6 January 1813, and news of the Emperor's return to Paris did not get through until 14 February. Thus Joseph had no conception of the ruin which had befallen the French armies in Russia. Even if he had, it is doubtful that events would have fallen out differently, for if 1812 had been a disastrous year for French arms in eastern Europe, it had not been exactly a startling success in Spain.

Napoleon's interest in Spain dated from a series of treaties in 1800, which obliged Spain to subsidise French military operations and which effectively transformed the Spanish armies, and more particularly, the Navy, into mere adjuncts of the French. The Treaty of San Ildefonso further allowed for the creation of a kingdom in Etruria for the son-in-law of Charles IV of Spain, in return for which Spain ceded her territories in Louisiana to France on condition that they would not be disposed of to any other party. This arrangement ended in disaster for Spain. The Louisiana Purchase in 1803 was a violation of the San Ildefonso treaty which Spain was powerless to prevent; and the naval co-operation ended with the destruction of the fleet at Trafalgar and the loss of colonies in the West Indies.

These losses stirred up much anti-French feeling in Spain, but in 1806, Napoleon was at the summit of his power and was in no mood to be defied. Anti-French sentiment gave him just the excuse he needed to consolidate his power over the whole of the Iberian peninsula and in so doing, complete his Continental System, exclude the British, and dominate the Mediterranean. He achieved his end by the device of the Franco-Spanish expedition against Portugal. With French troops in the Peninsula, it was only a step to the agreement of 5 May 1808, by which

Charles IV abdicated in favour of Joseph Bonaparte, and from thence a smaller step to the imprisonment of the rightful heir, Ferdinand VII, at Valençay. Thus Napoleon overran first Portugal and then Spain by treachery.

The chief consequence of Bonaparte's actions was not at all what he had intended. He managed to trigger first the popular revolt in Spain, and then the British intervention in Portugal, from which grew the Spanish Ulcer. The events of summer 1808, culminating in the Convention of Cintra, had freed Portugal from the French and allowed the country to be used as a base of operations against the French in Spain itself. This had begun with Sir John Moore's autumn campaign of 1808. Moore's intention had been to sever the French communications through Burgos, thus forcing them back towards Bayonne, but the plan had been allocated wholly inadequate forces and had failed.

Having driven the British off at Corunna, the French, commanded by Marshal Soult, had once more invaded Portugal only to be driven out by Sir Arthur Wellesley (hereafter referred to as Wellington), who had then himself invaded Spain. His move seemed successful when he had fought and won the Battle of Talavera, but a further advance on his flank by Soult's forces obliged Wellington to retire back into Portugal. During 1810 the French attempted to consolidate their position in the Peninsula but the following year, after emerging from the Lines of Torres Vedras, Wellington had at last succeeded in clearing Portugal of the French for good.

In retrospect, 1812 proved as much a turning point in Spain as elsewhere. At the beginning of the year, Wellington had successfully stormed the frontier fortresses of Badajoz and Ciudad Rodrigo and then, advancing rapidly, he had captured the siege and pontoon trains of both Marshals Marmont and Soult. However, Marmont had risen to the challenge and, using to the full the ability of the French army to march far and fast, he had successfully forced Wellington to consider retreat. But Marmont over-reached himself. Believing the allies to be already in flight he lunged in pursuit, became over extended on the line of march, and was caught by Wellington on 22 July at Salamanca. The allies rolled up Marmont's Army of Portugal, which lost 13,000 casualties including its chief. Only three weeks later, the allies entered Madrid. But the French were not beaten yet. General Souham and Marshal Soult were able to concentrate against the allies, repulse them at Burgos, and in November, push them back with loss into Portugal in a retreat which almost rivalled the retreat to Corunna in its severity.

Thus at the end of the year, the French military command still felt relatively in control as far as the British were concerned – at least on land. But after five years of hard campaigning, what had they to show for their pains? The frontier fortresses were in allied hands; Spain south of the Tagus had been lost; 20,000 prisoners had been shipped off to Britain in the last year alone, men desperately needed in Central Europe. General Foy wrote that

> Lord Wellington has retired unconquered . . . having restored the Spaniards the country south of the Tagus, and made us destroy our magazines, our fortifications – in a word all that we have gained by our conquest, and all that could assure the maintenance of it.[1]

In the longer term too, all was far from well. First, the army in Spain had already been heavily milked of manpower for the Russian campaign. As the campaigning season of 1813 approached, the army would again be plundered both of formed units and cadres of veterans as Napoleon desperately strove to rebuild his army in Central Europe. Second, the British exercised absolute control over the seas, so that all communications had to be across land. This laid them open to the third difficulty, the Spanish guerrilla war.

There were signs in 1810 and 1811 that French control was gaining ground in Spain, especially in Catalonia, and that the establishment of order and normal government was supported by local populations weary of war.[2] However, anti-French sentiment and support for the guerrilla war remained strong. It is hard to think of another war in which guerrilla forces did so much to tie down regular troops, except perhaps in the Balkans between 1941 and 1945, or Vietnam from 1946 to 1954 and 1965 to 1970. As French depredations in Spain had increased, so had Spanish hostility; in December 1808 the Spanish Council of Regency had given legal existence to the guerrillas, and after the allied victory at Salamanca in 1812 – a blow from which French prestige never recovered – the guerrillas were imbued with new confidence. Certain that Wellington would return, virtually the whole country was now in arms against the French.

The guerrillas, who numbered some 16,000 in Biscay and Guipuzcoa and 19,000 in Navarre, were able to surround and destroyed isolated French garrisons, as they did at Tafalla in February; throw down bridges; ambush marching troops; prey on supply convoys and depots, loot and burn whenever a weak spot was exposed. Many guerrilla bands were actually regular troops acting as irregulars; conversely, over time, the most successful guerrilla bands – or more accurately *partidas* – became strong enough to act as regular troops.[3]

So bad was the menace that in order to keep the communications open, every village along the main roads had to be garrisoned; every road regularly patrolled; every convoy – even down to dispatch riders – escorted in force. French reprisals only increased hostility, and the French system of forage – of living off the land – had played into the guerrillas' hands too, both in increasing their unpopularity in the countryside and in presenting targets for ambush. But when Marmont in 1812 attempted to institute a regular commissariat and supply system, so far had the internal security situation deteriorated that this too, with its reliance on supply routes, became an easy target for the Spanish irregulars.

The guerrillas probably maintained a force of around 50,000 men under arms at any one time, and their activities cost the French around 145,000 casualties over the five years from 1808 to 1813;[4] they were probably also responsible for the deaths of at least 30,000 *Afrancescados* – collaborators – which should be borne in mind when considering the Spanish civilian casualties at San Sebastian. The greatest contribution of the guerrillas was in helping to present the French with a tactical dilemma which they could not solve – what modern terminology describes as simultaneity – through the interaction of Allied regular and irregular forces. This was something which the Indians would also demonstrate in America, and quite simply, if the French concentrated to fight the allied main armies, they were vulnerable to the guerrillas; if they dispersed to contain the guerrillas, they became vulnerable to destruction by the armies. Wellington's great achievement in this respect was to induce the guerrillas to take part in a concerted plan and then during 1813, to bring them gradually into the regular army – Longa's division is a perfect example.[5]

It was because of this domination by the guerrillas that Napoleon's dispatches to his brother in early January did not reach Madrid until 16 February. These dispatches were of considerable importance to the Emperor, for they carried his instructions for the reorganisation of the French army in Spain and its role in supporting his coming life-or-death struggle in central Europe. First were details of the troops which Joseph was to send back to France: all the remaining Young Guard units; two or three complete infantry battalions and between 30 and 40 cadre battalions; 15 cavalry squadrons and a complete division of dragoons; six batteries of horse artillery; the majority of the German and Polish auxiliary units serving in Spain; and finally 25 picked men from every battalion of infantry and regiment of cavalry, and ten from every artillery battery, for the Imperial Guard. Next, Napoleon ordered his brother to concentrate the armies and to place the main head-quarters at Valladolid, only holding Madrid as an extremity of his line. He was also to divert large numbers of troops into Biscay and Navarre to put down the guerrillas and thus secure the lines of communication.

Thus by March 1813, the French army in the Peninsula was divided into five distinct formations. First, the Army of Portugal, under General Reille with his headquarters in Salamanca, numbered between 35,000 and 40,000 men divided into eight infantry divisions, a cavalry division and a division of dragoons. This army was deployed behind the Tormes and Esla rivers in order to watch the allied forces in northern Portugal and Spanish Galicia, but four of Reille's divisions had been diverted to assist the Army of the North in anti-guerrilla operations.

Next came the Army of the South which was now commanded by General Gazan, since its old commander Marshal Soult, along with Marmont, were both recalled by the Emperor. This army was at a strength of around 37,000 men, deployed behind the Tagus and Tietar rivers in order to watch the allied forces in central and southern Portugal and southern Spain.

Third, the Army of the North under General Caffarelli secured the line of communications back from Burgos to Bayonne. This army was at a strength of about 40,000, most of whom were tied up in fortresses and garrisons along the main routes and in the other fortresses of Biscay and Navarre, although Caffarelli did maintain a reserve division of 6,000 men at Bayonne. In February 1813, Napoleon replaced Caffarelli with General Clausel.

Fourth, the Army of the Centre under General Drouet d'Erlon numbered some 16,000 men and was given three tasks which were to a great extent contradictory: to cover Madrid; to connect the other armies by means of mobile columns; and to operate against the guerrillas in central Spain.

Finally there was the Army of Aragon and Catalonia under Marshal Suchet, tasked with holding the line of communications back through Perpignan. Suchet had about 64,000 men in all, but the majority were tied down in garrisons and in routine anti-guerrilla protection tasks, leaving him only some 18,000 men readily available for mobile operations.

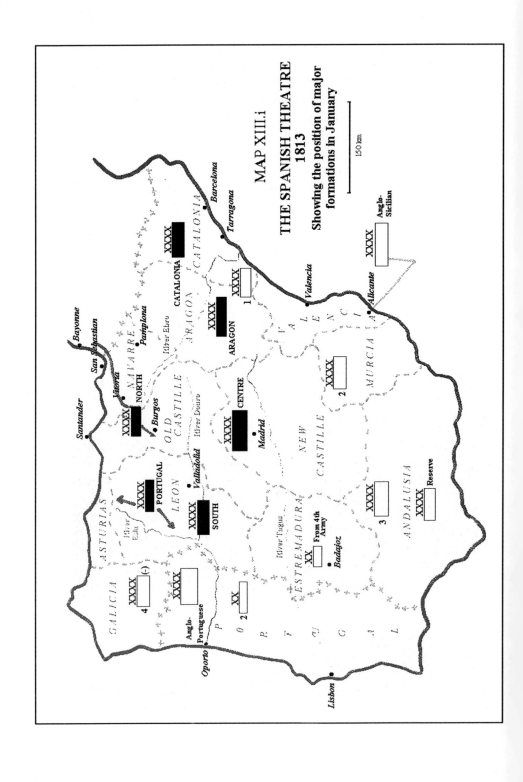

MAP XIII.i
THE SPANISH THEATRE
1813
Showing the position of major
formations in January

150 km

Anglo-Sicilian

XXXX 1

Barcelona
Tarragona
CATALONIA

CATALONIA

ARAGON

Valencia

ARAGON

V A L E N C I A

Alicante

Bayonne
San Sebastian
Pamplona
River Ebro

NAVARRE
NORTH

Santander
Vitoria
Burgos
OLD CASTILLE
River Duero

CENTRE

Madrid

MURCIA

XXXX 2

Valladolid
River Duero

NEW CASTILLE

PORTUGAL
LEON

SOUTH

ANDALUSIA

Reserve

XXXX 3

ASTURIAS
River Esla

River Tagus

ESTREMADURA

From 4th Army

Badajoz

GALICIA
XXXX 4 (-)

Anglo-Portuguese
Oporto

XX 0 2

River Tagus

P O R T U G A L

Lisbon

All these armies were predominantly French, but it is of note that there were still significant numbers of foreign troops present. There were, for example, several Spanish regiments – not all Spaniards hated Bonaparte and what he stood for; There were also two Italian divisions under Generals Palombini and Severoli;[6] the 7th Polish Lancers had been present, but were among the troops recalled to France; and despite

A Spanish cavalry general painted by the British artist Denis Dighton. His escort includes two lancers and a guerrilla chief on foot.

the withdrawal of many German units, there still remained Baden infantry and artillery regiments, Nassau infantry and cavalry and a battalion of Frankfurt troops all with the Army of the Centre. There were also infantry regiments from Würzburg, Nassau, Berg and Westphalia with Suchet's army in Catalonia.[7]

Napoleon's continued insistence on trying to command the Spanish theatre by remote control – especially given the guerrilla-infested communications – did little to help King Joseph, and this was made worse by the Emperor's consistent under-estimation of both the guerrillas and of Wellington. This was probably brought about by the undoubted fact that with the departure of Soult, Souham and Marmont for the central European theatre, there were few generals on the French side capable of manoeuvring a corps, let alone an army. Suchet could manoeuvre a corps, and Clausel had also proved his ability in 1812. But certainly such a task was far beyond the capacity of Joseph Bonaparte, as Napoleon well knew. However, the Emperor insisted that Joseph should make a demonstration towards Portugal in order to tie down the allies, a proposal which Joseph greeted with some heat:

> How am I to make a demonstration towards Portugal? To do so I must in the first instance concentrate the troops which is impossible owing to want of victuals. And what is the use of it, if I make such a demonstration? Wellington will not be deceived, for he knows that the whole Army is engaged in the north and that I have had to send large drafts to the Emperor . . . I hope Clausel may succeed, but I doubt it, and I am afraid that his divisions will be exhausted when they have to meet Wellington.[8]

Thus as the campaigning season drew on, the French army of 198,000 men was dispersed throughout Spain and Joseph could assemble at most 32,000 infantry, 9,000 cavalry and 100 guns without depleting his anti-guerrilla operations. This at a time when he knew that the allies had been reinforced and could be expected to move at any time. Nor, given the impossibility of scouting in guerrilla infested country, could he determine Wellington's intentions – so what should he do? Defend the Douro with his available striking force and risk destruction? Stop his anti-guerrilla operations and concentrate the army? Or retire behind Burgos, wait until the guerrillas had been smashed, and then advance? These questions were never answered – and soon it would be too late.

II. THE ALLIES

Despite the many problems faced by the French, they retained one considerable advantage: that of a unified command – although not, as will be seen, a unified command *structure*. The army contained Poles, Belgians, Dutch, Italians and Germans as well as French but it was to a large extent a single force with one chain of command, especially after Vitoria, although the armies in Catalonia and Aragon always remained largely autonomous.

This degree of unity was not the case for the opposing coalition forces, which comprised British, King's German Legion, Brunswick, Portuguese, Sicilian and Spanish formations. In theory, Wellington as the operational commander exercised supreme command over all allied forces, but such were the differing political aims of the partners that this was at times more a command in name than in fact – certainly as far as the Spanish were concerned. The differing views of the coalition partners have been well summarised thus:

> To the Spaniards it is the struggle of a whole nation rising against a tyran-nical foreign government, a movement in which our army plays but a marginal part. To the Portuguese it means principally the frustration of three cruel invasions: in this our share is fully acknowledged, but the climax of the war lies beyond the boundaries of national concern . . . the Peninsula claims *our* interest as the one theatre in which the military effort of this country [i.e. England] . . . was successfully exerted to contribute to Napoleon's downfall.[9]

Although a rather cavalier dismissal of British naval operations as well as the financing of military operations by the allies in Central Europe, the focus on differing allied perspectives is certainly valid and needs to be developed further, not neglecting the interference which Wellington continued to encounter from London in his handling of the army.

For the Spanish, the war had become a war of national liberation into which as we have already seen, the French had driven them. There was no ancient rivalry between France and Spain – indeed quite the reverse – and for 10 of the 12 years before 1808,[10] Spain had actually been at war with Britain and allied with France. Religious difficulties underscored national rivalries and above all the overweening pride of the Spanish nation made close co-operation with Britain difficult in the extreme. It must be ranked as a considerable French achievement that their policy and behaviour was so unacceptable as to have upset this situation – as General Francisco Castaños had remarked to his French prisoners after the Battle of Baylen, 'Let not Napoleon persevere in aiming at a conquest which is unattainable. Let him not force us into the arms of the English. They are hateful to us . . .'[11]

Almost equally hateful to the Spanish were their partners against the French, the Portuguese, with whom a series of wars had been fought since the sixteenth century. The revolt of the Spanish people had been given political expression and a voice in the councils of the allies by the assembly of a *Cortés* or parliament at Cadiz, representing the free parts of Spain and the colonies. This *Cortés* swore to uphold the Catholic religion, restore national territorial integrity, and remain loyal to the exiled King Ferdinand. The *Cortés* even promulgated a new constitution in 1812 which although a rather confused document, expressed the desire for a modern, liberal, almost democratic constitutional monarchy. It was also a statement of uncompromising resistance to Joseph Bonaparte, who although hated as a foreign usurper represented, by a supreme irony, a system which stood for many of the ideals which the constitution of 1812 had espoused. The same could hardly be said for the exiled Bourbons, whose first act on regaining the throne was to suspend this constitution.

The Spanish regular army, as opposed to the guerrillas, has generally received a bad press, which stems from the early years of the Peninsular War. Wellington had tried to co-operate with Spanish field armies but after a series of frustrations, let-downs, outright cowardice and major defeats of Spanish arms by the French, this had been given up at the end of 1809. At Talavera, an exasperated Wellington had reported how 'Two thousand of them ran off – not one hundred yards from where I was standing, who were neither attacked, nor threatened with an attack, and who were only frightened by the noise of their own fire.'[12]

Thereafter, Wellington preferred to keep Spanish formations at arm's length. However as time went on, both the Spanish armies and the guerrillas did improve and gradually became highly effective in keeping large numbers of French troops tied up, thus helping to create force ratios which were manageable in a pitched battle. By 1813, the Spanish regular army had improved to such a degree that it was quite capable of taking its place in the line and proved this time after time during the year: at Vitoria, Sorauren and San Sebastian, Spanish formations stood with the best of the allied units, and against the best veterans that the French could throw at them – and they emerged triumphant.

The field armies were, at least on paper, numerous: 1st Army under General Francisco Copons in Aragon numbered some 15,000; 2nd Army in Murcia under General Francisco Elio was around 30,000 strong; in Granada lay the 12,000 men of General the Duke of Del Parque's 3rd Army; General Castaños' 4th Army, the largest with a strength of 40,000, lay with one division in Estremadura and its remaining seven divisions in Spanish Galicia; finally the Spanish reserve corps of about 14,000 men remained in Andalusia. There remained some defects: the organisation was overstaffed and highly bureaucratic, and although Spanish formations were integrated into the allied field commands, this was never achieved below division level; conversely, with the exception of artillery batteries, it was rare for British or Portuguese formations to be integrated into Spanish formations.

A major change in the allied relationship had come after Wellington's success at Salamanca. On 22 September 1812, the *Cortés* had created him Generalissimo of the Spanish armies. This for the first time in four years gave him – in theory – real authority, at least to co-ordinate the activities of all the allied forces: but still he had no great confidence in the ability of his major partner in terms of political will or military high command, despite the growing fighting prowess at grassroots level. 'I do not', he wrote

> expect much from the exertions of the Spaniards. They cry *viva* and are very fond of us, and hate the French; but they are, in general, the most incapable of useful exertion of all the nations I have known; the most vain, and at the same time the most ignorant, particularly of military affairs, and above all of military affairs in their own country.[13]

Perhaps as a political ally of Britain, Spain was valuable as a theatre in which French forces could be diverted from central Europe; conversely in 1807 Napoleon had taken 15,000 Spanish troops to garrison north Germany and Denmark in order to free French troops and disrupt the Spanish Army.[14] From the British perspective at the beginning of 1813, as a military asset the Spanish were seen as being most valuable for limited operations in support of the Anglo-Portuguese main army and as guerrillas.[15] Wellington felt even at the beginning of the Vitoria campaign that he could not rely on them for battle on their own: 'The Spanish armies are neither disciplined nor provided nor equipped in such a manner as that they can perform any operation even of the most trifling nature if there should be any opposition on the part of the enemy.'[16]

How far this view changed during the year will be seen later, around San Sebastian. Thus Wellington had accepted the post of Generalissimo, pending the approval of the Prince Regent, with reluctance.[17] But having accepted, he was determined that his power over the Spanish armies must be made real and for this he intended to turn the financial screw – all future subsidies from Britain to Spain would be used only to support Spanish troops actually fighting alongside the Anglo-Portuguese army. He was also determined to control personally all senior appointments and promotions, and to have the power of dismissal over Spanish commanders. To assist him in this he determined on having a Spanish chief of staff appointed to his own headquarters. Finally he was absolutely set on having the large numbers of senior Spanish commanders and staffs reduced and the armies reorganised into proper fighting formations. These requirements he put in person to the *Cortés* in December 1812. Although they were unpalatable demands, especially coming from a not-too diplomatic foreigner, the *Cortés* accepted them with some variations.[18]

There was one significant problem. The Council of Regency with which Wellington struck his bargain was replaced in March 1813 by the *Cortés*, which appointed a puppet council while retaining all power itself. Effectively, therefore, when the allied armies took the field in 1813, Wellington was able to exercise command over only two Spanish divisions in his own army, and three more of the Army of Galicia. The reserve corps in Andalusia in particular did not join him until after Vitoria, so that only 90,000 out of 160,000 Spanish troops under arms were actually available for the decisive blow.

The British relationship with Portugal and the Portuguese Army was entirely different. Britain and Portugal were allies of long standing, the Portuguese economy relied heavily on British subsidy, and British prestige was high as a result of the expulsion of the French. People were generally well aware that freedom from French rule depended absolutely on the alliance, and the British policy of paying for all forage made the army generally popular, in contrast to the plundering French. As far as military relationships went, the Portuguese Army had been raised and trained by a British generalissimo, Sir William Beresford, who was also viceroy. Wellington's authority over it was absolute since being given the overall command by the Portuguese government in 1809 – a rare state of affairs indeed in coalition warfare.

> There was therefore no need to establish close personal relationships with the Portuguese: they had no field commanders of their own. The state was in ruins and the army was incapable [in 1809] of taking the field. Under these circumstances it is perhaps not surprising that the British were given a great deal of authority over the troops . . .[19]

The Portuguese government remained responsible for all aspects of supply, pay and equipment of their own national troops; but 'Wellington commanded them, Beresford trained them and they were led by British Officers.'[20] The troops were equipped and trained entirely to British standards and, formed into brigades, they were fully integrated into British divisions to the extent that, as Wellington said, '. . . it is nearly indifferent what the Portuguese government does; and I never give myself the trouble of writing to them, or of consulting their opinion on any subject whatsoever.'[21]

The relationship was not without difficulties. Under Beresford as viceroy, Portugal was almost completely militarised. This produced the only continental army capable of achieving consistent military victory over French armies, but the effort drained the nation. Its population, for example, fell from 3.2 million in 1807 to 2.9 million in 1814.[22] At local level the daily movement of troops and the inevitable lapses of discipline which went with such movements caused friction with the populace. The want of money to pay and supply the army was also a source of difficulty, for despite their responsibilities, the Portuguese government frequently neglected its troops, so that Wellington was forced to threaten appeal to the Regent of Portugal in Brazil unless action was taken.

This threat achieved the desired result, but one has to sympathise with the Portuguese: all available money went to the army, leaving the civil administration starved. Even so, large subsidies and loans were required from Britain just to maintain the status quo. This was made more galling to Portuguese pride by the fact that British officers filled nearly all senior command positions to the exclusion of the Portuguese themselves. It is hardly surprising, then, that as the campaign of 1813 progressed, and Portuguese troops fought further and further from home, enthusiasm for the alliance and for the coalition war, especially on behalf of Spain, began to diminish.

By 1812, the Portuguese element of the allied army was significant. It consisted of over 18,000 men formed into a Portuguese infantry division; a cavalry brigade of three regiments; an artillery battery; two battalions of *caçadores*, or skirmishers; two independent infantry brigades; and seven infantry brigades, each of two line battalions and a light infantry battalion, one brigade in each of the allied 2nd, 3rd, 4th, 5th, 6th, 7th and Light Divisions. These troops formed therefore around 35 per cent of the main army. This level of integration 'was only possible due to the long timescale (1808–1810), but it is a lesson that seemingly inferior troops can be made employable through an investment in time and effort.'[23]

In January 1813, after almost 20 years of fighting against the French, the total strength of the British Army was 255,000 men.[24] Some 65,000, or a quarter of the total available, were in Spain. Another 29,000 were in the East Indies, 23,000 in the West Indies, and 37,000 in the Mediterranean forming garrisons in Gibraltar, Malta, Sicily and the Ionian Islands, of whom 7,000 had been detached to Spain. A total of 80,000 men remained in Britain, including Ireland, of whom 55,000 were regulars and the rest embodied militia, but this total included not only the troops required for home defence, internal security and police duties, but also depots, recruits under training, and convalescents. The remaining 21,000 were distributed between Canada, the Cape, Madeira, New South Wales, West Africa, Heligoland, and the garrison of the city of Stralsund in Swedish Pomerania.

The Anglo-Portuguese Army in Spain was, after five seasons' campaigning, an experienced and highly capable force of eight infantry divisions, a light division and a cavalry corps. As already noted it contained significant numbers of Portuguese troops, as well as one brigade each of infantry and cavalry, with supporting artillery and significant numbers of light infantry, found by the mainly Hanoverian King's German Legion[25] (KGL) and the Brunswick-Oels contingent: in all, a truly multinational force.

The retreat from Burgos in the autumn of 1812 had caused considerable disruption and losses in the army, to which Wellington had turned his full attention during the winter. The normal turnover of manpower across the whole army was around 24,000 per year, an enormous problem to overcome even when militiamen were used for foreign service.[26]

Within the theatre, James McGrigor, his chief of medical staff, had cleared the hospitals, despite losses of 400–500 men per week during December 1812 and January 1813: indeed the returns for 1 January 1813 indicated a sickness rate of 30 per cent, reducing to 16 per cent by June after the decentralisation of the hospitals, which Griffith attributes to the high incidence of Walcheren fever.[27]

At the same time, the newly appointed Judge-Advocate, Francis Larpent, had cracked down on discipline, hanging and flogging deserters and plunderers. In this he was assisted by the creation of a new staff corps of 200 officers and men to take on military police duties. Between them, McGrigor and Larpent had managed to ensure that as many veterans as possible were returned to the colours.

This was highly necessary in view of the large numbers of new recruits coming into the theatre. Enlistment for the Army had done exceedingly well in 1812 and for the first time in the entire war a surplus – of 2,000 men – had been produced over and above the recruits needed just to replace battle and sickness losses. The scale of this achievement may be judged by the fact that the annual wastage of about 24,000 men could barely be met from recruiting and impress-ment, so that any increases in the army could usually only be made by enlisting colonials and foreigners. In 1804, there had been 17,000 of these, or 11 per cent of the army; by 1813, this figure had risen to 53,000, or 20 per cent, and included not only 8,000 KGL and Brunswickers, and 8,000 in the West India regiments, but also Canadians, Indians, West Africans, French exiles, Italians and, of all people, Albanians.

Better recruiting had been accompanied by adjustments to the Militia Laws in Britain which governed the employment of the 69,700 militiamen, with the result that many more regular units were being released from home service, so that by March 1813, only 25,000 regulars were retained for home defence. All these measures resulted in a substantial reinforcement to Spain, especially of cavalry, so that the British and KGL troops with the main army now numbered 52,000.[28]

Other improvements had been set in train to accompany the reinforce-ment. A proper pontoon train had been organised for river crossing; a train of heavy artillery and a small corps of sappers had been formed to assist with siege operations; the commissariat system had been improved by the Commissary-General, Sir Robert Kennedy and the Quartermaster-General, Major-General George Murray, who had been reinstated after a period of absence in Ireland. For the first time, for example, the troops were issued with tents. But the supply system depended absolutely on command of the seas and in 1813, this was being disrupted by American privateers.

As well as difficulties in the relationship among the allies, there also remained some problems in the relationship between Wellington and the Duke of York, the Commander-in-Chief in Whitehall. Even though Wellington had a staunch ally in the Military Secretary, Colonel Henry Torrens, one of the chief difficulties lay in the appointment of senior commanders: 1813 was the first year in which Wellington was able to send unsatisfactory generals home, and thus cut out some of the dead wood in his organisation. This was clearly a major advance. There also remained difficulties over regimental organisation, but in general terms this issue was also resolved to Wellington's satisfaction.

Finally, in addition to the main army, Wellington commanded an Anglo-Sicilian Army at Alicante, which consisted of 7,000 British, 2,000 KGL, about 1,000 Sicilians and 8,000 Spanish troops under the immediate command of Lieutenant-General Sir John Murray. All these except the Spanish were troops which Lord William Bentinck had despatched from the British garrison in Sicily, and which Wellington had received authority in August 1812 to take under his own command. Bentinck, as commander of the British army in Sicily, was not keen to see them go, as he had great plans for a descent on the Italian mainland during 1813, which the news from Russia only served to encourage. Wellington, however, was quite clear that the army in Alicante would have a vital role to play in tying down French troops which might otherwise be sent against him, and he put the case against their withdrawal in the strongest terms.[29]

Once again, Wellington won the argument although Bentinck succeeded in detaching 2,000 men in April 1813. More will be said later about this army, but it is worth noting that the British and KGL Hanoverian troops were as good as any in the armies and the Spanish were to prove exceptional fighters. The Sicilians, however, who included contingents of Croat and Swiss mercenaries, also contained large numbers of deserters and reformed prisoners of war from the French armies in Italy. Many of these attempted at various times to return to their old allegiance and were by no means reliable in battle.

In all, and despite the unreliability of the Sicilians, Wellington could count on having at his disposal an effective striking force of 113,000 allied troops for the campaign of 1813 – more if all the Spanish armies could be brought into play. He enjoyed command of the seas; the almost total support of the Portuguese and Spanish people; the ability

FIG. XIII.i

ALLIED COMMAND STRUCTURE IN SPAIN, MAY 1813.

xxxx
◻ Wellington

xxxx Anglo-◻ Portuguese	xxx Cavalry ◻	xxx Spanish ◻	xxx Anglo-◻ Sicilian
1 ⊠ *Anglo-* Howard *Hanoverian* *(1,1 - 4,854)*	Grant ⊿ *(1,624)* *British*	1 ⊠ *(15,761)* Copons Aragon	1 ⊠ *(4,036)* Clinton *Anglo-KGL-* *Sicilian*
2 ⊠ *Anglo-* Hill *Portuguese* *(3,1 - 10,834)*	Alten ⊿ *(1,005)* *British*	2 ⊠ *(30,505)* Elio Murcia	2 ⊠ *(4,045)* Mackenzie *Anglo-* *Italian*
3 ⊠ *Anglo-* Picton *Portuguese* *(2,1 - 7,459)*	Anson ⊿ *(819)* *British*	3 ⊠ *(12,591)* Del Parque Granada	⊠ *(3,901)* Whittingham *Mallorcan*
4 ⊠ *Anglo-* Cole *Portuguese* *(2,1 - 7,826)*	Hill ⊿ *(870)* *British (Heavy)*	4 ⊠ *(25,425)* Giron Galicia	⊿ *(1,179)* Adam *Anglo-KGL-* *Italian*
5 ⊠ *Anglo-* Oswald *Portuguese* *(2,1 - 6,725)*	Ponsonby⊿ *(1,238)* *British (Dragoons)*	5 ⊠ *(14,183)* O'Donnell Reserve	⊿ *(1,036)* F Bentinck *Anglo-KGL-* *Sicilian*
6 ⊠ *Anglo-* Pakenham *Portuguese* *(2,1 - 7,347)*	Bock ⊿ *(632)* *KGL (Dragoons)*		
7 ⊠ *Anglo-* Dalhousie *Portuguese* *(2,1 - 7,297)*	Fane ⊿ *(842)* *British (Dragoons)*		
Light ⊠ *Anglo-* Alten *Portuguese* *(2,1 - 5,484)*	D'Urban ⊿ *(685)* *Portuguese (Dragoons)*		
Silveira ⊠ *(0,2 - 5,287)* *Portuguese*	Campbell ⊿ *(208)* *Portuguese (Dragoons)*		
Morillo ⊠ *(5,129)* *Spanish*	Long ⊿ *(394)* *British*		
Longa ⊠ *(2,607)* *Spanish*			
1 Indep ⊠ *(2,795)* Bradford *Portuguese*			
2 Indep ⊠ *(2,492)* Pack *Portuguese*			

Note: In the 9 Anglo-Portuguese and Portuguese divisions, the first figures in brackets indicate the number of brigades, British first.

to harry the French communications and gather intelligence on their movements while concealing his own from intentions from his enemies. The force levels were relatively small beer when compared with those in Central Europe, but even so, these were advantages which he fully intended to use. 'I propose', he wrote 'to take the field as early as I can and at least place myself in Fortune's way.'[30]

NOTES

1. Foy, quoted in Fortescue, viii, p.624.
2. Broers, p.209.
3. Ibid. p.210.
4. Chandler, *Napoleonic Wars*, p.172.
5. Ibid.
6. See, for example, Oman v, p.239.
7. Serda, pp.117–18, 178.
8. King Joseph to Clarke, 6.v.1813, cited in Fortescue, ix, pp.5–6.
9. Ward, p.63.
10. 1796–1801 and 1804–1808.
11. M. Brialmont and G.R. Gleig, *History of the Life of Arthur, Duke of Wellington* (London 1858) i, p.186.
12. Wellington to Castlereagh, 25.viii.1809, cited in Oman, ii, p.514.
13. *Dispatches*, ix, p.370, 18.viii. 1812.
14. Muir, p.33.
15. Broers, p.245.
16. Wellington to Lord Liverpool, cited in C.J. Esdaile, *The Duke of Wellington and the Command of the Spanish Army 1812–14* (London 1990) p.1.
17. See especially his letter to Lord Bathurst in *Dispatches*, ix, pp.474–5, dated 5.x.1812.
18. The final terms are cited in Oman, vi, pp.210–13 and *Sup. Dispatches*, vii, pp.529–30, 546.
19. I. Cameron-Mowat, *Staff College Research Paper*, 1993, p.9.
20. Ibid. p.10.
21. *Dispatches*, viii, p.143, dated 24.vii.1811.
22. Broers, p.257.
23. J.W. Drage, *Staff College Research Paper*, 1993, p.15.
24. 260,000 by December. See Muir, p.14.
25. 54,000 strong by 1813. See ibid.
26. Ibid.
27. Griffith, p.59.
28. A detailed breakdown of the allied army is given in Browne, p.205.
29. Wellington to Lord Bathurst, *Dispatches*, x, pp.384–5.
30. Wellington to Graham. *Dispatches*, x, 67, dated 31.i.1813.

Chapter XIV

The Campaign of Vitoria

❧◉◉❧

I. SURPRISE AND SEA POWER

K ING JOSEPH MAY not have received the 29th *Bulletin* until January 1813, but Lord Liverpool had it on the smugglers' route on 21 December 1812, a mere five days after its arrival in Paris. He sent it on straight away to Wellington, to consult him on possible future courses of action, since no-one could yet be certain whether, in the face of the threat to his empire in Central Europe, Napoleon would leave an army in Spain at all. If the French did withdraw, Lord Liverpool and the allied governments would have to decide quickly what to do with the allied armies in the Peninsula. Although several schemes were discussed, this dilemma had, by March 1813, resolved itself when it became clear that Spain would not be abandoned, but it would be thinned out.[1]

There was, however, pressure from Hanover and Brunswick to send the KGL and Brunswick contingents back to Germany to support the war there. Wellington consulted his most trusted Hanoverian general, Charles Alten, whose view was that the 7,000 or so troops in question would be lost among the great hosts assembling in Germany, but they could make a considerable difference on a Peninsular battlefield – 'The best thing for England, for Germany, and for the world, is to make the greatest possible effort *here*.'[2]

Once Wellington became aware of the extent of the French commitment to anti-guerrilla operations, and of the scale of the thinning-out, he knew that the time was right to use his reinforced and battle-hardened army to strike a decisive blow. This would entail a change in the 'cautious system',[3] the waiting game which he had been forced to play since 1809. He had been forced to this system partly by the need to build up Portugal and its army, and partly because Britain could not replace the one-quarter of its entire army which Wellington commanded if he lost it. Wellington knew this well: 'I could lick those fellows any day, but it would cost me 10,000 men and, as this is the last army England has, we must take care of it.'[4]

Thus the allied army could undertake defensive operations based on strong positions, but no gambles could be contemplated. Salamanca had to some extent modified this view. It was an offensive battle which recalled Wellington's triumphs in India and brought home to the allies that they could fight offensive battles against the French and win.

Although he never wrote it down formally, Wellington's campaign plan for 1813 became clear from his correspondence. The campaign's aim was no less than the complete liberation of Spain which would follow as the natural consequence of the destruction of Joseph Bonaparte's armies in battle: 'I cannot have a better opportunity for trying the fate of a battle which, if the end should be successful, must oblige him to retire altogether.'[5] The campaign thus conceived would be an offensive at the operational and tactical levels of war, a deliberate and well-planned seizure of the initiative brought about by a series of enveloping moves on the French northern flank, by which they would be pushed back to the plain of Vitoria, pinned frontally, enveloped from the north-east, and destroyed.

To carry out this bold plan, two subsidiary operations were required. First, the Anglo-Sicilian Army at Alicante would engage in operations in Catalonia in order to tie down Suchet's army, prevent it from joining Joseph, and thus create favourable force ratios for the main army. It was for this task that Wellington had preserved this army against Bentinck's proposed expedition to Italy. Second, Lieutenant-General Sir Rowland Hill's 2nd Division at Coria would carry out a deception by threatening a possible advance up the Tagus to link up with Murray and turn the French left. To reinforce this, the Spanish armies would make demonstrations in La Mancha and Estremadura, thus confusing the French and preventing a concentration against the main allied army.

While these deceptions were in progress, the main allied army would be concentrated in northern Portugal and divided into two wings. The main effort would be placed with the left wing under Lieutenant-General Sir Thomas Graham, who would command a corps of six infantry divisions and one cavalry division. Graham's tasks were to outflank the easily defensible French positions on the Douro by crossing the river inside Portugal, then to move north and east across the Tras-os-Montes mountains and link up with the Spanish Army of Galicia. At the same time, the right wing, commanded by Wellington himself with the remaining allied and two Spanish divisions, would march on the River Tormes, link up with Hill at Moralaja, and force a passage over the Tormes.

Once communication had been established between the two wings, the whole army would then advance, with the main effort always on the left, so as to envelop the French from the north. The army would cross the Esla in its headwaters and traverse, with guns and wagons, one of the wildest and most trackless regions of Spain until, after a march of 300 miles, the allies would appear behind the French at Vitoria. If all went well, the French would be caught unconcentrated, and destroyed in detail.

This bold and essentially simple plan was worthy of the great Emperor himself at the height of his powers, and it shows Wellington in his true light, as a commander of genius. It was, moreover, a plan which depended on surprise and on sea power. To assure surprise, the allies depended on that intimate knowledge of French movements and dispositions, and corresponding ignorance of their own by the other side, which the guerrillas could give them. They depended too on the success of their deception operations, and on the detailed reconnaissance by their engineers and commissariat officers of the proposed route. This would help ensure a fast move to which the French, even if they realised what was afoot, would be unable to react in time.

Sea power was vital to cover the move of supplies, ammunition and heavy artillery by ship from Corunna to Santander on the northern coast of Spain, a port which the Royal Navy had seized and which the Spanish now held. For while Wellington threatened the French communications from Vitoria through Bayonne, he intended to secure his own. Once across the Esla, the base of operations would be transferred to Santander, shortening not only the land lines of communication, but also the vulnerable sea passage from Britain by 400 miles.

While the allied armies assembled in northern Portugal, the French certainly remained ignorant of allied intentions until a remarkably accurate report from a spy reached Joseph's headquarters on 20 May. Fortunately for the allies, Marshal Jourdan, lulled by the news that allied headquarters had not moved, issued no orders for any changes in dispositions. The armies thus remained well scattered on anti-guerrilla operations and along their lines of communication. This in itself presented one potential difficulty for the allies. As they pushed the French back on their own reinforcements, the French armies would grow stronger – there were 125,000 troops available in north Spain, 175,000 if Suchet could link up – while the allied strength would undoubtedly be weakened during the long march.

FIG. XIV.i
WELLINGTON'S MARCH TO VITORIA - SCHEMATIC

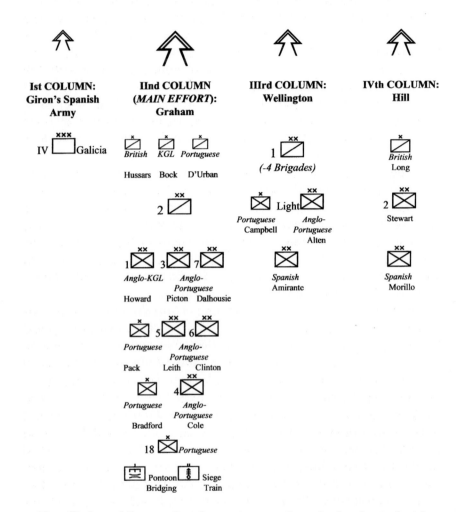

The allied need for speed and security was thus absolutely vital: either they broke the French decision-making cycle, or they would be defeated with no prospect of being able to withdraw. Thus the French must be confronted with a dilemma that they could not solve: remain unconcentrated to fight guerrillas and be destroyed by the allied armies; or concentrate and let loose the guerrillas. This dilemma would effectively ensure that, even with full knowledge of the allied intentions, the French would be quite unable to react in time and thereby would be surprised.

II. ON THE MARCH

As Napoleon pursued the allies after Lützen, the armies of the coalition began their march into Spain. Wellington had not expected the march across the Tras-os-Montes to be easy, but it proved even worse than had been feared. Even so on 22 May the right wing began its advance towards Salamanca. On the 26th, contact was made with the French division of General Villatte on the Tormes and a spirited fight went on all day as Hill's troops drove the French away from Salamanca towards the Douro. To Jourdan, everything seemed to point to an allied advance directly into Spain through Salamanca and he issued orders for a concentration to meet it.

This was no easy matter given the dispersion of the French armies. Reille's Army of Portugal had one division at Valladolid, another on its way there, its cavalry on the Esla and the rest of the army on the lines of communication or with the Army of the North, which was itself entirely engaged with the guerrillas. The Army of the South had one division on the Tormes at Salamanca and the rest of the army at Avila and Madrid. Finally D'Erlon's Army of the Centre was spread between Zamora, Toro and Valladolid.

But Wellington and Hill, on reaching the Tormes, halted, threw out a cavalry screen – and waited. They waited while the left wing completed its 200-mile outflanking march to the north. The going was hard indeed. The roads were few and scarcely worthy of the name, so that guns and wagons had to be hauled by hand over the rugged and precipitous terrain, and at frequent intervals had to be dismantled and carried, while men and horses scrambled for a foothold on the rocky crags. But by the 28th, Graham's corps, in three columns, had crossed the Spanish frontier and was marching hard for the Esla. The next day, they reached the flooding river which they crossed by pontoon and ford. A day later, the advanced guard entered Zamora, where Wellington himself had ridden to meet them. Before Joseph and Jourdan even knew what was happening, their right flank had been turned just as Wellington had intended.

It was too late for the French to do anything but withdraw. On 2 June, realising that the position on the Douro was untenable, the French evacuated Toro, closely followed by the allies: by 4 June, the whole allied army was north of the Douro. Losing no time, the army marched northeast in four columns 14 days without a halt across the easy going of the Castilian plain, a light cavalry screen out in front keeping in constant

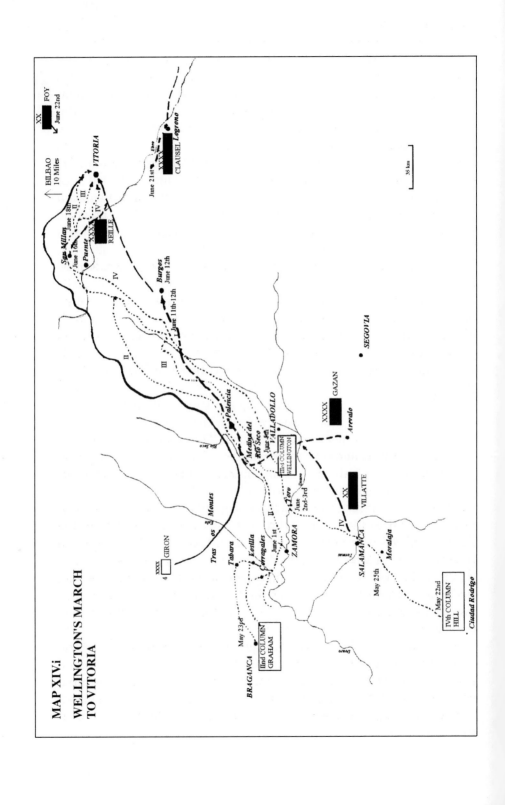

MAP XIV.i
WELLINGTON'S MARCH
TO VITORIA

touch with the retreating French. Despite the depredations of war and of the French occupation, supplies were plentiful and the people greeted the army as liberators. Knowing that the British always paid for their wants in gold, peasant farmers would hurry to greet the commissariat officers with chickens, pigs, hoarded grain, and wine. Against such a march, as speedy and audacious as anything the *Grande Armée* had ever carried out, the French were, as Wellington had foreseen, quite unable to react in time even though Gazan at least had correctly guessed Wellington's intention.[6] It was retreat or be cut off. Valladolid, headquarters of King Joseph himself, was evacuated on 2 June, Palencia on 7 June. Jourdan, accepting Gazan's advice, urged that all troops in the far north should be recalled and an attack mounted in strength towards the allied communications in Portugal, but Joseph would have none of it.

The allies had by now successfully linked up with the Spanish Army of Galicia, increasing their available strength to almost 100,000 men. This brought its own problems, principally demands from the Spanish for ammunition and supplies. Wellington's answer to these demands was characteristic: 'Either stay and do your best, or go back and I'll do my best without you.'[7] He was even sharper with the Spanish war minister:

> Here is an army which is clothed, armed and disciplined, but which cannot be brought into action with the enemy: I am obliged to keep it in the rear. How can troops march without provisions, or fight without ammunition?

But the French knew nothing of these difficulties. On 9 June Joseph at last sent word to Clausel to assemble every available man from the Army of the North, and join him. Clearly he hoped that the allies would advance from Valladolid towards Burgos by the main road, where they might be blocked. But Wellington was still pursuing his enveloping manoeuvre. On 12 June the allies halted to allow their supplies to catch up, for the Spanish troops were actually starving and had begun to plunder. Hill's column was, however, pushed forwards with most of the allied cavalry towards the city of Burgos, forcing the troops of General Reille, who was covering the approaches to the city, to withdraw. Once again, Joseph found himself confronted with the possibility of a battle before he had concentrated the army, or else retreat. Again he chose retreat. That night, the army left Burgos, blowing up the castle as it went.

Even as they did so, and as the armistice of Pleiswitz was concluded in Germany, Wellington once more ordered the left wing to push on across the Esla. Leaving only the cavalry screen across the main Burgos –Bayonne road, the army again left the plains for rough country. Wellington's intention, still maintaining his main effort on the left, was to march north, cross the Ebro River between Rocamunde and Puenta Arenas, then turn east and strike the French communications at Vitoria some 20 miles behind their main line of defence, thus completing his grand plan. For the next three days the army pushed on. Considering the broken, dry and hilly country through which they marched, and the scarcity of food and water, the advance was astonishingly rapid: 28 miles, for example, on 15 June alone,[8] the day on which the army again turned east to cross the Ebro. By 16 June the army had marched 300 miles into enemy territory, but it was still – at least the British, KGL and Portuguese – according to one witness '. . . in great fighting order, and every man in better wind than a trained pugilist'.[9]

Throughout these days, Jourdan had waited for news of the allied advance along the main road from Burgos, and his apprehension grew as his patrols found no signs. It was not until 17 June that his cavalry made contact with the allies near Puente Arenas, and Joseph gave orders to Reille to assemble the Army of Portugal at Osma, ready to move towards Bilbao. Next day, Reille's men met the allies heading east – not north as they had expected – at the village of San Millan. The French, caught off guard, received some very rough handling and the loss of 500 casualties. More important, however, Joseph realised that the Ebro was already outflanked. He could not risk the loss of his line of communications, nor the huge supply depots around Vitoria: there was nothing for it but to order a general retreat on Vitoria, where he hoped to find the army of General Clausel, the bulk of the Army of Portugal, and at least 4,000 men from the Army of the North.

D'Erlon and Gazan too were ordered to fall back on Vitoria, which both did with considerable skill, since the troops concerned could only get to Vitoria through the narrow pass at Puebla – and Wellington was far closer to the pass than they. Reille was therefore ordered to delay the allies in order to gain time for the move of the rest. Whether or not Wellington appreciated the opportunity he had of dividing the French forces and defeating them is uncertain, but by the time the army had arrived in the vicinity, the French were well on their way. Clausel too was on the march from Pamplona, with four divisions. On 19 June he was at Logroño, where he received news which made him believe that

Joseph was concentrating the armies on the upper Ebro. On 20 June he therefore marched north-west instead of north-east and thus failed to arrive at Vitoria on 21 June. Last of all, General Foy was ordered to evacuate Bilbao and he too was to march to Vitoria – but again, he had no chance of arriving before 22 June.

From the French point of view, therefore, the allies held all the aces. They could either besiege and mask Bilbao, and then march to cut the main road to Bayonne, a course of action which would force Joseph to march north and possibly evacuate Spain altogether as it would be impossible to feed and supply the armies. Or the allies might force a battle on favourable terms which if they won, would force the French to retreat on Pamplona over roads which were impassable to wheeled vehicles. Joseph, having ordered the concentration on Vitoria, was unable to decide which course the allies were most likely to follow, and therefore what measures he should take to pre-empt it – and so he did nothing.

III. THE DEFEAT OF JOSEPH

On the afternoon of 19 June the French Armies of Portugal, of the South and of the Centre, with a combined total of 57,000 men and with at least 20,000 camp followers in their wake, came pouring into the plain of Vitoria. It is a plain only in comparison with the rough ground all around, since it is an oval of rolling land about 12 miles long and 7 miles broad, funnelling towards the north-east into a bottleneck at the furthest extremity of the plain near Salinas. Here the little city of Vitoria stood on an isolated hill, clearly visible from all directions and dominating the plain with its two slim, graceful church spires.

The plain itself was drained by the tributaries of the River Zadora, which was a twisting, rocky mountain stream with alternating shoals and deep pools, fordable in places but with steep banks making passage difficult for horses, guns and wagons. The river flowed generally north-east to south-west; seven miles downstream from Vitoria it made a conspicuous hairpin bend, and here it was crossed by the bridges of Tres Puentes and Villodas.

Running south of the Zadora was the main Burgos to Bayonne road, overlooked by the ridge of La Puebla, which was the main French line of communication, and dominated opposite Villodas by a hill known as the Hill of Ariñez, a conical mound covered with shrubs and low bushes.

This hill was a feature which would be at the centre of the battle on 21 June. At Vitoria this road was joined by the main routes from Bilbao, Logroño and Pamplona, as well as by numerous small, rutted country tracks which crossed the Zadora and its tributaries by a series of fords and bridges in the plain.

Even though neither Clausel's army nor Foy's division had yet arrived, Joseph and Jourdan determined to take up a defensive position on the Zadora river. Clearly it would have made military sense to fall back on their reinforcements, but this was all but impossible owing to the enormous baggage trains which were slowly moving up the Bayonne road towards France, laden both with vital military stores and with the spoils of five years' plundering. Thus Joseph aimed to fight a purely defensive battle on a position from which he could either withdraw covering his baggage, or advance once reinforced. He hoped for the latter. His army had been continuously in retreat since late May in the face of an enemy whom few of the French troops had even seen. His own prestige was at rock-bottom, and worse still, he dreaded the rage which he knew would follow from his brother if he evacuated Spain and left France open to invasion.

Joseph had available 10 infantry divisions and one infantry brigade, mostly French but including some decidedly unreliable Spanish troops; 11,000 cavalry and dragoons; and 153 guns including those held by his artillery park. Altogether this force mustered around 57,000 men by most estimates,[10] a force inferior to the allies. To counterbalance this, however, Joseph had a reasonable superiority in artillery, reinforced by the presence of large magazines of ammunition and stores, in Vitoria itself. If Clausel could arrive, the French total would climb to 72,000; Foy's division would raise it to 76,000.

On 20 June Jourdan was taken ill so that the disposition of troops was left to Joseph himself. Clearly expecting the allies to attack up the main road from Burgos, he placed his main effort accordingly. The main army was drawn up in three echelons behind the Zadora, astride the main road. In the first echelon, across the road and west of the village of Ariñez, were placed three divisions of Gazan's Army of the South, supported by 54 guns, with their right on the river and their left on the heights of La Puebla. The second echelon was formed by the fourth division of Gazan's army, and General Pierre Soult's cavalry. The third echelon was formed by D'Erlon's Army of the Centre, consisting of two infantry divisions and a dragoon division.

Part of D'Erlon's task was to guard the bridges over the Zadora at

Tres Puentes and Mendoza on the Army's northern flank, but to do this he detached one weak cavalry brigade only. In reserve just west of Vitoria were placed the King's Guard Division; and a cavalry corps of three dragoon divisions, a chasseur brigade and two regiments of lancers which were well dispersed across the northern part of the plain. What he did not do was to place any troops on the opposite bank of the Zadora. As command of the stream varied from bank to bank along its length, just as with the Spree at Bautzen, this allowed the allies a free hand to dispose their troops for the assault.

Five miles north-east of the main army, on the upper Zadora just north of Vitoria, was placed the Army of Portugal. This army comprised only one infantry division, two cavalry brigades and a Spanish division and was placed to deny the northern approach to Vitoria across the bridges at Gamarra Mayor and Arriaga. The main effort of the army was south of the river, but an advanced guard of one infantry and one cavalry brigade was placed north of the river, later reinforced by the whole of the French infantry division. Finally the rather weak Spanish division, supported by artillery, was sent to guard the bottleneck on the Bayonne road at Salinas.

This army was by no means on the main effort, but the danger from the north was obvious. A cavalry reconnaissance up the Bilbao road on 20 June had identified some Spanish troops, but these were believed to be a deception. However on the night of the 20 June a Spanish deserter came in to the French lines bringing news of a large body of allied troops marching north, news which should have set alarm bells ringing. But the King was preoccupied with getting his treasure and supplies away to France. Despite this he remembered to order stands erected in the town for the benefit of the townspeople; however, having placed no troops across the Zadora, he did not remember to order the entrenchment of the position, nor the destruction of the bridges over the river.[11]

On 19 June the allies were only nine miles from Vitoria and here they rested throughout the 20th. Wellington's plan for the next day's battle was, like his campaign plan, bold and simple and he intended to crown his spectacular march with an equally spectacular battle; a decisive blow which would both cut the French withdrawal route and smash their armies. He disposed nearly 80,000 men in the main allied army, 100,000 if Lieutenant General Pedro Giron's Spanish Army of Galicia was taken into account, but with only 90 guns. His plan called for the army to be divided into four columns.

FIG. XIV.ii

FRENCH ORDER OF BATTLE, VITORIA

xxxx

Joseph Bonaparte

Marshal Jourdan

South xxx Gazan	**Centre** xxx D'Erlon	**Portugal** xxx Reille
1 xx Leval *(4,844)*	1 xx Darmagnac *(4,472)*	4 xx Sarrut *(4,802)*
3 xx Villatte *(5,874)*	2 xx Cassagne *(5,209)*	6 xx Lamartinière *(6,711)*
4 xx Conroux *(6,589)*	Dragoon Div xx Treillard *(1,038)*	xx Mermet *(1,801)*
6 xx Daricau *(5,935)*	Cavalry Bde x Avy *(474)*	Spanish xx Casalpalacios *(2,167)*
x Maransin *(2,927)*		**Reserve** xxx
Cavalry Div xx P. Soult *(1,671)*		xx Guards *(2,805 including cavalry)*
		Cavalry Bde x Spanish *(670)*
		1 Dragoon Div xx Tilly *(1,929)*
		2 Dragoon Div xx Digeon *(1,869)*
		3 Dragoon Div xx Boyer *(1,471)*
		Chasseur Bde x *(680)*
		Lancer Bde x

On the right, Hill would command a column of his own 2nd Division, Major General Francisco Silveira's Portuguese division, Major General Pablo Morillo's Spanish division, and a cavalry division of two brigades – 30,000 men all told. Hill's troops were to ford the Zadora well south of the French position, secure the defile and heights of La Puebla, and then push on up the main road, pinning the French main body.

Next to Hill, the main effort of the army would be in two columns totalling 31,500 men. While Hill pinned the French, these columns would envelop the right, or northern, flank of the enemy and complete the destruction. The right centre column was commanded by Wellington himself and consisted of 4th and Light Divisions and a cavalry division of four brigades. The column was to cross the Zadora by the bridges at Nanclares and Villodas and attack the flank of the Army of the South. On its left, the left centre column, commanded by Lieutenant-General the Earl of Dalhousie, contained 3rd and 7th Anglo-Portuguese Divisions. This column was to traverse the rough ground of Monte Arato, cross the Zadora near the bridge of Mendoza, and fall on the flank of the Army of the Centre.

Once he was sure that the French intended to stand and fight, Wellington intended that Hill's column should begin the attack at 8.00 am on the 21 June and that the other columns should be in position at the same time. This meant that the last column, Graham's, would have to make a night approach to cover the ground in time.

Graham's column was placed on the far left of the army and included the 1st Anglo-Hanoverian, 5th Anglo-Portuguese, and Longa's Spanish divisions, two Portuguese infantry brigades and a cavalry division of two brigades. It was Graham's troops which the deserter reported to Reille on the night of 20 June, marching north towards Murgia. Wellington had also sent word to Giron to march on the upper Bayas in support of Graham, and he did this probably because he had overestimated the strength of Reille's Army of Portugal and wished to add weight to Graham's attack.[12] In the event, Giron did not arrive until the battle was over.

The orders to Graham were certainly unclear. He was to maintain contact with the centre columns and be guided by what happened there; he was also told to avoid getting embroiled in a battle in or around Vitoria but concentrate on cutting the Bayonne road. This last objective was certainly Wellington's prime intention, as he himself stated: 'If . . . he observes that the troops forming the right of the [enemy] army continue to advance, he will . . . turn his whole attention to cutting off

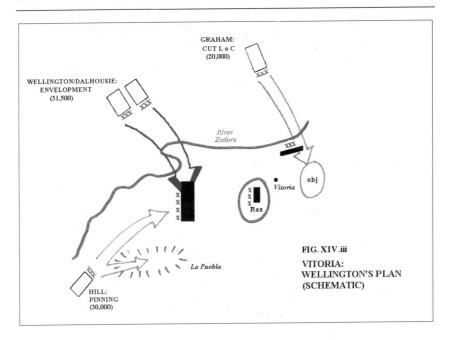

GRAHAM:
CUT L o C
(20,000)

WELLINGTON/DALHOUSIE:
ENVELOPMENT
(31,500)

*River
Zadora*

obj

• *Vitoria*

X
X
X
Res

X
X
X
X

La Puebla

HILL:
PINNING
(30,000)

FIG. XIV.iii

**VITORIA:
WELLINGTON'S PLAN
(SCHEMATIC)**

the retreat of the enemy by the great road which goes . . . to France.'[13]

But the stipulation to be guided by events in the centre must have caused Graham much anxiety. Thus the plan stood a good chance of success but it did contain two flaws: first, like Schwarzenberg's columns at Leipzig, the attack was to be mounted over rough ground with considerable distances between the various corps. Thus communication and coordination would be extremely difficult. Second, like Napoleon at Bautzen, Wellington had not made his intention to sever the enemy line of withdrawal completely clear to his subordinate. In the end, these flaws would prevent the complete destruction of the enemy army.

Early on the morning of 21 June, Marshal Jourdan, recovered from his fever, rode out with Joseph to inspect the battle position. Both were uneasy about the separation of the main army from that of Reille on the upper Zadora and they agreed that this could be overcome if the first echelon troops were removed and placed behind the present third echelon position. They had actually sent for Gazan to discuss this scheme when the first reports began to arrive of Hill's advance. It was clearly far to late to change positions now, and so the King and his retinue rode forward to the hill of Ariñez to observe events.

Hill's attack had gone in as planned but took some time to develop.

Morillo's Spanish division was pushed up to secure the right flank of the attack by seizing the high ridge of La Puebla, and at first, owing to the difficult going, the Spanish advance was slow: 'the ascent was so steep that while moving up it, they looked as if they were lying on their faces or crawling.'[14] Steep or not, the Spanish troops at length gained the ridge, and, driving the occupying French light troops before them, established themselves on the crest.

Gazan, seeing what had occurred, realised that a strong allied presence on La Puebla could envelop the whole of the first echelon of the defence from the south. He at once ordered his advanced guard brigade to counter attack, and sent two other brigades from the first echelon main position to support the move. This counter-attack almost succeeded, for the fighting was fierce, but Hill had reinforced the Spanish with Colonel Henry Cadogan's British infantry brigade and this was just enough to hold the position. The severity of the battle on La Puebla may be judged by the fact that Cadogan, the British brigade commander, was killed, and General Morillo severely wounded.

General Gazan had now seen two things. First, the rest of Hill's column had pushed on through the defile of La Puebla and occupied the village of Subijana without meeting serious resistance. Second, the movement of Wellington's own column were clearly visible across the Zadora around the village of Nanclares, threatening the French right. Gazan was sure, therefore, that the attack on La Puebla was not the allied main effort, and said as much to Joseph. Joseph, however, was still sure that the main attack would come up the main road and that Hill's moves proved it; Jourdan declared loudly that the movements on the right were a feint, and that the battle would turn around La Puebla.

Villatte's division from Gazan's army was therefore ordered to mount a further counter-attack on the heights, supported by two additional divisions, leaving only one infantry division of the first and second echelons actually on the main position. Hill had only so far committed one-third of his corps. His move onto the heights had opened up the French centre and by drawing attention to himself, was exactly fulfilling Wellington's intention.

But despite the slaughter, and the undoubted bravery of the Spaniards and British on the heights, the Battle of Vitoria was not decided there. It was now 11.30 am and Hill's attack had been under way for well over three hours. Wellington, although well satisfied with its progress, had received no reports of progress from either Dalhousie or Graham, both of whom had in fact made slow going over the rough terrain. Wellington

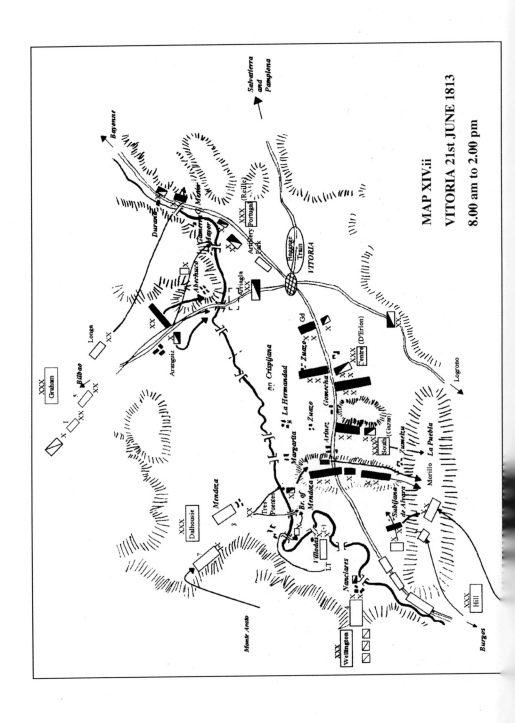

MAP XIV.ii
VITORIA 21st JUNE 1813
8.00 am to 2.00 pm

had decided that he could wait no longer and was about to order the Light Division to storm the bridge at Villodas, when a Spanish peasant appeared with the astonishing news that the bridge of Tres Puentes, about one and a half miles away, was unguarded. Wellington at once ordered a British brigade of the Light Division to follow the man and seize the crossing. Concealed from the French by the rocky ground, the brigade set off at a run; at Tres Puentes they found all just as the man had said, but while securing the position they were fired on by some French horse artillery in the vicinity – the second round blew off the Spanish peasant's head.[15]

As the riflemen had moved off to Tres Puentes, there were several other hopeful signs for the allies. First, the sound of cannon fire away on the upper Zadora announced the arrival of Graham's corps; second and more immediately, Dalhousie's column appeared on the slopes of Monte Arato. Dalhousie, a far from capable officer and a surprising choice as corps commander, refused to advance further than the edge of the hills, preferring to wait for formal orders to begin his attack. But Lieutenant-General Sir Thomas Picton, commanding 3rd Division, would have none of this. He could see the progress of Hill's troops, and could also see that the French were utterly unprepared for an attack across the Zadora. As time went on, his rage and impatience at the delay grew; by noon he could contain himself no longer and despite orders from Dalhousie that 3rd Division was only to take a supporting role in the eventual attack, sent word back to Wellington that '. . . the 3rd Division . . . shall in less than ten minutes attack that bridge [i.e. Mendoza] and carry it, and the 4th and Light Divisions may support if they choose.'[16] Turning to his division, and crying 'Come on ye rascals! Come on ye fighting villains!' Picton was away. The advance was furious; roaring across the front of 7th Division the troops surged across the river by the bridge and a nearby ford and, supported by the fire of the light brigade at Tres Puentes, threw back the light French covering force of cavalry and horse artillery.

As Picton attacked and Dalhousie dithered, Graham had advanced down the Bilbao road. On reaching the village of Aranguiz, the column had made contact with the French advanced guard division, and here it halted. Reille himself was with the French troops and was horrified to see the size of the allied column bearing down on him and rapidly reached the conclusion that here was not the place to fight. At noon, Graham had made up his mind to delay no longer and begin the attack, but as his assault brigades moved forward, the French withdrew in front of them back to their main position south of the Zadora. The French had, however, fortified the three villages of Gamarra Mayor, Gamarra Menor and Abechuco which could be supported by the fire of the army artillery south of the river. Graham therefore deployed his divisions to clear these villages, which he had to do in order to seize the crossings over the river.

On the left, Longa's Spanish division successfully cleared Gamarra Menor and pushed on to the Durana bridge where they came into contact with their compatriots in the Franco-Spanish division of General Casapalacios. As Longa's division was unsupported by artillery, and the Franco-Spanish division was well supplied with guns, it was not until after 2.00pm that Longa's men succeeded in storming Durana and cutting the main road. While the Spaniards battled it out, 5th Division had deployed in front of Gamarra Mayor and Abechuco which were stormed. The attackers had to fight hard and took considerable losses before they succeeded in clearing the villages, but even when they had done so, it proved impossible to advance across the river in the face of the deadly, accurate fire of the French artillery. So that although by the early afternoon, Longa's division had achieved its objective, the rest of Graham's column had been brought to a halt.

Even so, at 2.30 pm the allies were over the Zadora in strength and ready to settle the battle. Even King Joseph had now realised that the real threat was not that on the heights of Puebla. The rapid advance of Picton, supported by brigades from 7th and Light Divisions, now threatened to overwhelm the one remaining infantry division on the first and second echelon position, since the rest of the infantry from these positions was engaged against La Puebla and the third echelon position was nearly two miles to the rear. Wellington's own column too could now be seen moving towards the northerly of the two bridges at Nanclares – quite obviously, the entire centre of the French position would be smashed if something was not done quickly.

Immediate orders were sent to General Leval, who commanded the one remaining division on the main position, to fall back onto a blocking position on the hill of Ariñez. The remaining divisions were also ordered to abandon their attacks on La Puebla and concentrate behind the hill of Ariñez. Last, the third echelon – that is, the Army of the Centre – was ordered to advance and take up a blocking position between the hill of Ariñez and the Zadora, holding if possible the village of Margarita, but if not, then holding the village of La Hermandad. Thus a new line, two miles long, would be formed, but it would be no easy matter to execute these orders in the face of a determined enemy who could be expected to press home the attack. Moreover the new line was still vulnerable to outflanking movements from either La Puebla or from over the Zadora.

Villatte's division was still heavily engaged against the British and Spanish troops on La Puebla. At first, some headway had been made but the British brigade, two Scottish battalions, one English battalion and some Brunswick light troops, had rallied and driven the French back with great slaughter. It was just at this moment that Villatte received the recall order and broke off the attack, which effectively ended serious fighting on La Puebla – much to the relief of the allied troops, who had been in action for more than six hours.

Villatte began his move at once, but even as he did so, French hopes of forming a new position between Ariñez and the Zadora were frustrated by the speed of the allied advance. Within half an hour, the energy of Dalhousie's leading brigades (if not of their general himself) had swept the French out of Margarita and the troops were on their way to Zuazo. Picton, still leading 3rd Division, urging his men on and dressed in an old blue coat and round felt hat, all the while swearing 'as loudly as if he had been wearing two cocked ones.'[17]

Wellington's own column too was moving up the main road from the Nanclares bridge with infantry leading and cavalry in echelon behind. In the south, Hill's corps had pushed on past Subijana onto the ground evacuated by the withdrawal of the French first echelon and the troops on La Puebla, despite their fatigue, were ready to take the new French line in the flank. The allies were, however, still short of artillery for very few batteries had crossed the river and this caused some delay as guns were brought up. As they arrived, they were directed into the centre, onto the original ground of the French first echelon, forming a grand battery, and from there, the allied artillery began to pound the new French infantry position.

But Joseph had a still more powerful artillery arm. All the guns had been safely and smoothly moved from the original position and a great battery formed on the slopes of the hill of Ariñez. The cannonade from both sides was severe, but despite the proficiency of the French gunners it would be the infantry which would decide the issue. For it was clear now that the fate of the battle swung around Ariñez. Picton's troops coming in from the north clashed violently with the French, completely smashing one regiment and driving the rest of the enemy division, which had scarcely arrived, up the slopes of Ariñez hill in disorder.

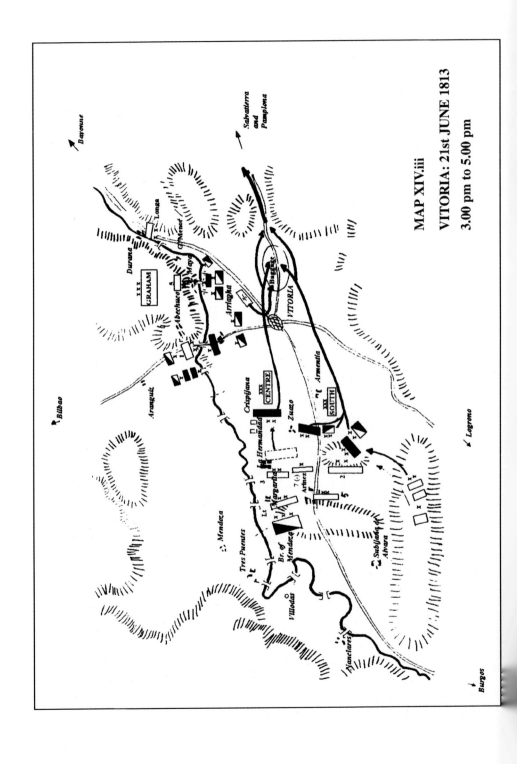

MAP XIV.iii

VITORIA: 21st JUNE 1813
3.00 pm to 5.00 pm

With their new position penetrated before it was properly established, the French had no option but to fall back onto a new line from La Hermandad, through Zuazo, to Ariñez. Again, their gunners showed great skill in extricating the artillery; they were fortunate too that the allied deployment was as yet incomplete. But this redeployment too was doomed before it was properly completed. A brigade of the Light Division now assaulted La Hermandad and in ten minutes, captured it and 12 guns from the defending Baden, Nassau and Frankfurt battalions. This penetration forced the French to yet another withdrawal, this time onto a line from Crispijana through Zuazo and on to Ariñez, a line which was now held by all the remaining infantry of the Armies of the Centre and the South in one body, with only the Guards infantry – about 2,500 men – in reserve. The French still possessed, however, plenty of guns and ammunition, and a considerable cavalry corps of 4,500 men in reserve.

Very soon the allied artillery too was brought fully into action and a new cannonade began to rake the French position. Both sides deployed about 75 guns in this position[18] and thus the artillery fire here was the fiercest ever seen in any Peninsular battle. The allied fire was quickly followed by a new infantry assault, it being now nearly 4.00 pm. The allied attack was mounted in three echelons. In the first echelon were Picton's 3rd Division, part of 7th Division (the rest never arrived until the battle was over), and Hill's 2nd Division. In the second echelon were 5th and Light Divisions; and in the third echelon, Silveira's Portuguese division and the bulk of the allied cavalry. On the right flank, Morillo's Spanish division and the one British brigade with it advanced along the ridge of La Puebla to get behind the new French line.

The attack was by all accounts a truly magnificent sight, recorded with admiration by those who watched from La Puebla or the hill of Ariñez. The French artillery fire was heavy and tore many gaps in the advancing lines, but their infantry defence was not resolute: having already been forced out of two positions, the French were in fact as good as beaten; they had no faith in their commanders; and worse still there were rumours that the Bayonne road had been cut by the allies and that they would soon be assaulted from the rear as well as the front. So as the allied infantry pressed in from the west and the south, the Army of the South began to retire – a retirement which was ordered by Gazan himself on no responsibility but his own, leaving Joseph and Jourdan to their fate. Jourdan later wrote with understandable ire that

General Gazan, instead of conducting his divisions to the position indicated, swerved violently to the right, marching in retreat, so as to link up with Villatte; he contrived to draw away, following the foothills of the mountain [i.e. La Puebla], leaving the high road to Vitoria far to his left, and a vast gap between himself and Count D'Erlon.[19]

Most allied narratives agree that from this point on, the French never made anything like a solid stand, and indeed this is borne out by the allied casualty lists. D'Erlon's men put up some resistance around Crispijana and Zuazo, but he was doomed if he stayed still. His troops were soon forced by the prospect of complete envelopment to retire to an intermediate position in front of Vitoria, where every available gun had been mustered. Yet again, a furious exchange of artillery fire broke out, as much to gain time for the French infantry to form, as to damage the allied attack, but it could only be for a few minutes: D'Erlon had received the King's orders for a general retreat towards Pamplona.

These orders stated that the baggage train and the artillery park were to move as soon as possible; the Army of the South would retire by the country roads south of Vitoria, and the Army of the Centre by the roads north of the city. The Army of Portugal was to hold its position until the main body had passed, and then it to was to retire, acting as rearguard. Since all the tracks and country roads specified in the orders converged on the Pamplona road just east of Vitoria, these orders ensured that total chaos would follow. In fact chaos followed even sooner than it might, for the orders to the baggage train and the artillery park had been issued far too late – two hours would have been needed to get them clear – so that all the routes were blocked with a struggling mass of wagons, carriages, and civilians. Batteries of artillery, released from the battle increased the confusion as they crashed into the traffic jam, trying to force a way through. It was impossible.

Around this great blockage the retreating army pushed its way in complete disorder, struggling over the six marshy-bottomed ravines and intervening wooded crests that lay in its path, and hotly pursued by the allied skirmishers. Gazan ordered all artillery to be abandoned to speed things up; the infantry threw off their packs and discarded their weapons, and by a supreme effort, the great straggling, struggling mass of the army, in terror of allied pursuit and in no recognisable formation whatever, managed to get away down the road, covered by the Army of Portugal which alone maintained some semblance of order.

In fact it was entirely due to the Army of Portugal that any French

The allied pillaging of the French baggage train east of Vitoria. British heavy dragoons keep up the semblance of pursuit.

troops at all got away. Longa's Spanish division had earlier managed to sever the Bayonne road and it was this significant success which had prevented the French from withdrawing in good order towards Bayonne. The rest of Graham's column had come to a halt soon after 2.00pm, with 1st Division, two Portuguese brigades and the cavalry in front of Arriaga and Abechuco; and 5th Division at Gamarra Mayor. Graham's failure to press home a serious attack across the Zadora, thus establishing himself in strength in the French rear, probably resulted from confusion in his orders over the need to conform to movements in the allied centre mentioned earlier. Although 5th Division made several vigorous attacks in the face of at least 20 French guns, the allied columns failed to breach the line of the Zadora.

Nor did Graham attempt to reinforce the success of the Spanish division by pinning Reille frontally with one division, and passing the rest of his infantry and his cavalry through Longa's position, and enveloping Reille from the north-east. Thus the real danger to Reille was the advance of the allied columns in the centre, which threatened to take him in the rear, rather than the static threat from Graham to his front. Even so, Reille kept his army in good order and, as much of his force was composed of cavalry and dragoons, two regiments were well able to act as rearguard in the narrow valley of the Pamplona road after the passage of the main body.

So far, there have been several striking similarities between Vitoria and Bautzen. Both envisaged a pinning action, an envelopment, and a move on the enemy lines of communication. In both battles a confusion in the orders led to only partial success by the troops moving on the enemy rear, allowing the escape of the enemy army. Here the similarities ended. At Bautzen, the allies effected an orderly withdrawal, and lost no trophies. At Vitoria, the French retreat was a shambles: another three hours of daylight would have clinched their destruction. What saved them as much as the approach of night was, paradoxically, their own baggage train. The pursuing allied cavalry just could not resist the lure of the spoil which, begun by straggling French soldiers, was afoot in the baggage train.[20] A pursuit of sorts was organised but it had to be called off after only five miles: growing darkness, broken ground and sudden, torrential rain made a properly organised pursuit impossible.

Since pursuit was out of the question, the exhausted allied infantry, many of whom had marched 20 miles since the previous evening, were allowed to rest during the night of the 21st in and around Vitoria. Rest they did not, for their minds were more on loot than on sleep. The story of the plundering of Joseph's baggage train has been told often enough, so it is enough to say that an orgy of truly bacchanalian proportions developed as the soldiers of four nations helped themselves to the accumulated treasures of Joseph's train: clothes, paintings, church plate, jewels, food and wine, and money: the pay of the French armies, five million dollars in silver, had arrived at Vitoria shortly before the battle; only 100,000 dollars found its way into Wellington's war chest.

> The consequence was, that they [i.e. the allied troops] were incapable of marching in pursuit of the enemy, and were totally knocked up. The rain came on and increased their fatigue, and I am quite convinced that we have now out of the ranks double the number of our loss in the battle . . . I am very apprehensive of the consequences of marching our soldiers through the Province of Biscay. It may be depended upon, that the people of this province will shoot them as they would the French, if they should misbehave.[21]

Wellington had aimed not just to defeat the French at Vitoria, but to destroy them. In this he was not completely successful, for the bulk of

Boney Receiving an Account of the Battle of Vitoria. A contemporary British cartoon by George Cruikshank. 8 July 1813. The allied sovereigns take heart in the middle. [BM Catalogue no. 12.069]

the army had escaped, but even allowing for this Vitoria was a smashing success for the allied cause not just in the Peninsula, but in Central Europe too.

Losses were comparatively light on both sides: the French lost around 8,300 casualties, the allies 5,158 of which 3,675 were British and Hanoverian, 921 Portuguese and 562 Spanish. But the French lost 151 guns, their entire artillery save one gun and one howitzer; 415 caissons and 14,000 rounds of ammunition; almost 2 million musket balls and 40,688 lb (140 tons) of powder – that is, enough ammunition for 60 rounds per man for almost 33,000 infantry soldiers; 100 wagons; and one colour.[22] Finally Jourdan's own marshal's baton was picked up among the wreckage and sent to the Prince Regent. In return, he sent Wellington the baton of a Field-Marshal of England.

NOTES

1. *Dispatches*, x, pp.125, 177, 207.
2. *Sup. Dispatches*, vii, pp.601–2.
3. Described in Griffith, pp.31 – 6.
4. Stanhope MS cited in Fortescue, vii, p.547.
5. Wellington to Lord Bathurst, *Dispatches*, x, p.372 dated 11.v.1813.
6. *Archives*, Gazan to King Joseph, 27, 28 and 29.v.1813.
7. *Dispatches*, x, pp.413–15.
8. Fortescue, ix, p.154.
9. Smith, i, p.97.
10. See, for example, Oman, vi, p.388, Napier, p.134 and Glover, p.107.
11. Browne, p.212.
12. *Dispatches*, x, pp.449 and 450.
13. *Ibid.* p.450.
14. Diary of an officer of the 43rd Regiment, cited in Oman, vi, p.112.
15. A painting by T.J. Barker (1815–1882) which is held by the British Army Staff College illustrates this sequence of events.
16. Oman, vi, pp.410–11.
17. Glover, p.123.
18. Oman, vi, p.428.
19. Jourdan, *Mémoires*, p.479.
20. Browne, pp.213–14.
21. *Dispatches*, vii, p.473.
22. Glover, p.124. By comparison at Vitoria Wellington's 50,000 infantry fired 3,675,000 ball cartridges and his 90 guns almost 7000 rounds, see Henegan, pp.344–6. The captured French musket balls were used in part by Wellington's troops until their own reserve supplies arrived tardily by sea via Santander, see *Dispatches*, x, p.495.

Chapter XV

On the Frontier

I. THE PURSUIT OF JOSEPH

A T 10.00 AM ON 22 June the allied advanced guard moved out of Vitoria in pursuit of the French. Contact had been lost the previous evening in the dark and rain and those troops not engaged in plundering – there were some, like the heavy cavalry and 5th Division, for example, who recalled the night after the battle only as one of short rations and cold, wet, weather – had bivouacked four or five miles east of the city. As the French had continued their flight far into the night until too exhausted to go any further, a gap between pursued and pursuers had already opened, made worse by an exceedingly leisurely start by the allied cavalry on the morning of 22 June. Coming on top of the plundering this was scarcely likely to improve Wellington's temper, and it is hard to understand, for out of nine brigades of cavalry available, only two had actually been in action on 21 June. The tardy cavalry was followed by the plunder-laden, drink sodden infantry at such a pace that the French had a breathing space in which to gather themselves together; as early as the morning of 22 June their battalions, regiments and divisions began to reassemble.

Wellington's plan for the pursuit was that the Spanish army of Giron, reinforced by Longa's division, would move north into Biscay, if possible capture the last convoy out of Vitoria, sever the main road to Bayonne, and isolate the French troops in the region – these being Foy's division and the garrisons of the Biscayan fortresses. While the Spanish moved north, the rest of the allied army would follow Joseph towards Pamplona. There was a distinct danger that Clausel's Army of the North, which was known to be near Logroño, would continue its march on Vitoria and find there the allied hospitals and all the spoils of battle, and so 5th Division and a cavalry brigade were left to guard the city, pending the arrival of 6th Division which had taken no part in the battle of 21 June.

The main allied army marched once more in three columns. The centre column, formed by the corps of Wellington and Dalhousie, marched on the main road; the corps of Hill marched on the side roads through El Burgo and Alegria; while the corps of Graham marched on Arzubiaga and Audicana; but all these routes converged at Salvatierra, where the mountains blocked the exit from the plain of Vitoria. George Murray suggested, in view of the likely congestion, that one column should march north across country to assist Giron and Longa by cutting the Bayonne road behind the system of French fortified posts, thus intercepting either the convoy, or Foy's division, or both. Wellington adopted this suggestion at once, intending that Graham should either destroy the French in Biscay, or force them back across the Bidassoa into France, and sent out orders accordingly.

Unfortunately the poor roads and confused situation of the army caused considerable delays in the transmission of the orders so that Graham's column fell behind its proposed schedule, and became badly disorganised too, with its cavalry stuck behind the infantry. The delay which this confusion inflicted was subsequently to prove significant.

As Graham did his best to sort out his column, the rest of the army pushed on. On 23 June the allied light cavalry caught up the tail of the French column, which was moving at great speed, as only French troops could, and skirmished rather ineffectually with the rearguard division. On 26th, the allies approached the fortress of Pamplona, which was strongly garrisoned, having maintained at least some contact with the French. That day, the rearguard division had been brought to battle properly at Araquil near Yrurzun and after a running fight, some 200 casualties had been inflicted on the predominantly German troops of General Darmagnac's division, and one of the army's two remaining guns captured.

But the rearguard did its work well, for the bulk of the army was beyond Pamplona and marching hard for the frontier: Joseph had paused briefly at Yrurzun and issued orders directing the Army of the Centre to march through the pass of Roncesvalles to St Jean Pied-de-Port; the Army of the South to march by the Col de Velate and the pass of Maya to the Bastan, where it was to establish a blocking position; and the Army of Portugal to march north to Santesteban and the lower Bidassoa, (parallel with Graham's march, as it happened, although neither was aware of the other across the intervening mountains) in

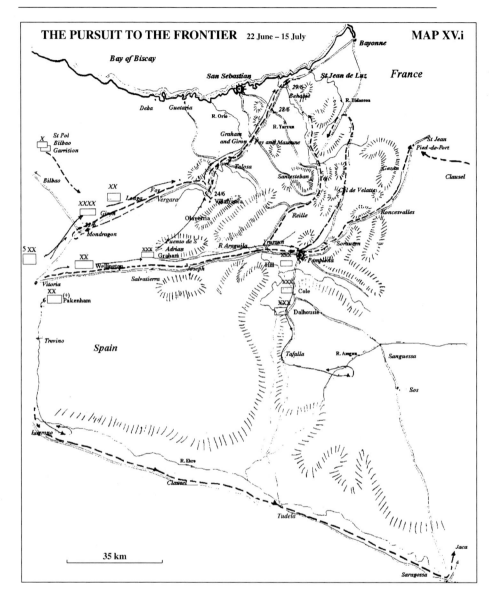

THE PURSUIT TO THE FRONTIER 22 June – 15 July MAP XV.i

order to link up with Foy and prevent a *coup de main* invasion of France in the north.

Meanwhile, on the morning of 23 June, while still some distance short of Pamplona, Wellington had received some surprising news: Clausel had not heard of the French defeat at Vitoria and was still marching on the city. The 6th Division had arrived safely at Vitoria, but the 5th had at once marched off to join Graham, so that the defending force was likely to face odds of at best three to one. The acting commander of 6th Division, Major-General Edward Pakenham, at once sent word to 5th Division and to Longa, both of whom were still only a few miles away, to return at once.

Pakenham, however, need not have feared. Clausel had reached Trevino on the evening of 22 June and there heard news of the battle. Here he halted, and sent forward his cavalry, which in due course reported a substantial body of allied troops in battle formation. This was more than enough for Clausel, who had no intention of risking a battle, but wished only to get away and rejoin King Joseph as soon as possible. His first idea was to march by the direct route to Pamplona, but as he gathered more news of the scale of the defeat at Vitoria, and as guerrilla activity increased and news came in of allied troops heading towards him, he retraced his steps to Logroño, picked up the garrison there, and headed for Pamplona by a more roundabout route.

It soon became clear, however, that all routes to the north-east were well blocked by Mina's guerrillas; Clausel's fears of allied troops approaching were also growing, and so he turned away from Pamplona, and on 26 June crossed the Ebro at Lodosa. He had now abandoned any idea of rejoining Joseph and instead decided on a move south-eastwards to link up with Suchet in Aragon. He had already lost much time in counter-marching, which was wearing his troops down, and thanks to the guerrillas, Wellington was well aware of his movements and had already sent troops to try to intercept him.

Wellington had seen the chance of cutting Clausel off from his line of withdrawal and smashing him, after receiving a dispatch from Mina on the night of 25 June. The orders for the next day were hurriedly changed: Lieutenant-General Sir Lowry Cole, with a corps of two infantry divisions and a cavalry brigade, was to move as quickly as possible along the Tudela road to Mendavil, and find Clausel. Dalhousie's corps, also of two infantry divisions and a cavalry brigade, was to follow as soon as Hill's corps had come up. Hill, for his part, was ordered to relieve Dalhousie and invest Pamplona. The 5th Division was ordered to march to join Graham. Concurrently 6th Division, now commanded once again by Major-General Henry Clinton, with two brigades of heavy cavalry, was ordered to abandon Vitoria and march with all speed down the Logroño road. Clinton did as he was ordered. On 27 June he arrived at Logroño to find Clausel two days' march ahead of him and already across the Ebro, and he realised that there was little chance of catching up. Nevertheless, he continued the pursuit as far as Lerin before abandoning it, marching his cavalry back to Logroño and his infantry to Pamplona.[1]

The only real chance of catching Clausel now lay with either the guerrillas, or with the four divisions marching on the Tudela road – but Clausel was marching hard and had a good start. On reaching Tudela on 27 June he picked up the garrison and dropped the bridge; he marched 20 miles on 28 June, and the same on 29 June. On 30 June he reached Saragossa. Wellington had realised on 28 June that interception was most unlikely, but had issued a modification to his orders.[2] From Mina's reports it seemed that the only chance of intercepting Clausel now was to turn the pursuit eastwards into the valley of the River Aragon, and so catch the French at Jaca. The modified orders therefore concentrated the most mobile elements of the pursuit, the cavalry and artillery, onto the main road and pushed the infantry onto country roads, in order to increase the speed of at least part of the force. But by the evening of 29 June, Wellington decided to call off the pursuit. He had no real expectation now of success, and was very afraid that more pressure on Clausel would push him faster towards Suchet, rather than over the frontier.

There was also a very bad problem of straggling in the allied pursuit, which had resulted in a loss already of nearly 3,000 British and 1,500 Portuguese soldiers[3] on top of the losses of battle and its aftermath. Clausel, meanwhile, had allowed his three divisions a rest of three days at Saragossa and on 2 July began his march on Jaca, which he reached on 6 July, hoping to make contact with Suchet and if possible, effect a union in or near Saragossa. By the 11th, this prospect had disappeared with the abandonment of Saragossa by its garrison after attacks by the guerrillas and so the next day he crossed the Pyrenees. By 15 July, he had succeeded in rejoining the main force at St Jean Pied-de-Port, with a strength of 11,000 infantry, 500 cavalry and six guns. He had lost 1,500 men on his march, mostly from guerrilla activity, which indicates that the allies might have been better advised to leave Clausel entirely to the guerrillas, instead of dissipating their strength away from the pursuit of the main army. Indeed, having abandoned Clausel at last, Wellington gave the army a day's rest on 30 June, meaning to resume the pursuit of Joseph. But such was the dispersion of the army, this would now take some days to prepare.

In contrast to the pursuit of Joseph and Clausel, the pursuit of Foy had been a brisk affair for the corps of Graham and Giron. Like Clausel,

Foy too had failed to arrive in time for the battle of 21 June. On 19 June he had received dispatches indicating that he should rejoin the main army, but these orders were vague and indefinite, so that instead of concentrating his forces – 5,000 men would have made a welcome addition to the French armies at Vitoria – he dispersed them between Villafranca de Orio, Deba, and Vergara, while ordering the garrison of Bilbao to evacuate the town and join him at Vergara.[4]

On the evening of 21 June the last convoy out of Vitoria, extravagantly escorted by an entire infantry division under General Maucune, bivouacked at Vergara. Maucune told Foy that a heavy cannonade had been in progress all day, but he had no other news. Scarcely had the convoy left next morning than the first fugitives from the battle began to come in bringing news of disaster. On hearing this news the commanders of the three forts between Vitoria and Vergara had abandoned their posts and marched the garrisons to Vergara, pursued at first by Giron and Longa. The news of Clausel's approach had caused Giron to turn back, but once the danger was passed the Spaniards had turned around once more. But much time had been lost and the army was exhausted, hungry and wet; only Longa's division had pressed on and it was now far ahead of Giron, so that Foy had only five battalions immediately facing him.

It was nearly enough to undo him. Foy had decided that he must in all duty delay the inevitable allied pursuit for long enough to allow the convoy to escape, and was angry at the abandonment of the forts. He therefore gathered up the fort garrisons and the two available battalions of his division, and marched down the Vitoria road towards Mondragon. Just south of Mondragon he met Longa's five battalions: Longa, unsure of Foy's strength and out of touch with Giron, advanced cautiously; Foy fell back steadily in front of the Spanish division, losing 200 men in action, and halted for the night two miles north-east of Mondragon.

That night a further three French battalions arrived raising Foy's strength to 3,000 men, and he decided to make a more determined stand until the garrison of Bilbao and St Pol's Italian brigade came in. So next day he waited for Longa – but in vain. Longa too had decided to wait until Giron came up; when he did so, Giron decided that the attack would be put off until the following day, 24 June, so that by the time the Spanish began to advance on Vergara, Foy had collected his missing brigades and had retired.

Foy had also sent word to Maucune to drop the convoy at Tolosa crossroads and move back with his whole division to a line between

General Francisco Longa (1770–1831), one of the prominent and successful Spanish commanders in 1813. He had started as a Cantabrian guerrilla leader of 100 men in 1809 and here wears a hussar uniform. His division of five battalions numbered 3,130 on 1 June 1813.

Villafranca and Olaverria from where he was to cover the retirement of Foy's troops – for Foy now had news that not only was Giron on the move, but so was Graham.

Giron had received the same news – but too late, for it was not until the night of 25 June that a dispatch reached him from Wellington urging him to engage Foy as closely as possible and delay him, so that Graham could have time to march up from the south and fall on the French rear. Graham had finally sorted out the confusion in his convoy and had struck northwards across the Puento de San Adrian; on 24 June his cavalry had made contact with Maucune, although much of his infantry was still strung out on the march. He could see Maucune's covering force division, and also the head of Foy's approaching column; he could also see that Giron was some way behind the French: he decided to attack at once with what forces he had.

These consisted of two Portuguese infantry brigades and one KGL brigade – insufficient to force Maucune off his position. The allied troops fought well and gained some ground, but Maucune was able to stand his ground for long enough to allow Foy's division to get past. By 3.00

pm, most of Graham's infantry were up and he was beginning to turn Maucune's position around Villafranca, moreover Giron's troops at last hove into view, at which Maucune, having successfully fulfilled his mission, skilfully broke contact and executed a retirement towards Tolosa.

During the late afternoon of 24 June, Graham and Giron collected their forces around Villafranca. There were now some 5,000 British, 4,500 Portuguese, and 16,000 Spanish troops available, plus another 6,500 British and Portuguese of 5th Division on the march, facing around 16,000 French and Italian troops under Foy and Maucune.[5] It was clear to Graham that the plan to intercept Foy had failed, so he decided to limit his operations to pushing the French back over the Bidassoa river into France, inflicting what damage he could in the process.

On 25 June the allies began to advance towards Tolosa crossroads, where Foy had taken up a strong defensive position. He had done this in the belief that Joseph's main army might be heading towards him[6], and so he sent off the convoy under escort of four battalions, and disposed the rest of his force for battle. The position itself, anchored on the well-fortified town and a defile in the road, was very strong against frontal attack and difficult to envelop except by a long flank march to the south.

It was this movement which Graham decided to make. Deploying the bulk of the allied infantry to pin the position frontally, he dispatched two outflanking forces: Longa's division and one other Spanish division were sent on the long southward hook, while a small detachment of one Spanish and one Portuguese battalion were sent to try to outflank the position from the west and north. Last, Graham sent word to the Biscayan guerrilla forces to move onto the Bayonne road and cut the French escape route.

Throughout the day there was little activity in front of the French position, although one Portuguese brigade managed to seize and hold the high ground overlooking the Pamplona road,[7] and likewise the outflanking move to the north was unable to make much progress due to the rugged terrain. But at 6.00 pm, distant firing announced the arrival of the Spanish outflanking movement, and Graham ordered a general attack. This attack produced some extremely fierce fighting, for the French were well positioned and determined, and the assault on the town itself failed completely. East of the town, however, the combination of frontal assault and flank attack drove the outlying three French brigades back into the town, while the guerrillas too began to appear in the French rear, and even the outflanking movement to the north at last succeeded in making headway.

Foy was in real danger of being completely surrounded and, probably with only 30 minutes at most to spare, he ordered a general retreat. It was just in time. Graham's artillery had blown in the main gate of the town, and his KGL brigade was actually inside the fortifications – but with darkness coming, the French were able to break clean and slip away up the main road.[8] Each side lost about 600 men.

Graham did not press them, wishing only to see the French back over the frontier. Foy continued to retire next day, picking up his convoy escort and a Spanish regiment on the way, and also discovering the presence of Reille's two divisions which Joseph had ordered to Vera. Both Reille and Foy had been entirely in the dark about each others' movements, and Reille was mightily relieved that the Biscayan garrisons had been saved, for a reasonable force was now available to defend the Bidassoa.

He ordered Foy to retire on Oyarzun in order to cover the frontier and keep open the communications with the fortress of San Sebastian, since this fortress was a cause of considerable concern. Its defences had for long been sadly neglected, it was poorly provisioned and armed, and its garrison was a mere 1,200 men of various assorted units. Worse still, it had a population swollen by 7,000 or so French and Spanish refugees. The new Governor, General Rey, had only just been appointed and he set about setting the place in order. Foy himself made a flying visit on 28 June and as a result he had replaced the garrison with a brigade of 3,000 regular troops as well as removing all the refugees under escort of the old garrison. The next day, Foy was ordered back across the Bidassoa; he had been gone only three hours when the Biscayan guerrillas invested the fortress.

By 30 June, San Sebastian, with Santona and Pamplona, were the only isolated outposts of French power remaining in the whole of northern, southern and western Spain. The French armies, with the exception of Suchet in Aragon and Catalonia, had withdrawn across the frontier, not even attempting to maintain bridgeheads over the Bidassoa. However Joseph and his lieutenants, for all their many mistakes, had managed to save a considerable army from the wreckage of Vitoria. Although short of cavalry, guns and ammunition, there were altogether at least 70,000 men available to defend the southern frontier of the empire even without counting a similar number available to Suchet and the National Guard battalions in France; it was their success in saving these that made it necessary for the allies to fight the battles in the Pyrenees.

II. A DILEMMA

Once the French armies had been driven back over the frontier it became clear that for the allies, an operational pause was both necessary and desirable, since the present line of operations could not be developed further. This was so for four distinct reasons. First, although the change of base from Lisbon to Santander had taken place as envisaged, the supply situation had not caught up. Wellington's view was that this was due to a lack of escort ships and the depredations of American privateers, and their absence meant that the allied armies were having to live off the land, something Wellington in particular did not like.[9] So before any further moves north were put in hand, the supply situation must be resolved.

This view does not, however, stand up to close scrutiny. Despite the difficulties, convoys to and from the Peninsula generally made safe passage, especially where military stores and reinforcements were concerned. It is probable that, because of Wellington's complaints, the successes of the Royal Navy have received insufficient credit.[10] Large stocks of supplies had been built up in Lisbon by the summer of 1813 and in answer to Wellington's charges that convoys were not being sent speedily enough, the Admiralty pointed out that a convoy was dispatched whenever eight or ten ships were assembled.[11]

Second, Wellington also wished to clear the French garrisons from the fortresses of San Sebastian and Pamplona – there were other minor forts holding out, but these two were strongly held, and could interfere with his lines of communication both with the north coast (and so to England) and back towards Portugal. Wellington's complaints against the perceived lack of success of the Royal Navy along the Spanish coast which he felt had impeded the flow of supplies to the allies again do not seem to be particularly well founded. His siege train had arrived at Santander by 29 June and was landed at Passages for San Sebastian from 7 July onwards.[12] Captain Sir George Collier's squadron began the blockade of San Sebastian on 3 July, and supported the siege with six heavy guns and 60 sailors from the fleet.[13] By September this squadron totalled 3 frigates and 15 sloops and brigs.[14] To resolve Wellington's complaints, Rear-Admiral Byam Martin was sent to Wellington's headquarters where at a meeting on 13 September 1813[15] he showed Wellington a list of 22 convoy escorts, not including Collier's squadron, which had made Passages during August alone. Wellington '. . . admitted a feeling of astonishment at such activity in support of his operations and overall the tone of the meeting was harmonious'.[16]

Wellington may be forgiven, perhaps, for some of his complaints on the ground that despite the Royal Navy's best efforts the French had been able to put right the poor provisioning of San Sebastian.

Third, as well as national problems there was a minor but irritating dispute to be resolved among the allies. At the end of June, the Spanish Regency in Cadiz removed Generals Castaños and Giron from their commands, a prerogative which was supposed to be in the gift of Wellington alone as Generalissimo. Wellington wrote at once to his brother, the ambassador, in Cadiz[17] to urge him to try to prevent any further occurrences of this kind. But he evidently decided that as the armies approached an invasion of France, the preservation of allied unity was all-important. So although distinctly displeased, he confined himself to a series of protests only.[18]

Last, and most important of all, there was a great deal of political uncertainty caused by the negotiations in Prague, for the attitude of Metternich was well understood. If Napoleon should make peace with the allies in Central Europe, who could tell what might happen if he turned all his ire towards Spain? If on the other hand war was resumed, then the best service that the allies in Spain could offer to the whole coalition effort would be to continue to tie down as many troops as possible, preventing their redeployment to Napoleon's strategic main effort. Wellington himself put this dilemma, and his solution, very succinctly in his despatches:

> My future operations will depend a good deal on what passes in the north of Europe: and if operations should recommence there, on the strength and descriptions of the reinforcement which the enemy may get on our front . . . I think I can hold the Pyrenees as easily as I can Portugal.[19]
>
> . . . If the war [in Central Europe] should be renewed, I should do most good by moving forward into France . . . If it is not renewed, I should go into France only to be driven out again.[20]

This was certainly a policy of which Napoleon himself approved: 'It is certain that Lord Wellington had a very sensible scheme. He wished to take San Sebastian and Pamplona before the French army could be reorganised . . .'[21]

It was as well that the success of Vitoria had given Wellington even more stature to deal with interference from London and to some extent, dictate his own campaign. For the old scheme of diverting resources away from Spain had never entirely died, and now Wellington found himself receiving suggestions that with the French expelled from most of Spain, or at least held north of the Ebro, their armies could be kept at bay by Spanish and Portuguese formations, stiffened with a few British brigades, while the bulk of the Anglo-Hanoverian army – perhaps 50,000 veteran troops – might be shipped to Germany. The presence of this body of troops would, it was felt, induce the allied sovereigns to offer supreme command of the armies to Wellington; thus Britain would hold the chief command as well as the purse strings and could thus dictate allied policy. What chance then for a separate continental peace? And if the worst came to the worst, and war was not renewed in central Europe, perhaps Napoleon would settle for a frontier on the Ebro in return for concessions elsewhere?[22] Wellington would have none of this,[23] and such was his position now that the ministry bowed. His wisdom was proved within a few weeks by Soult's attack.

The allied intentions for the time being therefore called for the adoption of a wait-and-see policy, based on a strong defensive line. With the return of Soult, there could be no doubt that a French counter-attack would be launched,[24] and so the field armies were for the most part positioned along the frontier to cover the likely approaches to the two main fortresses of Pamplona and San Sebastian. As the allies had only sufficient siege guns and engineers for one major siege at a time, and as Wellington was sure that Soult was most likely to try to relieve San Sebastian first by the easy approach route across the Bidassoa, the main effort was placed in the north. Here, the corps of Graham and the Spanish army of Giron were to cover the Bidassoa river and capture San Sebastian. Next, a corps under Dalhousie held the passes of Echalar and the heights of Santa Barbara above Vera. Hill's corps held the pass of Maya and the minor passes as far east as Les Aldudes. On the right, a corps under Cole held the pass of Roncesvalles.

The Spanish reserve corps of Andalucia, under the Irish-Spanish General Henry O'Donnell, had now at last come up, having on its way successfully stormed the French forts at Pancorbo, west of Vitoria.[25] This formation was designated to invest Pamplona, if possible starving it into surrender, thus releasing 3rd and 6th Divisions to be held in army reserve at Olague and Santesteban respectively.

Finally the bulk of the cavalry, which would not be needed in the mountain terrain, was quartered at Vitoria. Wellington still had concerns about his right, however unlikely the prospect might be of any moves by the main French army to effect a junction with Suchet in Catalonia, since this would leave him vulnerable to a move up the Ebro.

Two additional deployments were ordered to deal with this possibility: first, Mina's guerrillas, now embodied as a regular formation, were ordered to screen the Ebro valley; second, orders were sent to Bentinck in Alicante to launch a demonstration in Valencia province to engage Suchet's attention once more.[26]

Thus disposed, the allied forces numbered 70,000 British, Hanoverians and Portuguese; and at least 25,000 Spaniards, of whom 10,000 were engaged in the sieges. But the defensive line was a long one, and vulnerable to a rapid French concentration since the road network was as good on the French side of the mountains as it was poor on the Spanish; and this was exacerbated on the Spanish side by the high ridge of the Sierra de Aralar, which tended to isolate the corps of Cole on the right. Wellington was not completely happy with the scheme, as he himself wrote, 'There is nothing I dislike so much as these extended operations, which I cannot direct myself.'[27] Events were to prove his uneasiness well-founded, but at the time there was no real alternative, and he was at least reasonably confident that with these dispositions, the forward divisions would be able to hold on long enough for him to concentrate the rest of the armies, and counter-attack.

III. THE COMING OF SOULT

Napoleon received the news of Vitoria at Dresden on 1 July. He had no doubts about the effect of the victory on allied willingness to renew the war in Germany, hence his agreement next day to the extension of the armistice of Pleiswitz. For this reason as much as for the loss of his territories and his prestige in Spain he was furious, forbidding any mention of it in the press, indeed he could scarcely believe that any allied commander – let alone the despised and underrated Wellington – could be capable of a campaign of such rapidity and of such devastating consequences. He had firmly believed that all was well in Spain, and even as late as 24 June he had demanded the withdrawal of another 12 regiments of cavalry from Spain to make good the deficiency in his own army which had been one of the reasons for his agreement to the armistice in the first place. There could, to Napoleon, be only one explanation for this disaster, and that was criminal negligence in the high command. That same day, he sent orders for the resignation of Joseph, and authorised the appointment of his ablest available lieutenant, Marshal Soult.

Soult had already spent five years in Spain and he took with him now a commission as 'Lieutenant of the Emperor', as well as letters of credit for one million francs; a warrant for the arrest of Joseph if he saw fit; and orders to throw the allies back beyond the Ebro: to 're-establish the Imperial business in Spain and save Pancorbo, Pamplona and San Sebastian'. He was also secretly authorised, if things went badly, to open negotiations with the Spanish Regency for the return of Ferdinand VII and the removal of all French troops in return for a separate peace and the abandonment of the coalition by Spain.[28] The last measure was indeed taken up by Napoleon himself in December 1813, but to no avail. As to his other instructions, it was already too late for Soult to save Pancorbo, and Joseph was permitted to retire quietly to the country, as was Jourdan.

For Joseph, whose personal dislike of Soult was intense and who had campaigned long and hard – without success – to have Soult removed from Spain, the return of this marshal must have been unbearable. Joseph considered Soult untrustworthy, perverse and dangerous – no wonder, then, that he left the theatre with haste and almost in secret. But with these, to him, peripheral issues settled, Soult applied himself with vigour to his task. Soult was not much liked by the army, not merely for his well-known taste for loot, but also because although a master of organisation and of the operational art, he was too often beaten on the battlefield. In the present circumstances, though, his good qualities seemed to outweigh the bad, hence his appointment.

Soult had lost no time in reaching the frontier, indeed he arrived only 11 days after leaving Dresden, and he at once set about resurrecting the army. His actions and his energy were little short of inspired: first, he re-established discipline and morale, placing the blame for past defeats on the shoulders of the discredited high command, and issuing a proclamation to the troops urging them to revenge the defeat of 21 June and sweep the allies back behind the Ebro – 'Let the account of [this] success be dated from Vitoria, and the birthday of the Emperor [15 August] celebrated in that city.'[29] This proclamation was a clever piece of work, for the majority of the troops were old soldiers with a good fighting record, although they were now dispirited by long marches, poor rations, and defeat. One British prisoner noted after Vitoria, how the French soldiers cursed their generals, and vowed revenge.[30] Soult appealed basically to their own good opinion of themselves, and succeeded in convincing them that they had not been given a fair chance to defeat the allies.

Leaving aside the National Guard and the troops with Suchet, Soult had available 72,000 French infantry, 12 foreign battalions (Spanish,

Italian, and German), but only 7,000 cavalry. Overall, the force ratios were roughly even, but either side had the ability to create a local superiority, and the advantage in this respect lay with the French in view of the better communications and the allied commitment to sieges. Soult immediately set about reorganising the army as his master had ordered. Napoleon wished to end the old division of the army and create a new, unified Army of Spain organised into three corps-sized formations (although in his instructions to Soult, Napoleon had expressly forbidden the formation of titled *corps d'armée*), a large reserve division including most of the foreign troops, and two cavalry divisions. Each infantry division was to have two brigades each of 4,000 men, as well as divisional artillery.

Although Soult carried out the changes in the structure, there remained considerable differences in the size of divisions. He was able, however, to make good much of the deficiency in artillery, a task made easier by the large reserves of cannon and ammunition held in the arsenal of Bayonne which was able to supply 140 guns of all calibres to the army. He was less successful with supplies, so that the army resorted to its usual practice of plundering – this time in its own country. The condition of the troops can be judged from the fact that they had to be beaten off the bullocks, which Soult had secured to pull his guns over the mountains, to prevent them killing and eating the wretched animals on the spot.

With his army back in some semblance of order, and this achieved within the incredible time of two weeks, Soult turned his attention to the operational plan. Suchet indicted no wish to pursue a joint project, and so Soult had three lines of operation open to him: first, he could attack across the Bidassoa and relieve San Sebastian; second, he could attack in the centre through the pass of Maya and on to Pamplona; third, he could attack through Roncesvalles, destroy the isolated corps of Cole, and then swing towards Pamplona. He had received news from Rey in San Sebastian that all was well there, and so he decided to place his main effort against Pamplona.

In the north, the reserve division under Villatte would pin the allied formations there by demonstrations and deceptions, which would include bridging operations on the river and the positioning of his two cavalry divisions on the Nive and Adour rivers. In the centre, the corps of D'Erlon would force the pass of Maya, and then seize and hold the passes across the Sierra de Aralar, thus securing the main army against an allied flank attack. But the main effort would be on the left, both to

FIG. XV.i

SOULT'S REORGANISATION OF THE ARMY OF SPAIN, JULY 1813

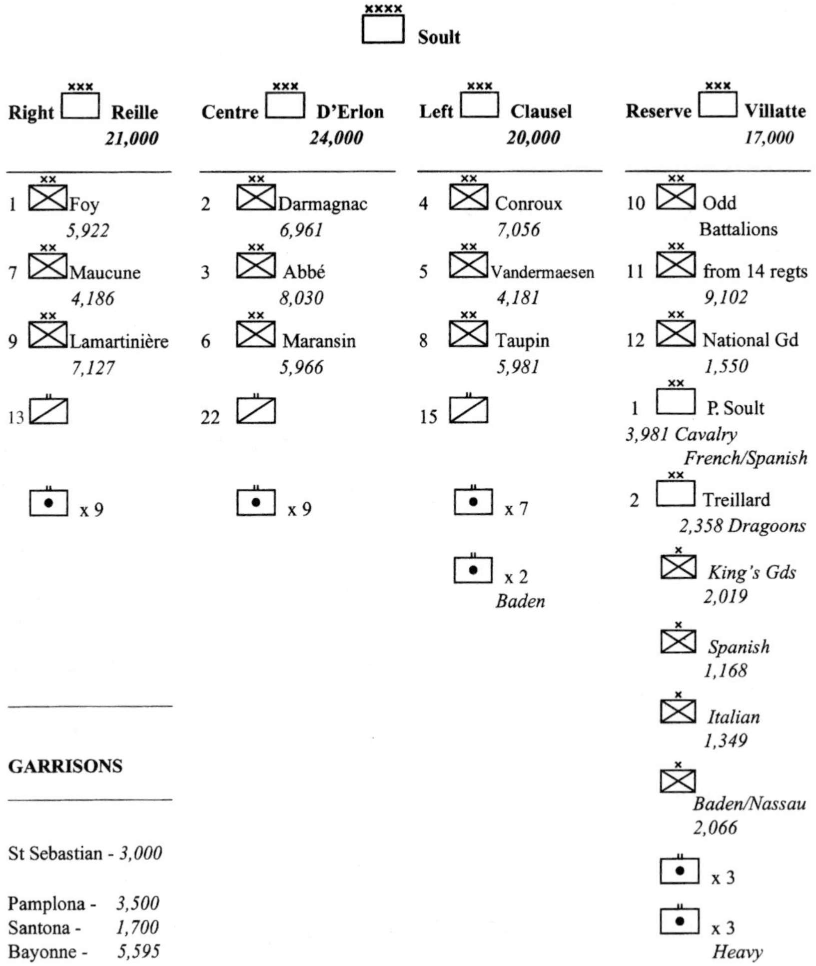

XXXX
☐ Soult

XXX	XXX	XXX	XXX
Right ☐ Reille	Centre ☐ D'Erlon	Left ☐ Clausel	Reserve ☐ Villatte
21,000	24,000	20,000	17,000

Right	Centre	Left	Reserve
1 ⊠ Foy **5,922**	2 ⊠ Darmagnac **6,961**	4 ⊠ Conroux **7,056**	10 ⊠ Odd Battalions
7 ⊠ Maucune **4,186**	3 ⊠ Abbé **8,030**	5 ⊠ Vandermaesen **4,181**	11 ⊠ from 14 regts **9,102**
9 ⊠ Lamartinière **7,127**	6 ⊠ Maransin **5,966**	8 ⊠ Taupin **5,981**	12 ⊠ National Gd **1,550**
13 ▱	22 ▱	15 ▱	1 ☐ P. Soult **3,981 Cavalry** *French/Spanish*
▣ x 9	▣ x 9	▣ x 7	2 ☐ Treillard **2,358 Dragoons**
		▣ x 2 *Baden*	⊠ King's Gds **2,019**
			⊠ Spanish **1,168**
			⊠ Italian **1,349**
			⊠ Baden/Nassau **2,066**
			▣ x 3

GARRISONS

St Sebastian - *3,000*

Pamplona - *3,500*
Santona - *1,700*
Bayonne - *5,595*

▣ x 3
Heavy

maintain communications with Suchet and to make use of the road network to concentrate rapidly against what Soult saw as the isolated corps of Cole. This corps was some 11,000 strong, although Soult underestimated its strength, and against it he planned to move the two corps of Reille and Clausel. Reille was ordered to force the narrow pass of Roncesvalles, while Clausel moved to the east through the even narrower Val Carlos. These two corps would destroy Cole's formation, press on before the allies had time to make a counter move, and relieve Pamplona.

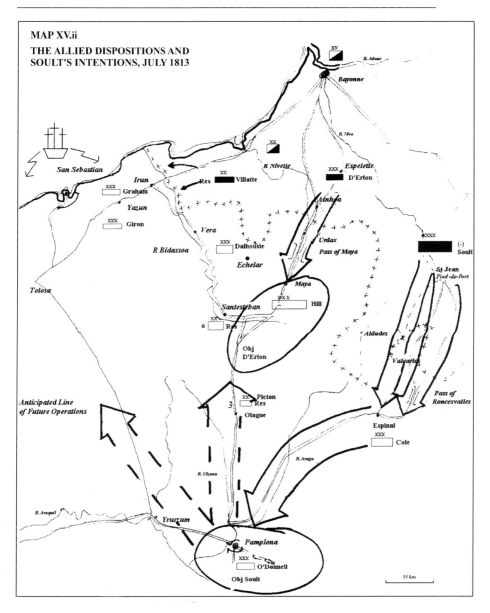

MAP XV.ii

**THE ALLIED DISPOSITIONS AND
SOULT'S INTENTIONS, JULY 1813**

From here Soult would command the main roads, so that he could quickly destroy the allied divisions in the centre and then either move against the rear of the allied forces on the Bidassoa in conjunction with his own Reserve, or else raise the siege of San Sebastian, or both. Thus the allies would be forced, like the French during Wellington's march to

Vitoria, to retire or be destroyed in detail. Soult began his preliminary moves on 20 July and hoped to begin the attack on 24 July. It was a daring plan which fully recognised the weaknesses of the allied position: but it demanded surprise, fast marching through difficult country, hard fighting against a determined enemy, and a good system of supply. This last was a fatal flaw from the beginning, for the army was still desperately short of wagons and held only four days' supplies with the troops: if the army could not capture the stores of the besiegers at Pamplona within that time, the troops would begin to starve.

NOTES

 1. *Sup. Dispatches*, viii,p.39 and *Dispatches*, x, p.501.
 2. *Dispatches*, x, 470–1 and *Sup. Dispatches*, viii, p.33.
 3. *Dispatches*, x, pp.477, 496 and 501.
 4. Foy, pp.393–4.
 5. Oman, vi, p.476.
 6. Foy, p .400.
 7. Ibid.
 8. This account is drawn from *Sup. Dispatches*, viii, p.44.
 9. See especially *Dispatches*, x, p.495.
10. See, for example, Forester, *Fighting Sail*, pp.70–1, and Hall, *Royal Navy* p .406.
11. *Dispatches*, xi, 17–19, dated 19.viii.1813; Hall, ibid.
12. Hall, p.411.
13. Ibid. Collier's ships captured 6 of the at least 50 US privateers taken by the Royal Navy in 1813, see list in John Norie, *The Naval Gazeteer, Biographer, and Chronologist* (London 1827) pp.532–3.
14. Hall, p.412.
15. Ibid.
16. Ibid.
17. *Dispatches*, x, p.491.
18. Ibid. pp.473–4, 475, 496.
19. Ibid. pp.523–4.
20. Ibid. pp.553–4.
21. *Lettres*, No. 28.
22. *Sup. Dispatches*, viii, pp.17–18 and 64–5.
23. *Dispatches*, x, pp.524, 568, 596.
24. Ibid. p.559.
25. See the report of this brave and daring series of attacks in *Dispatches*, x, p.478.
26. Ibid.
27. Ibid., p.602.
28. Related by Vidal de la Blanche and cited in Oman, vi, p.551.
29. The Dispatch is cited in full by Vidal de la Blanche, and quoted in Glover, p.135 and Oman, vi, pp.587–8.
30. Browne, pp.214–15.

Chapter XVI

Nine Days in the Pyrenees

⟡⟡⟡

I. THE BATTLES OF 25 JULY:
SAN SEBASTIAN, MAYA AND RONCESVALLES

A S SOULT MADE his preparatory moves, Wellington, still sure that a
French attack would come, nevertheless believed that the French
main effort would directed towards relieving San Sebastian. Soult's
deception measures on the Bidassoa were well thought out in this
respect, fuelling as they did this strongly-held opinion:

> I have undoubted intelligence that Soult has moved the greatest part of his
> force towards St Jean de Porte Pied leaving at Urrugne the boats, which are
> two complete bridges. It would appear, therefore, that he entertains serious
> designs to draw our attention from the side of Irun [on the Bidassoa] and
> then attempt to pass the river.[1]

Thus Wellington felt no compunction in ordering the storming of San
Sebastian to proceed. Like Soult's attack, this was due to take place on
24 July and was also put off until 25 July.

The fortress of San Sebastian sat on a sandstone plug about 400 feet
high, surrounded on two sides by the ocean, on one side by the estuary
of the River Urumea, and connected on the fourth side to the land by a
low sandy spit just over half a mile long. The plug itself was crowned
by the old castle, but the real defences were lower down. On the
landward side these were formidable, and were supplemented at the
landward end of the spit by additional outworks based around the old
fortified monastery of San Bartolomé. Since the seaward side was unassailable, the weakness of the fortress lay on the eastern side, on the
estuary, which was easily fordable at low tide and covered by sand hills
opposite which lay within gun range. From this side, Marshal Berwick

had successfully breached the walls and forced the surrender of the fortress and although this breach had been repaired, the defences were little different in 1813 from what they had been in 1719. Wellington had delegated the conduct of the siege to Graham, and the General's plan called for first, the capture of the monastery; second the breaching of the walls in the same place as Berwick had done so, and third the storming of the town at low tide across the open ground, since no approach trenches could be dug in the tidal flats.

The besieging troops had originally been General Gabriel Mendizabel's four battalions of Biscayan irregulars, but these had rapidly been replaced by Major-General John Oswald's 5th Division and an additional Portuguese brigade under Bradford,[2] and the Spaniards sent to blockade Santoña.[3] The troops had moved into position on 7 July and some 40 guns, assembled from the army artillery reserve, supplemented by guns shipped in and guns dismounted from HM ships, had been assembled. A rather irregular blockade was established at sea by a small naval force, but this was not enough to prevent the French running in small boats every night throughout the siege, filled with reinforcements, food and ammunition. The battering of the outworks had begun on 14 July and after two days an assault had been tried, and repulsed. Another two days of firing was more effective, and a heavier assault by the Portuguese on 17 July successfully stormed and captured the monastery.

The batteries were now erected for the main attack and the barrage opened at 8.00 am on 20 July. Good progress was made, but French counter-battery fire was also effective. By 23 July, 50 yards of wall had been dropped, and a second breach also made as a distraction; the engineers had also discovered and mined an old aqueduct shaft running under the main defences across the spit: had an assault been made straight away, it would probably have succeeded, but the delay of two more days allowed the defenders time to throw up effective inner defences. As it was, the assault was planned for 24 July but the artillery had caused such fierce fires in the streets around the breach, that Graham had to put off the attack for 24 hours. General Rey inside the fortress saw quite well what had occurred, and was well able to anticipate the assault.

The attack was planned for 5.00 am – low tide, and just before daybreak. The signal for the attack would be the blowing of the mine which, if successful, would be followed up by the Portuguese while the main attack would be mounted across the estuary. The mine was duly fired as planned, and did much more damage than had been expected,

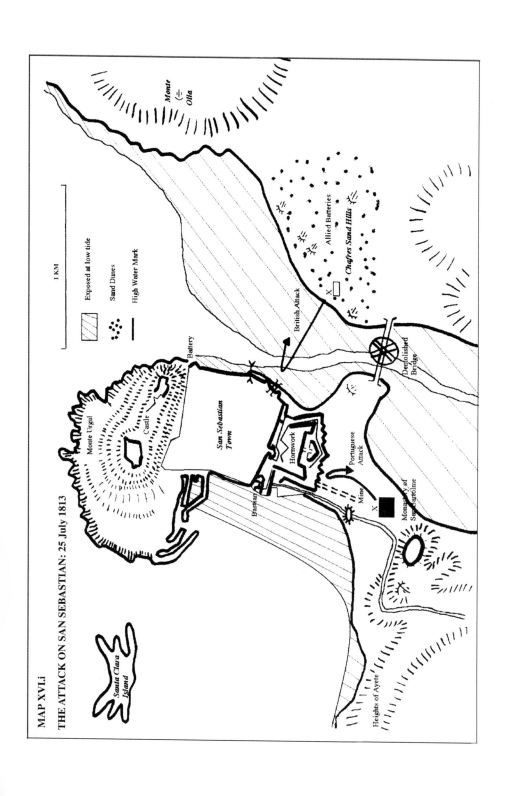

MAP XVI.i

THE ATTACK ON SAN SEBASTIAN: 25 July 1813

1 KM

Exposed at low tide

Sand Dunes

High Water Mark

Monte (= *Olia*)

Allied Batteries

Chofres Sand Hills

British Attack

X

Demolished Bridge

Battery

Monte Urgul

Castle

San Sebastian Town

Hornwork

Portuguese Attack

Mine

X

Monastery of San Bartolme

Bastion

Santa Clara Island

Heights of Ayete

but the assault was unsupported, and was repulsed. The main assault columns, meanwhile, had issued slowly out of the support trenches and stumbled in the dark across the slippery estuary. The troops reached the breach alright, but could go no further as there was a drop of 20 feet from the lip of the breach down into the town and scaling ladders were needed. As soon as the leading assault troops halted, the French opened a devastating fire which killed every man in the breach: with the first impetus lost, any chance of success vanished and after 30 minutes of fruitless effort, the troops were ordered to retire. The casualties had been severe: 571 killed in the breach, 330 from the Royal Scots alone.[4]

While the assault was in progress, Wellington had remained at his headquarters in Lesaca, not wishing to interfere with Graham's conduct of the battle, but listening to the sound of the guns and trying to judge whether the assault had been successful. At 11.30 am a message reached him to say that the assault had failed. Wellington at once ordered his horse and galloped off to San Sebastian to confer with Graham; the two concluded that the siege must be continued using new guns and more ammunition which were expected from England, and that these would be used to batter down the main defences, allowing an assault from the landward side. While he was gone from the headquarters, George Murray the Quartermaster-General heard distant firing coming from the east; soon after a dispatch arrived from Dalhousie at Echalar to say that the Pass of Maya had been heavily attacked but was holding – Murray therefore sent a warning order to 7th and Light Divisions and some additional artillery to reduce their notice to move, but made no other changes to the dispositions.

Wellington was back by 8.00 pm and he approved Murray's orders, but without more information he too felt unable to issue further orders. At 9.00 pm a report came in from Cole, which had taken eight hours to get back, saying that the Pass of Roncesvalles had also been attacked, but it too was holding. Wellington still believed that Soult's main effort would come across the Bidassoa, and he therefore sent a message to Graham warning him to stand by for attack; to ship his siege guns – doubtless the example of the other Murray at Tarragona was in his mind – and to be prepared to mask the fortress while fighting a defensive action. For Wellington could 'hardly believe that, with 30,000 men, he [Soult] proposes to force himself through the passes of the mountains'.[5]

He did, however, take the precaution of sending orders to O'Donnell to detach one division from the siege of Pamplona and support Cole; he also sent word back to Vitoria for the cavalry to move up to Pamplona. These orders sent, he went to bed.

Wellington had slept for only two hours when a dispatch from Hill awoke him. Hill's troops in the pass had been in contact all day and had been driven from the pass with the loss of four guns and 1,300 casualties. Only the intervention of a brigade of 7th Division had averted disaster; Hill had withdrawn, but was still in a position to stop further progress by D'Erlon. Soult's real plan was at last revealed and Wellington issued orders accordingly. The 6th Division was to leave one brigade to secure the town of Santesteban while the main body marched to Elizondo to establish contact with Hill; 7th Division was to march to Sumbilla, and establish contact with the 6th; the Light Division was to be prepared either to reinforce Graham, or to march east.[6]

With these orders sent, Wellington rode off with his staff to Irurita, where he found Hill, well posted with 9,000 men and no French troops in sight, and there he heard of the events at Maya. Hill's force had consisted of 2nd Division, one Portuguese and two British brigades under Lieutenant-General William Stewart; and Major-General Francisco Silveira's Portuguese division of two brigades. The corps was well dispersed, with the two British brigades in the pass of Maya; the Portuguese brigade of 2nd Division, under Brigadier-General Charles Ashworth, in the pass of Ispegui some seven miles east of Maya; and Silveira's division further east still, maintaining contact with the troops at Roncesvalles. To the north and west of Maya, 7th Division held the Puerto de Echelar, the Light Division was at Vera, and 6th Division at Santesteban.

D'Erlon's corps of three divisions had been concentrated for the attack at Maya well in advance, with an advance guard at Urdax and the rear services at Espellette. D'Erlon was instructed to push the allies hard, as Soult assumed that with success at Roncesvalles, the troops at Maya would be forced to withdraw or be isolated; D'Erlon was then to seek to unite with the main army as soon as possible. Given the poor communications on the Spanish side of the frontier, this is a rather odd assumption to say the least – the allies did not fall back until night, and thus ensued one of the bloodiest battles of the Peninsular War.

The attack had opened with a demonstration by some National Guard troops towards Silveira's Portuguese, which was thrown back, but it did have the effect of drawing Hill away from Maya to investigate. This was perfectly natural; what was not natural is that Stewart, who was responsible for Maya, left his command and also went to see what was happening. He was sought in vain once the real action started, so that command at Maya devolved onto Major-General William Pringle, a brigade commander who had arrived from England only two days before. Considering that Stewart must have been aware of D'Erlon's force; that Maya was his main effort; and that Wellington had issued clear orders that the passes were to be held, Stewart's absence was, to say the least, negligent.

Nor was Stewart's disposition of troops at Maya a triumph of tactical planning. The position was a broad, grassy saddle about one mile long and 2,000 feet high, flanked by peaks reaching another 1,000 feet higher. The road from Urdax to Elizondo crossed the saddle at the western end, and a track from Maya to Espellette, joined the road by a lateral track at the highest point of the saddle, crossed it at the eastern end. Another track running away westwards, still called the *Chemin des Anglais*, allowed communication with 7th Division. The main road was guarded by a British infantry brigade under Lieutenant-Colonel John Cameron, supported by a Portuguese artillery battery, but the eastern track was covered only by a company from the other British brigade under Pringle which was posted on a knoll called the Aretesque, while the main body was held in Maya village, 2½ miles or one hour's march away. Posted halfway between the brigade and the picqueting company were four light companies, about 300 men. There was much dead ground on the approaches to the position, but Stewart had made no provision for any screen or covering force and thus the French had plenty of opportunities to scout the allied position thoroughly.

As a result of his reconnaissance, D'Erlon decided to place his main effort on the eastern track, where two divisions would attack in echelon, with the third division held at Urdax. By 10.00 am on 28 July some movements had been observed sufficient to cause Pringle to order the light companies up to Aretesque Knoll. They had only just arrived when the first of the four phases of the Maya battle opened as D'Erlon's attack came in: at 10.30 am, a swarm of *tirailleurs* advanced onto the Aretesque position, followed by the leading division in column. The speed of the French advance caught the defenders by surprise and forced the small garrison of Aretesque into a tight perimeter on the knoll, where it held out stoutly for an hour until 260 of the 400 men were casualties, at which point the rest surrendered.

The rest of the lead French division meanwhile marched up and began to deploy across the saddle, at the same time as Pringle's brigade came up from Maya. Their approach signalled the start of the second

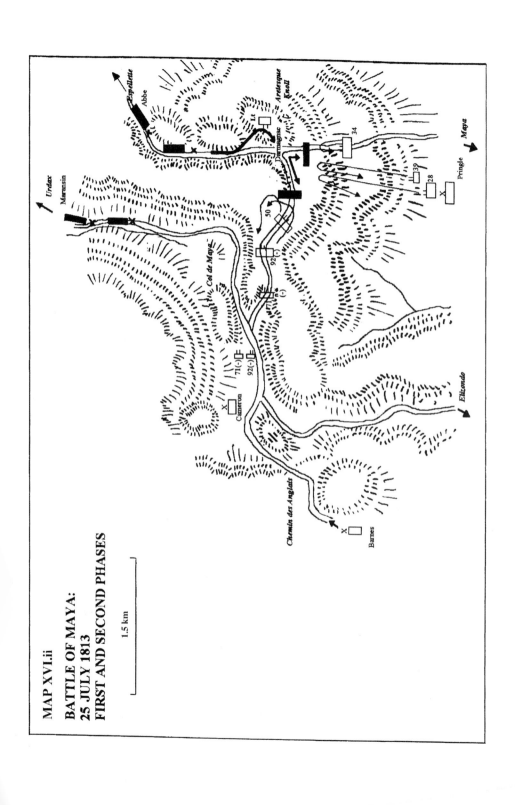

MAP XVI.ii

BATTLE OF MAYA:
25 JULY 1813
FIRST AND SECOND PHASES

1.5 km

phase of the action, a series of piecemeal attempts by the three battalions of Pringle's brigade and supporting troops from Cameron's brigade to dislodge the French. The first two battalions from Maya were rapidly brought to a standstill by French fire; one of Cameron's battalions, the 50th Foot, had some limited success but it too was brought to a halt. Finally the third battalion from Maya and half of the 92nd Foot from Cameron's brigade were led by Pringle personally in an attack on the French right flank. A horrific fire fight ensued, at a range of no more than 120 yards, in which the French suffered more casualties than the British, but with odds of 20:1, the British force was shot to pieces – within a few minutes, 60 per cent of the two battalions were casualties. This repulse brought the end of the second phase, the withdrawal of the remnants of Pringle's brigade towards Maya and of the 50th and 92nd back onto Cameron's position.

Cameron's brigade too was soon in trouble. The third phase of the action opened with the French pushing along the lateral track from the Aretesque, while simultaneously the third French division, that of General Maransin, began to move up the road from Urdax. Cameron had attempted to block the lateral with another half-battalion, the 71st, leaving only two half-battalions (71st and 92nd) to block the main road. The half battalion on the lateral did succeed in bringing the advancing French to a temporary halt, but it was soon enveloped on both flanks and forced back.

It was now 2.00 pm and it was obvious that the allies had no chance of stopping D'Erlon on the Maya position; at this point, Stewart at last appeared, to survey the wreckage of his division. To his credit, he saw that the only hope of avoiding annihilation was to conduct a delay battle on the main road to allow time for the arrival of 7th Division, to which urgent messages for help had been sent. Stewart immediately gave orders for the formation of a new blocking position three quarters of a mile further south, and this was achieved, although the four guns of the Portuguese battery were lost in the process, the only guns lost by the Anglo-Portuguese Army in the whole Peninsular War. Fortunately the French did not press home the attack just yet, and this allowed Stewart a pause of perhaps 30 minutes.

From this new position, the fourth and final phase of the battle was opened. On the French side, the lead division, that of Darmagnac, had been successful but the stubborn allied defence had depleted its numbers. D'Erlon therefore ordered an echelon change; Maransin's division took

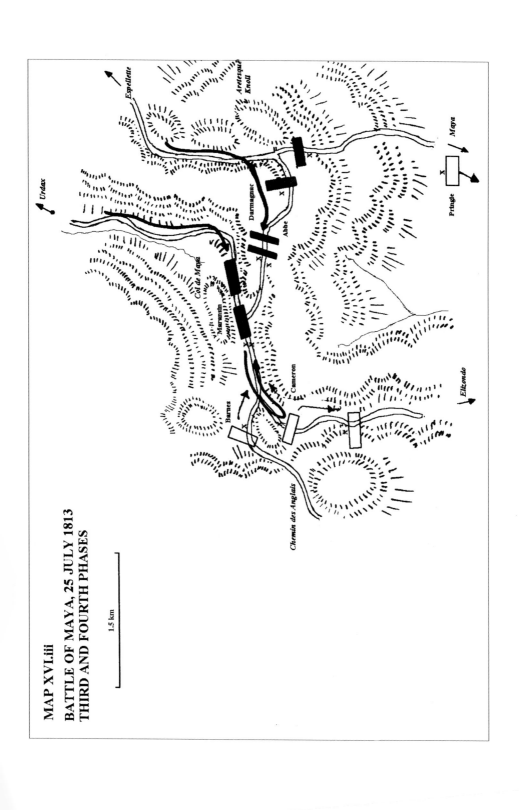

MAP XVI.iii
BATTLE OF MAYA, 25 JULY 1813
THIRD AND FOURTH PHASES

1.5 km

Urdax

Espellette

Aretesque Knoll

Darmagnac

Abbe

Col de Maya

Maransin

Barnes

Cameron

Chemin des Anglais

Elizondo

Pringle

Maya

up the lead, with Abbé in support, and a new attack was launched at 3.00 pm.

In the new position, the British brigade had formed two firing lines about 300 yards apart, each of which delivered a volley and then retired behind the other. This effective fire, and the irresistible temptation to loot the allied camp sites, checked the French advance for over an hour; when the attack was resumed, it was met with a counter-attack, for the lead brigade of 7th Division had arrived. This counter-attack was temporarily successful, but once again a small-scale allied response met with failure against the formidable force ratios involved. Slowly, the British troops gave way. By 6.00 pm it seemed that all was lost, but at that moment, the second brigade of 7th Division, consisting of only one British and one Brunswick battalion under Major-General Edward Barnes, marched up. Although the brigade mustered only 1,500 men, Barnes at once led it in a crashing counter-attack onto Maransin's right flank which, catching the French completely unprepared, totally flattened the lead battalion.

The remains of Cameron's command at once gave a loud hurrah and took up the charge: the result was quite astonishing – Maransin's leading brigade dissolved and fled, taking the supporting brigade with it so that the whole division was soon running hard back uphill towards the saddle. D'Erlon assumed that the whole of 7th Division must have arrived and he threw a brigade of Abbé's division across the saddle. But Stewart did not intend the press the matter, content to have checked the French advance, and as dark came at 8.00 pm the firing died away.

The day's losses had been horrific, especially on the allied side. 1,500 British were casualties or prisoners out of a force of 6,000 engaged. The French losses had been heavier, 2,100, but this was out of a force of 20,000. D'Erlon reported to Soult that the battle was won, but it had been the most desperate he had ever seen. The British troops had fought for ten hours, facing odds approaching 20:1 at times, and they were so exhausted that they had scarcely strength to move. But when Hill himself arrived at 9.00 pm he brought news that Roncesvalles had been attacked and Cole was retiring: the weary soldiers must therefore summon their strength and march back to Elizondo, six miles away, or risk being surrounded.

It was there that Wellington met the corps, and told Hill in no uncertain terms to stand fast and to keep in contact with 6th and 7th Divisions. D'Erlon did not pursue. After the counter-attack late on 25 July he was certain that on the 26th the allies would come at him in strength and that he would have to fight a defensive battle. All day on 26 July he made only reconnaissance moves towards Elizondo and Vera, and when that evening he received news from Soult that Roncesvalles had been evacuated, Hill had been given 24 hours start. This in itself was enough to wreck Soult's plan.

With Hill in no imminent danger, Wellington decided to amend his orders. The 7th Division would support Hill in place of the 6th, and the 6th would march towards Pamplona.[7] Since most of 7th Division was already close by, this made sense. Wellington himself, mightily perturbed at the news of Cole's retirement, rode on over the crest of the Col de Velatte to see for himself what had occurred. News of Cole's retirement, which had been the cause of Hill's withdrawal from Maya, had reached Wellington almost by chance at 8.00 pm on the 28th.[8] The dispatch made depressing reading.

Soult had selected two routes for his attack at Roncesvalles. Of these, the main road through the pass was quite passable for guns, wagons and horses and this road ran up from Venta d'Orisson on the French side, across the watershed and down into Spain past the Abbey of Roncesvalles, where lay the tomb of Roland. This route was allocated to the corps of Clausel. The second route, allocated to the corps of Reille, was a different matter entirely. Separated from the main route by three miles across the deep Val Carlos, there was no chance of mutual support between the two corps. The route itself was no more than a herdsmen's track, quite impassable for wheeled vehicles as it wound along the steep, narrow Airola ridge until it joined the main watershed at Linduz. From Linduz a lateral track running along the Ibaneta ridge connected the two routes. Also at Linduz, a second lateral track ran off to the west towards the Alduides valley, and thus the area was a convergence of a series of ridges, commanding sweeping views of the French side of the mountains.

Because of this, Soult knew that the allies had already seen Clausel's concentration, and that an attack up the main road was expected, but he hoped that Reille's attack would achieve surprise. This would be vital, for given the going, Reille's three divisions would have to leave its cavalry, artillery and wagons with Clausel's corps on the main road, and then advance in a column with a frontage of *two men* over a length of three miles. The only available artillery support would come from eight mountain guns carried on mules. On the main road, Clausel's corps was to be committed in echelon of divisions, followed up by the cavalry, then the guns and transport of both corps. It too was a very

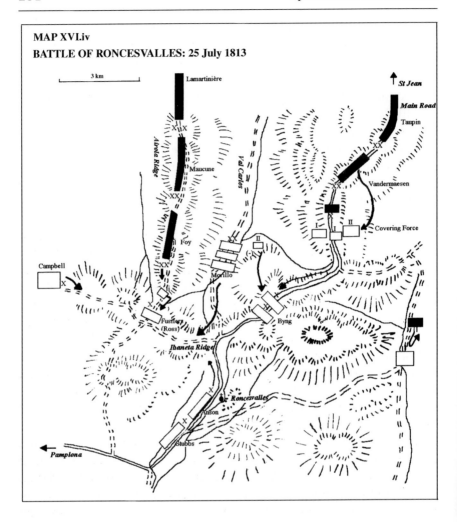

MAP XVI.iv

BATTLE OF RONCESVALLES: 25 July 1813

long column indeed, but the road was good and the slopes each side allowed at least some deployment.

On the allied side, Cole, in his first command at corps level, had been left in no doubt about his higher commander's intention. On 23 July a dispatch from Murray, the Quartermaster-General, had instructed him that

you should support Major-General Byng in the defence of the Passes as effectively as you can . . . you will be good enough to make arrangements further back also, for stopping the enemy's progress towards Pamplona, in the event of your being compelled to give up the Passes . . . A sure communication should exist with General Sir Thomas Picton . . . in order that he may make such arrangements . . . for giving support . . .[9]

This had been followed up by a still sterner order on 24 July from Murray:

Lord Wellington has desired that I should express still more strongly how essential he considers it that the passes in front of Roncesvalles should be maintained to the utmost, And I am to direct you to be so good as to make necessary arrangement for repelling effectually any direct attack that the enemy may make . . .[10]

Responsibility for the pass of Roncesvalles had originally been delegated to Morillo's Spanish division and Byng's brigade of 4th Division. Subsequently, Cole himself had assumed personal command. The original dispositions had wisely placed the main effort of the defence on the main road. Byng and Morillo between them disposed a total force of 2,000 British and 3,800 Spanish troops which were deployed with a covering force of three British light companies and a Spanish light battalion well forward; two British and two Spanish battalions were deployed across the main route two miles behind the covering troops, with a further Spanish battalion detached to guard the flanks a small path on the allied right flank. The rest of Morillo's division, reinforced by one British battalion, was down in the Val Carlos.

On assuming command, Cole had brought up additional forces: the British Fusilier Brigade was moved to Espinal, about two hours' march away; the rest of 4th Division – one British and one Portuguese brigade, plus an additional Portuguese brigade, were all within six hours' march. On the night of 24 July Wellington's dispatch had been received and the covering troops had been engaged in some skirmishing, and then a Spanish informer brought news of a likely French attack up the track to Linduz. Cole had therefore very wisely ordered the Fusilier Brigade to occupy the area of Linduz, and this move had been achieved in the dark so that by 6.00 am on 25 July the brigade was in position.

The first firing began soon after the Fusiliers had arrived. This was the deception attack by the National Guard which had attracted the personal attention of both Hill and Stewart. A second deception attack was mounted on the Spanish battalion holding the allied right, but neither attack achieved any noticeable effect. At 7.00 am the head of Clausel's column appeared in front of the allied covering force and tried

General Pablo Morillo (1777–1838) fought the British as a marine at Cape St Vincent (1797) and Trafalgar (1805). Officer rank came to him for bravery against the French in 1808. A guerrilla chief in Murcia and then Galicia, his 1813 division (4,551 strong on 1 June) was one of the most disciplined Spanish formations.

to sweep it aside, but the initial attack failed completely. For three hours, the allied light troops pinned the leading French brigade so effectively that the whole of Clausel's column came to a halt and began to pile up. Both Spanish and British troops stood immovable, well concealed in the rough terrain – inspired too, no doubt, by the personal presence of General Morillo. One officer who was present, Second Lieutenant George L'Estrange of the 31st Foot, described the action thus:

> As soon as we could distinguish anything to the front, we saw that the French were coming up . . . They continued to bring up their columns for several hours. I conclude that the miserable state of the roads did not admit of any very rapid movements . . . General Morillo . . . sent out a lot of the Spaniards to skirmish in the front; and we were ordered to defend our position to the last extremity. . .[11]

Eventually the whole of the lead French division had to be deployed in a long turning movement to the east across the steep hill sides and seeing this, Byng ordered the covering force to break clean before it was cut off, and to withdraw. This movement was achieved in good order: the delay imposed had been remarkable, for it was now approaching 3.00 pm, and allied reinforcements were well on their way. To the dismay of the French, the allied main position was even stronger than that of the light troops, and Clausel had decided that the only possible avenue of approach was another long turning movement to the east. But at 5.00 pm, a dense fog came down, obscuring everything and making all movement impossible so that the allied main position remained intact.

At the western end of the position, at Linduz, fighting had been much heavier. For nearly four hours the 2,000 Fusiliers had rested after their night march, listening to the sounds of firing on the main road. General Cole himself rode past, with the encouraging news that another British brigade and a Portuguese brigade were marching up in support. At midday, signs of approach up the track were seen and heard, and Robert Ross, the brigade commander, sent forward a company of Brunswick light troops and part of one British battalion to reconnoitre. The Germans got to within 200 yards of the approaching troops, and saw that they were French, but in no particular formation after the hard climb – just a straggling herd coming up the path at a point where the crest was only 30 yards broad and well covered with trees and shrubs. The leading French battalion, seeing the Brunswickers, deployed and opened fire, forcing the 60 or so Germans to retire. Needing more time to deploy his brigade, Ross ordered the British troops he had sent forward, a company of the 20th Foot, to charge with the bayonet. Its commander Captain George Tovey, described the affair:

> . . . we came so suddenly on the head of the enemy's infantry column . . . that the men of my company absolutely paused in astonishment, for we were face to face with them and the French officer called to us to disarm; I repeated 'Bayonet away! Bayonet away!' and rushing headlong among them, we fairly turned them back into the descent of the hill . . .[12]

After only a minute Tovey, seeing the rest of the French battalion coming up, broke off the action and retired – but he had gained the time needed: the whole of the 20th Foot was deployed in line, and opened a steady fire on the approaching French column, causing heavy casualties. But the French strength continued to mount and the fire fight increased in intensity, at a range of no more than 100 yards, until the 20th was forced back behind the rest of the brigade which was also now fully deployed on the Ibaneta ridge. As the French followed up the 20th, devastating volleys from 7th and 23rd Fusiliers felled first the leading battalion, and then the rest of the leading brigade. After that, Foy's division made spasmodic attacks all afternoon, but all failed, and no attempt was made to outflank the British position. At 3.30 pm, Reille's second division, that of Maucune, began to appear, but by 5.00 pm it was still incomplete when the fog came in.

So neither Clausel nor Reille had made the slightest progress. And even if they had succeeded in forcing out the initial allied defenders, Cole's reserves had come up soon after noon. The battalions from the Val Carlos had also withdrawn onto the main position so that the allies presented a continuous line of 11,000 troops on a three-mile front, a formidable position, probably unassailable without artillery, and made stronger still when Major-General Archibald Campbell's Portuguese brigade (2,700) appeared on the allied left flank. The morale of the allied troops was also high after a successful action – but Cole was less than happy. He estimated the French strength – correctly – at more than 30,000, nor did he expect support from Picton's division, marching up from Olague, before early on 26 July at the very best. Unnerved too by the fog, under cover of which anything might be happening, he took counsel of his fears. despite his successful defence and strong position, he decided 'that he could not hope to maintain the Passes against the very great superiority of the forces opposed to him – amounting to between 30,000 and 35,000 men'.[13]

This being so he must retire by night under cover of the darkness and fog. Surprisingly, perhaps, Byng agreed with him, although Wellington clearly felt that Cole was wrong:

> Sir Lowry Cole . . . retired, not because he could not hold his position, but because his right flank was turned . . . all the beatings we have given the French have not given our generals confidence in themselves and in the exertions of their troops. They are really heroes when I am on the spot to direct them, but when I am obliged to quit them they are children.[14]

And indeed, in view of Wellington's distinct and explicit orders, followed by a successful defensive battle, Cole's decision is impossible to understand. But in the early hours of 26 July the whole position was abandoned. The French did not hear the movement and by dawn the whole corps was marching towards Pamplona, aiming for a junction with Picton's 3rd Division at Zubiri.

All in all, the day's fighting had ended in a far from satisfactory state of affairs for either side. The allies had abandoned or lost the vital passes, whose possession would guarantee the time which Wellington needed to concentrate his dispersed army against Soult. But Soult too was in trouble. He had banked on an easy passage of the mountains; instead the French had been forced to fight hard and had taken heavy losses. Surprise had been lost, but worse still, so had valuable time. As Napoleon remarked before Jena, space can be recovered, but time – never.

II. THE ALLIED CONCENTRATION

After the withdrawal of Cole, Wellington had sent explicit orders to Picton, telling him that the French must at all costs be held in front of Zubiri, where 3rd and 4th Divisions would be reinforced by the 6th and one of O'Donnell's Spanish divisions from Pamplona, and where he himself would come to take command.[15] But this scheme was rapidly overtaken by events. When the fog had come down at Roncesvalles, Soult must have felt his position to be hopeless; but as day broke on 26 July he realised from reconnaissance reports that, amazingly, the allies had slipped away.

His dispatch by semaphore to Napoleon at Mainz was thus one of victory: the passes were forced, D'Erlon had captured four guns and several hundred prisoners, and he hoped to be in Pamplona by 27 July. The news reached Napoleon by semaphore on 1 August at the same time as the news of Rey's repulse of the storming of San Sebastian. Napoleon, in optimistic mood, sent to the Foreign Minister, Maret, in Paris telling him that

> You had better circulate the news that in consequence of Marshal Soult's victory over the English [*sic*] on July 25th, the siege of San Sebastian has been raised and thirty siege guns and 200 wagons taken. The siege of Pamplona was raised on the 27th: General Hill, who was in command at that siege, could not carry off his wounded, and was obliged to burn part of his baggage. Twelve siege guns (24-pounders) were captured there. Send this to Prague, Leipzig and Frankfurt.[16]

Such a message was, of course, aimed as much at the congress of Prague, which was still in session, as at public opinion in France.

Soult's orders to the main army for 26 July were an exact replica of those which had failed on 25 July, and one has to speculate on the carnage that would have ensued if the allies had stood fast. Reille was ordered to force the pass at Roncesvalles and then follow the mountain crest in order to support D'Erlon by taking the allied troops at Maya in the rear – 17,000 men in single file on a steep crest spread over six miles. Reille tried to follow these orders, but the fog was still thick and the column came to a halt. The Basque guides did not speak French and in despair, the leading division, that of Foy, took the most obvious path. After two miles, this brought the corps down to the main road at Espinal where the troops tagged on to the rear of Clausel's corps, ignoring the orders to move towards D'Erlon. In front of Reille's men, Clausel's corps advanced to the abbey of Roncesvalles but found no sign of the allies; cavalry patrols were sent forward and these soon came up to the allied rearguard, which was bivouacking at Espinal. Clausel gave orders for the infantry to pursue, but the fog was still heavy and it was 3.00 pm before Taupin's division could be got up. As it did so, the fog lifted, revealing the whole corps of Cole in a good blocking position on the high ground behind the Erro River around Linzoain.

Here Picton arrived between 3.00 and 4.00 pm, with his division only three miles behind him. Picton was looking even more eccentric than at Vitoria, wearing a top hat and blue frock coat, and carrying a rolled umbrella. 'Here comes old Tommy' was the word passed down the ranks of 4th Division, 'Now boys, make up your minds for a fight.' But there was no fight on the Erro. Picton, after conferring with Cole, agreed that the position was too liable to be turned on both flanks, especially by an enemy 35,000 strong. Picton decided to hang on until night, as the French were obviously well strung out on the line of march, and then slip away again. He sent word to this effect, but it was of course contrary to Wellington's instructions to hold the enemy. Picton however had decided that the only defensible position was on the heights of San Cristobal, only just east of Pamplona. So by 11.00 pm the whole corps was on the march: Wellington's message to hold the ground it had abandoned did not arrive until the column was approaching its destination.

The position chosen by Picton was in itself a good one, but it was only a mile from the hostile fortress of Pamplona, allowing no depth to the deployment and making the defence vulnerable to a sortie from the fortress in conjunction with a frontal assault. Cole therefore suggested that the position be moved two miles further north, between Sorauren and the River Arga. This would make use of an excellent position along a steep ridge, 1,000 feet high and two miles long, dominated by the heights of Oricain, and connected to the outlying ridges of the Pyrenees

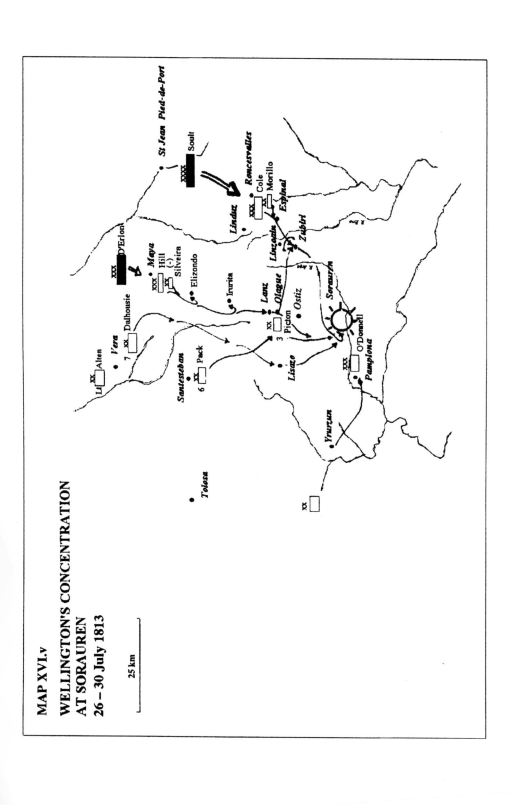

MAP XVI.v
WELLINGTON'S CONCENTRATION
AT SORAUREN
26 – 30 July 1813

25 km

massif by a prominent col. This ridge offered a strong defensive line on reverse slopes, with secure flanks anchored on two river lines.

The deployment was a defence in two echelons. Forward of the first echelon a covering force of *Caçadores* and British light troops was thrown out; next, the first echelon was placed along the Oricain feature, with two British and two Portuguese brigades in line, supported by KGL artillery and a third British brigade on the highest part of Oricain. The extreme right of the line was anchored on the hill of Zabaldica, which was held by two Spanish battalions sent up by O'Donnell. The second echelon was placed along the original line of the heights of San Cristobal. This was held on the left by a division of O'Donnell's Spanish corps, the rest of which masked the fortress of Pamplona; Morillo's Spanish division in the centre; and on the right, the two British and one Portuguese brigades of Picton's 3rd Division. The extreme right of the second echelon was protected by a cavalry division of four brigades which Wellington had earlier ordered up from Vitoria.

The dispositions had been completed well before the French appeared, for they had been badly held up by traffic congestion on the one decent road through the rough country – by implication this was excellent terrain for delay, and should not have been given up so easily by the Allies. At 9.00 am on 27 July Clausel's leading division came up in front of the Zabaldica but Reille's corps, having detoured off the main road to try to avoid the congestion, had made even slower going, across country, than Clausel. Clausel at once put his corps into assault formation on a ridge opposite the allied first echelon. He could see troop and vehicle movement in the area of Pamplona and felt sure that the allies were raising the siege: the position opposite him must therefore be designed only for delay. He sent to Soult straight away to ask permission to attack, but Soult did not believe that the allies would give up Pamplona so easily, and rode forward himself to see what was happening. As it happened, his arrival coincided with that of Wellington.

As he had ridden on eastwards, rumours of Picton's and Cole's continued retreat reached Wellington and so alarmed him that he sent a galloper back to Hill to warn him that if things went badly, a retreat to the Yrurzun–Tolosa line north-west of Pamplona might be necessary; but no moves were to take place without his specific orders. In the meanwhile, though, 6th Division was ordered to march to Olague, Silveira's Portuguese division was to march to Lanz, and both divisions and the Light Division were to be ready to move fast if needed.[17] Further down the road at Ostiz, Wellington met Major-General Robert Long with his brigade of light dragoons. Long confirmed that Picton had abandoned his position at Linzoain and now intended to fight close to Pamplona. The French were in pursuit, and a fight might start at any moment. Ostiz is only four miles north of Sorauren: there might just be time to get to Picton before fighting began.

Wellington left George Murray to direct troops as they came up, and galloped off with his staff, gradually outpacing them all except Lieutenant-Colonel Lord Fitzroy Somerset, his Military Secretary. As he came towards Sorauren, roughly parallel to the French line of advance, he could see the whole position, and the French advance was less than a mile from him. He dashed on to Sorauren bridge where, in the face of the oncoming enemy, he stopped, dismounted, and wrote out a dispatch for Murray. With Spanish peasants all around crying out that 'The French are coming, the French are coming!' Fitzroy Somerset dashed off with the order; it warned 6th Division and all available artillery to approach by a safe but roundabout route to the Sorauren position, where it should arrive the next morning; 2nd and 7th Divisions were to move up to Lanz and Lizaso. Murray had the order 30 minutes later.

Wellington, now alone, rode on up the steep track out of Sorauren just as the French cavalry came in to the village at the other end. As he rode into the allied position he was at once recognised by the Portuguese covering force troops, who set up a cry of 'Douro, Douro!', which was soon joined by cries of 'Nosey!' and 'Our Arthur!' from the British. It was not long before these dreaded cries, as feared by the French as the cries of *'Vive l'Empereur'* were by the allies, drifted across to the assembling French divisions.

Wellington could now see that only half the French army had arrived. He said afterwards that if only Cole had sent back proper information at regular intervals then much trouble could have been avoided, the army concentrated, and the French stopped much sooner.[18] It is certain that with the French separated and attempting to deploy across his front, Wellington contemplated launching an attack himself;[19] and indeed an attack might well have succeeded for Soult utterly refused Clausel's appeals for a French attack. Instead, he took his luncheon and a *siesta* while Clausel, leaning against an oak tree, was literally beating his forehead with suppressed rage and muttering 'who could go to sleep at such a moment?'

All that was eventually attempted by the French on 27 July was, first, a reconnaissance by combat onto the Zabaldica, which was crushed by

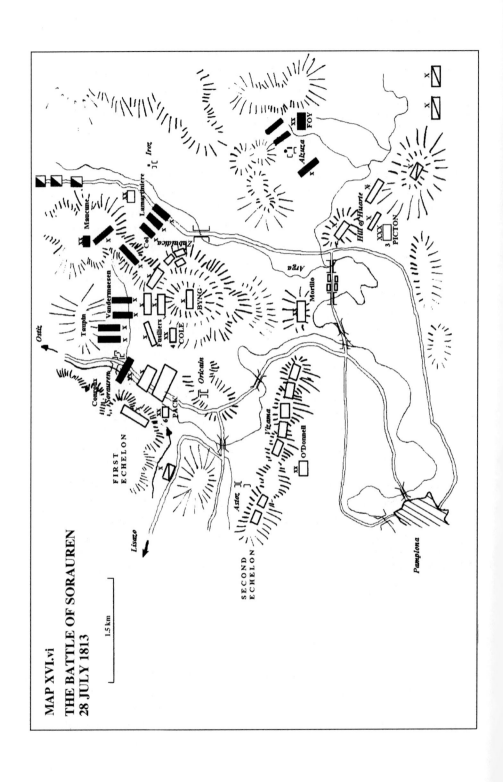

MAP XVI.vi
THE BATTLE OF SORAUREN
28 JULY 1813

1.5 km

the defending Spanish battalions, and then an advance by Foy's division against the right of the allied second echelon on the hill of Huarte. The two French regiments sent forward suddenly found themselves facing an entire Anglo-Portuguese division – and they retired in haste. As they went, a violent thunderstorm swept down from the mountains, effectively ending all activity for the day.

While these skirmishes had been in progress the opposing commanders had been refining their plans for the real contest next day. Soult, after conferring with his senior commanders decided that the division of Foy would hold its position to screen the Anglo-Portuguese division on the hill of Huarte – it was Picton's – while the remaining five divisions would mount a general attack on the allied first echelon position. The main effort would be on the right, where Clausel's three divisions would attack between Sorauren and the col, while Reille's remaining two divisions would attack the col itself and the Zabaldica position. Most of the army artillery and the cavalry was still jammed on the road and so very little was available to support the attack, nor did it seem likely that D'Erlon's corps would put in an appearance. Thus success depended on a sudden, all-out blow before allied reinforcements arrived.

Wellington meanwhile made very few changes to the initial dispositions, for his concern was to get away orders to hasten the arrival of 6th and 7th Divisions, the whole of Hill's corps, and the artillery. These he sent off at 4.00 pm:[20] 6th Division, followed by all the available artillery, was to march by country roads to the River Ulzama close by the left flank of the allied first echelon; it must at all costs arrive and not be delayed or distracted on the way. The 7th Division and the corps of Hill were to concentrate around Lisazo, eight miles north-west of Sorauren, on the night of 27/28 July, and should then follow 6th Division as soon as possible. All baggage should be sent to Yrurzun, presumably because Wellington had no wish to ease Soult's supply problems by offering him the chance of plunder. With these arrangements made, Wellington went to bed and slept well.

III. SORAUREN

The Battle of Sorauren was to last, in one way or another, for three days and was in the end to be perhaps more decisive than Vitoria, for by the end of the battle and the subsequent pursuit, the French army would almost cease to exist. The first day of the action, 28 July 1813, dawned fine and clear after the storms of the previous day, so that the allied covering troops had an excellent view of the whole French position. The morning was largely spent by Soult in bringing up and laying out his assault divisions, disentangling his cavalry from the traffic jams on the approach road, and bringing up four howitzers and some mountain guns which were the only French artillery employed that day.

On the allied side, 6th Division had marched early and fast, and reported itself in position by 10.00 am. Wellington ordered the division forward onto the left of the first echelon around Sorauren village, thus securing his left flank against what would obviously be the French main effort. Dalhousie and Hill, however, had been badly slowed by the storm in the mountains, and so did not appear at all on 28 July.

The 6th Division began to appear in line at noon, just before the time fixed by Soult for the main attack. The approach of the division caused Clausel considerable alarm, for he feared that he was about to be attacked in the flank; thus the first move of the battle was an advance by Conroux's division across the Ulzama against the approaching 6th Division at 12.30 pm. But this attack was lapped by allied fire on three sides and was quickly forced back into Sorauren village, at which point the battle paused. Not for long. At 1.00 pm the grand attack began. The French came up the steep slope, nearly 1,000 feet high, towards the allied position, in echelon of brigades, preceded by double their customary cloud of skirmishers. The timing of the attack was by no means simultaneous, indeed it rippled from west to east, but Clausel's initial momentum on the allied left drove in the covering troops and actually reached the summit in front of the Fusilier Brigade before being thrown back in disorder by allied volley-fire and counter attacks. In only one place did Clausel's corps manage to breach the allied line, between the Fusiliers and Campbell's Portuguese brigade. And although a penetration was achieved, the attacking troops had lost all cohesion: the severe climb, the devastating effects of volley fire, and the high casualties among the officers caused the disintegration of the French formations into groups of individuals.

By this time, Reille's attack on the main position was in progress across the col: it never reached the allied line but was everywhere thrown back with terrible losses. Seeing this, Wellington decided to put an end to Clausel's penetration and he ordered two British battalions to charge the French left flank, while Byng's brigade was brought up from the support position to block the penetration frontally. The counter-attack came in at the run, and such was the impetus that the French, although in superior numbers, were swept away down the hill in disarray.

Subsidiary attacks on the flanks fared no better. The division of Lamartinière had attacked the Spanish troops on the Zabaldica, supported by the available artillery. This attack was directed by Reille in person, but was a complete disaster: the Spanish met the oncoming troops with such a blast of fire that three assaults were all thrown back with loss. The 6th Division around Sorauren had meanwhile maintained contact with Conroux's division, and as the French fell back into the village the allies tried to follow up and take the place. In the fighting the divisional commander, Major-General Denis Pack, was badly wounded in the head and Wellington himself called off further moves.

But now the crisis of the day had passed. Fighting went on for another hour or more as French officers tried to reform battalions and commit them once more to hopeless assaults – all was futile. By 4.00 pm the day's fighting was over and the French retired to their original positions; there was no allied pursuit at this juncture, for Wellington was still expecting the arrival of additional formations without which the force ratios were not favourable for an allied attack: the French were beaten, to be sure, but not broken, and the ground was no more favourable for an allied attack than it had been for the French.

The first day of Sorauren had been a classic defeat of column by line, and a classic demonstration of Soult's tactical ineptitude. Wellington said of it that it was 'fair bludgeon work',[21] and certainly the casualty figures were high: 1,358 British and Germans; 1,102 Portuguese; 192 Spanish; and between 3,000 and 4,000 French.

While the battle of the 28th was being fought out at Sorauren, D'Erlon, Hill and Dalhousie were all trying to obey the orders of their superior commanders and achieve a union. Hill had received Wellington's orders by mid-afternoon on 27 July and had marched at once for Lisazo with two British and one Portuguese brigades of his own division; Silveira's division, which mustered only one brigade; and one British brigade of 7th Division. Dalhousie too had received his orders and marched with his remaining one British and one Portuguese brigade. But the thunderstorm which had struck the troops at Sorauren struck the marching troops even harder.

Hill's column had dropped Ashworth's Portuguese brigade with orders to delay D'Erlon's advance, and was on the roughest part of the road near the crest of the pass of Velate, when a positive deluge blew down, blotting out the light and practically sweeping the troops off their feet.

The column became so entangled with carts, guns, struggling horses and panicking mules, that in the darkness there was no chance of going any further; there was nothing for it but to sit down in the cold and dreary mud and wait for the dawn. When it came, the column struggled off again, and limped into Lisazo, where Hill collected the troops and sent word to Wellington that he had no chance of arriving at Sorauren before early on 30 July.

Dalhousie on the other hand had fared rather better. Marching all night, he left only one Portuguese light battalion to watch his rear, and reached Lisazo at noon on 28 July. Here he picked up his detached brigade from Hill and after six hours' rest, marched his division on to Sorauren, where it arrived that night – complete, after a remarkable feat of marching over two nights on extremely rough roads.

The storm which had befouled Hill's advance had also kept D'Erlon from discovering the move of the allies. When he did at last push forward reconnaissance early on 29 July, it was to find Hill gone. He began to move his corps forward at once, pushing the Portuguese delaying brigade in front of him, and collecting allied wounded and stragglers as he went. His light cavalry soon made contact with Hill's main column and also established communications with patrols from Soult's main army, but D'Erlon did not press Hill, as he greatly overestimated the strength of the allied corps. Nor did he follow Soult's orders of 23 July which had specifically instructed him to 'seek to reunite as soon as possible with the rest of the army'.

Dawn on 29 July had found Soult's main army in the same positions as on the previous evening, with D'Erlon's leading division still more than ten miles away at Lanz. The allied situation was far better, for 7th Division was close by and Hill's corps was now within reach: by the end of the day, Wellington was sure of having superior numbers. Soult too must have known this, and probably planned to withdraw after the battle of 28 July: certainly he sent off his guns and baggage towards Roncesvalles that night. Equally certainly, 29 July was the last day for which French rations were available.

But the Marshal's outlook changed dramatically when he received the news that D'Erlon was only half a day's march away: this caused him to plan a very risky stroke indeed, for given the nearness of D'Erlon and the concentration of allied forces around Pamplona, Soult felt justified in switching the line of march from Pamplona towards the objective of imposing his army between those of Wellington and Graham, forcing Graham to lift the siege of San Sebastian. D'Erlon would act as advanced guard of the army, attack Hill's corps, turn the allied left flank, and cut the main Pamplona–Tolosa road. The rest of the army would march to link up with D'Erlon, and here was the risk, for to do so the main army would have to march across the front of the allied army, at a distance of only half a mile.

This was a gross tactical error by any standards: having obliged Wellington with another Busaco on 28 July, Soult was about to present the opportunity for a second Salamanca on 30 July. Soult also calculated that despite the lack of rations, supply convoys were on their way – but again this was a risky assumption given the state of the roads and the sheer size of the supply problem. Foy thought that the plan was designed chiefly to save Soult's face with the Emperor,[22] rather than as an legitimate act of war, but the plan was laid.

D'Erlon was reinforced with a division of dragoons and ordered to attack Hill at Lisazo; Clausel was to leave Conroux's division in Sorauren to cover the move of his other two divisions, and Conroux would be relieved by Maucune who would cover the move of the rest of Reille's corps. The whole move was to be made in the dark during the early hours of 30 July and by dawn the army would, Soult expected, be clear of Sorauren. The result was not as expected – an extended series of battles over a frontage of ten miles ending in ignominious retreat.

The allies for the meanwhile remained on the defensive, but their strength was increased by two significant arrivals. The 7th Division came up and was placed in a concealed position on the left of 6th Division,[23] and with the 7th arrived much of the allied artillery, which was deployed with its parent divisions. Wellington also issued new instructions to Hill, accepting the delay in his arrival. Clearly Wellington had assessed Soult's options, and so directed Hill to establish a blocking position around Lisazo to prevent a French envelopment of the allied left, using his own division, and was to detach the brigade of Silveira's Portuguese division to support 7th Division. Orders were also sent to the Light Division and an additional cavalry brigade to march to an unspecified location near the Tolosa–Yrurzun road.

The French move began at midnight on 29/30 July when Clausel's rear two divisions moved off leaving their fires still burning. By dawn they were on the Sorauren–Ostiz road, waiting for Conroux's division to catch up, as it had not been relieved as planned. The relief was actually in progress at dawn, much later than Soult had wished, and there were two entire divisions in and around the village of Sorauren. Foy's division was following Maucune, but Lamartinière had not moved off.

In this vulnerable position, the French army suddenly received wholly unexpected salvoes of artillery fire, which brought ruin and confusion everywhere, for the allies were in a perfect position from which to punish Soult's error.

What had happened was that the night move had been overheard and the whole allied army stood-to an hour before dawn. Wellington himself was abroad early, and seeing the French movement, he had only to issue the order for a general attack, which he did. The 6th Division and Byng's brigade attacked Sorauren village, while the rest of 4th Division and the Spanish troops on Zabaldica went for Foy's column. Picton's division advanced towards Lamartinière's division up the main Roncesvalles road, intending to cut off the French withdrawal route northwards. Most of the French army was thus caught by artillery fire and infantry attack in march column, quite unable to fight back effectively:

> We had not been intending to fight, and suddenly we found ourselves massed under the fire of the enemy's cannon. We were forced to go up the mountain side to get out of range; we should have to retreat, and we already saw that we should be turned on both flanks.[24]

At least Foy's men could fall back, the troops in Sorauren could not. Surrounded on three sides by British and Portuguese troops, one brigade managed to get clear but the rest of the two divisions were practically exterminated: the total casualties out of 8,000 men amounted to 3,400 killed and wounded, and 1,700 prisoners.[25] The remnants rallied to Foy up on the hillside.

Further away, Clausel had halted his two divisions at the village of Olabe, halfway between Sorauren and Ostiz, and deployed a two-battalion flank guard above the Ulzama River on his left. But at 8.30 am 7th Division came up from its concealed position, pushed the flank guard aside, and began to close in on Clausel's column, pouring in a withering fire on the stationary column. Clausel could not stay still, nor could he go back to Sorauren: there was only one thing to do. Disengaging as best he could, he marched his column up the Olague road away from D'Erlon, and towards France.

While the initial assault was in progress, Wellington had time to issue fuller orders. Picton was ordered to continue his enveloping movement towards Roncesvalles; Cole was to continue to pin the enemy frontally by attacking between the rivers Ulzama and Arga; 6th Division,

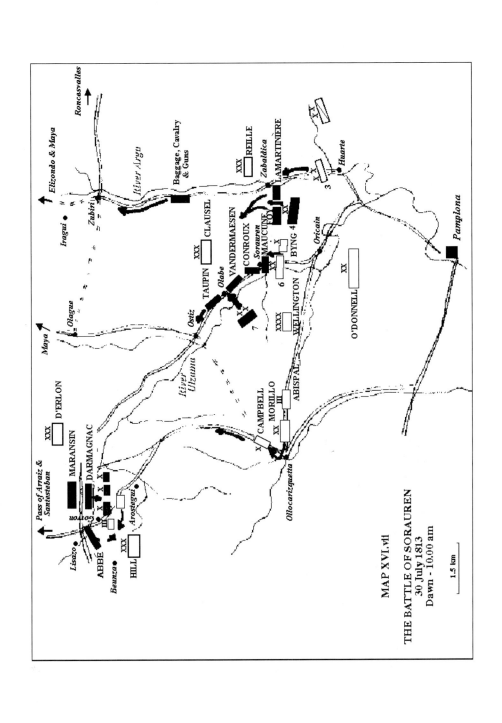

MAP XVI.vii

THE BATTLE OF SORAUREN
30 July 1813
Dawn - 10.00 am

1.5 km

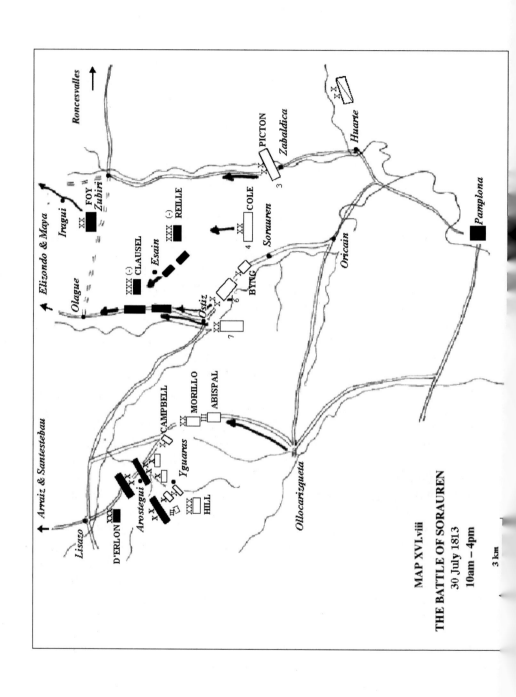

MAP XVI.viii

THE BATTLE OF SORAUREN

30 July 1813

10am – 4pm

3 km

O'Donnell's Spanish division and Byng's brigade were to pursue up the Olague road, co-operating with 7th Division which was to remain on the east bank of the Ulzama. The same orders were also sent to Hill, telling him to move towards Olague and Lanz if at all possible. Hill was also allotted Silveira's Portuguese division, Morillo's Spanish division, and the Spanish regiment of Abispal, detached from O'Donnell, to support him, although 7,000 of these supporting troops were located at Ollocarizqueta, ten miles to his rear, and although they marched towards Hill, they arrived late in the day.[26] These orders clearly mark an abandonment of the defensive, and the re-assumption of the offensive based on the belief that the French would now have to retire and that this would chiefly be through the pass of Maya.

As the allied attack developed, things went no better for Reille than for Clausel. Abandoning Maucune's division to its fate in Sorauren, he tried to form a position with the divisions of Foy and Lamartinière, but the approach of Picton threw him into a panic. Terrified at the prospect of being surrounded, Reille gave orders for the immediate withdrawal of the corps across country. The corps practically fled, so that by 1.00 pm Reille's men had escaped their pursuers and had halted near the village of Esain. After restoring some kind of order and gathering up a mass of stragglers, Reille headed off towards Olague, which he reached at dusk with a mere 6,000 men: for Foy's division had disappeared completely.

This division had in fact lost its way and marched by way of Iragui; from there, Foy continued his retirement the next day to Cambo in France, taking no further part in any fighting and losing 550 men. As the French fell back towards Olague, so the allies followed up both on the road and east of the River Ulzama, turning every blocking position which the French tried to occupy, so that by dusk, Clausel was at Olague where he was joined by Conroux's few survivors – a total force of perhaps 8,000 men out of his original 17,000 – and Reille's 6,000.

What of D'Erlon and Hill, and Soult himself for that matter? Soult was not actually present at Sorauren on 30 July for he had ridden to join D'Erlon very early, before dawn, and so missed the wreck of his army. Reports from deserters and prisoners told him that three allied divisions were to reinforce Hill, and Soult therefore wished to ensure that his planned advanced guard should crush Hill as soon as possible. Hill was, however, well aware of D'Erlon advancing towards him and had drawn up the 9,000 British and Portuguese troops available in line on a wooded ridge half a mile south of Lisazo, throwing out a covering force of light troops in front of his main position. D'Erlon, with 18,000 men available including the division of dragoons, planned to fix the allies with a frontal assault by Darmagnac's division, then envelop the allied left flank with two divisions attacking in echelon – Abbé leading, followed up by Maransin. With such a superiority, success seemed certain.

Darmagnac's attack began as planned, but instead of fixing the allies, the French tried to press home the attack and penetrate the position. With an unfavourable local force ratio, this frontal attack was repulsed. Abbé's first attack also went awry; advancing through the woods, the division missed its way and it too assaulted the allied position frontally. It too was repulsed. But seeing his error, Abbé sent another brigade further round the allied flank and this brigade would have succeeded completely but for the committal of Hill's reserve brigade, which threw back the attack and gained enough time for the whole allied division to withdraw.

This movement was conducted very steadily across a valley and through a stream, closely pressed by the French, until the allies came to a halt on a new line just in front of the village of Yguras where yet another frontal assault by Darmagnac's division was thrown back. It was now 4.00 pm and D'Erlon was forming up his corps for a further attempt when at the critical moment, the Portuguese and Spanish troops from Ollocarizqueta marched up: this was enough to cause D'Erlon to break off the action for the day.

Certainly, he had forced the allies back, and gained a local tactical success, but he had not beaten them as Soult intended that he should have done – but with a force ratio of only 2:1, it is unlikely that he could have done more than he did. And what he had done counted for nothing, since Soult's main army was a disorganised wreck camping miserably and without rations around Olague. Allied battle losses on the 30th totalled 1,083 to the French 4,000.

This unpleasant truth dawned on Soult as he rode towards Olague. In effect, D'Erlon's corps was his only effective combat force. Food and ammunition were running low, and morale was in tatters. There was nothing for it but to abandon the grand plans, and retreat as fast as possible back into France, using D'Erlon's corps not as advanced guard, but rearguard. The quickest route for the shattered main body was from Olague to Elizondo and Maya – the route which Wellington had surmised – but instead of taking this course, Soult's orders called for D'Erlon to hold his position and for the rest of the army to march across country to Lisazo, and from thence to the pass of Arraiz and Santesteban. This was another very risky move, but it clearly aimed to rely on the steadiness of D'Erlon's men, and to give the slip to what would doubtless be a merciless allied pursuit.

The three-day battle around Sorauren is often compared with Busaco (1810), but in fact it might more usefully be compared with Vitoria. Soult had certainly aimed to inflict on the allies the sort of crushing defeat which they had handed to Joseph in June, but there was no chance that Soult, with his bull-headed forcing of the passes, loss of security, and logistic fragility could hope to emulate the speed, security and brilliance of Wellington's flank march to Vitoria.

Nor could Soult match Wellington's mastery of the tactical battle. In both cases the defenders had been drawn up in echelon on ground suitable for the defence, although Joseph had had a secure fortress at his rear, while the allies were forced to mask Pamplona and its hostile garrison; but the two attack plans again demonstrate that the jibes at Soult were well deserved: Soult's clumsy, brutal, frontal attack with unfavourable force ratios cannot stand comparison with Wellington's imaginative enveloping attack. But both battles had one thing in common: at the end of the fighting, the French army was in full retreat towards the mountains. This time, the allies had no intention of letting them slip away unhindered.

IV. THE PURSUIT TO ECHALAR

At 1.00 am on 31 July the tired remnants of Clausel's and Reille's shattered corps marched off as best they could, leaving a trail of stragglers as they went. D'Erlon hung on until daybreak, then sent the divisions of Darmagnac and Maransin off, leaving Abbé's division on the high ground north of Lisazo as rearguard. Surprising as it may seem, Soult's risky plan appeared to be paying off, for Wellington was still working on the assumption that the French line of retreat would be through Elizondo. His orders were issued accordingly.[27] Picton was to continue his pursuit on the Roncesvalles road; Pakenham was to take 6th Division and Campbell's Portuguese brigade from Olague across country to co-operate and if necessary link up. Thus a corps was effectively committed to a blow in the air.

The main effort of the pursuit would be commanded by Wellington

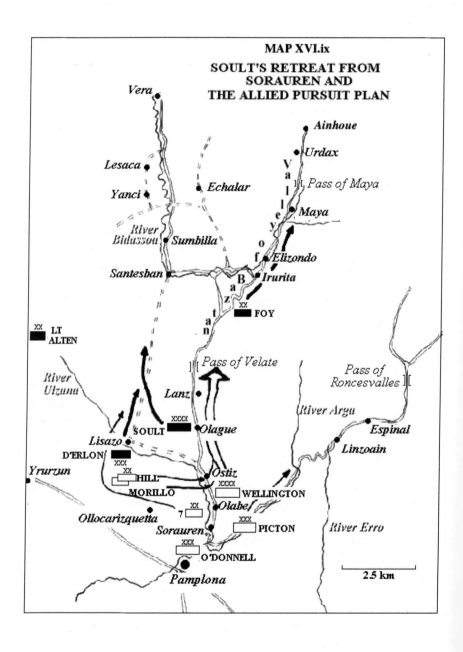

MAP XVI.ix

**SOULT'S RETREAT FROM
SORAUREN AND
THE ALLIED PURSUIT PLAN**

himself, following the direct route through Maya, with Hill's 2nd Division, Cole's 4th Division, the remainder of Silveira's Portuguese division, the Spanish division of Morillo, and the regiment of Abispal. Only Dalhousie with 7th Division was to follow the route through the pass of Arraiz, and this not to pursue, but as a possible outflanking movement to support the main effort.

Separate orders were also sent to Alten's Light Division to march back to Zubieta,[28] ready to co-operate with 7th Division if necessary. Thus with these orders, well over half the available allied troops were dispatched down routes on which there was no enemy at all.

By the end of the day, this situation had become clearer. Picton soon found that the enemy on the Roncesvalles road was really just a mass of 4,000 stragglers which had turned towards the pass of Aldudes the night before. Cole on the Maya road found that Foy was a full day ahead and could not be caught and Wellington, pressing on to Irurita, discovered that at most, 1,000 French troops had passed through. On the other hand, news came in that showed the French main body to have made for the pass of Arraiz, with Hill and Dalhousie after them. This was not a large enough force to press the enemy heavily, especially since 2nd Division was very weak after the hard fighting over the preceding days, nor was the position of the Light Division known accurately – it could be well placed to deliver a flank attack.

It had in fact taken Hill some time to discover that the whole French army was passing in front of him, for Abbé's division maintained an effective blocking position. But when he did discover the real situation, and with the news of the smashing victory over the main French army at Sorauren the previous day, he decided to attack at once despite the poor condition of his division, for he realised that the French could not stand for long.

The attack began at 10.00 am on the 31st, by which time, fortunately, 7th Division was close by. This delay was, however, invaluable to Soult, whose disorganised army was badly jammed on the roads and quite unable to fight: the narrow defiles were blocked with baggage, mules and horses, and once Hill's attack was heard, Reille's infantry made matters worse by trying to force a way through. It was as well that D'Erlon's rearguard under Abbé was staunch: it gave ground slowly and repelled two allied attacks with dreadful losses, made worse when General Stewart insisted on mounting needless frontal attacks. By the time that 7th Division was fully up, it was late in the afternoon and as at Roncesvalles, a dense fog came down which stopped the fighting and allowed the French to move off. Stewart's brigade ended the day with an effective strength of 800 men.

Hill now committed a serious blunder. Having identified the enemy, he thought it necessary to stick to the letter of his orders rather than fulfil Wellington's *intention* of pursuit in a changed tactical situation. He therefore marched his division towards Maya, leaving only 7th Division to follow Soult. Wellington himself, despite the growing indications of the real situation, made only minor changes to his original orders: during the afternoon he sent further orders to the Light Division to intercept Soult's probable withdrawal route through Santesteban[29] and Sumbilla, and that evening he ordered 4th Division to link up with the 7th.

Why was this? In fact, having allocated the three divisions to the direct pursuit of Soult, Wellington had a much more ambitious scheme in mind, aimed at the encirclement and complete destruction of Soult's army. Byng's brigade was ordered to march from Elizondo to Maya, and then to occupy Urdax on the French side of the mountains; Hill at Irurita was then to follow up, pass through Byng, and press on as far as Ainhoue on the Nivelle river, supported by Silveira and 6th Division.[30] Thus a large body of allied troops would envelop the French, while the three pursuing divisions fixed them frontally. Finally, Graham was ordered to be ready to co-operate in this move by crossing the Bidassoa and engaging the French reserve division with his and Giron's whole force.[31]

As we shall see, this daring scheme was not put into effect. But even with just the pursuing forces to deal with, Soult was feeling hard pressed. He was aware of allied forces behind and around him, but he was unsure of any detailed dispositions as he had no cavalry or reconnaissance forces to speak of; and there was no news of any activity by his own reserve division on the Bidassoa facing Graham's corps. In his own estimation, he faced the definite possibility of annihilation if he did not get out of the narrow passes around Santesteban as soon as possible.

Because of the continued misdirection of the allied pursuit, the opportunity to escape completely presented itself on the night of 31 July/1 August and the method would be a march along the gorge of the Bidassoa River. As on the previous day, the march began early, at 2.30 am, with Reille's infantry leading, then the entire cavalry and baggage with the remains of Clausel's infantry, and finally D'Erlon's corps as rearguard once more. On this line of march, the only allied troops capable of moving to block the route were Longa's Spanish division on

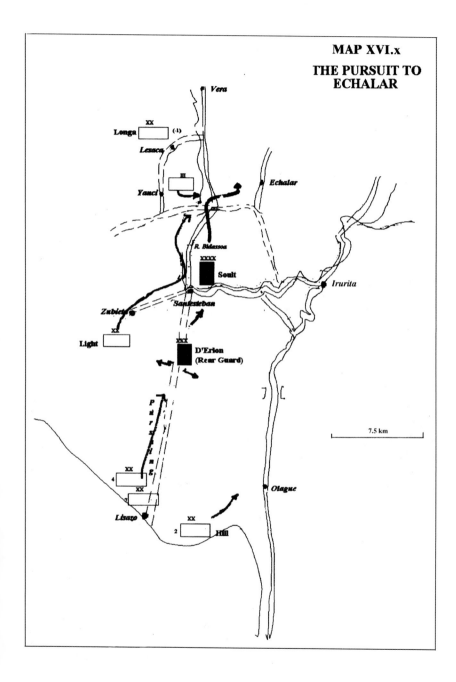

the heights of Vera, with a detached brigade at Lesaca and a regiment at Yanci.

The allied pursuit too began early on 1 August and by 7.00 am 4th Division had marched across and was already engaging the French rearguard, followed by 7th Division. The French infantry, marching on the slopes around the road to avoid the baggage were rapidly enveloped by the allied infantry which, bypassing the rearguard, gained the ridges above the centre of the column. After an hour of confused fighting around Sumbilla, the whole of Clausel's command was scattered in disorderly flight across the hills towards Echalar.

At the head of the French column too there were troubles. Slow but steady progress was made until late morning when the column arrived at the bridge of Yanci, where Longa's men held the bridge and the village. The French line of march was not across the bridge, but turned eastwards by it towards Echalar. When Reille's leading battalion reached the cross roads by Yanci bridge it was fired on by the Spanish troops there, which caused considerable confusion and a complete stoppage of the whole column. Reille's leading troops assaulted the Spanish position, but the firing was misinterpreted further back down the column as an allied attack: dragoons panicked and galloped off down the road, getting hopelessly mixed up with the baggage and infantry.

It took Reille himself to sort out the turmoil and get the column moving again but the Spanish, having been forced off the bridge once, returned and continued firing on the passing French. Soon the two companies on the bridge were reinforced by the rest of their regiment, which mounted a vigorous attack on the French which once again caused complete anarchy down the column as far back as Sumbilla, where the combat was in progress with 4th Division. At last a whole French brigade was committed, which pushed the Spanish back after a battle in which the unsupported Spanish troops acquitted themselves like heroes.

It seemed that, although practically a mob, the French would now get away across the mountains, for by late afternoon, Darmagnac's division, the last of D'Erlon's rearguard, had reached Yanci. But suddenly a furious burst of firing broke out as a swarm of green-jacketed skirmishers rushed towards the French: it was the Anglo-Portuguese Light Division.

After three days of march and counter-march, hearing always the sound of distant firing, the Light Division had received Wellington's

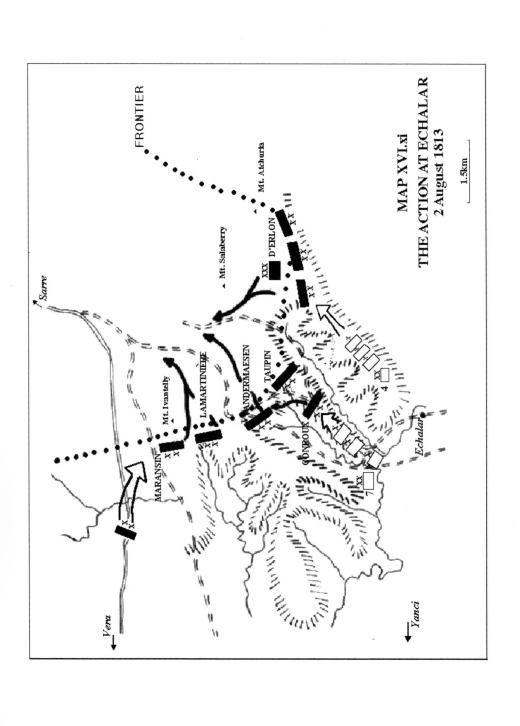

MAP XVI.xi
THE ACTION AT ECHALAR
2 August 1813

1.5km

FRONTIER

Mt. Atchurla

D'ERLON

Mt. Salaberry

↑ Sarre

Mt. Ivantelly

LAMARTINIERE

VANDERMAESEN

TAUPIN

MARANSIN

GONROUK

Echalar

↑ Vera

↓ Yanci

order to intercept Soult. The order came in to Major-General Alten at Leyza in the hours before dawn on 1 August. He was fully 15 miles from Yanci along heartbreaking roads, the division was already tired and short of food, and the weather was blazing hot August sunshine. Even so, the division marched at dawn. At 4.00 pm it reached Sumbilla and saw the enemy rearguard engaged with 4th Division. Alten decided to push on the remaining seven miles to Yanci, but his troops were completely blown. After a short rest, one brigade pressed on, and so came to Yanci in time, where till dark, the riflemen poured a dreadful fire into the retreating French until 4th Division came up. As a result, the rearguard division lost 500 killed and 1,000 surrendered, and the rest of Darmagnac's troops had scattered over the mountains in their attempts to escape. But there was no question of further pursuit: the exhausted men of the 4th and Light Divisions slept where they dropped.

That night, Soult gathered up the wreckage of his army on the mountain slopes behind the village of Echalar, along the frontier. With the allies so close, he could not risk being caught in march column and had no option but to turn at bay and adopt a defensive position. He placed the remains of Clausel's divisions in his centre astride the road from Echalar, with Reille's command extending his line westwards, while D'Erlon's three divisions held the eastern part of the line. Altogether, he had only about 25,000 tired, hungry and dispirited men on his position: the remainder were killed, wounded, or in allied hands – or else were scattered far and wide across the countryside.

Wellington himself had come across to take command of the operation at Echalar, where he now mustered only 12,000 men in three divisions. Wellington decided to assault the formidable French position, some 1,500 feet high and against odds of two-to-one, which under normal circumstances would have been suicidal. But the allied troops were in tremendous spirits, despite their tired condition, and all were sure that the French were as good as beaten before fighting began. Wellington's plan was that 4th and 7th Divisions would fix the French by frontal attack while the Light Division made a long flank march through Vera, to envelop the right flank.

The 4th Division began its attack early next morning, 2 August, but its move was slowed by massive amounts of discarded French baggage in front of the position,[32] and so it was 7th Division marching to the east which came up to the French first. Dalhousie saw straight away that the enemy was completely unprepared for an attack – soldiers were sleeping, or cleaning weapons, or in the case of a lucky few, cooking breakfast – and so rather than wait for his whole division to come up, he launched the leading brigade at once. As it happened, this was under Barnes, whose charge had saved the day at Maya. Once again the 1,500-strong brigade charged and although it suffered 300 casualties in a few minutes as it closed with the French, Conroux's estimated 3,000 troops would not stand. As the British came on, the French turned and ran, taking Vandermaesen's division which was in support of them.

As they ran, 4th Division began to press in on D'Erlon's wing and almost simultaneously, the Light Division appeared on the other flank – with the same effect. With both his flanks disintegrating, Soult could only order a retirement; the army broke contact as best it could and fell back on Ainhoue.

So the army was back once more on French territory. Its condition was nothing short of appalling – exhausted after nine days' hard marching, hungry, and sadly depleted, its morale was now broken by defeat. Soult wrote to Paris that

> I deceived myself . . . that the troops had their morale intact and would do their duty. I mistook the sentiment of shame for their recent disaster [i.e. Vitoria] for that of steadfastness. When tested, they started with one furious rush, but showed no power of resistance . . . since I first entered the Service I have seen nothing like them . . . The spirit of these troops must be terribly broken . . .[33]

Thus did Soult shift the blame for defeat from himself to his troops. One can only speculate on what would have happened if Wellington had pressed ahead with his plan for an encirclement, for his army would certainly have destroyed Soult's remaining force. But Wellington had withheld the orders at the last moment, and the reason he did so is clear from his correspondence:[34] the Congress of Prague was still in session and however tempting, there would be no allied invasion of France until it was certain that war had been resumed in central Europe.

So the allies settled down once more to the sieges and in the Pyrenees after an interval of six days fighting which had cost them 7,096 casualties and the French almost 13,000 (including 3,000 prisoners and virtually *one third* of their infantry officers), and which had been, as Wellington himself remarked of it, ' . . . rather alarming, certainly, and it was a close run thing'.[35]

NOTES

1. *Dispatches*, x, p.563.
2. Ibid. p.512.
3. Ibid. p.525.
4. Browne, p.226.
5. *Dispatches*, x, p.566.
6. *Sup. Dispatches*, viii, pp.120–1.
7. Ibid. p.121.
8. Ibid. pp.124–5.
9. Ibid. p.113.
10. Ibid. p.114.
11. Recollections of Sir George L'Estrange, cited in Harman, *Roncesvalles*, p.26.
12. Captain George Tovey 'The Charge of a Company of the XX Regiment at Roncesvalles' in *United Service Journal* (Nov. 1839) cited in Harman, *Roncesvalles*, p.27.
13. *Sup. Dispatches*, viii, p.127.
14. *Dispatches*, x, p.596.
15. *Sup. Dispatches*, viii, p.259.
16. *Lettres*, No. 3.
17. *Sup. Dispatches*, viii, pp.122, 259–60.
18. Larpent, p.242.
19. Ibid. p.243; Oman, vi, p.663.
20. *Sup. Dispatches*, viii, p.123.
21. Longford, p.330.
22. Foy, p.219.
23. *Sup. Dispatches*, viii, p.151.
24. Foy, p.221.
25. An account is in Browne, pp.229 –31.
26. *Sup. Dispatches*, viii, pp.154–5.
27. Ibid. pp.152–3.
28. Ibid. p.154.
29. *Dispatches*, x, p.574.
30. *Sup. Dispatches*, viii, p.164.
31. *Dispatches*, x, p.574.
32. See Larpent, p.214 for a description.
33. Soult to Clarke, 2 and 6 Aug. 1813, cited in Oman, vi, p.736–7.
34. *Dispatches*, x, pp.591 and 611.
35. Larpent, p.304.

Chapter XVII

News from Prague

I. SIEGE WARFARE

W ELLINGTON'S CAUTON IS understandable, for although it was only
ten days after Echalar that the armistice of Pleiswitz was ended,
the vagaries of communication meant that it was not until 3 September
that word came that the armies of Austria now marched alongside the
allies. As far as Wellington was concerned, his was the only allied army
actively engaged against the French – and now was not the time to
strike, for the situation was no different from that which had made him
hold back before Soult's attack. And besides, an invasion of France
would only succeed if mounted from several directions simultaneously.

Now was the time to repair the damage to the armies, and prepare.
The strength of the allied armies in the northern Spanish theatre was
now 59,500 British, German and Portuguese[1] troops, and 25,000
Spanish. Of these, Graham's corps, consisting of 1st Anglo-Hanoverian,
5th Anglo-Portuguese, and Longa's Spanish divisions, still besieged San
Sebastian, and with Giron's Spanish corps of three divisions it also held
the line of the lower Bidassoa. O'Donnell's reserve corps and Morillo's
division blockaded Pamplona, while the rest of the Anglo-Portuguese
divisions held the frontier. The 2nd Division, much reduced during the
recent fighting, was posted at Roncesvalles where no activity was
expected, supported by Silveira's Portuguese division. The 6th Division
held Maya, supported by 3rd Division at Elizondo; the Light Division
held the heights of Santa Barbara; and 7th Division was posted between
the 6th and the Light; 4th Division was held back in support of these
three divisions.

The main effort of this defensive posture was placed on the coast, in
order to cover the siege of San Sebastian, and here the bulk of reinforcements were sent as they came in. These included the 1st British Guards

Brigade from Oporto, a new infantry brigade from England and Gibraltar, and some 800 individual reinforcements. Longa's Spanish division was also strengthened with the addition of three battalions from O'Donnell's corps. As well as these forces, the Anglo-Sicilian Army was still very much in being in Catalonia, for Wellington remained concerned that Suchet would march his 30,000 available troops across to join Soult. He need not have worried, for Suchet valued his independence too highly; nor would Napoleon contemplate leaving the approach into south-east France unguarded. But advice and guidance to Bentinck nevertheless took up much of Wellington's time.

As well as rebuilding the strength of the army, in which he was remarkably successful, for by mid-August the armies were only 1,500 men short of their strength in July, Wellington had to deal with continuing difficulties with the Spanish alliance. The dispute of June over the usurpation of the Generalissimo's powers of appointment and dismissal was now resolved: Wellington agreed that Castaños would not be replaced, and that Giron would be succeeded by General Don Manuel Freire – who was to prove a fortunate choice. Giron was moved to the command of the Andalusian reserve corps in place of O'Donnell: ostensibly, O'Donnell had applied for sick leave, but in reality he had retired to nurse his wounded pride. O'Donnell had suggested the creation of a unified corps including all Spanish troops in the allied army, under his command. In the light of his experiences since 1808, Wellington saw no reason to disturb the present highly satisfactory arrangement, and said so. O'Donnell departed. Concerns remained, however, over the state of Spanish formations, ill paid and supplied by their own government, and maintained with rations and ammunition which should have gone to British and Portuguese troops.

But Wellington's main concern lay with the two sieges. That of Pamplona was a blockade rather than a siege, being conducted by the 10,000 men of Giron's reserve corps. This corps consisted of two Andalusian infantry divisions, which were subsequently replaced by a division from Del Parque's 3rd Army and by Carlos d'España's Castilian division, and a corps cavalry regiment. It was not the 10,000 men actually tied up by the blockade that really mattered, it was the need to replace Hill's men at Roncesvalles with Spaniards in order to release the Anglo-Portuguese formation for service on the Bidassoa. But there was little chance of an early end to the blockade, for the Spaniards had no heavy siege artillery and could only hope to starve the garrison out.

The governor of Pamplona, General Cassan, had no intention of

FIG. XVII.i
ALLIED COMMAND STRUCTURE IN SPAIN
SEPTEMBER 1813

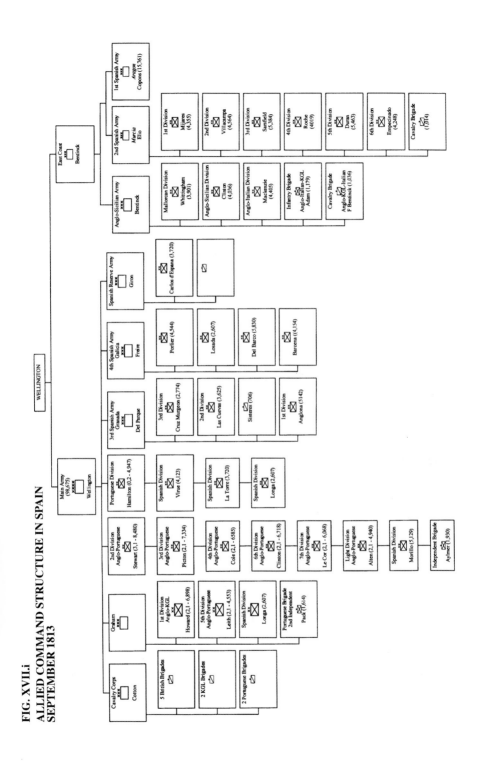

giving in without a fight. Frequent sorties were made by the 3,000-strong garrison into the surrounding agricultural land to gather food, and seeing the preparations for the Battle of Sorauren on 27 July Cassan attempted a serious sortie which was only thwarted by the vigilance of the besiegers. For the next two days, the garrison was held in readiness to sally out and fall on the defeated allies, but to no avail, and it says much for Cassan's strength of character that he kept his men going for another three months after this disheartening anti-climax.

By the end of September the garrison was on half rations, and food in the surrounding fields had disappeared; all the horses were gradually killed and eaten, then the dogs, cats, and rats. by mid-October, desertion was rife, and on 24 October Cassan began surrender negotiations. On 31 October the ragged skeletons of the garrison marched out into captivity.

The siege of San Sebastian had meanwhile begun again in earnest with the arrival from England of 28 new guns, 62,000 round shot, and 7,500 barrels of powder. Although it had been intended to mount a new attack from the landward side, the engineers considered that the principal attack again be mounted across the estuary, to which Wellington agreed. New batteries were thrown up, supplemented by mortars and howitzers to fire on troops behind cover, although Wellington forbade a general bombardment of the town, as it was principally occupied by Spanish civilians.[2]

The bombardment of the defences began again at 9.00 am on 26 August and the fire was overpowering, not only damaging the walls but also silencing the French guns so that there was almost no effective counter-battery fire. After four days pounding, a major breach of 300 yards had been made in the south-east wall, and a smaller breach further north. An assault could not long be delayed.

General Oswald, commanding 5th Division, held the view that an assault across the estuary would only repeat the slaughter of 25 July and Wellington therefore proposed to call for volunteers from 1st, 4th and Light Divisions to storm the place.[3] A total of 750 men came forward, but Oswald was so infuriated at the insult that he swore that they would be nothing but supports to his own division, which would take the place. Unhappily, Oswald was due for relief, and his replacement, Sir James Leith, actually arrived only two days before the assault: Oswald with great selflessness stayed on as honourary ADC to Leith to assist him in his planning. This plan called for an assault by Major-General Frederick Robinson's British brigade of 5th Division, supported by the 750 volunteers, two Portuguese brigades, and 5th *Caçadores* to act as sharpshooters. The assault would be mounted in two columns on the main breach, with a Portuguese column assaulting the smaller breach, and the time was fixed for 11.00 am on 31 August – low tide was at noon. Thus the assault was in broad daylight, and was watched as if it was a demonstration by an immense crowd of military and civilian onlookers.

Inside the town, the garrison was down to a strength of 2,500, but Rey's men had managed to maintain the sheer drop from the lip of the breach by clearing away all rubble, and had strengthened their new stone inner wall. Rey had also kept several guns masked to cover the breach, and had placed a large mine actually under the breach, meaning to blow up the assault. Fortunately, this failed to go off as the fuze had been disrupted by the bombardment. The morning of the assault was one of heat and haze.

All the allied batteries kept up their fire until 10.55 am when the storming columns emerged from the trenches at a run. The French response was immediate: accurate musketry and artillery fire, so that just as on 25 July the assault troops reached the lip of the breach and stopped, only to be shot down. The casualties were heavy, and included Lieutenant-Colonel Sir Richard Fletcher the chief engineer, who was killed, General Oswald, who was wounded, and General Leith who was blown from his horse.

By 11.35 am the assault was well and truly stalled, but the Portuguese put in their attack on the lesser breach. They too were halted. General Graham realised that the whole assault was about to fail and only drastic action would save the day. He therefore ordered all batteries to fire over the heads of the assaulting troops, which they did for ten minutes with great effect, for the defences were packed with French soldiers and the slaughter was terrific. When the fire lifted again, the assault brigade was able to gain entry to the town; by 1.00 pm the allies were in San Sebastian in strength.

The defenders resisted fiercely, and counter-attacked, but were gradually bayoneted back; by 1.35 pm, prisoners were being brought out, and after another hour, the allies had cleared the town, assisted by an explosion in the French main magazine which blew up just as the allied reserve brigade was committed. About 1,300 men of the garrison escaped with General Rey into the old castle, taking with them 450 wounded and 350 allied prisoners; but by this time, the general disorganisation of the assault, heavy casualties among the officers, and a sudden heavy storm put an end to the fighting – and started the sack of the town.

All the plunder, drunkenness, rape and destruction of Badajoz and Rodrigo were repeated, although the extent was deliberately overstated by the Spanish authorities, and when a raging fire broke out, which destroyed most of the town, Wellington was accused of having started it deliberately, out of commercial jealousy.

The old castle held out for another nine days. For three days, allied mortars and howitzers pounded the rock, destroying all the buildings and causing heavy casualties. On 3 September Rey was offered surrender terms, but refused, so to bring him to his senses, Wellington ordered heavy guns to be brought up. On 8 September, 61 guns, howitzers and mortars opened up: after two hours, Rey hoisted the white flag and the garrison marched out into captivity.

So ended the siege, which had not been a happy episode at all for the allies. Two attempts had been made, the 10,000-civilian population had lost their homes, and the casualties had been severe, with the unusually high proportion of one-third dead to two-thirds wounded. Most authorities agree with Jones's assessment in his *Peninsular Sieges*:

> The operations against San Sebastian afford a most impressive lesson on the use of science and rules in a siege. The effort made to overcome and trample on these restrictions caused an easy and certain operation of twenty days to extend to sixty, and cost the besiegers a loss of 3,500 officers and men.

II. THE HEIGHTS OF SAN MARCIAL

Even before the assault on San Sebastian had begun, the sound of gunfire could be heard from the lower Bidassoa, heralding the start of Soult's final attempt to relieve the fortress: it was an attempt which Wellington had expected. Soult was in daily touch with the garrison, but was unable to make any move earlier in August because of the state of the army after the battles in the Pyrenees. However, the lack of an allied pursuit into France gave him four weeks of invaluable time. He recovered 8,000 stragglers, brought in drafts of conscripts, and filled up his depleted corps from the reserve division. So by late August he had a force of 53,000 men and 97 guns, organised in nine French infantry divisions (two virtually reformed), two cavalry divisions, and Villatte's reserve division – which now contained the old

Royal Guards, and the three foreign brigades of Spanish, Italian and German troops.

Soult knew that the allied army was well dispersed along the frontier, with the bulk of the British divisions in the centre and right of the line, beyond Vera. He was coming under increasing pressure from Paris to assist Rey, whose repulse of the allies had gained Napoleon's admiration, and to guarantee the integrity of French territory. This rather forced his hand: the most direct approach to San Sebastian, across the lower Bidassoa, involved negotiating some very rough country and dealing with three lines of allied defences; but on the other hand the defenders were only Spanish troops, the fortress lay only one day's march from the frontier, and the river was fordable in several places. Moreover in 1794, a French army had successfully forced the Bidassoa in this area, and it was this operation which Soult intended to repeat.

His plan called for a direct, frontal attack by the corps of Reille with the three divisions of Villatte, Maucune and Lamartinière, across the fords of the Bidassoa to pin the Spanish Galician corps on the heights of San Marcial between the river and the town of Irun. The corps of Clausel would represent the main effort of the attack, with the four divisions of Vandermaesen, Taupin, Maransin and Darmagnac crossing the river below Vera to smash Longa's Spanish division, and then envelop the Galicians who would be forced to retire or be annihilated.

To protect this enveloping movement from the British and Portuguese troops at Maya, a strong flank guard formed by the corps of D'Erlon, with the divisions of Conroux and Abbé, would be placed on the line from Sarre to Ainhoue, Urdax and Espellette. Foy's division had originally also been part of this corps, but the day before the attack it was removed and held with the cavalry in army reserve behind the corps of Reille.

The drawbacks of the plan were serious: a direct attack was to be mounted on a well defended and difficult piece of terrain across a river obstacle by columns which were so well separated that communication between them would be tenuous to say the least. The force ratios were unfavourable, and the need for a flank guard, as well as the positioning of Foy's division on the right of the attack, meant that the main effort was by no means strong enough to be certain of making a breakthrough.

Unfortunately for Soult, the movements of his army westward during August had been discovered by the allies, and Wellington had guessed

Soult's intention. Wellington wrote to his division and corps commanders that

> The enemy appears to have assembled a very considerable force towards Irun, opposite our left, and also to have added something to their strength near Vera . . . All rumours from them agree that they mean to make an attempt for the relief of San Sebastian.[4]

Wellington had divined both the pinning attack and the main effort, and issued orders accordingly. The attack on San Marcial would be held by Freire's Galicians and Longa's Cantabrians, supported by the Anglo-German 1st Division and the two British brigades of 4th Division. These were all seasoned troops, who were completely confident of their ability to defeat the French. On Longa's right came a long stretch of unfordable river, then a series of four fords between Enderlaza and Lesaca. These fords were covered by the Light Division, supported by the Portuguese brigade of 4th Division and a British brigade from 7th Division. On the extreme right, 6th and 7th Divisions, supported by a division from Giron's reserve corps and 3rd Division, were ordered to make a demonstration as if to attack D'Erlon's corps.

Soult had originally intended to attack on 30 August but the non-arrival of his pontoon bridging caused a delay of one day, during which the allies were able to observe the large masses of French troops. Even so, the heat haze of 31 August enabled the corps of Reille to move down to the river and cross it unobserved, and to place a battery of 36 guns south of Hendaye to support the attack. Thus it was only when the Spanish piquets were driven in west of the Bidassoa at 6.00 am that the alarm was raised. However while the haze concealed the actual crossing, it prevented the French from forming up and pressing on over the rough ground of San Marcial and so the allied troops were able to stand-to.

By 9.00 am, Reille had two divisions across the river, and Soult urged him to press on without waiting for Villatte or Foy to cross. Reille therefore ordered Lamartinière to assault the centre of the heights, and Maucune to assault the western end. The two divisions climbed the hill in column, just as at Sorauren. But Freire had kept his troops in mixed order two-thirds of the way up the slope with a covering force of light troops deployed well forward. When the French, disordered and tired by the stiff climb, approached the line the Spanish gave a volley and charged. This sudden attack rolled the French columns downhill so fast that they did not stop until the river was reached once more, while the Spaniards immediately reformed and reoccupied their position.

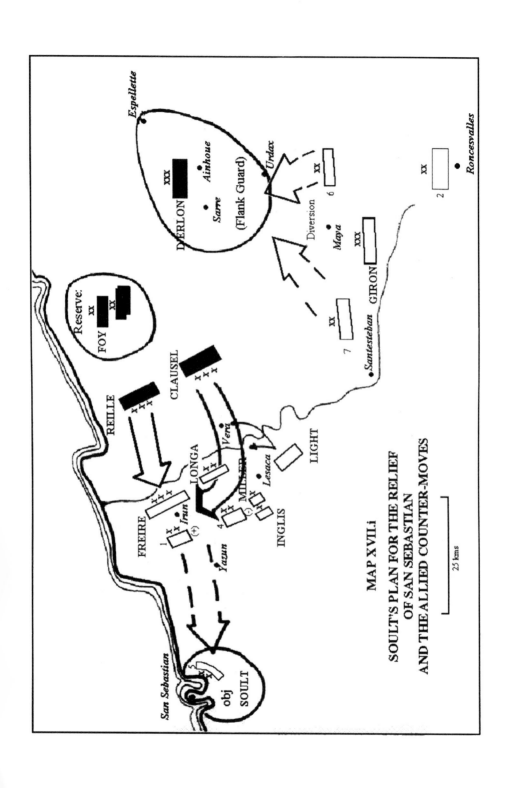

MAP XVII.i

SOULT'S PLAN FOR THE RELIEF
OF SAN SEBASTIAN
AND THE ALLIED COUNTER-MOVES

25 kms

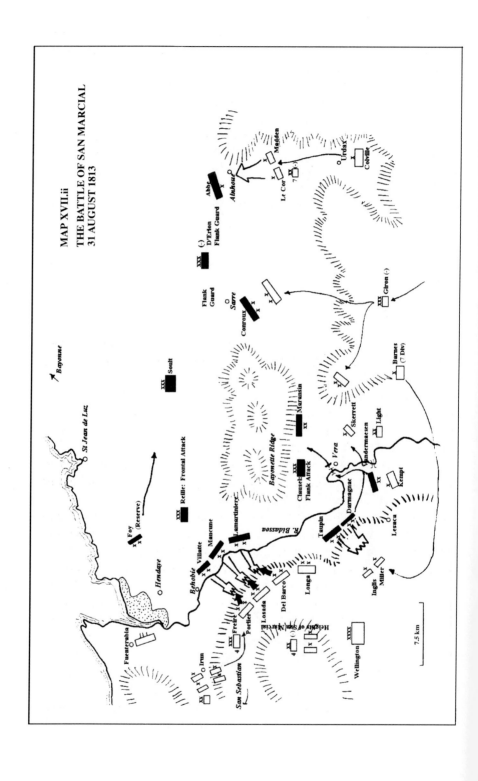

MAP XVII.ii
THE BATTLE OF SAN MARCIAL
31 AUGUST 1813

At 11.00 am Villatte's division had crossed the river and Reille prepared to attack again, this time with three divisions in line: Villatte on the right, Maucune in the centre, and Lamartinière on the left. As the French came on, the Spaniards again repeated their tactic, and again rolled back Maucune and Lamartinière without difficulty. Villatte's men, however, made a more determined attack and gained the summit opposite the weakest of the three Spanish divisions. Wellington, who was watching, ordered up a British brigade from Irun to support the Spaniards but refused to commit a whole division as Freire asked, as he could see that the French penetration was only local. He was quite right: Villatte's men, seeing that they were unsupported, gave way to the next Spanish counter-attack and fled. One watcher wrote

> This was the only time I ever saw the Spanish Army behave like Soldiers. The 31st August is one of their proudest days . . . their conduct in repelling the . . . attacks of the enemy had been admirable . . . the Spanish were not assisted, and repulsed the enemy alone.[5]

This time, the French fled so hard that they did not stop at the river, broke the pontoon bridges by overcrowding them, and could not be rallied for several hours. They left behind 2,500 dead and wounded, and a victorious Spanish corps. It is said that Wellington replied to Freire's request for a full division in support: 'If I sent you British troops, it would be said they had won the battle. But as the French are already retiring, you may as well win it by yourselves.'[6]

Any further French moves here were prevented by the same storm which swept over San Sebastian, and by disquieting news from further east which required the move of Foy's reserves.

Clausel's attack upstream had been less costly, but no more successful than Reille's. Again concealed by the haze, three divisions forded the river, while Maransin's remained on the French bank. Having crossed, Vandermaesen's division was also dropped off as a flank guard on the left of the corps, so the attack was made with the divisions of Taupin and Darmagnac only: the main effort, such as it was, was fatally dissipated. As the haze lifted around 8.00 am, the French pressed forward and soon pushed back Colonel James Miller's Portuguese brigade towards Major-General William Inglis's British brigade. But as Clausel's divisions followed up, the Anglo-Portuguese 4th Division also moved forward. Seeing this, Clausel hesitated, and halted.

An hour later he received orders from Soult to recross the river, as it appeared that D'Erlon's corps was being attacked in the flank. By now it was 3.00 pm and as the two divisions began to retire, the storm swept down so that the columns became both disorganised and lost. After much blundering, they eventually reached the river towards dark, where the water level was rising rapidly. Clausel himself with the two lead brigades got across, but soon a raging stream six feet deep prevented any further crossing, so that the rear brigades of Taupin and Darmagnac, and the whole of Vandermaesen's division, were marooned on the far bank.

Vandermaesen realised that if he was still there next morning, he would be destroyed by the allies and so marched the 10,000 troops to Vera to cross by the bridge there. At 2.00 am, the troops reached the bridge, which was held by a company of the Light Division. This company at once opened fire from barricaded positions, bringing the column to a halt and inflicting severe casualties. This firing was heard by Major-General John Skerrett, in command of the nearby Light Division brigade, who nevertheless refused to send any assistance. For an hour the battle continued; Vandermaesen himself was shot and killed, but in the end, numbers told and the French forced the bridge. Thus four French brigades escaped certain destruction; Skerrett was never forgiven for this incident by the Light Division.

The cause of the order for Clausel's retreat and Foy's move eastwards was the demonstration by 6th and 7th Divisions against D'Erlon. Dalhousie, with 7th Division, was so encouraged by the results of the initial skirmishing that he put in a real attack on the French brigade at Zagaramurdi, which pushed them back to Ainhoue. Although this was contrary to Wellington's orders, it certainly fulfilled his intention, for D'Erlon was sure that he was being attacked all along his line. It was only an order to Dalhousie to disengage and march to support the block in front of Clausel's corps that broke off any further action.

And thus ended Soult's last battle in Spain. With only 45,000 troops in the actual attack, after the requirement for flank guards and reserves, it never really stood a chance against a concentrated allied army of almost 70,000. The attack cost Soult 4,000 casualties which he could ill afford, including the deaths of Vandermaesen and Lamartinière and the wounding of three brigade commanders. The allies lost 2,524 casualties of which 1,679 were Spanish, but Wellington was content to have foiled the attack, especially as the brunt of the action had been borne by the 12,000 Spanish troops, who, despite several days of short rations, had been as steady in action as the best of the allied or French formations. Next day, Soult learned that San Sebastian had fallen, and that his battle had been fought – and lost – for nothing.

III. THE PASSAGE OF THE BIDASSOA

This was certainly a good time for the long-delayed allied advance. Soult blamed his generals and the troops for the failure at San Marcial, the generals blamed Soult's plan, and the troops had lapsed into the habit of defeat. By contrast, allied morale was high both in Spain and at home, so that when the news of renewed war came on 3 September[7] Wellington was ready – despite the defeat of the allies at Dresden:

> . . . I shall put myself in a situation to menace a serious attack, and make one immediately I see a fair opportunity, or if I hear that the Allies [in Central Europe] have been really successful . . . I see that (as usual) the newspapers on all sides are raising public expectation, and that the Allies are very anxious that we should enter France, and that the government has promised that we shall do so, as soon as the enemy has been finally expelled from Spain. So I think that I ought, and I will, bend a little to the views of the Allies, if it can be done with safety to the Army. Notwithstanding, I acknowledge that I should prefer to turn my attention to Catalonia as soon as I have secured this frontier.[8]

Soult was very much surprised that after San Marcial, the allies had once again not followed him into France. With the breathing space thus offered, and with the inability to persuade Suchet to cross over from Catalonia, Soult had opted for an operational and tactical defensive. He was sure that with autumn approaching, he would be attacked soon, and he thus bent the energies of the army to fortifying a line of defences from Maya to the sea. This front of 23 miles ran along the foothills of the Pyrenees and was divided and dominated by the bulk of the mountain known as the Grande Rhune, a *massif* rising 2,800 feet above Vera. From the Grande Rhune eastwards stretched a chain of lesser features of which the largest was the Petite Rhune at 900 feet, until the mountain of Monderrain was reached, which rose 2,000 feet above Roncesvalles. Westward the hills ran down gradually towards the coast following the line of the Bidassoa which formed the frontier.

Soult felt that the most likely allied approach lay towards his centre left, east of the Grande Rhune, and here he placed his main effort. Six divisions held the line here: D'Erlon, with the divisions of Abbé, Darmagnac and Daricau occupied two lines of defences between Ainhoue (now called Ainhoa) and Monderrain, based on five strong redoubts linked by a continuous system of trenches in the first line, with a second line of entrenchments running from Espellette to Amotz. Clausel, with the divisions of Conroux, Maransin and Taupin held the front from Ainhoue to the Grande Rhune, including the ridges of Insola, Commisari and Bayonette. Of these divisions, those of Conroux and Maransin were well entrenched with two large redoubts east of the Grande Rhune, while Taupin, equally well dug in, lay to the west. The Rhune itself was only lightly held.

Supporting the main effort, Villatte's reserve division occupied a fortified camp around Ascain, ready either to move forward or act as a second tactical echelon in the defence. To form this main effort, Soult had had to make economies on his flanks. To the east, Foy's division was at St Jean Pied de Port acting as flank guard, supported by Paris's rump division from Saragossa which still held the pass at Jaca. To the west, Reille's corps with the two small divisions of Maucune and Boyer (formerly Lamartinière's) held the tidal estuary of the Bidassoa: Maucune was in the front line, occupying three redoubts at Biriaton, the hill known as Louis XIV, and another height rejoicing in the name of *Café Républicain*; while Boyer was held in reserve at St Jean de Luz.

Thus on what he felt to be the main area of threat, Soult had massed 29,000 men supported by a reserve of 8,000, while the flanks were held in the east by 8,000 men and in the west by 10,000. Four-fifths of the army was deployed in a single tactical echelon without either an effective second echelon or a reserve large enough to block large allied penetrations – quite a contrast to the excellent arrangements made by Wellington which had led to Soult's defeat at Sorauren.

It was a plan which could hardly have suited Wellington's intentions better if he had dictated it himself, for the allied C-in-C intended only a limited operation, designed to be the precursor of his large-scale invasion, and aimed not at a trial of strength but at Soult's weakness. His plan was based on deception, on reinforcing Soult's belief that the main attack would come in the left centre and would aim to drive the French towards the coast. To this end, Campbell's Portuguese brigade made a demonstration attack on D'Erlon on 1 October which brought Soult himself over, greatly concerned. On 5 October Wellington issued the orders which would ensure this deception worked: The corps of Hill, with 2nd Division at Roncesvalles, 6th Division at Maya and Morillo's division in support would hold fast; the Portuguese division, now commanded by Major-General John Hamilton (for Silveira on sick leave), would hand over in Alduides to Mina's irregulars and move to Maya;

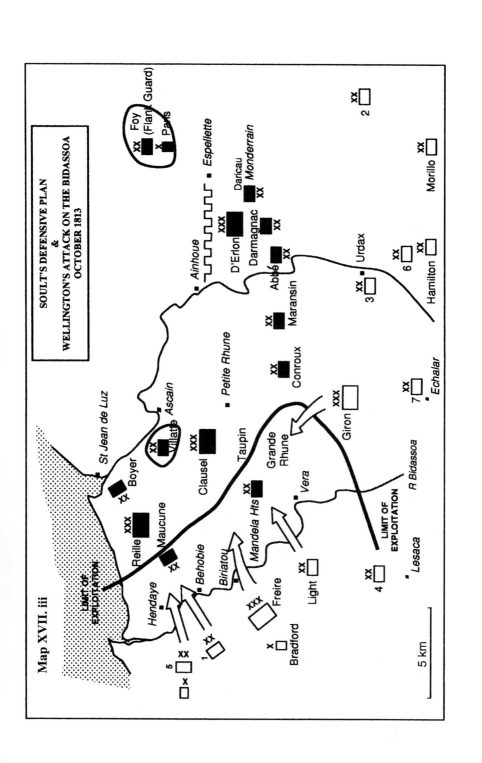

Map XVII. iii

SOULT'S DEFENSIVE PLAN
&
WELLINGTON'S ATTACK ON THE BIDASSOA
OCTOBER 1813

Picton's 3rd Division would march to Zagaramundi (now called Zugar-ramurdi) and Dalhousie's 7th Division to Echalar, and both would support Giron, who was to attack the eastern side of the Grande Rhune; finally a corps under Alten, with his own Light Division and Longa's Spanish division, supported by 4th Division, would attack in two columns on the southern and south-western sides of the Grande Rhune. Thus a force of nine British, Portuguese and Spanish divisions would attack on a frontage of four miles with an approximate force ratio of 1:1, easily enough to induce Soult to believe that this was the allied main effort.

But in reality, the main effort would be across the tidal estuary of the Bidassoa, where the French defenders were weakest and where there were few well-prepared defences, and here a much more favourable ratio of forces was generated. The defenders felt secure in this area, behind the three-quarter-mile broad tidal estuary of the river. But Wellington knew that as well as the three fords near Irun which were passable by infantry at low water, and others around Biriatou upstream, there were three fords known to the local shrimp-fishers near Fuenter-rabia which were easily negotiable at low tide.

Along this front, therefore, against the 4,000 men deployed in the front line by Maucune, Wellington assembled 24,000 British, German, Portuguese and Spanish troops of 1st and 5th Divisions, and Freire's corps. Under cover of night, 5th Division was to move up to Fuenter-rabia and at low tide was to make a dash across the estuary to seize Hendaye; it was then to move inland and head for the heights of Croix des Bouquets, a known French rallying point two miles north of the river. Simultaneously 1st Division was to make for the fords of Irun, seize Béhobie and the redoubt of Louis XIV; while engineers built a pontoon, the division was also to head for the high ground above the river. Freire, with two divisions, was to cross the river around Biriatou in two columns; engineers would build another pontoon here while the Spanish troops seized Green Hill Ridge and the Mandela heights. In reserve were held Aylmer's British and Bradford's Portuguese brigades.

Throughout the night of 6/7 October the allied troops completed their final approach march, covered by the now obligatory thunder-storm. At 7.25 am on 7 October, covered by the fire of their batteries, 5th Division crossed the exposed sands of the estuary at the run and entered the Bidassoa – it was only waist deep. They were across before the French could stand to, and the paltry defending force was soon swept away. Within two hours, 5th Division had reached Croix des

Bouquets. On its right, 1st Division made equally fast progress and as the 5th moved up to Croix des Bouquets from the west, the 1st approached from the south. Here a French brigade had assembled, joined by fugitives from the front, and Reille himself had ridden up to join it. But before Boyer's division could be summoned, Croix des Bouquets was stormed and captured.

The allied success was completed by Freire's corps which made the same fast progress, linking up with 1st Division and extending as far east as the Col du Poirier. By 9.00 am the heights above the Bidassoa were secure, and by noon Wellington had halted any further moves except for the Spanish and Portuguese light troops which continued to harry the retreating French for the rest of the day.

While this quick and easy victory was being won, a heavier but no less successful fight was in progress around Vera and the Grande Rhune. The attack began at 7.00 am with a demonstration aimed at fixing D'Erlon's corps while Longa and Giron moved up. Giron's leading division advanced on the eastern side of the Rhune, up the ridge of Fagadia and after several hours' struggle with four determined French battalions, gained the summit. Alten's Light Division on Giron's left advanced from Vera in two columns: Major-General James Kempt's brigade against the pass of Vera, and Major-General John Colborne's brigade – both brigades were composed of British and Portuguese battalions – against the Bayonette ridge. Between them, a broad wooded ravine was occupied by a detachment of Longa's division, the bulk of which advanced against the Grande Rhune itself on Alten's left.

Facing the Light Division, Taupin's whole division was in the line, occupying two redoubts: the redoute de St Benôit and the aptly-named redoute de la Bayonette. Between them lay an entrenchment, and the whole was occupied by 10 battalions (4,700 men) who prepared for the assault of 13 allied battalions (6,500 men).

Kempt's column was able to gain the summit of Commisari ridge with no great loss, for the French seemed to have no stomach for the fight. Colborne had more difficulty, for the whole of his brigade was needed to force the St Benôit redoubt, and then the entrenchments took time to clear out before the troops, preceded by a swarm of riflemen and *Caçadores* moved on to the redoute de la Bayonette. But to Colborne's surprise the defenders of the redoubt would not stand, so that his brigade gained the summit of the ridge just as Kempt's brigade reached its objective, and the two formations linked up immediately. A fresh French battalion happened to be moving forward at the same time, but the

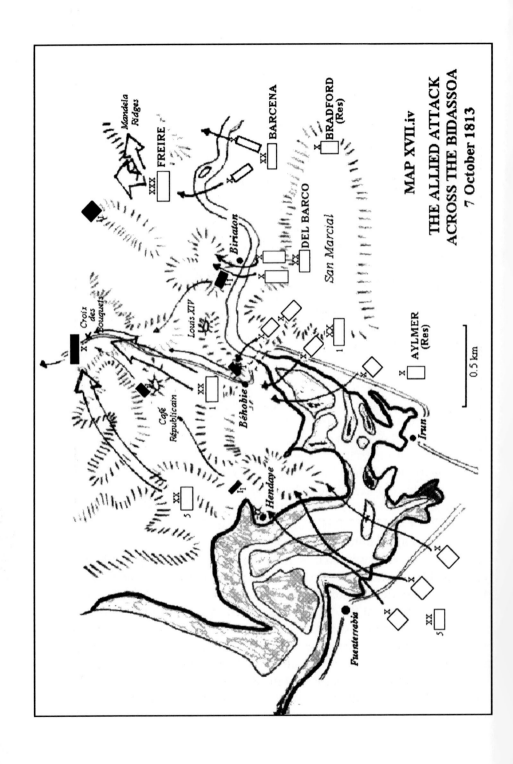

MAP XVII.iv

THE ALLIED ATTACK
ACROSS THE BIDASSOA
7 October 1813

0.5 km

FREIRE

BARCENA

BRADFORD
(Res)

DEL BARCO

San Marcial

AYLMER
(Res)

Mandela Ridges

Biriaton

Louis XIV

Croix des Bouquets

Café Républicain

Béhobie

Hendaye

Irun

Fuenterrabia

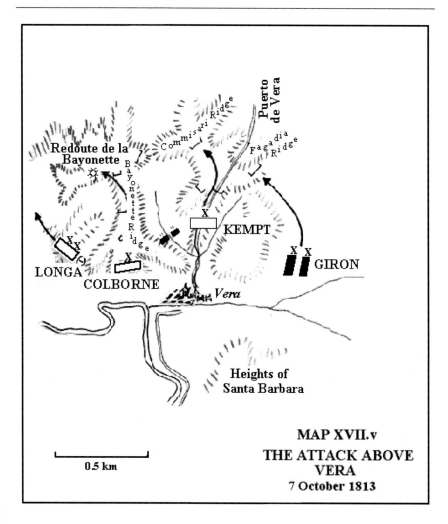

Redoute de la
Bayonette

Puerto
de Vera

Commisari Ridge

Fagadia Ridge

Bayonette Ridge

X
KEMPT

X X
GIRON

LONGA

X
COLBORNE

Vera

Heights of
Santa Barbara

0.5 km

MAP XVII.v
THE ATTACK ABOVE
VERA
7 October 1813

sudden arrival of both allied brigades forced it to surrender, although
the rest of the French garrison fled so fast that most did not stop running
until they reached Villatte's reserve division at Ascain.

The penetration of the French position by the Light Division allowed
Giron's division to establish itself on the upper slopes of the Grande
Rhune, but by this time the summit had been reinforced, and all
attempts to carry it by assault failed. It was not until the following day
that the threat of envelopment from the west by Freire and from the
east by 6th and 7th Divisions forced the French to abandon the whole
position.[9]

Wellington and his multinational staff at the crossing of the Bidassoa, 7 October 1813. An ADC is reporting to the allied C-in-C who holds a telescope.

The operation on the Bidassoa cost the allies over 1,600 casualties – 800 from Giron's division on the Grande Rhune – and the French a few score more including almost 600 prisoners, plus the loss of nine field guns and all the mounted pieces in the forts and redoubts. Wellington's plan had worked exactly as he had intended, but Soult, while adopting a tactical and operational defensive, had lost sight of the principle of offensive action which Napoleon had employed to such good effect at Dresden. To all intents and purposes, Soult and his troops were beaten before any fighting began: afterwards, the Marshal, just as after Sorauren, blamed everyone but himself.

NOTES

1. *Sup. Dispatches*, viii, p.176.
2. *Dispatches*, xi, p.32.
3. Ibid. pp.33 and 46.
4. *Sup. Dispatches*, xiv, p.281.
5. Browne, p.236.
6. Cited in many authorities, see especially Oman, vii, p.48, and Browne, p.236.
7. *Dispatches*, xi, p.74.
8. Ibid. p.124.
9. There is an account in Browne, p.248.

Chapter XVIII

The War in the Mediterranean

എൻൈ

I. THE CAMPAIGN IN CATALONIA

I N ADDITION TO his main army, Wellington also commanded an Anglo-Sicilian force at Alicante, which consisted of 7,000 British, 2,000 KGL, about 1,000 Sicilians and 8,000 Spanish troops under the immediate command of Lieutenant-General Sir John Murray. All these except the Spanish were troops which Lord William Bentinck had dispatched from the British garrison in Sicily, and which Wellington had received authority in August 1812 to take under his own command. One pre-requisite of success in the campaign of Vitoria was that the French army in Catalonia, under Suchet, should be prevented from marching to join King Joseph.

The task of tying down this force had been entrusted primarily to the Murray. His force was heterogeneous in the extreme, consisting of six British, three KGL, four Italian and two foreign infantry battalions in British pay; two cavalry regiments, one British and one Sicilian; and some British and Portuguese artillery. Added to it were two Spanish divisions, one under Major-General Samuel Whittingham (a Briton in Spanish service), called the Mallorcan (Majorcan) division, which was entirely in British pay, and a second under General Philip Roche which was part of the Spanish forces, making a total force of 21,000 men – more numerous than Suchet's available field army, but weak in cavalry and artillery and, as was mentioned earlier, having some units of highly doubtful character.

More serious for Suchet was the added presence of the Spanish Army of Murcia under General Francisco Elio, which raised the total allied strength in eastern Spain to 52,000 men. Facing this force, the nominal strength of Suchet's army in Aragon and Catalonia was close to 75,000 men but of this total all but about 15,000 were permanently employed on anti-guerrilla operations or guarding the lines of communication back through Aragon to Madrid, and through Perpignan into France.

Since February 1812 Catalonia had been annexed to France herself and thus Suchet enjoyed a great deal of autonomy from the high command in Spain. But with the removal of King Joseph's headquarters to Valladolid, Suchet was in an isolated and potentially dangerous position. In general, however, the region was relatively peaceful and he was determined to hold on to his position. While the bulk of his army remained dispersed, he concentrated what striking force he had on the line of the Xucar river, in order to guard the province of Valencia from the one enemy force he really feared – the Anglo-Sicilian Army. Thus simply by being there, the allied army had gone a long way towards fulfilling Wellington's intention.

By late February, Murray had good information regarding the French deployments, and he decided to begin his active campaign in March, by

FIG. XVIII.i

ORDER OF BATTLE, FRENCH ARMIES OF ARAGON AND CATALONIA

XXXX Suchet

XXX **Aragon** **Suchet**	XXX **Catalonia** **Decaen**	XX **Cavalry** *1839*
XX 1 Musnier *(4,975)*	XX 1 Quesnel *(3,625)*	
XX 2 Harispe *(4,115)*	XX 2 Lamarque *(3,628)*	
XX 3 Habert *(4,975)*	XX 3 Matthieu *(6,365)*	
XX 4 Paris *(4,450)* To main Army Sept 1813	X Petit *(1,619)*	Additional men in fortresses and garrisons:
	X Espert *(3.077)*	Figueras - *3,860* Tarragona - *1,514* Lerida - *1709* Detached - *395* Sick - *6089*
XX Italian Severoli *(3,909)*		

MAP XVIII.i

East Coast of Spain

Gerona

Saragossa Lerida

Barcelona

R. Ebro

Tarragona

Tortosa

Castellon de la Plana

Bruñol

Valencia

R. Xucar

Alcira

Chinchilla

San Felipe de Xativa

Yecla

Alicante

Cartagena

0 50 100 150 200 250 km

Source: McDonald, 'Exeunt Omnes', *Miniature Wargames* no. 122 (June 1993)

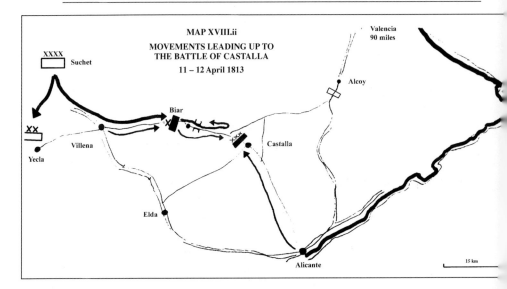

attacking and destroying the French brigade at Alcoy, a considerable town in a fertile agricultural region, whose loss would be a blow to the French. The scheme foundered, allowing the enemy to slip away and although it seemed to everyone that Murray intended to press forward and challenge Suchet to a general action, his real intention was, having distracted Suchet's attention, to make a dash for Valencia and seize that city in co-operation with the Spanish Army of Murcia.

This scheme too foundered, chiefly for reasons of allied politics in Sicily which will be dealt with later, but which necessitated the withdrawal of two battalions – one British and one KGL – from Alicante, but at the same time, Murray received dispatches from Wellington which ordered him to wait for detailed orders before embarking on any further expeditions.[1]

II. CASTALLA

In the meanwhile, Suchet had decided to take advantage of Murray's seeming indecision and go over to the offensive himself, and for this he concentrated three infantry divisions and half his available cavalry, forming two columns. The first column was directed at the isolated Spanish division in Yecla; the second aimed to sever communications between Murray and the Spanish army. The blow against the Spanish was launched on 11 April and was a masterpiece of surprise which resulted in the destruction of half the Spanish division after a spirited fight.

Fighting had broken out early in the morning and by noon, news of the battle had reached Villena, 15 miles away, where by chance, Murray was in conference with General Elio. News of the second French column also came in and it seemed that this was headed directly for them. It was clear that Villena would have to be evacuated immediately and all available troops concentrated for a defensive battle. Elio needed some days to collect his command, and Murray decided to retire towards the strong position at Castalla through the pass of Biar in which he placed the 2,200 men of the allied brigade of Colonel Frederick Adam.[2] with orders to delay the French in order to gain time for the concentration of the army at Castalla. This brigade was further supplemented with a light cavalry screen of one squadron of foreign hussars between it and Villena.

Suchet reached Villena that same evening, and finding a Spanish battalion still in the castle there, bombarded the place and forced its surrender next morning. He intended now to press on to Castalla and defeat the allied force there before Elio's Spaniards could march to join them. His cavalry had quickly identified Adam's covering force and he gave orders for the troops at Villena to attack at once and push this puny force aside, while the second column was ordered to march from Yecla and link up as soon as possible.

Adam's delaying action in the mountain pass of Biar, in face of a force ratio of nearly five to one, was one of the most successful delaying actions of the whole Peninsular War. With skill and bravery, this polyglot allied formation held the French advance in check for five hours on 12 April with the loss of only 300 casualties, so that when the French emerged from the pass it was far too late in the day to attempt any further moves on the allied main position before the next day. Thus

Adam gained a full 24 hours for his commander. Whittingham, who saw the later stages of the battle, described it as

> ... a beautiful field-day, by alternate battalions: the volleys were admirable, and the successive passage of several ravines conducted with perfect order and steadiness. From the heights occupied by my troops it was one of the most delightful panoramas that I ever beheld.[3]

The delay allowed Murray time to select and prepare a strong position on which to meet Suchet's advance, using a line of rugged hills and the bed of a steeply cut, precipitous torrent, anchored on the old castle of Castalla. The torrent, which had been damned up, had flooded to the extent that an area of swamp now protected not only the allied right, but a proportion of the centre as well. The approach, over low ground, was dominated by the ridge and a projecting spur which, along with an intermediate ridge called the Cerro del Doncel, effectively divided any attacking force.

On the left of the position, well entrenched, Murray placed Whittingham's Mallorcan division; in the centre, he placed Adam's brigade and Major-General John Mackenzie's division of British and KGL troops, supported by the bulk of the artillery. The right flank, on lower ground, was held by an Anglo-Sicilian division under Major-General William Clinton, with part of Roche's Spanish division holding an advanced post on rising ground in front of the centre-right supporting a covering force of Spanish and Italian cavalry. The remainder of Roche's troops and the allied cavalry were held in reserve behind the castle of Castalla. Altogether, the force numbered 17,080 infantry and 1,036 cavalry, with 30 guns.

Suchet, with an available force of 11,848 infantry, 1,424 cavalry and 24 guns, seems to have planned an infantry attack at noon in the centre by the divisions of Generals Robert (*vice* Musnier) and Habert against the strongest part of the allied line, supported by a move with five companies of his *voltigeurs* against the allied left, while enveloping the allied right with his considerable cavalry. The infantry division of General Harispe was held in reserve. This plan seems to have been founded on the absolute conviction that the allied troops, especially the Spanish and Italians, would not stand: a conviction which was about to be rudely disproved.

The advance of the French light troops against Whittingham's Spanish was easily beaten off; the attack by Robert's division on the

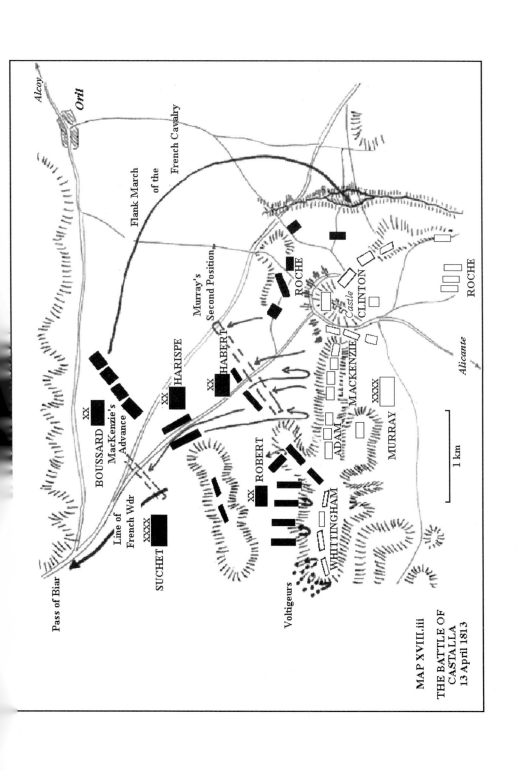

Alcoy

Onil

French Cavalry

Flank March of the

Pass of Biar

Murray's Second Position

BOUSSARD
XX
MacKenzie's Advance

HARISPE
XX

HABERT
XX

Line of French Wdr

SUCHET
XXXX

ROBERT
XX

ROCHE

Castle
CLINTON

ROCHE

Alicante

ADAM

MACKENZIE

MURRAY
XXXX

1 km

WHITTINGHAM

Voltigeurs

MAP XVIII.iii
THE BATTLE OF
CASTALLA
13 April 1813

centre developed in five columns which, after crossing the Cerro, seem to have drifted to their left and thus three of the columns actually attacked Whittingham and only two attacked Adam, supported by the move of Habert's division on Mackenzie's position. Although this was a strong attack, the allied troops stood their ground. The French columns actually reached the summit in several places but in every case, the assaulting troops were thrown back with loss.

With his cavalry out to a flank, Suchet found himself in a perilous position, for a determined counter-attack by the allies would have destroyed his whole force. Fortunately for him, Murray was not of the stamp to take such an opportunity and Suchet was able to regroup his mauled force and retire unmolested through the pass of Biar. By the time that Murray belatedly organised a pursuit, the French rearguard had taken up a position in the pass and was able to do to the allies just what Adam had done to the French. Thus Suchet, mauled and with 1,300 casualties, escaped overnight.

Although it was by no means a shattering victory, the Battle of Castalla brought great credit to the allied armies on the east coast, especially the Spanish, who had borne much of the fighting and had shown a steadfastness and determination which only a few years before would have been unthinkable. Better still, for only 440 casualties (over half Spanish) it broke Suchet's reputation and made easier the operations of Elio's army and the guerrillas. For his part, Murray made only one further feeble attempt to follow up the success at Castalla and after a few days, returned to await instructions from Wellington. As it happened, these were already on the way.

III. TARRAGONA

The time was now drawing near for Wellington to begin his advance on Vitoria. His intentions for the Anglo-Sicilian Army in tying down Suchet have already been mentioned, but he had other, more positive plans as well. These were that, in conjunction with Elio's and Del Parque's Spanish armies, the army would embark on a campaign to clear French power from the whole of south-east Spain. To achieve this state of affairs, Murray was given a series of objectives,[4] for which the overwhelming British naval superiority in the Mediterranean held the key. First, he was to capture the province of Valencia; second, establish a secure base on the east coast; and third, force the French back from the lower Ebro.

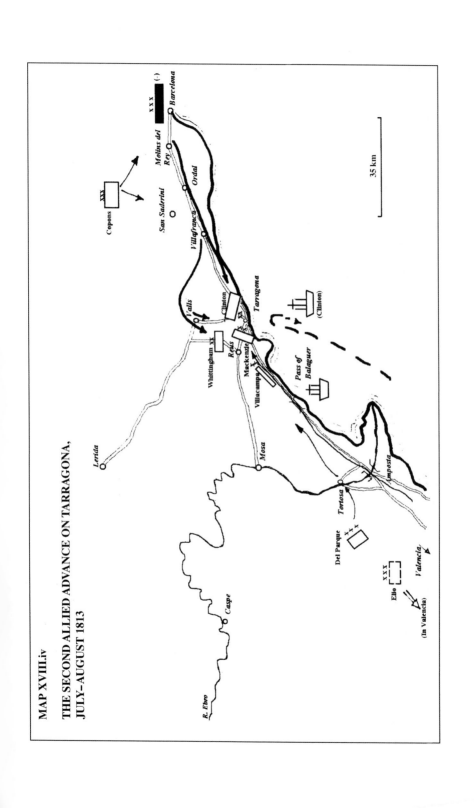

MAP XVIII.iv

THE SECOND ALLIED ADVANCE ON TARRAGONA,
JULY–AUGUST 1813

35 km

However, the total force ratios were unfavourable to the allies for offensive operations, and so in order to achieve the first of these objectives, Suchet must be induced to weaken his forces against Elio and Del Parque, and this is where sea power would play a part. Murray was ordered to embark 10,000 men on transports and move them by sea to the city of Tarragona in Catalonia, which was to be besieged and captured. If Suchet descended in force on the siege, Murray was to re-embark and induce Suchet to follow him, thus wearing out the French by constant marching and exposure to guerrilla attacks. Murray was also ordered that on no account was he to risk defeat in the field.

Murray began his embarkation at Alicante on 18 May in a fleet of about 180 ships of all kinds under Rear-Admiral Benjamin Hallowell. Because of a shortage of horse transports, Murray had to leave behind his Sicilian and Spanish cavalry and some artillery draught animals. The fleet sailed on 31 May and with favourable winds he arrived at Tarragona on 2 June. The greater part of the army landed at Salou Bay, about eight miles from Tarragona, while 1,000 men under Colonel William Prevost landed at the Col de Balaguer in order to capture the important fort of San Felipe, blocking the road 20 miles south of the coastal city.

> Tarragona . . . is seated on a rock of considerable height, isolated and scarped on the north, east, and south. Towards the west and south-west the ground slopes . . . towards the port and the Francoli [fort]. The upper town is surrounded by ancient walls crowning the summit of the rock, the contours of which are followed by a second enclosure, provided irregularly with bastions. The east side with the road to Barcelona [is] moreover, covered by five lunettes, forming a line . . . supported . . . upon the sea. Two other large lunettes [protect] . . . the north side. These two fronts [present] to the besiegers nothing but . . . bare rock, upon which [an] attack would [be] extremely arduous; whereas the side next to the [River] Francoli [offers] gentle . . . slopes, and a deep soil favourable [for the attacker] . . .
> The lower town was encompassed by a second enclosure . . . defended by three regular bastions and some other works. Thus the general outline of the two towns, upper and lower, formed a large parallelogram twice as long as broad.[5]

In addition, two forts had been constructed in 1811 and a third, Fort Olivo, on the Olivo heights to the north. However, such was the state of the fortifications and so degraded was the garrison. that a determined siege and assault could certainly have captured the place within a few days. The garrison consisted of an Italian battalion, a Piedmont battalion, a Spanish company, two artillery companies and the crews of three ships blockaded in the harbour, a total of about 1,500 men commanded by the governor, General Bertoletti. Murray set about the siege in a decidedly leisurely way. Adam's and Mackenzie's troops deployed to the west of the town, Whittingham's Spaniards to the east, and the remainder on the Olivo.

The first move was to capture the outlying forts and to construct two batteries. On 6 June these batteries and the fleet began to bombard the town. By 7 June, Fort Royal had been silenced and much of the town's defences blown away. But rather than capture the lower town at once, Murray now constructed two more batteries and the bombardment continued. By the night of 11 June, the garrison realised that the assault was at hand. While all this was in progress, Fort San Felipe had been captured and Prevost's force had blocked the likely approach route of any relief for Tarragona.

A series of reports now began to come in – all to a greater or lesser extent false – which convinced Murray over the next five to six days that Suchet was about to attack him. General Decaen, in Catalonia, had heard of the siege and had sent all available troops – two brigades – to join General Maurice-Mathieu the governor of Barcelona. Maurice-Mathieu pushed these 6,300 infantry towards Reus in order to link up with Suchet, but threatened by Major General Francisco de Copons' 7,000 Spaniards, withdrew. Suchet himself had been unable to push more than an advanced guard division under General Pannetier over the inland mountain roads which on the morning of 12 June lit some beacons to signal to the defenders that help was at hand, but the force was in no position to interfere.

Murray lost his head. The reports of movement by Pannetier and Maurice-Mathieu were misinterpreted as Decaen and Suchet. On 12 June, with no enemy in sight, Murray re-embarked his army, losing in the process 18 precious siege guns, and set sail to pick up the force at the Col de Balaguer. As these troops were embarking, Suchet himself appeared at the Col but was bombarded by the fleet and, seeing himself outnumbered, he withdrew.

Only three days later, on 15 June, Murray decided to disembark once more at the Col with the idea of intercepting the leading brigade of Suchet's army and co-operating with Copon's small Spanish army. Copons, in contrast to the disgraceful behaviour of Murray, had actually engaged the French main body despite being heavily outnumbered, and sent repeated messages to Murray urging him to fall on the leading French formations.

It was all to no avail. Murray was now so seized with indecision that he could not be depended on for any resolute action at all. On 17 June the Anglo-Sicilian Army re-embarked once again, but without bothering to inform their Spanish allies, and sailed back to Alicante. Thus this expedition must be counted a failure in all respects but one. The allies had made no gains, had lost 18 guns which Wellington had spared from his own precious siege train, as well as 600 casualties, and numerous horses and mules. Much worse, allied unity had been badly damaged by Murray's poltroonery, especially after Wellington's exertions earlier in the year to establish control over the Spanish armies.

In 1814, Murray was tried by court-martial on charges of 'Disobedience to orders, neglect of duty, highly to the prejudice of the service and detrimental to the British military character'. He was acquitted of these charges and found guilty only of an error of judgement. He was '. . . never indicted for his worst offence – the callous betrayal of the Spanish colleague who had done his best to serve him'.[6] The only advantage which this campaign brought was that, despite Murray's incompetence, his movements and the bravery of the Spanish forces did achieve the objective of tying Suchet down at a time when his army could have made a great difference at Vitoria.

IV. SUCHET ABANDONS VALENCIA

Even as the embarkation from Col de Balaguer had been in progress on 18 June Bentinck himself had arrived from Sicily and had at once taken over command of the army from Murray. He was appalled by what had happened, but could see nothing for it but to proceed with the evacuation as the troops were clearly no longer in a fit state to fight after continual disembarkation and re-embarkation. The troops were in good spirits but horses and mules were in a bad state and much materiel had been lost. The expedition sailed for Alicante that same day, but a storm dispersed the convoy. Fourteen ships were lost of which four had to be burned. The remainder reached Alicante on 28 June where Bentinck found, to his extreme annoyance, that Murray had dispersed the land transport which had been collected in the spring, so that time was lost while it was re-assembled.

Meanwhile further south, Del Parque and Elio had not exactly been active. Suchet had left a force of 14,000 men and 40 guns under General Harispe to defend Valencia, of which 2,000 were tied down in garrisons. Facing them were two Spanish armies with double Harispe's strength: first, 3rd Army of the Duke Del Parque, which Wellington considered the best Spanish formation in the field. It consisted of 12,000 infantry, 700 cavalry, and 12 guns. These were all experienced and battle-hardened troops skilled in mountain warfare, divided into three infantry divisions commanded by Generals the Prince of Anglona, Marquis de las Cuevas, and Cruz Murgeon. Second, there was the 2nd Army or Army of Murcia under General Elio, which mustered 17,000 regular infantry, 900 cavalry, 22 guns and some 10,000 guerrillas operating in New Castile. The army was divided into four divisions under Generals Roche, Sarsfield, Mijares and Villacampa: the division of Roche was trained, paid and led by the British and was reckoned excellent, especially after Castalla; the rest were of lesser quality.

Wellington had ordered the Spanish commanders to manoeuvre Harispe out of his position on the Xucar river by a flank attack delivered by Del Parque's army, while Elio pinned the French frontally. Unfortunately, Elio persuaded Del Parque to exchange roles, and also gave him Roche's division, with the result that a weak flank move was made by the worst troops. Moreover the change of roles meant that when Murray had sailed for Tarragona on 31 May the Spanish operation did not begin until 9 June. Not surprisingly, the flank attack, although achieving some success, was pushed back by Suchet's troops moving down to the Xucar. Worse still the frontal assault failed completely having been caught during the approach march by a French counter-attack on 13 June which cost 1,500 casualties and which forced Del Parque to withdraw.

As the Anglo-Sicilian Army regrouped at Alicante, Elio dispersed, and Del Parque occupied Murray's old blocking position at Castalla, Suchet was concentrating his forces on the Xucar river ready for a counter move which should have caught the allies in complete disarray. But for the news of Vitoria, the war on the east coast might have ended then and there. But this news changed the tactical situation completely. Bentinck had been contemplating some kind of outflanking movement inland by all three available allied armies, but realised immediately that, with the main French army now behind the Pyrenees, Suchet would have to retire behind the Ebro or risk being cut off by an allied advance from Saragossa down the Ebro. Accordingly he decided to march the

Anglo-Sicilian Army on the direct road to Valencia, keeping in contact with the all-important British fleet, while Del Parque marched parallel and Elio moved on Valencia from the rear.

Bentinck was quite right. Even before the news of Vitoria, Suchet had been considering a retirement, and his mind was made up when he received the news from Clausel's columns, retiring through Saragossa. He put his intention into action without delay: on 4 July the divisions of Harispe and Habert, with the cavalry, were pulled back to Valencia; on 5 July the fortress was blown up and the whole army marched back to Saguntum. From there, the army marched along the coast, and reached the Ebro on 9 July, joined on 12 July by Musnier's division and Severoli's Italian division which had been guarding the inland flank against Elio.

This evacuation of the province of Valencia was accomplished with speed and precision, and the army was well placed either to fall back into Catalonia or march through Saragossa to join in operations against Wellington. This last had clearly been Suchet's preferred option, for he had kept the division of General Paris at Saragossa. The continued retirement of Clausel, however, cancelled any possibility of a union of the armies, and Suchet ordered Paris to join him on the Ebro. This Paris, much harassed by a formidable force of 14,000 guerrillas under Mina, was unable to do: he retired instead over the Pyrenees by way of Jaca, and eventually joined Soult's main army.

Thus on the Ebro, Suchet commanded a force of 18,000 men, with another 8,000 or more in General Decaen's Army of Catalonia engaged against Copons' Spanish army. This was a large force on paper, but Suchet had already begun to repeat the mistake that Napoleon was making in Central Europe, by tying down numbers of troops in fortress garrisons in the expectation of recovering them at some future date. The main field army was assembled around Tortosa, with the divisions of Severoli and Musnier detached at Caspe. But when the news of Paris's retreat came in, Suchet decided to continue his retirement towards Tarragona, which was reached on 17 July but the strength of the army was depleted still further by the detachment of more garrisons: Tortosa, for example, was garrisoned with 4,800 men, Lerida with 2,000.

But once in Catalonia, Suchet took over the command of Decaen's divisions too, for he knew that the allies would soon follow up his retirement. Thus his available field force, allowing for garrisons and convoy escorts, was 25,000 men in six divisions of infantry and one of cavalry.

V. BENTINCK'S ADVANCE TO TARRAGONA

Bentinck had begun to follow up the retiring French as soon as he could complete the refurbishment of his army and gather sufficient transport. On 9 July Adam's brigade, again acting as advanced guard, entered Valencia four days behind the French but the Spanish armies had scarcely moved. It was not until 13 July when Suchet was already north of the Ebro, that Bentinck agreed a new plan with Elio and Del Parque. Bentinck was sure that Suchet would abandon Catalonia if pressed, and thus while Elio was to reduce the Valencian fortresses with the divisions of Roche, Mijares and Sarsfield, the main army, reinforced with the division of Villacampa, would go by the coast road towards Tarragona. The division of Clinton was to be embarked on the fleet and if Tarragona was unoccupied, it was to land and seize a bridgehead where the main army would link up with him, and with the Spanish army of Copons. Del Parque was to reduce the fortress of Tortosa and then co-operate with the main army. Thus the allies prepared to attack with 16,000 Anglo-Sicilian troops and 8,000 Spanish, against 25,000 veteran French troops who had no intention of giving in.

The Anglo-Sicilian Army advanced slowly along the coast as far as Vinaroz, 15 miles south of the Ebro, where it halted on 20 July to await Del Parque and Villacampa, and to gather intelligence on Suchet's movements: large bodies of troops were reported moving towards the Pyrenees.

The allied advance began on 26 July. Clinton's division duly embarked, but found Tarragona well garrisoned and so had to return. Suchet had 15,000 men close to Tarragona ready to fight; Decaen had another 10,000. Adam's brigade, Mackenzie's and Whittingham's Mallorcan divisions and the cavalry all crossed the Ebro at Amposta, followed by Villacampa who had been provided with 100,000 rations of flour to feed his troops. Del Parque's main body followed up two days' march behind. On 30 July Bentinck began his approach to Tarragona and on reaching it, blockaded it with his two Anglo-Sicilian divisions, placing Whittingham's Mallorcans at Reus to watch the approach from inland.

The Spanish armies began to close up, and Copons began to raid the French communications; for two weeks, there was no French response. Suchet could have fallen on the allies with 20,000 men from Villafranca within two days, but had mistaken Bentinck's boldness for strength and was waiting for the return of Decaen. All seemed to be going well for Bentinck, although mindful of Murray's disaster, the siege train was not disembarked. It was just as well. On 14 August Suchet moved, pushing the two divisions of Harispe and Musnier down the coast, the two divisions of Habert and Severoli from Villarodona, and two divisions under Decaen towards Reus.

Bentinck realised that he had insufficient time to concentrate all the allied armies, and ordered a general retirement so that when Suchet's three converging columns linked up as planned, they found the allies gone. Suchet pushed on at once and on 17 August he reached the Col de Balaguer again, where he found the British fleet offshore in strength and the allies occupying a strong defensive position. Deciding therefore to content himself with the second relief of Tarragona, Suchet wisely drew back.

For the time being, the allied advance into Catalonia was checked. Bentinck sent Del Parque's force back south of the Ebro as despite the strength of the Balaguer position, it relied on supply by the fleet; the capacity of this system was insufficient for the whole force and so Del Parque recrossed the Ebro at Amposta, beating off a sally by the garrison of Tortosa as he did so. Suchet meanwhile retired and began to dismantle the fortress of Tarragona, then retired on Villafranca and sent Decaen's divisions back north.

This news reached Bentinck as a rumour that Suchet had sent half his army back to France. He thus felt obliged to obey a provision in Wellington's orders[7] to send Del Parque's army across to join the main allied force. Del Parque marched at once and reached Tudela on 15 September where his army joined the blockade of Pamplona. This unnecessary re-deployment seriously weakened the available allied strength for no marked gain in the north. It was a move Bentinck would later regret.

VI. SUCHET AND SOULT

During August and September Suchet carried out a thorough review of his possible options. Considering that his total force was around 57,000, the available field army of 25,000 represented an enormous commitment to static garrisons and convoy escorts. His best course would certainly have been to abandon everything south of the Fluvia river, hold this with a corps of observation, and concentrate a field army of 40,000 men which could reinforce Soult. This was certainly what Wellington expected, and feared.[8] But Suchet did not take this course. His chief reason for not doing so was political: if Napoleon won in Central Europe, his ability to dictate a continental peace might be weakened by further allied gains in Spain.

There were concerns too about a Spanish invasion of Languedoc and Rousillion, although in fact Wellington himself was opposed to this on the grounds that, first, it was logistically unsustainable, and second, a largely Spanish army on French territory might behave in such a way as to stir up civil resistance, thus making the future invasion of France by the main allied armies that much more difficult.

After the disaster at Sorauren, Soult wrote several times to Suchet urging a union of their forces at Jaca, from where their force of 80,000 men could strike north-westward. Failing this, Soult suggested a union at Pau inside France, and an attack through the pass of Somfort. But Suchet was under no illusions about the state of Soult's army and the magnitude of Soult's defeat; he also had a long-standing grudge against Soult; and finally, probably rightly, he saw Soult's proposals as impracticable. Suchet believed that the terrain was so bad and the difficulties of supplying such a large army so severe, that the proposed union of forces would lead to disaster. The dispute rumbled on for months, but long before it was settled, the Battle of Leipzig had been fought and lost, and Wellington was over the Bidassoa into France.

VII. VILLAFRANCA AND THE COMBAT OF ORDAL

Bentinck was much encouraged by the belief that Suchet was sending troops into France and despite his detachment of Del Parque, he decided to move once again into Catalonia. His intention was to seize and repair the fortress of Tarragona and use it as a naval base from which to launch subsequent operations. If the French army appeared sufficiently depleted, he intended then to advance and capture Barcelona as a prelude to engaging and defeating Suchet's field army.[9]

On 28 August the army, accompanied by the fleet, marched for Tarragona which was reached two days later. Work began at once to repair the fortifications and remount the spiked guns. On 1 September Bentinck received a visit from General Copons who gave information which appeared to confirm the French moves to the north. Copons promised to bring his 6,000 men into action against Barcelona as the allies advanced. In addition to these, Bentinck could count on only the 22,000 men of his own army and Sarsfield's Spanish division, since the rest of Elio's divisions were engaged in blockading the Valencian fortresses.

The move forward to Barcelona began on 5 September: the main army marched to Villafranca leaving the Spanish division of Sarsfield at Valls,

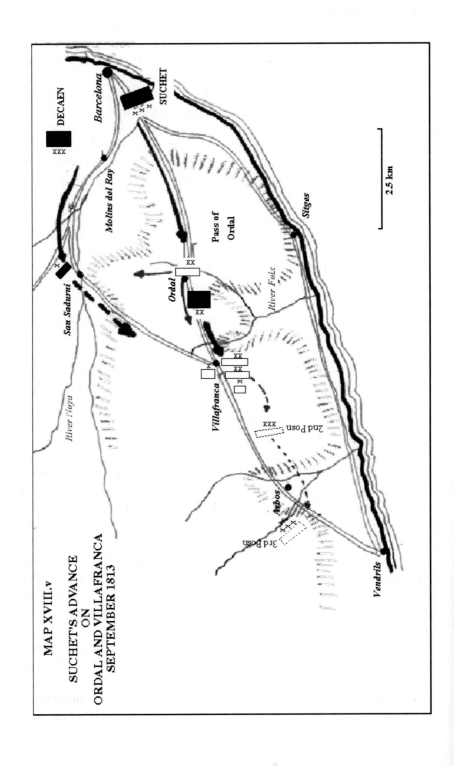

MAP XVIII.v

SUCHET'S ADVANCE
ON
ORDAL AND VILLAFRANCA
SEPTEMBER 1813

DECAEN

Barcelona

SUCHET

Molins del Rey

San Sadurni

River Noya

Pass of
Ordal

Ordal

River Foix

Sitges

Villafranca

2nd Posn

Abos

3rd Posn

Vendrils

2.5 km

and Whittingham's Mallorcans at Reus. On 12 September the move resumed again with Adam's brigade acting as advanced guard occupying the pass of Ordal, where the Barcelona road crosses a mountain ridge.

Adam's brigade consisted of 1,500 British, Brunswick, KGL, Sicilian and Italian troops, and occupied a strong position protected by a ravine, over which the road was carried by a narrow bridge. The brigade occupied an old fortification and threw out a cavalry screen, but saw no sign of the French, although it did establish communications with Copons's nearest units five miles to the north at San Sadurni.

In the late afternoon, 2,300 men of Sarsfield's division marched up and joined Adam on the position and although Bentinck had told Adam that the main army would also march that day, he had subsequently changed his mind. For the time being, the Spaniards occupied the centre of the position at Ordal, with Adam's men on either side, but the cavalry screen was pulled in.

Suchet meanwhile had been reassembling his army at Molins del Rey. Here he formed two columns: three infantry divisions and the cavalry under his own command – 10,000 infantry and 1,500 cavalry – and the remaining two French and one Italian infantry divisions under Decaen, with a strength of 7,000 infantry. His intention was to make a sudden, bold descent with his own column marching through the pass of Ordal to attack the allied main body at Villafranca from the front, while Decaen attacked Copons in the valley of the River Noya, then turned the allied flank from the San Sadurni–Villafranca road.

During his preparations, Adam and Sarsfield had occupied Ordal, and with a force of 4,000 troops supported by artillery should have been able to inflict on Suchet the sort of treatment which Soult had received at Roncesvalles. But Suchet decided to push on anyway, and his boldness was rewarded. His column marched at 8pm on one road by night for 10 miles and after three hours reached Ordal. There were no covering troops, and the French were over the bridge soon after 11pm and on the defenders before they were discovered. The French troops stormed the first line of defences and pushed on, were counter-attacked by the Spanish brigade with great ferocity and thrown back, reformed and attacked again.

The Spanish resistance was fierce, but numbers told. With the centre forced, the right wing turned, and casualties – including Adam himself – heavy, the defence broke. The Spanish mostly got away in the dark to join Copons, taking most of the British infantry with them; the rest of the British cut their way through to Villafranca – only 150 men out of 400 made it. The Italians and Brunswickers retired on Villafranca in good order, but the four British 6-pounders, moving back down the main road, was overtaken and captured by the pursuing French cavalry. The retreating allies left behind 635 casualties and 222 prisoners, and the defile in Suchet's hands.

While Suchet rested his tired infantry, the French cavalry pursued the retreating allied force, and was soon scouting Bentinck's position at Villafranca. Suchet had thought it likely that Bentinck, warned of his approach, would have slipped away unless Decaen's column had managed to close up on the allied flank. Neither situation had in fact developed, and the French cavalry found the allies drawn up in two echelons of divisions, with a Spanish brigade in reserve, south of Villafranca. The town had been evacuated and the bridge thrown down, and the position was protected from the front by the Foix river: Bentinck was well informed of the approach of both Suchet and Decaen.

But the French cavalry found no sign of Decaen's men, for they had made slow progress. Copons's troops had delayed them early on, and then the retreating troops of Adam and Sarsfield had caused a false alarm, so that by dawn on 14 September the column had only just reached San Sadurni. Here another fight was necessary to clear out a brigade of Elio's corps and the fugitives from Ordal who were there. By this time, Decaen's infantry was exhausted and needed rest before tackling the rough mountain road from San Sadurni to Villafranca; Bentinck, knowing therefore that he was faced only by unsupported cavalry, realised that he had a chance to escape the trap.

During the morning of 13 September the allied main body retired by divisions, covered by its cavalry and artillery. The 1,500 French and Westphalian cavalry, in two brigades with a horse artillery battery, tried to harry the withdrawal and turn it into a rout, but a courageous and skilful counter-attack by the 800 allied cavalry – led by Lord Frederick Bentinck, the commander's brother – threw the French back with loss.

This allowed the allies to take up a second position halfway between Villafranca and Arbos, where another attack was made by Suchet's cavalry; again, the attack was thrown back by a counter-charge of great dash and courage from the smaller allied cavalry brigade. As the French drew off, the allies retired again to a third position behind Arbos, where the bridge over the river was burned. Here the French 10-mile pursuit halted around noon; it was never renewed. Within nine days, Suchet had dispersed his army once more and hearing of this, Lord William Bentinck handed over his command to the unadventurous General William Clinton, and sailed for Sicily.

VIII. BENTINCK IN SICILY

The situation in Sicily although bearing only slightly on the war in Spain, does provide an interesting illustration of the way in which, in coalition war, grand strategic political considerations influence military operations even down to the tactical level. Sicily, which before Napoleon's annexation of Italy had included both the island and the kingdom of Naples, was in 1813 Britain's principal Mediterranean base. Sicily was vital to British strategy in the Mediterranean theatre, providing a good naval base and a base for possible offensive operations against the French in Naples, Corfu, Sardinia, Illyria, Corsica, and Catalonia.

There was therefore a constant worry for the Royal Navy that the French Toulon fleet would attempt to collect troops in Naples and support an invasion. The cost of maintaining the base was high. Britain had undertaken to provide a force of 10,000 men to garrison the island,[10] but the strength of the garrison usually stood between 15,000 and 20,000. This was a considerable drain on military resources and only a small portion of this force could safely be allocated to offensive operations. Wellington had been promised four battalions in 1810, but these had not been sent due to the threat of French invasion and a refusal by the King of Sicily to place his own troops under British command.

While London's objective was to maintain the base, the domestic political situation of Sicily was one of some turmoil. The King and his Court, and his government, were unpopular; Sicilian nobles resented the prominence given to Neapolitan and French exiles; the King, Ferdinand IV, was weak, and government business was largely run by Queen Maria Carolina, who was anti-British, strongly suspected of being in correspondence with the enemy, and who had made numerous attempts to obtain Russian or Austrian troops to replace the British.

In late 1810 Lord William Bentinck was appointed by London both as envoy to the government and military commander. Bentinck was the second son of the Duke of Portland and had wide military and diplomatic experience in Austria and Spain.[11] Bentinck's inclination had been for forceful British intervention in the affairs of the island but the then Prime Minister Spencer Perceval had persuaded him to a more conciliatory line.[12] On arrival, he had assured the Sicilian government that he had no intention of interfering in the internal politics of the island, but had argued for concessions to the opposition as a means of stabilising the volatile political situation.

Achieving no result he determined to return to London at once to urge a change of policy. His return caused a sensation, but as a result Bentinck was given control of the subsidy to Sicily and the authority to suspend it until effective measures were put in place to train the Sicilian Army and place it under his own authority;[13] to release imprisoned nobles; and to introduce more Sicilians into the government. Additionally, if these measures were not achieved, Bentinck was given authority to withdraw British forces. The aim was, therefore, to convince and reform the Sicilian government. Like Portugal, it depended absolutely on British protection to prevent French invasion.

Bentinck carried forward these moves during 1812 in the teeth of delaying tactics, as well as pushing forward support for an insurrection in the Ionian islands. But Bentinck's real passion was and remained the liberation of Italy; he saw reform in Sicily as a means of achieving this. Since the King of Sicily had also been ruler of Naples, the emergence of a more enlightened rule in Sicily might, he felt, be a spur on anti-French revolt on the Italian mainland. Conditions in Italy, however, continued to be unfavourable to the allied cause and this had moved him to dispatch Murray's expedition to Alicante.

In March 1813 the King, Ferdinand, at the instigation of his Austrian Queen, instigated a sort of mild *coup d'état*, issuing a proclamation which declared the re-establishment of the *ancien régime* in the kingdom. It seemed highly likely that civil war would follow. Bentinck resolved that a strong show of force, showing British support for constitutional reform and thus leading to the withdrawal of the proclamation was the only way to end the crisis. He therefore demanded the return of two battalions from Murray. Bentinck's political instincts were absolutely correct: the mere threat of the arrival of troops was enough to oblige the Royal party to back down – but in the meanwhile, the troops and naval forces for Murray's planned seizure of Valencia had been effectively tied up to the extent that he had felt obliged to cancel the project.

Bentinck himself took command of the force in Catalonia as has been outlined. His return to Sicily, mentioned above, was brought about by another political crisis this time in the parliament, which again threatened the process of reform. The new parliamentary opposition had blocked the proposed budget; anti-British feeling was growing; and there were serious food riots. Bentinck returned to Palermo and, unable to persuade the parliament to pass the budget, had the parliament suspended. Bentinck now became ruler of Sicily, during which time he made a suggestion that the island should be annexed to the British Crown.[14]

The Sicilian Court protested strongly to the British government which disclaimed any such intentions, since these were untrue and moreover likely to have a bad effect on Portugal and Spain, as well as causing annoyance to Austria and Russia. Fortunately this episode was not made public until 1814, so no damage was done except to Bentinck's reputation. This and his judgement were further called into question by the non-appearance of any anti-French revolt in Italy and this reinforced London's firm intention not to be further distracted from the maintenance of Wellington's main army, or the financing of the 6th Coalition.

Despite the non-appearance of a revolt in Italy, Napoleonic rule had in fact begun to disintegrate in central Italy during 1813. Heavy conscription quotas produced a breakdown of law and order and widespread brigandage.[15] As Napoleonic rule collapsed in 1814, Murat absorbed the remnants. In January 1814, Austria signed a peace treaty with Murat confirming his possession of Naples in return for Murat's co-operation against Napoleon, thus depriving the King of Sicily of his mainland dominions. The allies made this move because Murat's rule was seen as more effective than the Bourbons, with an efficient bureaucracy and a formidable army of 30,000.

Bentinck opposed this as he mistrusted Murat. In March 1814, acting against his instructions, Bentinck mounted a small expedition to Livorno and Genoa to try to revive hopes of an insurrection.[16] However, without effective means of furthering his aim, and having incurred the wrath of Metternich by intruding into an Austrian sphere of influence, Bentinck withdrew to Sicily in June. But he was proven right in the end by Murat's subsequent behaviour in supporting Napoleon during the Hundred Days. At the Congress of Vienna, Naples was restored to the Bourbons and the Kingdom of the Two Sicilies revived.

IX. CONCLUSION

Thus ended the campaign in the Mediterranean. Although at the end of 1813 Catalonia was still in French hands, the considerable French forces there were tied down just as Wellington had intended that they should be. They had been tied down by probably the most heterogeneous allied force in the whole Spanish, Portuguese and Mediterranean theatres of operations, which says much for Bentinck's skill in orchestrating not only his own polyglot corps, but those of three Spanish generals as well, at the tactical level.

This campaign also says much about the value of joint operations by land and sea on remote coastlines, and gives an illustration of the difficulties faced by a commander at the operational level in allocating scarce resources to support his main effort.

Wellington complained frequently about the inadequacies of the Royal Navy on the north coast. He could of course have accepted a diminution of the naval effort in support of the campaign in the Mediterranean in order to provide more support for the main army, but had he done so it is conceivable that the campaign in the Catalonia would have proved unsustainable. How then would a union of 40,000 of Suchet's veterans with the army of Soult have been prevented in the aftermath of Vitoria?

NOTES

1. *Dispatches*, x, p.162.
2. This brigade consisted of a composite KGL battalion, a British battalion, an Italian battalion and the Calabrese Free Corps supported by a battery of four mountain guns. See Oman, vi, p.287 for more details.
3. Whittingham, cited in Oman, vi, p.289.
4. *Dispatches*, x, pp.357–8.
5. Suchet, *Memoirs*, cited in McDonald, p.122.
6. Oman, vi, p.522.
7. *Dispatches*, x, p.635.
8. Ibid.; xi, pp.39–41 and xi, pp.83–4.
9. *Sup. Dispatches*, viii, pp.219–20.
10. Muir, p.167.
11. Details of Bentinck's career and personality are given in Roselli, Chapters 2, 3 and 5.
12. On Anglo-Sicilian relations see Gregory, Rosselli, and Muir.
13. Most British officers viewed the Sicilian Army with the same disdain as the Spanish. See Broers, p.263.
14. Muir, p.273.
15. Broers, p.249.
16. Muir, p.306.

Chapter XIX

Upon the Sacred Territory

❧❦❧

I N 1808, GEORGE CANNING had remarked that one day, a British army
would stand on the Pyrenees and look down into France. And so it
was now. One soldier described it thus:

> From these stupendous mountains we had a most commanding view of a
> vast extent of highly cultivated French territory, innumerable villages, and
> the port and town of St Jean de Luz. We could also see our cruisers sailing
> about near the French coast which gave an additional interest to the view
> before us.[1]

A pause of a month followed the crossing of the Bidassoa until on 31
October Pamplona surrendered thus releasing all British, Portuguese
and German troops, as well as the best of the Spanish, for offensive
operations into France. Soult's new defensive position on the line of the
Nivelle river was forced by the allies on 10 November, but both it and
the battle on the Nive, where Soult's terrible counter-attack almost
broke the allies, properly belong to the story of the invasion of France;
an invasion which Napoleon had made inevitable by his refusal, on the
day before the Nive, of the allies' offer to guarantee the natural frontiers
of France.

It was not only Pamplona that had caused the allies to pause once
more. The news of Dennewitz, Kulm and the Katzbach had trickled in
but Wellington was waiting for a greater sign. He got it after the Nivelle.
On the night after the battle, Wellington had invited the captured
commander of the French 88th Regiment to dinner. A rather brusque
interview by his staff had met with only morose silence, but Wellington
felt that a good dinner and a bottle of Madeira might do the trick. After
dinner, Wellington casually asked after the location of Napoleon's
headquarters. 'Monseigneur', replied the Frenchman, 'Il n'y a plus de

quartier général.' He related the first news of the calamity of Leipzig, which had just been received. 'Then' wrote Wellington 'I saw my way clearly to Bordeaux and Paris.'[2] The German troops in Soult's army clearly felt the same way – at the Nive, the whole brigade deserted to the allies except for one battalion which was disarmed and interned.

After Leipzig, the invasion was a strategic and operational certainty, the only question was, when? Napoleon was known to have retired behind the Rhine, but would the allies follow at once? If so, Wellington would be obliged to co-operate; but if the armies went into winter quarters, Napoleon might order the evacuation of Catalonia, reinforce Soult, and make the drive on Bordeaux that much harder. Wellington therefore needed to know more of Metternich's and Tsar Alexander's intentions, especially in the light of the Frankfurt proposals, and therefore the Nivelle and the Nive operations were only limited.

The position of the Bourbons was also in question: was Napoleon so hated that the French people would return to the old allegiance? Émigré emissaries from London assured Wellington that this was so, but his own feeling was that although the French might be tired of Napoleon and might not support him actively, rapacious conduct by the invading armies might yet convince them that he was still their best prospect. His dispatch of 21 November says much:

> The Allies ought to agree on a Sovereign for France instead of Napoleon, if it is intended that Europe should ever enjoy peace . . . [but] Possibly all the Powers of Europe require peace even more than the French. If Buonoparte [*sic*] became moderate, he would probably be as good a sovereign as we could desire in France. If he did not . . . he would find himself engaged single-handed against an insurgent France as well as all Europe.[3]

But without certain knowledge of allied political intentions, Wellington faced the task of trying to win over the French provinces without offering either freedom from Napoleon or any alternative, and of trying to adapt his military policy to an uncertain political direction.

Even in this overall perspective, the future invasion was also a tactical certainty, for Wellington had now shown that with Soult on the defensive, the allies could concentrate anywhere at a time of their choosing and break any position Soult took up. Surveying the Nivelle position, Wellington said as much to his subordinate commanders: 'Those fellows think themselves invulnerable, but I shall beat them out, and with great ease . . . I can pour a greater force on certain points than they can concentrate to resist me.'[4]

There was no matching confidence on the French side: 'The men are fighting badly. They are no good. At the head of such troops we shall certainly come to shameful grief.'[5] But if the French army had no more stomach for the fight, Wellington was always afraid of the potential of the civilian population to turn guerrilla: '. . . in France every man is or has been a soldier. If we were five times stronger than we are, we ought not to enter France, if we cannot prevent the men from plundering.'[6] For in order to maintain any kind of favourable force ratio against the remaining French field army, as well as satisfy the needs of winning over the population, Wellington could spare no troops for internal security, lines of communication duties, or garrisons. Thus before winning his next victories against Soult, he had first to win the battle for discipline in his own army, once it had 'infringed upon the Sacred Territory',[7] thus winning over the French population.

This would be no easy task with an army containing large numbers of Portuguese, Spanish and German troops who had seen their own homes pillaged and burned, and their families driven out or murdered. Many were sworn to revenge. But pillage was also a necessity for the Spanish divisions, most of whom were literally starving because of their own government's continuing neglect. On the night after the Nivelle, Longa's Cantabrians indulged in an orgy of looting and burning in Ascain, which prompted an immediate riposte from Wellington:

> I despair of the Spaniards. They are in so miserable a state, that it is really hardly fair to expect that they will refrain from plundering a beautiful country, into which they enter as conquerors; particularly adverting to the misery which their own country has suffered from its invaders. I cannot therefore venture to bring them into France, unless I can pay and feed them . . . If I could bring forward 20,000 good Spaniards, paid and fed, I should have Bayonne. if I could bring forward 40,000 I do not know where I should stop.[8]

The upshot was that after the Nivelle, most of the Spanish divisions except for those of Morillo and Carlos d'España were left on the frontier or investing the Catalonian and Valencian fortresses. As Wellington clearly wrote: 'I am not invading France to plunder; thousands of officers and men have not been killed and wounded in order that the survivors might rob the French.'[9]

Much to the relief of the inhabitants of the French borderlands,[10] Longa's division was sent to Medina Pomar in Old Castile, Giron's corps to Elizondo, and Freire's corps to San Sebastian and Vera. Here they were to gather supplies, and recover the numbers of sick – up to a quarter of their fighting strength – from the hospitals. Thus Wellington made a conscious decision to reduce his own strength by 20,000 men who had fought with skill and bravery, and deny himself another 20,000 who had not crossed the border.

In the event, his determination to preserve discipline was greatly helped by the addiction of the French army to plunder even in its own country, so that the invaders could be made to appear as liberators. Discipline amongst the allied troops was ferociously enforced, all forage was paid for, local mayors were invited to dinner by Wellington himself – no French general, child of the Revolution or not, would have done such a thing! Such conduct amazed and delighted the French population, who could scarcely believe such a manner of making war; soon they were coining money by selling foodstuffs to the commissariat, whose stores bulged with fodder, grain, meat and good drink. The allies, it was said, waged war not on honest men, but only on those who carried weapons. In vain Soult issued proclamations to the people to rise: the only guerrillas were those who took up arms against his recruiting parties. Thus Wellington, by this remarkable success, added at least an army corps to his field army.

As well as the difficulties with the Spanish field armies, other difficulties remained to be settled at government level before the main invasion of France could be carried forward. In September, Wellington had written to the Council of Regency,[11] that as his recommendations for promotions and dismissals were continually overturned, he would offer his conditional resignation as generalissimo. The Regency, far from backing down, referred the matter to the *Cortés*, which as a new assembly was to meet on 1 October, in turn referred the matter. This new *Cortés* was far more representative of the whole nation – the result of the allied liberation of the entire country except Catalonia during 1813 – and had decided to move from Cadiz to Madrid. It in turn referred the matter of the military command to the Council of State, not the Regency, for a decision, and this council on 8 November issued a censure of the Regents upholding Wellington's authority.[12]

But even with this satisfactory resolution, minor irritations continued. The Spanish press continued the accusation that Wellington had ordered the burning of San Sebastian, and even that Castaños had offered to make Wellington King of Spain if he would but turn Catholic! Spanish customs officials too were found to be interfering with the supply of the armies through Bilbao and Passages. As Wellington said, in a comment which reveals the underlying political view of the alliance as a short-term necessity: 'The officers of the government would not dare to conduct themselves in this manner, if they did not know that their conduct was agreeable to their employers.'[13]

Problems with the Portuguese government too rose to the surface. There was a clear feeling that the war was now far from the national frontier, and that the burden of military spending was growing intolerable. The recruiting laws were allowed to lapse and recruits and convalescents were held back at the depots, so that many battalions in the Pyrenees were reduced to 350 men. Beresford was sent back to Lisbon to in September to try to resolve matters, but found the Regency there in truculent mood.

The real grievances seemed to be that with the transfer of the military base to north Spain, customs receipts at Lisbon – and thus the money to pay for the army – had dwindled. There were clearly some worries about Spanish designs, and hurt that recent dispatches had emphasised the role of Spanish troops while neglecting that of the Portuguese. Spain was, after all, the ancient enemy, and although differences had been settled for the greater need of the coalition, national priorities were once more beginning to surface as the unifying fear of the French receded.

The Regency therefore proposed to Beresford that Wellington should form all ten Portuguese infantry brigades, with the supporting cavalry and artillery, into a national corps under a Portuguese general. Wellington, despite the excellent conduct of the Portuguese units, was aghast at this proposal: 'Separated from ourselves they could not keep the field in a respectable state, even if the Portuguese government were to incur ten times the expense.'[14] But Wellington took good care to be louder in his praise of the Portuguese in his dispatches thereafter. The underlying success of the integration of Portuguese and British troops could not, and was not, denied by anyone. If proof were needed, it came in 1815 when Wellington made an urgent but fruitless application for a Portuguese contingent to fight in the Netherlands.

While the allies prepared their moves across the Rhine and the Pyrenees, Napoleon had one last shot to fire at allied unity: the Treaty of Valençay. After his return to Paris after the Battle of the Nations, Napoleon took up the idea of releasing the imprisoned Ferdinand VII and restoring him to the Spanish throne (Joseph Bonaparte was contemptuously thrust aside) in return for a treaty favourable to France.

Ferdinand VII of Spain in French captivity with his uncle and brother at Valençay (Talleyrand's Château). In the 1813 treaty of that name he gained his freedom and double-crossed Napoleon.

The driving force behind the treaty was the need for the 100,000 veteran French troops still on the Spanish frontier, which Napoleon considered the only force now capable of stemming the main allied invasion across the Rhine: their obvious lack of enthusiasm for further battle seems not to have registered at all. To release them, Napoleon was prepared to offer Ferdinand his freedom, and all the territory and the fortresses still occupied in the annexed territories of Valencia and Catalonia.

In return, Napoleon asked for no less than Spanish withdrawal from the coalition, a free pardon for all collaborators, the hated *Afrancesados*, and the removal of all allied troops from Spanish territory. Thus Spain would cease to be a base for allied operations, and Wellington's army would be confined to its small bridgehead in France between the Bidassoa and the Ardour rivers, with the port of St Jean de Luz as its only supply base.

On paper this was an excellent scheme, but Napoleon completely failed to understand that Ferdinand would agree to anything in order to gain his freedom, but, such was his hatred of Napoleon, with no intention of keeping his word. Napoleon gambled on the Spanish attitude of hostility to the British, but entirely misunderstood the intense anti-French feeling which had followed the French annexation and the five years of repression which followed: this after the devastating effects of the Spanish guerrilla war.

How he could have believed that such an agreement was possible clearly shows how far Napoleon's grasp of reality had slipped – both in Spain and in terms of its effects on the allies. Ferdinand, in prison, understood the true situation better than Napoleon. But on 22 November 1813 a draft treaty was presented to Ferdinand which after two weeks' discussion and much feigned reluctance, Ferdinand signed.

Next day, 11 December, Ferdinand's envoy the Duke of San Carlos rode to Madrid with the treaty, but also with the King's private instructions, which were that even if the Regency and the *Cortés* ratified the treaty in part, nothing was to be agreed contrary to the alliance; the British government was also to be fully informed that as soon as the King returned home, the treaty would be declared void. Quite independently, the *Cortés* also presented to the Regency its determination that nothing signed by the King in captivity could be considered legal or valid, so that when the treaty was laid before the *Cortés* on 2 February 1814 it was thrown out.

Throughout December 1813, Napoleon had acted under the belief that the Treaty of Valençay would be accepted. He considered it highly likely that the bulk of the Anglo-Portuguese Army would be shipped to the Netherlands to support the rising there, a plan which had certainly been suggested by Lord Liverpool,[15] and one which Wellington had been obliged yet again to fend off:

> I am now as a commander sitting on the most vulnerable frontier of France
> . . . Does any man believe that Napoleon would not feel an army in such a
> position more than he would feel 30 or 40,000 British troops laying siege
> to one of his fortresses in Holland?[16]

But in this firm if misplaced, belief, Napoleon had begun to draw off quantities of troops from the armies of Soult and Suchet. Wellington can hardly have believed his good fortune: the loss of the Spanish divisions had reduced the main army to 76,000 men in France, not including the cavalry which was yet to come up, only slightly superior to Soult's total, while the Anglo-Sicilian Army and the three Spanish corps in Catalonia, a total of 36,000, were again a rough parity with Suchet.

But three weeks after Christmas 1813, half of Soult's cavalry with its horse artillery, two infantry divisions with their artillery, and a large number of officers and NCOs to form cadre battalions, began to march for Paris. These 14,000 troops and 35 guns were followed by an infantry division and a cavalry brigade (10,000 troops and 12 guns) from Suchet – which, with the commitment to garrisons, reduced the Army of Catalonia almost to impotence.

At the same time, the Spanish brigade was disbanded, and the Italian brigade sent back home, so that by the early spring of 1814, Soult was reduced to 60,000 men including cavalry, National Guard and garrison troops, with 77 guns; and Suchet to 18,000 and 24 guns in his field army after the garrisons had been extracted, of whom at least 9,000 were fully employed on the lines of communication. After that, it was only a matter of time: the war ended on 17 April 1814.

In Spain Napoleon had made his first mistake, an act so insulting and so treacherous that it drove Spain into the arms of her ancient enemy. As Napoleon himself later said on St Helena, 'the whole affair was too immoral'. Certainly, the Battle of Baylen and the Convention of Cintra in 1808 had an effect throughout Europe not matched again until the brilliant campaign of Vitoria and in the meantime, the genius of Wellington, the endurance of the allied troops, and the perpetual Spanish insurgency proved a fatal combination: the course of the war in Central Europe could well have been substantially different with the addition of 200,000 extra French troops.

The Peninsular War too made both Wellington and Castlereagh important figures in the allied counsels: leaving aside the matter of subsidies, the British record of resistance to Napoleon and of success in the field could hardly be matched. Then the victory of Vitoria, stiffening the resolve of the allies at Pleiswitz, pointed the road to Leipzig – and so was Pitt's prophecy after Trafalgar fulfilled, that 'England has saved herself by exertions, and will (I trust) save Europe by her example.'

NOTES

1. Simmons, p.335.
2. *Dispatches*, xi, p.275.
3. Ibid. xi, pp.304–7.
4. Smith, i, p.142.
5. Villatte to Thouvenot, 7/8.x.1813, cited in Oman, vi, p.137.

6. *Dispatches*, xi, pp.169–70.
7. Bragge.
8. *Dispatches*, xi, p.306–7.
9. Wellington to Freire, *Dispatches*, xi, p.296.
10. See especially Vidal de la Blanche, ii, p.130, cited in Oman, vi, p.219.
11. *Dispatches*, xi, pp.214–15.
12. *Sup. Dispatches*, viii, pp.355–6 and 406.
13. *Dispatches*, xi, p.326.
14. Ibid. xi, p.185.
15. *Sup. Dispatches*, viii, pp.414–15.
16. *Dispatches*, xi, p.385.

PART FOUR

AMERICA

Chapter XX

Mr Madison's War

⋰⊙⊙⊙⋱

I. A MATTER OF MARCHING

P RESIDENT MADISON'S ADDRESS to the US Congress on 1 June 1812, which preceded the declaration of war on Britain, set out the grievances for which the United States felt obliged to fight: the impressment of American seamen from US ships; the violation of US territorial waters by the Royal Navy and a succession of incidents between ships, like that those between *Chesapeake* and *Leopard*; the inadequate notice given before the imposition of 'mock blockades'; and the regulation of trade with Europe by a neutral nation through the Orders in Council.[1] The tone of the address was hostile to Britain, but not especially friendly towards France, for Madison had a vague feeling that somehow, Napoleon had manoeuvred the British and US governments into conflict – a conflict whose purpose was to put an end to the interference with US trade and shipping, but whose method was to be the largely unrelated business of a land war against the British and their allies in Canada.

The timing for such a war seemed right. Bonaparte was at the height of his power and was preparing to attack Russia: only Sicily, Sardinia, Sweden and Portugal were outside his influence, and it could be only a matter of time before the British and their few clients were forced to their knees, as they had been in 1783. The natural consequence would be that, just as the American colonies had moved to a republican form of government then, so would Canada now, under the guidance and tutelage of Washington.

What Madison overlooked was the nature of Bonaparte's government. It was no longer, and had probably never been, the sort of enlightened republicanism envisaged by the revolutionaries of 1789, but a despotism as absolute as anything seen before or since. Had Britain been defeated, the Napoleonic policy of continual expansion might soon have repudiated the Louisiana Purchase and sought to subvert both French Canadians, and French and Spanish colonists in Florida and Louisiana, thus bringing an open confrontation with the USA.

For these reasons, and the very real dislike of Mr Madison and his policies, as well as of Bonaparte, there were many people in the USA who had no enthusiasm for Mr Madison's war. This was particularly the case in Vermont and New York, which in addition fared very well commercially from those contracts which accounted for two-thirds of the supplies bought by the British army in the Canadas. With the coming of war, this valuable trade could easily be lost.

But for others, especially in the south and west of the USA, there was no doubt about the identity of the enemy. To establish the US in a position of advantage, from which its grievances could be righted, there seemed only one correct course of action. Since any naval war would, given the sheer strength and size of the Royal Navy, only ever be an inconvenience to Britain, it was proposed to conquer the Canadas using naval forces to control the Great Lakes, and the US Army to conquer territory. The vociferous Kentuckian Congressman Henry Clay, the original War Hawk, had declared that 'I trust I shall not be presumptuous when I state that I verily believe that the militia of Kentucky

President James Madison, 4th President of the USA (1809–17). He led 18 disunited and unprepared states into a war many opposed.

are on their own competent to place Montreal and Upper Canada at your [Madison's] feet.'[2] While ex-President Thomas Jefferson had at the same time declared his belief that an advance on Quebec would be 'a mere matter of marching'.

The entire establishment of the US Army which was to accomplish this mere matter of marching was, in 1812, only 10,000 regulars, organised into 25 infantry regiments but unsupported by any staff system or logistic infrastructure. This establishment was duly increased by Congress to 36,000, or 45 regiments, by January 1813, plus 50,000 volunteers – an enormous force far exceeding the small British garrison, but almost totally lacking in competent officers and NCOs. Most of the former were either raw young men or elderly veterans of the Revolutionary War. The army was equally deficient in training and in practical experience, and although it tried to adopt a new, flexible, system of manoeuvre,[3] this never succeeded during the war.

Equipment too was in short supply, for much of the army's clothing and equipment usually came from Britain. The national fortresses – especially the frontier forts at Plattsburg, Sackett's Harbor, Oswego, Niagara, Schlosser, Detroit, Mackinac and Presqu'isle – the port defences, and the arsenals, were all neglected.

True, there was the Militia, which at a theoretical strength of 100,000, was the traditional bulwark of the American people against oppression. It was this citizen army which, according to popular mythology, had wrested victory from the redcoats and Hessians (the massive French and Spanish assistance of the later years of the Revolutionary War was conveniently forgotten). Post revolutionary America had no love for a regular army, but every man between the ages of 18 and 45 was theoretically liable for service in the militia. But years of peace had eroded the capability of the militia, which was in any case under state, not national, control: its discipline and training was lamentable, leading to much friction with regular units; its officers were elected; and men with farms to run were unwilling to tramp off to Canada. However, not all was gloomy – there remained a strong core of hardy men well skilled in shooting and fieldcraft – although in general terms, the ability of the militia to conduct even limited operations was greatly in doubt.[4]

Unsurprisingly, despite the confidence of Clay and Jefferson, the attack on the Canadas in 1812 had not gone well. A poorly planned, three-pronged invasion had met with disaster at Detroit, Queenston and Lake Champlain. At Detroit, Brigadier General William Hull had meekly

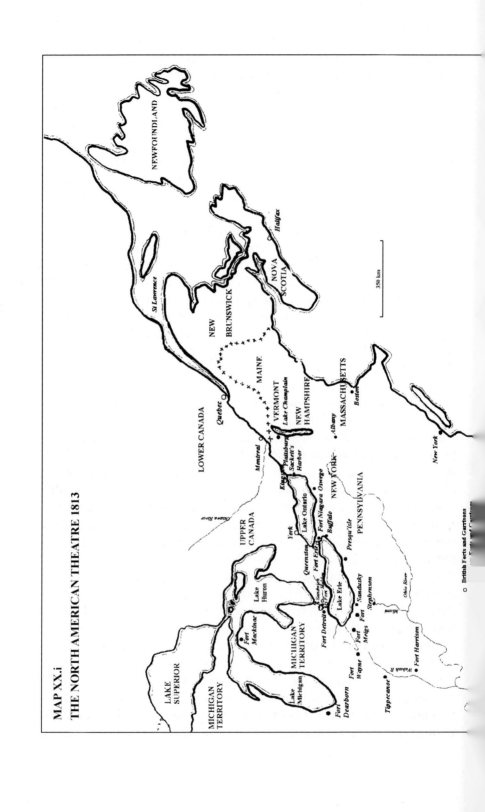

MAP XX.i
THE NORTH AMERICAN THEATRE 1813

350 km

○ British Forts and Garrisons

surrendered the fort and 2,300 troops to Major-General Isaac Brock, who commanded a mere 730 British and Canadian regulars and 600 Indians. At Queenston on the Niagara river frontier, the allies had suffered a severe blow in the death of Brock, but Major General Stephen Van Rensselaer's invasion force of 2,270 militiamen and 900 regulars had been thwarted by 1,000 allied troops and Indians, who had annihilated the American regulars while the militiamen refused to cross the Niagara. The same sort of refusal had brought the abortion of Major General Henry Dearborn's expedition on Lake Champlain in November.

In contrast, the British had captured the forts at Dearborn, Detroit and Mackinac, and had consolidated their alliance with the Indians and the French Canadians. This *débâcle* was a shattering moral and physical blow to those who had expected an easy victory, and had reinforced the anti-Madison lobby; had it not been for the considerable US naval successes in 1812, public opinion might well have swung decisively against war. As it was, the defeats on land, contrasted with success at sea, caused widespread rage in the pro-war states which paradoxically did wonders for recruiting.

By the end of 1812 it was abundantly clear to the US administration that future success depended absolutely on control of the Lakes. Brock's attacks on the American frontier forts had been founded on this, and these successes had bound the allies together. It was also realised that better commanders must be found; and an operational plan which directed the military effort at decisive points leading towards the defeat of the allies must be formed. The first improvements, the leadership, were at government level after Madison was elected for his second term. William James replaced Paul Hamilton as Secretary of the Navy. John Armstrong, a republican from New York who had been minister to France and a brigadier general in the US Army, assumed the post of Secretary of War. Six new major generals were appointed, but with an average age of 57 they were no more up to the rigours of campaigning than their predecessors, a deficiency which was only slightly offset by a younger and more vigorous set of brigade commanders.

At the operational level, the control of the Lakes as the pre-cursor to a successful invasion of Canada was entrusted to Captain Isaac Chauncey, who began in late 1812 to build up squadrons on Lakes Eire and Ontario. The necessary land operations would be undertaken in two areas of operation: west and north. In the west, a force of 7,000 men under Major General William Harrison would assemble at

Sandusky on Lake Eire and would recapture the lost Michigan territory including Fort Detroit, before seizing the Canadian settlement at Amherstburg. But the American main effort on land would be in the northern area of operations. Here, a force of 10,000 men would be assembled under Major General Dearborn at Sackett's Harbor and Buffalo; the initial plan called for 7,000 men to assemble at the former and 3,000 at the latter in April 1813. In co-operation with Chauncey's naval squadron, the force would capture first Kingston, then York and the British naval contingent there, and subsequently Fort George and Fort Eire in the Niagara peninsula.

This was essentially a sound plan which would secure naval supremacy by controlling the freshwater routes and the lake ports, and which would also sever allied communications westwards. But winter alarms during late 1812 called for the plan to be modified, as Dearborn was far from confident about his ability to capture the well-garrisoned fort at Kingston. Instead, the force from Sackett's Harbor would embark in Chauncey's ships, strike at York first and then capture Fort George; the force at Buffalo would take Fort Eire and Chippewa, and then link up with the main body after which the whole army would advance against Kingston. It would be supported by a third force of 4,000 men under Major General Wade Hampton, which would move west of Lake Champlain to threaten Montreal, linking up with Dearborn's army after the capture of Kingston.

Some success was vital, not only to restore credibility at home, but also because in the long term, the position of the US was precarious: the Orders in Council had been repealed even before war broke out, thus removing one significant source of grievance; and now, with Bonaparte defeated in Russia and the allies holding firm in Canada, a vigorous allied counter-offensive against America at sea and on land seemed a definite future possibility.

II. STRANGE BEDFELLOWS

The coalition forces which had inflicted such sharp defeats on the Americans in 1812 were strange bedfellows indeed: British; native Americans (generally referred to at the time as Indians, by which name they will be referred to hereafter); and Canadians, of whom a large percentage were, ironically, French. The assembly of such a coalition must therefore be counted as one of the most remarkable achievements

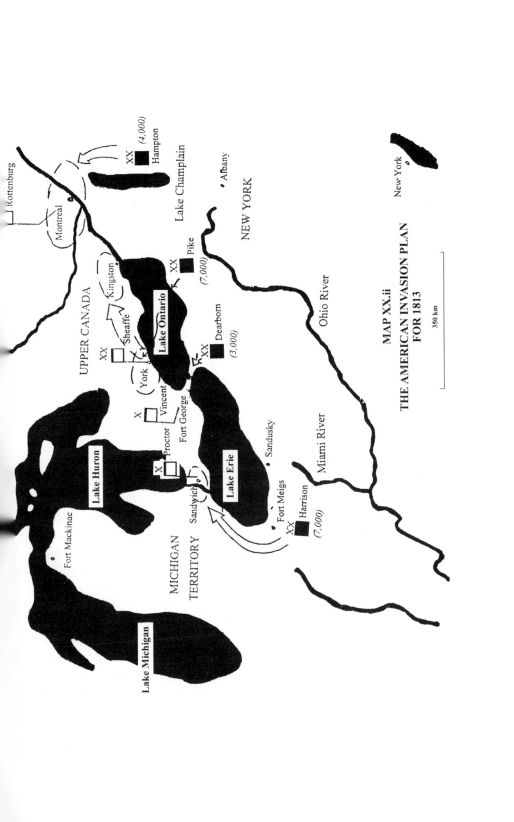

Kottenburg

(Montreal)

XX ■ (4,000)
Hampton

Lake Champlain

Kingston

Sheaffe

XX □ Vincent

Fort George
Proctor

UPPER CANADA

(York)
XX □
XX ■ Dearborn
(3,000)

XX ■ Pike
(7,000)

Lake Ontario

Albany

NEW YORK

New York

Ohio River

Lake Huron

Fort Mackinac

MICHIGAN
TERRITORY

Sandwich

Lake Erie

Sandusky

Fort Meigs

XX ■ Harrison
(7,000)

Miami River

Lake Michigan

MAP XX.ii
THE AMERICAN INVASION PLAN
FOR 1813

350 km

of British colonial rule in America. These forces held the 1,100 miles of frontier between the United States and the two provinces which formed that part of British North America, which were generally referred to as the Canadas.

The province of Upper Canada, with a population of 80,000 and with its capital at York, consisted of the territory west of the Ottawa river. Most of the population here lived in scattered farmsteads, and contained a high percentage of Americans who had migrated since the Revolution, and whose sympathies were generally in the USA.

The province of Lower Canada, by contrast, was more densely populated, with around 330,000 people of whom over 250,000 were of French origin. Its capital, Montreal, lay some 300 miles east of York. Another 400 miles eastwards, and separate from the Canadas but closely associated with them, were the maritime provinces of New Brunswick, Newfoundland, Prince Edward Island, and Nova Scotia. Here the population was either English, Scottish, or empire loyalists who had migrated from the USA after the Revolutionary War, and all of whom supported the British cause to the hilt: the 9,000 or so loyalists, for example, provided six battalions to the allied army before the end of the war, as well as maintaining links to the anti-war states in New England from where the army continued to be supplied.

If the loyalists in the maritime provinces were utterly dependable, what of the French in Upper Canada? The coming of the French Revolutionary War had brought great fear among the loyalist and British settlers in Canada, especially the former – had they not lost everything in the American Revolution, and did the same fate perhaps await them once more at the hands of the French? The ethnic tensions which this fear had created were if anything heightened by the introduction of the Constitution of 1791, which created a representative form of government for the first time in the Canadas, since it tended to over-represent the non-French element of the population. Scare stories of invasion by French fleets, or from Vermont, only made things worse.

But the beginnings of a *rapprochement* were created as early as 1793 by the lay, but more especially by the clerical, leaders of French Canada, who had quickly seen the French Revolution for what it was. In November of that year Bishop Hubert of Quebec issued an unequivocal circular letter which stated that the 'bonds which attached them to France had been entirely broken, and that all the loyalty and obedience which they formerly owed to the King of France, they now owed to His Britannic Majesty.'[5] This was followed by loyal manifestos in Quebec and Montreal and further reinforced by votes of money from the provincial assemblies for the prosecution of the French war. Thus it was the French Revolution which first broke the link with France, even though the distinctive French culture and language survived.

Even after the overt break with France, ethnic tensions remained, which were made worse under the governorship of Lieutenant-General Sir James Craig from 1807. 'Craig's reign of terror', as it became known, seemed capable of seeing only the possibility of treason and latent Bonapartism in the French community;[6] indeed Craig went so far as to propose the revocation of the Constitution of 1791 and the reorganisation of the Canadas in order to nullify French influence – even at the cost of favouring American settlers, who were much misliked by the French and whose loyalty was highly dubious. The French in Canada disliked these settlers partly because they stood for the same breakdown of established authority as the revolutionaries in France, and partly because they feared being swamped by a hostile population.[7]

It was certainly true that as the probability of an Anglo-American war grew, Bonapartist agents actively tried to make capital from the feelings of ill-will that Craig created, but their efforts were brought to nothing by the efforts of Craig's successor, Sir George Prevost. Prevost was a French-speaking British Lieutenant-General, of Swiss origin. He had previously been Governor of St Lucia and had successfully conciliated the French population there. In 1808, he had been transferred to Nova Scotia. On moving to Quebec in September 1811 he embarked on a policy not merely of conciliation, but of recognition for the French Canadians as a dominant ethnic group in Lower Canada, who had no desire to be submerged either by British or American influences. Prevost established excellent relations with the Assembly of Lower Canada, which by the outbreak of war had become so co-operative (in contrast to that of the Upper Province), that it voted almost $100,000 for the war.

It was equally supportive in the matter of the militia. Both Isaac Brock in Upper Canada and Prevost in Lower Canada pushed hard to raise the capability of the militia and in French Canada, such was the strength of support for Prevost, that the assembly agreed to embody 2,000 militiamen for 90 days training, extended to a year's service on the outbreak of war, provided the men were not enlisted into British regular regiments. Finally, when Lieutenant Colonel Charles de Salaberry raised the *Voltiguers Canadien* in April 1812, the ranks were filled within a matter of days.

Thus under Prevost's enlightened leadership, any proposed alliance between Napoleonic France and the USA gained no sympathy in French Canada: the newspaper *Le Canadien*, for example, led the way in opposing adventures by any outside power and went so far as to refer to Bonaparte as 'the lawless leader of France'.[8] So strong had dislike of both Bonaparte and of America become by 1812, that any inter-ethnic quarrels were effectively submerged.

These successes did little, however, to alleviate the short-term difficulties of the military situation in the Canadas. In 1812, the British regular army in the Americas numbered some 35,000 men, but of these, 23,000 were permanently stationed in the valuable colonies of the West Indies. Only 11,000 men formed the garrison of the Canadas and the maritime provinces. Of these, around half were in the five British regular battalions and the eight companies of artillery,[9] and half in the eight regular Canadian regiments which formed part of the British Army.[10] Some 5,000 of these troops were deployed in the maritime provinces, 1,200 in Upper Canada under Brock, and 4,000 in Lower Canada under Major-General Baron Francis de Rottenburg, a former

A contemporary caricature of Lieutenant-General Sir George Prevost (1767–1816) which well captures his cautious style of command. *McCord Museum, McGill University*

officer of the French Royal Army, who had for 20 years been in the British service.

In late 1812, two additional units had been sent to Canada,[11] and in early 1813 a more substantial reinforcement was found. This consisted of a cavalry regiment (19th Light Dragoons), an additional artillery company and some drivers, a company of Engineers, nine additional infantry battalions,[12] and drafts to bring the existing regiments up to strength. But no forecast could be made of when these extra troops would actually arrive in theatre.

Backing up this small force was the much larger militia, some 4,000 strong in Upper Canada, 6,000 strong in Nova Scotia, and potentially 60,000 strong in Lower Canada. For the most part these men were unarmed and untrained and affiliated to sedentary units of similar capability to their counterparts in the USA; but some units of trained militia did exist, and Brock in Upper Canada had been able to embody two companies per battalion for extended service anywhere in Canada.

Much of the available force was tied down in the main garrisons of Quebec, Montreal, Kingston, Halifax, York, Fort George, Fort Eire and Amherstburg; still others in many small militia posts, blockhouses and batteries. This, combined with the enormous distances, the appalling state of the roads, and the reliance on waterborne transport made concentrating any sizeable force extremely difficult. Thus the battles of 1813 in North America, although sometimes fought against odds of 20:1 and involving marches of almost superhuman effort, scarcely register when compared with the titanic struggle being waged in Europe. The lessons of coalition war are, however, no less valid.

Despite the reinforcement, America remained an afterthought for the British government, which is hardly surprising: the provinces could not hope to draw the full attention of London when overshadowed by the momentous events in Europe; nor was any weakening of the effort in Spain either possible or desirable. As early as 1807, Lord Castlereagh had laid down the basic elements of British strategy in North America:

> There are only two capital objects which could fully repay the expense and danger of an [American] expedition. One, the seizure of the town and harbour of Halifax in Nova Scotia . . . the most important naval station in the North American continent, the other the capture of the fortress of Quebec, which would place them in the sovereignty of His Majesty's Canadian Possessions.[13]

This policy had led to the neglect of all other fortifications – at least until the advent of Brock. But oddly enough, no compromise peace was sought after the relative success of 1812. In February 1813 a parliamentary debate on the American war upheld, with peculiarly insular logic, the almost indefensible position on impressment – this after the repeal of the Orders in Council. If Madison thought after 1812 that a face-saving compromise might be offered, he was much mistaken, and the vote in the House of Commons was for continued war, prosecuted principally by naval blockade.

To prevent the Americans from seizing control over the Lakes, Captain Sir James Yeo was sent from the West Indies with a cadre of 447 seamen to build up what was essentially a transport service into a fighting force, but insufficient resources were devoted to this project, which if pursued to the exclusion of all else could have guaranteed the security of the Canadas, and thus control of the Lakes was in due course to be lost to the Americans, with serious consequences.

On land, a strategic and operational defensive was to be maintained, for establishing economy of effort here was the only way to support the main effort in Spain: once Bonaparte was defeated, attention would turn to Mr Madison, but not before. As late as the middle of 1813, an exchange of letters between the Sir George Prevost and the Secretary for War and the Colonies Lord Bathurst confirmed this. Prevost wrote that 'Your Lordship must ere this be well aware that I have not been honoured with a single instruction from His Majesty's Government upon the mode of conducting the campaign . . .'

To which Bathurst, in tones which clearly indicate astonishment that any clarification of the position should be necessary, replied that

> His Majesty's Government felt that to present you a specific plan of campaign . . . was a measure only to add to your embarrassments and to fetter your judgement . . . more especially as the correct view which you expressed on the two points most essential to the defence of the Canadas, the maintenance of naval superiority on the Lakes and the uninterrupted communication with our Indian allies.[14]

These Indian allies were, for the British and Canadian military, the only way of evening up the likely force ratios against the Americans. As with the French Canadians, the alliance with the Indians was brought about through the subordination of national interest in the face of a unifying threat; and like the French Canadian alliance it was also the product of patient diplomacy over many years.

During the eighteenth century, both the British and French had sought alliances with the Indians, who were after all experienced warriors well used to the local conditions. For their part the Indians, and especially the most influential group in the north-west, the Iroquois – a term which itself means a confederacy or league of Indian nations embracing the Seneca, Cayuga, Oneida, Onondaga, Mohawk and Tuscarora tribes – had been nominally allied to the British by the Treaty of Utrecht in 1713, but had used alliances with both the British and French to serve their own interests. The Iroquois had in general preferred alliance with the French, whom they saw as less of a threat to the hunter-gatherer way of life, but after the triumph of the British they began to prefer them to the American colonists for very much the same reason.[15]

The Iroquois had a strong tradition of communal ownership of property and a well-developed political structure based on matrilinear families, both of which would come to the fore in 1812. The eventual triumph of the British in North America brought one highly significant political development, the Royal Proclamation of 1763, which was aimed at the avoidance of conflict. This important measure was to have a profound influence on subsequent history, for it laid down that Indian land could not be sold except to the Crown, and that the Indian hinterland was closed to agricultural expansion. Explicitly, the treaty stated that it was essential to the interests of the Crown

> . . . and the security of our colonies, that the several Nations or Tribes of Indians with whom we are connected, and who live under our Protection, should not be molested or disturbed in the Possession of Such Parts of Our Dominions. Territories as . . . are reserved to them . . . any lands whatever, which, not having been ceded to or purchased by Us as aforesaid, are reserved to the said Indians . . . And we do hereby strictly forbid . . . any Purchases or settlements whatever, or Taking Possession of any of the lands above reserved, without our especial leave and licence.[16]

Not unnaturally this proclamation was heartily loathed by the American colonists and became one of the acts used to justify the American Revolutionary War. Certainly, during that war the Iroquois fought on the side of the British in pursuit of their own interest once more. In later years, this proclamation was to be used as part of the Indian argument for recognising aboriginal title to unceded lands.[17]

With the end of the first American war, the Treaty of Paris brought the surrender of all British, Canadian and Indian claims south of the Great Lakes and a large-scale resettlement of Britain's Indian allies in Canada – a large group of Iroquois, for example, led by Joseph Brant, settled on the Grand river; and after Jay's treaty in 1794, 3,000 more were settled in Ontario. To underline this, in 1788, the US Congress passed the North-West Ordinance, which opened up the land west of the Ohio river to settlement by white-owned land companies, speculators and farmers. At first, few people made the trip and Indian tribal disunity prevented any serious opposition to the newcomers. But once European settlement began to gather momentum, Indian raiding soon developed into all-out war.

Thus from early days, America was identified in the Indian mind with oppression: the Iroquois term for the US President was – and remains – the same as 'town destroyer'.[18] Andrew Jackson's campaign against the Creek Indians in the Floridas, in full swing by October 1813, served only to underline this perception. But Canada, where the Great King offered sanctuary and protection, and trade with the North-West Company and the British Indian Department, was identified with the traditional Indian hunter-gatherer's way of life.

By 1809, a 40-year-old Indian chieftain had begun his rise to prominence in the Indian nation. This was Tecumseh, who was perhaps as great a statesman as any in North America at that time. The son of a Creek mother and a Shawnee father, he had been brought up in what was to become the Ohio territory of the USA. As a result of his experiences there as white settlement developed, he became convinced that there had to be a better strategy for the Indian nations than random raiding. This led him eventually to the concept of territorial security through racial unity, a development of the existing Iroquois tradition. Joined by his brother, who was generally known simply as the Prophet, they established the settlement of Prophetstown on the Tippecanoe river.

Here, in 1809, Tecumseh first propounded the view that no Indian had the right to concede land to white men without the consent of the whole Indian nation. This idea gained ground so rapidly that, although he eventually agreed to put the view to the US President, William Harrison, governor of the territory (later to become known as 'Old Tippecanoe'), decided that a salutory lesson was needed. This lesson, the destruction of Prophetstown in November 1811, was duly delivered.

In its aftermath, Isaac Brock realised that such an uncompromising attitude had driven the already pro-British Indians, athirst for revenge, into his arms. This was not so of the whole Indian nation: the Grand river tribes, for example, worn out by war with the Americans, elected to stay neutral. However, Brock's early attacks on Detroit and Mackinac were aimed as much at persuading Indian opinion as at striking the US, and in this they were successful – so many Indians showed up for the attack on Mackinac in the hope of booty that the British could not employ them all.

Brock and Tecumseh met for the first time on 12 August 1812 at Amherstberg. The meeting is well documented, and clearly the two made a deeply favourable impression on each other. Tecumseh is reported to have said to Brock, 'I have fought against the enemies of our great father, the King, and they have never seen my back. I am come here to fight his enemies on this side of the great salt lake, and now desire with my warriors to take lessons from you and your soldiers.' Then, turning to his companions, he indicated Brock and said to them, 'This is a *man*.' Brock's pleasure was deep indeed. At the time, he presented his general's silk sash to Tecumseh (it was bartered within a short time), and later wrote that 'a more sagacious or gallant warrior does not, I believe, exist'.

News of this meeting, and of the allied successes at Detroit and Mackinac, spread rapidly among the tribes, and soon it was said that 'Tecumseh now openly holds that the Great Spirit intended the Ohio River for the boundary between his white and red children, but that a cloud hung over the eyes of the tribes and they could not see what the Great Spirit meant. General Brock has now torn away the cloud.'[19]

There is an interesting parallel between the Indians and the Spanish guerrillas, in that both were likely to come off badly in formal battles, but used properly, could present an opponent with an insoluble tactical problem: the interaction of regular and irregular forces creates circumstances in which an enemy army can deal with a guerrilla force by dispersing in garrisons, guarding routes and convoys – all to the detriment of maintaining any concentrated force to contend with the opposing regular army. But should that same army try to concentrate against another army, and ignore anti-guerrilla operations, then it will find its communications raided, its depots looted and its isolated outposts made untenable.[20]

The death of Brock in action at Queenston on 13 October 1812 had dealt the allied cause a serious blow, and his successor, Major-General Roger Sheaffe, was not a man to inspire great loyalty. But even so, at the end of the year the allies still maintained a tenuous superiority on the lakes, and thus their lines of communication over the 1,100 miles of frontier and with the 6,000 Indians who, by early 1813, had declared for the allied cause. Of all his many achievements, this was perhaps Brock's most significant.

NOTES

1. Muir, pp.232–3 provides an excellent and balanced summary of the dispute.
2. Lloyd, p.30.
3. See Duane, *Hand Book for Infantry*.
4. Muir, p.234, characterises the US government's decision to go to war as 'stark folly'. Or as Lord Liverpool put it, 'the war on the part of America had been a war of passion, of party spirit, and not a war of policy, of interest, or of necessity.'
5. Wade, p.99.
6. See especially Wade, p.110.
7. See Lanctôt, *Quebec*, p.131.
8. See especially ibid. p.135.
9. These were battalions of the 8th, 41st, 49th and 100th Regiments, plus the 10th Royal Veterans Battalion, a garrison unit.
10. These were the Royal Newfoundland Regiment, the Royal Nova Scotia Regiment, the King's New Brunswick Regiment, the Royal Canadian Volunteers, the Queen's Rangers (of Revolutionary War fame), the Glengarry Light Infantry, the Canadian Fencibles, and the *Voltiguers Canadien*. Some independent troops of cavalry from the Canadian Light Dragoons were also present in Upper Canada.
11. The 102nd Regiment, and the *Chasseurs Britannique*, formed from French prisoners captured in Spain who had changed sides.
12. These were from the British 13th, 41st, 70th, 89th, 98th, 101st and 103rd Regiments; and the foreign regiments of De Watteville from Cadiz and De Meuron from Malta.
13. Stanley, p.75.
14. Coles, p.110.
15. Miller, p.68.
16. Berger, p.62.
17. Miller, p.73.
18. Ibid. p.76.
19. Lloyd, p.77.
20. See Miller, p.62 for a description of the style of Indian war.

Chapter XXI

The Invasion of the North-West

I. RAISIN RIVER

MAJOR GENERAL WILLIAM Harrison was appointed to command the North Western Army of the United States on 17 September 1812. His directive placed him in command of all regulars, rangers, volunteers and militia of the states of Kentucky, Ohio, Indiana, Pennsylvania and Virginia. The directive also ordered him first to form a new north-western army, since the existing one had been lost by Hull at Detroit, then to retake Detroit and the Michigan territory, and only then to embark on an invasion. Harrison was determined to begin operations as soon as possible in 1813, or better still, before the close of 1812. But he needed time to assemble and train his 7,000 available troops; and he also needed time for the establishment of naval superiority on Lake Eire.

Once this was achieved, Harrison planned an advance in three columns. On the left, Brigadier General James Winchester's brigade of Kentucky militia and some regulars would advance down the Maumee river from Fort Wayne. In the centre, the Ohio militia brigade, with the army's supply train, would advance from Urbana following Hull's route of 1812. Finally on the right, the Pennsylvania and Virginia brigades would advance down the Sandusky river. The whole army would converge at the Maumee (Miami) river rapids and continue the advance north to Detroit.

The hazards of such a campaign were not so much the allied field army, but rather from the harsh terrain, especially a huge swamp stretching from the Sandusky river to the Auglaize which barred the passage of wagons and heavy guns. There were also problems arising from the extremely cold weather, from harassment by Indian raiders, and the immense problems of organisation, transport and supply. All

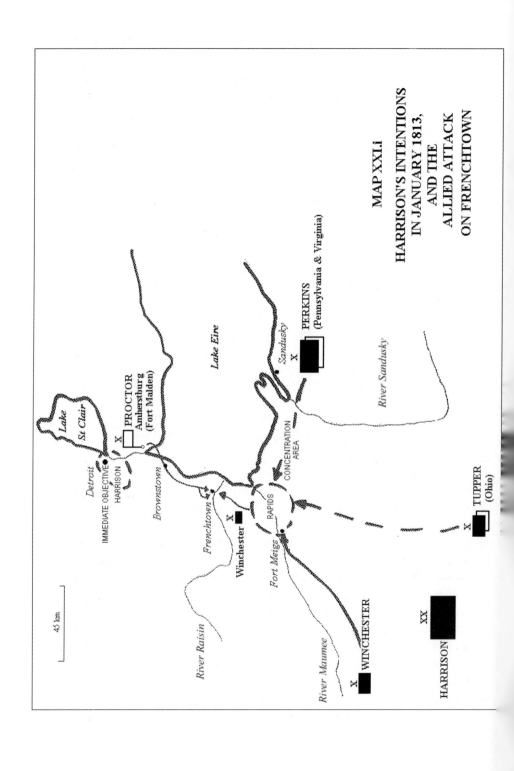

MAP XXI.i

**HARRISON'S INTENTIONS
IN JANUARY 1813,
AND THE
ALLIED ATTACK
ON FRENCHTOWN**

45 km

Lake St Clair

Lake Eire

Detroit

IMMEDIATE OBJECTIVE

HARRISON

X PROCTOR
Amherstburg
(Fort Malden)

Brownstown

River Raisin

Frenchtown

X Winchester

Fort Meigs

RAPIDS

CONCENTRATION
AREA

Sandusky

X PERKINS
(Pennsylvania & Virginia)

River Sandusky

X TUPPER
(Ohio)

River Maumee

X WINCHESTER

XX

HARRISON

these required Harrison's whole attention for months, before some kind of order was achieved. By this time, an autumn campaign had become impossible and Harrison decided to wait for the mud and wet to freeze.

By early December 1812, the assembly of the three parts of the army was well under way, although the needs of blockhouse building, anti-guerrilla operations against the Indians, and the assembly of supplies still caused difficulties. The onset of winter brought further problems. The American troops were inadequately clothed, sheltered and fed, and the bitter December conditions treated the soldiers cruelly: that they did not either mutiny or desert in droves says much for their determination. With conditions like these, Harrison decided he could not wait while his army deteriorated and so on 20 December he ordered Winchester's column to move and secure the Maumee rapids. Though the snow was two feet deep, Winchester's brigade reached its objective on 10 January 1813 and began to lay out a fortified camp on the north side of the river.

Some 35 miles north-east lay a small settlement called Frenchtown, on the Raisin river, and from here, messages were received indicating that American settlers and a large store of food was in need of rescue from a garrison reported to be about 50 Canadian militia and 100 Indians. After so much waiting, the chance to strike a blow was irresistible. On 17 January two columns, one of 550 men under Colonel William Lewis and another of 110 men under Colonel John Allen were dispatched, and by nightfall on the following day, Lewis had seized the town. The Canadian garrison withdrew with its 3-pounder field gun, having conducted a skilful delay battle for several hours.

But Winchester belatedly realised that his force was now divided, and half of it was only 18 miles from the strong British garrison at Fort Malden (Amherstburg). He marched at once with an additional 300 men to join Lewis so that by 20 January there were around 1,000 Americans at Frenchtown, but no artillery, and although Winchester's dispatches speak of a breastwork,[1] no real fortification of the position seems to have been undertaken. Moreover, his own headquarters was placed some way from the main position, on the other side of the river, and worse still, no covering troops were deployed against surprise. These arrangements greatly shocked Colonel Sam Wells, the only regular officer present, but he could do little to improve matters.

Wells's fears were well founded. The Canadian garrison at Frenchtown had sent word of the American attack to Colonel Henry Proctor commanding the allied troops at Amherstburg, and by 18 January

The Massacre at the Raisin River; a contemporary American woodcut portrays Indians drinking, and scalping their US prisoners. About 30, too badly wounded to walk, were murdered on 23 January 1813 when taken from the blockhouses. The British camp appears pointedly to the left.

Proctor was fully aware of the situation. Without delay, Proctor called up the militia to take over the defence of Detroit and Amherstburg, and assembled all available troops for a counter-attack. These troops consisted of 273 British regulars, 273 Canadian militia, three 3-pounder field guns, and 600 Indians led by Chief Roundhead.[2] Proctor moved the force across the ice to link up with the expelled Frenchtown garrison and then marched to within three miles of the Raisin river.

Although the force ratios were approximately even, Proctor had the clear advantage of surprise, so that an immediate attack before sunrise on 22 January would certainly have brought success. But Proctor chose instead to fight a set piece battle: he drew up his 273 regulars and his guns in his centre, a small body of militia on his left, and his 600 Indians and the rest of the militia on his right. These dispositions were eventually noticed by the American sentries, and Winchester's army stood to arms in two divisions, 600 men on the right, protected by a breastwork, and 400 on the left.

Having allowed his enemy time to form up, Proctor's assaults on the American right – the strongest part of the line – were three times beaten back with loss. But the Indians and militia on the right were able to turn the American left flank and produce a chaotic retreat in which both Winchester and Lewis were captured, and Allen killed. Winchester was taken first to Chief Roundhead, who relieved him of most of his clothes, and then to Proctor. Although the American right was still holding firm, Proctor convinced Winchester that a massacre was imminent, and Winchester ordered an immediate surrender.

About 500 Americans were taken, and 100 escaped, but almost 400 were killed or wounded by Winchester's own admission.[3] Proctor's losses too had been heavy – 185 of his 546 British and Canadians – and he promptly withdrew to Brownstown leaving from 60 to 80 wounded American prisoners at the Raisin river. Most of these were subsequently scalped and murdered by Indians, providing a propaganda coup for the American press: 'Remember the Raisin!' became the rallying cry of the North-Western Army, and Proctor was held personally to blame.

It is, however, doubtful if Proctor could have prevented the massacre and if he could, it is more doubtful still that he would have risked a rupture with his Indian allies over it. In all the Raisin river battle and the American defeat, although by no means decisive, did strengthen the allied resolve and delay Harrison's advance. It also taught Harrison to treat the allies with a great deal of respect and to exercise proper caution when advancing against them.

II. PROCTOR'S COUNTER-OFFENSIVE

Once news of Winchester's movements had reached Harrison, he himself moved as quickly as possible to the Maumee rapids where on 22 January he heard of the defeat at Frenchtown. Thus deprived of over 1,000 men, and with the enlistment terms of many of the Kentucky militia drawing to a close, Harrison had no choice but to delay his offensive; thus the initiative passed to Proctor. But Harrison did heed the lessons of the Raisin river, and he at once began work on a firm fortified base, which would prevent any allied penetration of Ohio, and from which he hoped to resume the offensive in due course.

The site he chose was on the south bank of the Maumee river, below the rapids, on rising ground which was well protected by a ravine and a stream on two sides and by the river on the third. Here he employed most of his 1,300 available troops by building a strong fortified redoubt which he named Fort Meigs, while he went off to Cincinnati to raise recruits in the knowledge that as the ice was breaking up it would be some time before an attack could be mounted from Amherstburg. He also expected the arrival of Brigadier General Green Clay with another 1,200 troops to boost the strength of the garrison to 2,500.[4]

Meanwhile Proctor was determined to follow up his success at Frenchtown which had earned him promotion to brigadier-general. He knew of the new fort on the Maumee from the reports of his Indians, and he was sure that a successful assault, destroying the fort before it could be completed and routing the American army, would both stabilise the Eire frontier for the rest of the year, and secure the valuable Michigan Territory. In addition this would allow him to release the militia men, who were needed on the farms to ensure adequate food stocks for the next winter. Proctor therefore requested more troops, while Tecumseh gathered the Indians. But the weather was as much against the allied commander as it had been against Harrison; a wet spring delayed any movement until April, by which time Fort Meigs was complete and Clay's relief column was only days away.

Nothing daunted, Proctor assembled his available troops and on 23 April he embarked 522 regulars, 461 militia, eight guns and two mortars on board six ships.[5] The force was further augmented by 1,500 Indians and two escorting gunboats. By 28 April, after a combination of boat transport, marching, and hauling the guns along difficult, muddy roads the force reached the site of an old fort, Miami, just below Fort Meigs. From here the gunboats harassed the fort while Proctor constructed two batteries on the north bank of the river and a third on the south, from where a bombardment was opened on 1 May.

Inside the fort, Harrison rapidly formed a plan to raise the siege. He knew that Clay was now close by, and so sent him a message ordering him to dispatch 800 men down the river on rafts to capture the batteries on the north bank and spike the guns, and then re-embark while the rest of Clay's force was to drive the Indians away from the fort and link up with the garrison, which would make a sally and destroy the remaining battery. The combined army would then attack Proctor's force and drive it off.

On the morning of 5 May Clay's leading regiment led by Colonel William Dudley duly appeared and spiked the British guns north of the river as arranged. But instead of re-embarking, the American troops set off in pursuit of some Indians, who led them towards the British camp at Miami. Proctor, assuming this landing to be the American main attack, drew the bulk of Tecumseh's Indians away from Fort Meigs and sent them to block Dudley's attack, supported by as many of the regular troops and militia as could be assembled. The result was that the Americans found themselves in a trap, from which only 150 escaped:

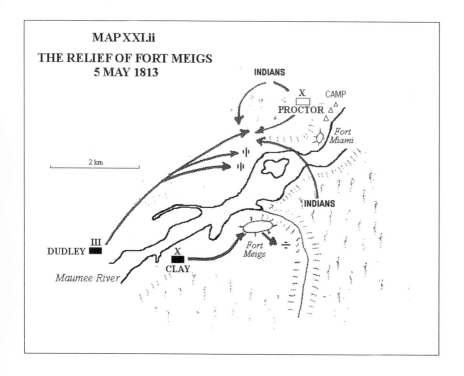

MAP XXI.ii

THE RELIEF OF FORT MEIGS
5 MAY 1813

200 were killed, 450 were made prisoner, and it took the personal intervention of Tecumseh to prevent a repeat of the Raisin river massacre.

On the south bank, the withdrawal of the Indians allowed the relief force to enter the fort and an American sally to seize the battery and drive off the remaining Indians, but the loss of Dudley's regiment prevented any further exploitation. The sally ended the fighting for that day, and indeed for the next two days there was little activity: half of Clay's men were inside the fort, and although the allies recovered and repaired their guns, and captured many of Clay's boats filled with supplies, there seemed little prospect of a successful assault. Indeed the seizure of supplies by the Indians was followed by the disappearance of most of them, laden with their plunder, and once the militia began agitating for a return home, Proctor had no choice but to lift the siege.

By 9 May the allied force was back at Amherstburg having won a tactical victory, but having surrendered the initiative once more to Harrison who had retained his base of operations. That said, Harrison's offensive had once again been subjected to delay, and any time was valuable to the allies. As his opponent wrote, 'If the enemy had been permitted to receive his reinforcements and supplies undisturbed, I should have had, at this critical juncture, to contend with him for Detroit, or perhaps for this shore.'[6]

Proctor knew that an American offensive was inevitable; he also knew that any further reinforcement of his own forces was out of the question and that if necessary, Upper Canada would be abandoned in order to concentrate all available forces against an American attack on the Lower Province.[7] He was also painfully aware of the limitations of his militia and the Indians, and it seemed to him that if he was to keep the Indians interested – and at the same time keep Harrison tied down – further offensive action was the only course open despite the limited resources. To sit still and wait would only invite destruction.

As it was, the siege of Fort Meigs was followed by a pause of two months. Harrison continued to gather and train recruits, and at the same time he conducted considerable reconnaissance with his newly-arrived mounted infantry regiment. As he did so, the new American squadron ominously neared completion at Presqu'isle. Ideally, Proctor would have liked to attack this fleet but his resources were far too slim. Instead, Tecumseh suggested another attack on Fort Meigs: this time, the available force was smaller than in May – only 400 regulars, 100 militia and 1,000 Indians, and only three six-pounder guns which were useless for a siege. Added to this, the fort had been much strengthened, and was now even better able to stand a siege.

Tecumseh's plan was therefore based on deception. The garrison would be lured out of the fort by a sham battle staged in the forest, which would convince Clay that another relief column was close by, and then encircled and destroyed by the allies. Under normal circumstances this plan would probably have worked, but on 20 July Clay had received word that no troops were to be expected for some time. This was the very day on which the allied force landed, near their old camp site, and thus when the attempt began, there was no movement from the garrison. On 28 July Proctor and Tecumseh were obliged to lift their siege and most of the Indians returned home.

Proctor however did not go home. His alternative idea had been to attack Fort Stephenson on the Sandusky river, and this he now decided to carry through. On 1 August his force, embarked in Captain Robert Barclay's squadron, landed early in the morning on the lake shore and erected a battery against the north side of the fort. This fort was a small wooden redoubt on the western side of the Sandusky river with a garrison of 160 regulars and one 6-pounder gun under the command of Major George Croghan. Against even this primitive structure, the bombardment of Proctor's light guns was ineffective; Proctor therefore decided to mount an assault. But although this assault on 2 August was pressed home with great determination by the British regulars, the garrison held its position, and forced Proctor to withdraw having suffered 96 casualties. This reverse effectively put an end to allied offensive activity and with the completion of the American squadron at Presqu'isle, the situation was about to change dramatically.

III. MORAVIANTOWN[8]

On 10 September 1813 the decisive battle of the year in the north-west was fought not on land, but on Lake Eire. In this three-hour battle, the US naval forces, nine ships under Captain Oliver Perry, captured the six-vessel British flotilla under Captain Barclay. Proctor had repeatedly warned of the dangers of allowing the Americans to construct their fleet but neither Major-General Baron de Rottenburg (now in command of Upper Canada), nor Prevost, nor Yeo felt able to divert more than slender resources away from the main effort of the defence of the Niagara peninsula and Lower Canada. Ironically, reinforcements had

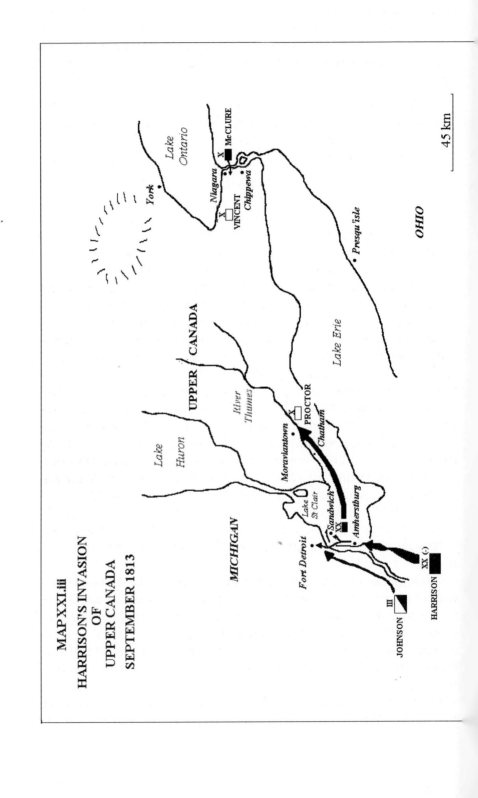

MAP XXI.iii
HARRISON'S INVASION
OF
UPPER CANADA
SEPTEMBER 1813

York

Lake
Ontario

Niagara
McCLURE
X

VINCENT
X
Chippewa

Presqu'isle

OHIO

Lake
Huron

UPPER CANADA

River
Thames

Lake Erie

Moraviantown

PROCTOR

Chatham

MICHIGAN

Lake
St Clair

Sandwich
XX
Amherstburg

Fort Detroit

JOHNSON
III

HARRISON
XX (-)

45 km

trickled in to Proctor's army during August, but he was in no doubt about the effect of the American victory would be on his communications:

> The loss of the fleet is a most calamitous circumstance . . . I do not see the least chance of occupying to advantage my present position, which can be so easily turned by means of the entire command of the waters here which the enemy now has, a circumstance that would render my Indian force very inefficient. It is my opinion that I should retire on the Thames without delay.[9]

Prevost clearly agreed, and on 22 September he ordered Proctor to withdraw from the Detroit frontier, directing that Rottenburg was to move forward to assist him. On 24 September, having delayed a week already, Proctor abandoned Detroit without waiting for Prevost's orders to reach him. Amherstburg was also abandoned and burned, and the allied army with such Indians as were prepared to go along, marched to Sandwich, linking up with the retiring Detroit garrison. From Sandwich the entire force of about 400 British troops, less than 100 militia, and about 400 Indians, marched north for the River Thames. All were thoroughly demoralised by the retreat, feeling no doubt that their hard campaigning during the previous year had come to nothing.

On the American side of Lake Eire the naval victory unleashed some frantic activity. Harrison now had some 5,000 men available for the invasion of Canada, including a mounted regiment of 1,000 Kentucky riflemen in two battalions, and Perry's supporting squadron. His intention was to send the mounted troops by road to Detroit, while the rest of his army would embark in the ships, land near Amherstburg and seize the fort there before marching on to Sandwich to link up with the mounted troops. This plan was put into operation on 27 September and American troops marched into the smoking ruins of Amherstburg hard on Proctor's heels.

Two days later Harrison reached Sandwich and occupied Detroit, but did not linger: it was clear that the allied force was within reach, and so a vigorous pursuit was pressed. On 2 October the whole American army, escorted by three gunboats, began to march south of Lake St Clair and along the south bank of the Thames, meeting no resistance, but finding all the signs of a hasty withdrawal: abandoned stores, burned buildings, and groups of stragglers.

Proctor had originally intended to make a stand at a small settlement called Moraviantown, where an excellent defensive position was

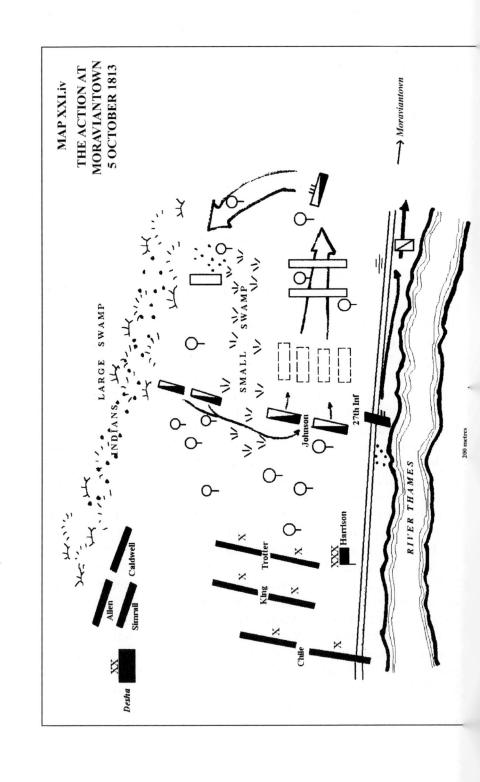

MAP XXI.iv
THE ACTION AT
MORAVIANTOWN
5 OCTOBER 1813

→ *Moraviantown*

LARGE SWAMP

SMALL SWAMP

INDIANS

Johnson

27th Inf

Desha

Allen

Caldwell

Simrall

King

Trotter

Chile

Harrison

RIVER THAMES

200 metres

available on a small plain, its front guarded by a wooded ravine, its left flank secure on the river, and its right flank covered by thick woods which would suit the tactics of the Indians. Proctor certainly intended to fortify this position, and had left all his artillery, save one gun, on it – but he had not withdrawn his main body to occupy the position. Instead the tired and hungry troops had been left two miles west of the village in an intermediate position which although secured on the flanks by the river and a large swamp, was open to a frontal attack by superior forces.

No orders were issued, nor was Proctor's intention known, so that when the 3,500 Americans appeared in front of the position on 5 October, the allied troops formed up as best they could. The 430 British formed two lines 200 yards apart with the single 6-pounder gun and 20 Canadian dragoons on the left, while the 600 Indians occupied the swamp. Harrison decided on an immediate attack. Placing most of his infantry on his left to prevent an envelopment by the Indians, he flung Lieutenant Colonel Richard M. Johnson's mounted regiment directly at the British troops. Being in open order, both lines were ridden down: Proctor and a few mounted Canadians fled, but most of the rest of the troops had no choice but surrender.

The mounted troops then wheeled onto the Indians' flank and dismounted as the American infantry attacked frontally; the Indians resisted fiercely for almost an hour longer, encouraged by Tecumseh who, although wounded, refused to give up the struggle until he was killed. With their ammunition exhausted, the Indians gradually withdrew into the swamp, taking Tecumseh's body with them. Where he was buried remains a mystery. The Indians left 33 dead on the field. The US casualty bill totalled 45.

The victory at Moraviantown was as complete a success as it could possibly have been. Proctor's command was virtually annihilated with the complete loss of 634 officers and men and all his eight or nine guns captured, including some which had originally been taken at Saratoga in 1777, and recaptured at Detroit. Moreover the Indians, dispirited and dismayed, retired to their hunting grounds: without Tecumseh, the Indian alliance was to all intents and purposes, dead.

Yet this complete tactical victory did not lead to operational success. Had the Americans pressed on and occupied the Burlington heights which lay between Lakes Eire and Ontario, they would have forced the allied forces in the Niagara peninsula to retire or be destroyed, and severed Upper and Lower Canada. Thus Moraviantown was potentially one of the decisive battles – if not the decisive battle – of the war.

The Battle of Moraviantown (or the Thames), 5 October 1813 in an 1833 American Lithograph. Dismounted Kentucky riflemen engage the Indians in the forest fringe. Their commander Lt. Col. Richard M. Johnson (US vice-president 1837–41) shoots dead Tecumseh, the great Shawnee chief.

But fortunately for the allies this was not to be, and it remained only a tactical success. Harrison had already outmarched his supplies, and any further advance was now impracticable anyway in the worsening autumn weather. By 14 October, the eve of Leipzig, Harrison had withdrawn his army to Detroit; on the same day he signed an armistice with the Indians and, like Proctor before him, began to issue them rations:

> . . . five nations of Indians, viz – Ottawas, Chippewas, Pottewatamies, Miamis and Kickapoos . . . have come in for peace; and I have agreed that hostilities should cease, for the present, on the following conditions: – they have agreed to take hold of the same tomahawk with us, and to strike all who are, or may be enemies to the U. States, whether British or Indians.[10]

On 17 October Harrison turned over the civil and military command to Brigadier General Lewis Cass, and made a triumphal progress to Washington. Here he was met only with official enmity and jealousy, and sent to a minor command in Cincinnati. When he offered his resignation in protest at this, it was accepted, and thus the USA lost the services of the one general who had so far won a significant victory on land, who had after two campaigns finally driven the British from western Upper Canada, and who had severed the British and Canadians from their Indian allies.

NOTES

1. Fay, p.76.
2. Hitsman, p.113 and Fortescue, viii, p.546.
3. Dispatch to the Secretary of War dated 23.i.1813 in Fay, p.74.
4. Fortescue, ix, p.324.
5. James, ii, pp.195–6. These ships were not, strictly speaking, yet under Yeo's or Barclay's command.
6. Dispatch by Proctor, cited in Wood, iii, p.35. His losses were only 61 killed and wounded.
7. See especially Proctor's letters dated 14.v.1813 and 19.vi.1813 in the Canadian Public Archives. In June Proctor was promoted major-general and his tiny command misleadingly designated the 'Right Division'.
8. This account is based on the descriptions in Fortescue, ix, pp.334–5 and Harrison's dispatch in Fay, pp.136–9.
9. Proctor to Prevost, 12.ix.1813 cited in Coles, p.129.
10. Gen. Duncan McArthur to the Sec. of War, 6.x.1813 in Fay, p.129.

Chapter XXII

Dearborn's Invasion of the North

I. YORK

WHILE HARRISON'S ARMY threw the allies back from Fort Meigs, the American main effort against Upper Canada was being developed on the northern front. After a change of plan described earlier, Dearborn accepted the notion of attacking York (later Toronto), the provincial capital of Upper Canada and so on 22 April, 1,700 regular soldiers and volunteer militia embarked in Chauncey's flotilla of 14 vessels after the winter ice broke. The town of York, although the capital of Upper Canada, was much smaller than Kingston and in 1813 it consisted of

> a pleasant little town, the houses generally of wood, and containing some good shops. Being the seat of government of the Upper Province, it has a house of assembly, court house, etc. It is situated at the lower end of a long bay formed by a narrow peninsula stretching up the lake, parallel to the shore, about two miles. On the extremity of this, called Gibraltar Point, stands a lighthouse, and exactly opposite to it, on the mainland, the garrison . . .[1]

York was not strongly garrisoned. Brock had planned a fort, but only a temporary blockhouse, magazine and ditch had been built along with some barracks and protective batteries. The available troops, commanded by Major-General Sir Roger Sheaffe, consisted of three companies of embodied militia, three companies of Canadian regulars and two of British regulars, some Royal Artillery gunners, and 50 to 100 Indians: in all, about 700 men.

The American assault force, commanded by Brigadier General Zebulon Pike, landed from 8 a.m. on 27 April, having been sighted as they passed Gibraltar Point. Some artillery and infantry at the landing site would probably have repelled the initial assault at least, but Sheaffe

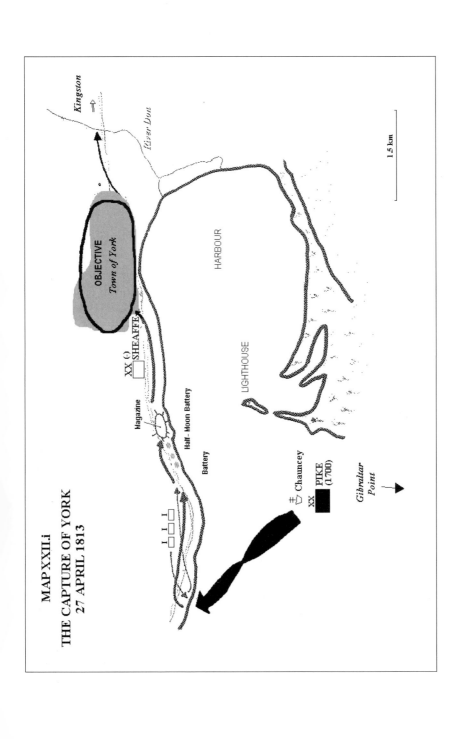

MAP XXII.i
THE CAPTURE OF YORK
27 APRIL 1813

Kingston

River Don

OBJECTIVE
Town of York

SHEAFFE
XX (-)

Magazine

Half - Moon Battery

Battery

HARBOUR

LIGHTHOUSE

Chauncey

PIKE
(1700)
XX

Gibraltar
Point

1.5 km

committed three companies piecemeal, all of which were thrown back by superior forces. By 11 a.m., the allied troops had withdrawn to the cover of their batteries and when one of these was accidentally blown up, morale began to crack. It was soon clear to Sheaffe that Pike's much larger force, supported by field artillery and the guns of the flotilla, would soon close up to the batteries and outworks, and Sheaffe saw no advantage in defending these against heavy odds. Gathering up all his regulars and some of the militia – 300 were left to become prisoners, he evacuated York, burning on the stocks a new frigate under construction, which was to be called *Sir Isaac Brock*, and blowing up the magazine.

The Americans entered the fortifications just before the explosion, which was devastating: casualties were heavy and included Pike himself; 260, as opposed to only 46 battle casualties.[2] This, and the excitement of their otherwise easy success, inflamed the Americans to loot and burn the town, an outrage which produced yet another item in the list of charge and counter-charge which so embittered the war. Sheaffe himself was held partly to blame by the people of York although his troops had incurred 156 killed and wounded, and it was many years before the sack of York was forgiven.

Sheaffe meanwhile hurried east to Kingston, a distance of almost 170 miles on rough and dirty roads, through country which was largely populated by American settlers none too friendly to the allied cause. After 14 days of ceaseless rain, the troops, with a considerable following of civilians, arrived at Kingston – seemingly little the worse for their long march.

While Sheaffe had turned east, Dearborn's men re-embarked in Chauncey's ships and on 8 May sailed west. Later that day the contingent disembarked near the US Fort Niagara, for here it was proposed to rest the force, while collecting all other available troops from Sackett's Harbor, Utica, Rome and Oswego: 'my intention', wrote Dearborn to Secretary Armstrong, 'is to collect the main body of the troops at this place and, as soon as Commodore Chauncey returns and the forces from Oswego arrive, to commence operations in as spirited and effectual a manner as practicable.'[3]

II. THE INVASION OF THE NIAGARA PENINSULA

Only two weeks later, Dearborn was ready to carry forward his plan for the seizure of the Niagara peninsula. The allied troops in this area consisted of just over 1,300 British and Canadian regular troops, up to 300 militia, Provincial Light Dragoons and some Indians, all under the command of Brigadier-General John Vincent.[4] There were few militia in the area, since this too was an area of considerable American settlement, and even fewer Indians. Sir George Prevost had ordered the move of two regular infantry battalions from Upper Canada to reinforce the Niagara frontier, and one of these, the 104th Regiment, had marched over 700 miles from New Brunswick to Kingston, *via* Quebec, in 44 days, a tremendous physical feat of winter warfare.

In the Niagara region, the two main forts, Eire and George, were old and in poor condition. Fort George was defended by only four guns and there were few batteries in between. Against these thin defences, the Americans could throw a force of up to 7,000 troops in two divisions, supported by a flotilla of ships which gave them a degree of tactical surprise, although they did not possess operational or strategic surprise since some kind of attack was expected.

After two days of preliminary bombardment with hot shot from Fort Niagara, the American guns again opened up on the foggy morning of 27 May, supplemented by fire from three schooners. Their target was Fort George, and under cover of the bombardment Dearborn's assault brigades in their barges were towed onto the lake shore behind Fort George, whose guns were either trained on the Niagara river, or were silenced by the American fire. Once the fog cleared and Vincent saw the assault force around 9 a.m., he dispatched all his available light troops, three companies, supported by one regular infantry battalion, to dispute the landing. But two battalions could do little against five brigades supported by naval gunfire and the allied force was gradually forced back.

Vincent realised that if he did not evacuate the fort, he would be encircled. Having fought for three hours and lost 358 casualties,[5] he spiked his guns, blew up his magazine, and withdrew south towards Queenston. As he did so he sent word to the garrisons of Fort Eire and Chippewa to abandon their posts, blow up their magazines, and join him at the supply depot at Beaver Dams, leaving Dearborn, who had suffered only 150 killed and wounded, to take possession of both the British-Canadian forts.

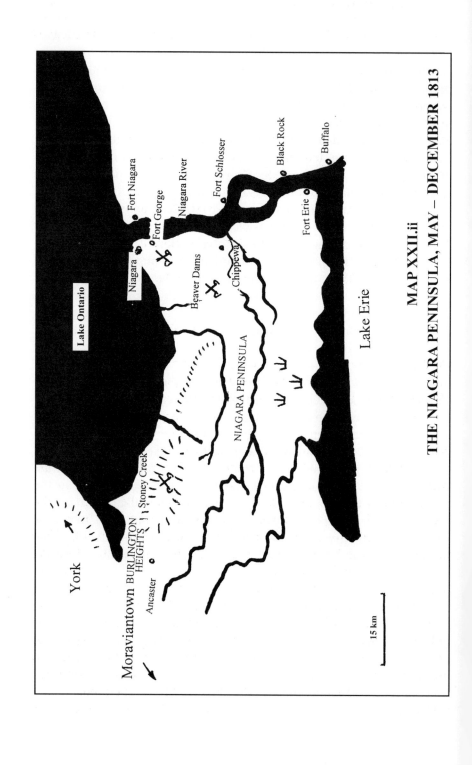

MAP XXII.ii

THE NIAGARA PENINSULA, MAY – DECEMBER 1813

Dearborn clearly thought that Vincent would make a stand at Chippewa and dispatched troops both to fix the Allied force there and to cut off any withdrawal westwards,[6] but in this he was mistaken. Vincent called up all available wagons, but allowed the militia to return home, and marched hard for Burlington heights. This he knew to be the vital ground in the region and he was determined to occupy it, knowing that in doing so he could both deny it to the Americans, while also keeping open his communications westwards to Proctor, and eastwards to York and Kingston. By 29 May he had reached the heights and there occupied a defensive position with his 1,600 men.

Against Vincent, Dearborn still possessed the great advantage of tactical mobility which Chauncey's flotilla conferred. This mobility he hoped to use in order to intercept Vincent's march somewhere along the lake shore,[7] but he was frustrated by contrary winds and by a surprise stroke at his own base of Sackett's Harbor.

III. SACKETT'S HARBOR

On the night following the American attack on the Niagara peninsula, Sir George Prevost ordered a diversionary attack onto Dearborn's base of operations at Sackett's Harbor, a stroke very similar in conception to the American attack on York. The attack was made possible by the arrival at Kingston, on 15 May, of Commodore Sir James Yeo and a cadre of 150 experienced officers and seamen. Yeo put together a force of five ships, two gunboats and 30 bateaux carrying 1,000 allied troops, with two field guns, and sailed for Sackett's Harbor.

Although the amphibious force arrived off its intended target on the evening of 28 May, light winds slowed the approach thus giving the American commander, Colonel Jacob Brown, time to summon 500 militia to supplement the 400 men of the regular garrison. Thus the 870-strong allied landing after dawn on the 29th was stoutly resisted until the fierceness of the assault threw the defenders back into their fortifications.

Thinking all was lost, an American naval officer set fire to the important navy yard; this was to say the least premature, for Prevost quickly realised that his two 6-pounder guns were quite incapable of breaching the defences, nor could Yeo's ships come in close enough to fire effectively. Prevost accordingly called off the attack, after over three hours' fierce fighting in which both sides lost 240 to 260 men.

This action did little direct damage, but the indirect consequences were immense. The first of these was that Chauncey, in mortal fear of losing his base of operations, withdrew the bulk of his ships from supporting Dearborn, and returned them to guard Sackett's Harbor, thus depriving Dearborn of both mobility and firepower. The second consequence was that, with Chauncey thus determined at all costs to preserve his squadron – including ships being built at Sackett's Harbor – the US Navy reverted to a defensive posture on Lake Ontario.

Repeated skirmishes were to take place all year between the two squadrons, but at the end of the war, Yeo could very reasonably claim that he had maintained enough control over the lake for allied troops to operate in the Niagara peninsula. Dearborn must have rued the day that he switched his initial attack from Kingston to York: had one of Zebulon Pike's brigades occupied the allied naval base at Kingston, then all allied operations in the north-west would have been seriously curtailed.

IV. THE ALLIED COUNTER-ATTACK

Vincent's position on Burlington heights was a good one, but he knew that he could not afford to stand still for long. Supplies were low, and to the west, Proctor's position was increasingly threatened: a vigorous American attack might well have forced him to retire on Kingston, but Dearborn was not the man to press the attack. Dearborn has been variously described, usually as 'feeble and sickly,'[8] and certainly the two brigadier generals, William Winder and John Chandler, to whom the pursuit of Vincent was entrusted, were far from energetic. The pursuing force of two infantry brigades (about 3,400 troops), a detachment of 150 dragoons, and eight or nine guns,[9] did not reach the area of Stoney Creek – about seven miles from Vincent's position – until 5 June.

Here it was located by allied scouts and that night Lieutenant-Colonel John Harvey, who had suggested the idea, led a force of about 700 British troops in a night attack on the American camp. The attacking force succeeded in surprising the sentries, but in spite of orders, the troops began shouting and firing before they were properly formed for the attack. This gave the Americans a few moments to stand to arms and thereafter, the fighting became confused and bloody. Just before daybreak on 6 June the British broke off the attack and withdrew, having lost 214 casualties but having inflicted 105 killed and wounded and taken 120 prisoners and four guns. Among the prisoners were both American brigadiers.[10]

The effect of Stoney Creek on the morale of both sides was dramatic: the allies were greatly encouraged, the militia began to turn in and Indians to appear, while the American commander, Colonel James Burn, decided on an immediate withdrawal to Forty Mile Creek.

On arrival there on 8 June he was joined by Major General Morgan Lewis, who since the temporary withdrawal of Dearborn himself on grounds of health,[11] now commanded in Niagara. Both were dismayed to see Yeo's squadron offshore, which had come from Kingston with supplies and 220 reinforcements for Vincent. Seeing the Americans, Yeo sent in two ships to bombard them while taking 16 boatloads of US supplies. Believing he was about to be caught between an amphibious assault and a pursuit by Vincent, Lewis ordered an immediate and precipitous withdrawal.[12] As they went, the Americans were harassed constantly by Yeo's ships on the lake, and on their flanks and rear by the increasing numbers of militia and Indians.

Lewis fell back as far as Fort George, not only abandoning the Niagara peninsula but also the positions at Chippewa and Erie which had been occupied without a fight on 28 May. Erie was burned on 9 June and the bulk of the American army concentrated around Fort George, whose fortifications were strengthened with new earthworks, and where boats were placed for a possible evacuation. The Americans also abandoned vast quantities of much-needed stores which were seized by the allies: 500 tents, as well as wagons, food, ammunition, muskets, and guns.

Clearly the Americans were morally beaten already, and Vincent was, unlike Dearborn, anxious to reinforce his success. By 23 June the allied force was deployed around Fort George with troops astride the road westward at Twelve Mile Creek and Twenty Mile Creek, and also astride the St David's road, while Yeo's seven ships and six gunboats cruised the lake and the straits unchallenged all that month in capturing five supply vessels and two depots. Thus a force of at least 6,000 Americans had allowed itself to be penned in by a force of no more than 2,500 allies, including 550 Indians and militia.

Steadily, Vincent began to tighten the noose, although in view of the force ratios he felt unable to risk a direct assault on Fort George itself. Instead he resorted to guerrilla tactics, using an *ad hoc* force of three companies of light troops, some provincial light dragoons and about 400 Indians, who fell on American outposts, foraging parties and patrols. These tactics provoked an American expedition, aimed at destroying the allied base at Beaver Dams from where the raiding operations were directed.

This expedition, consisting of 570 troops under Lieutenant Colonel Charles Boerstler, set out for Beaver Dams on the morning of 23 June. It was quickly seen and reported by the Indians, as predicted by the famous Laura Secord, to the British troops on the St David's road: on the 24th, the American column marched into a 400-strong Indian ambush at about 9 a.m. in the beech woods. The Indian force kept up the fight for three hours until the arrival of British troops, after which a demand for surrender was issued by the allies, no doubt playing on American fears of another Raisin river massacre, which was duly accepted.

It is fair to say that Beaver Dams was essentially an Indian victory: the first British commander on the scene, Lieutenant James FitzGibbon, afterwards wrote that

> ... not a shot was fired on our side but by the Indians. They beat the American detachment into a state of terror, and the only share I claim is taking advantage of a favourable moment to offer them protection from the tomahawk and the scalping knife. The Indian Department did all the rest.[13]

A total of 510 American soldiers were made prisoner and the remainder, being 30 militia, were paroled. The trophies included two guns, two wagons, and the colours of the 14th US Infantry.[14]

The action at Beaver Dams encouraged the allies to keep up the pressure on the Americans, and to extend the scope of their raiding across the frontier. From 19 June, General Rottenburg took over the command in Upper Canada from Sheaffe, and for a while moved his headquarters to Twenty Mile Creek. Rottenburg placed a strong detachment on Burlington heights to secure the position against an amphibious *coup de main* attack, and then proceeded to mount a succession of raids on American bases across the Niagara river. By the end of July, the Americans were feeling their humiliation keenly. One commentator noted that

> ... we have had an army at Fort George for two months past, which at any moment of this period might by a vigorous and well-directed exertion of three or four days have prostrated the whole of the enemy's force ... and yet this army lies panic-struck, shut up and whipped in by a few hundred miserable savages, leaving the whole of this frontier ... exposed to the inroads and depredations of the enemy.[15]

The news of Beaver Dams created a far greater consternation in Washington than in Fort George, so much so that Secretary of War Armstrong ordered Dearborn's permanent dismissal on 6 July and his replacement by Major General James Wilkinson. For a drastic change of direction in the conduct of the war was being contemplated: no further moves would be made in the north or north-west – hence the lack of any exploitation of Harrison's success at Moraviantown – but all American forces would be concentrated at Sackett's Harbor. From here, an attack could be mounted on Kingston, or else the force moved down the St Lawrence to link up with Major General Wade Hampton's Lake Champlain army for an assault on Montreal. The Erie and Niagara frontiers would thus become economy sectors, and although Wilkinson himself did not favour this plan, it was accepted in late July 1813.

From then on, the 4,000 American regular troops in the Niagara peninsula were gradually replaced by about 1,200 New York militia, and about 70 renegade Canadians, under militia Brigadier General George McClure. But any immediate pressure on them was relieved by the news of Proctor's defeat at Moraviantown. Prevost and Rottenburg had by now returned to Kingston and from here, Prevost ordered the evacuation of all Upper Canada west of Kingston. But Vincent clung to his belief in the importance of the Burlington heights, fearing what would happen if Harrison was allowed to advance rapidly to occupy the position. After some reflection, Prevost agreed with him and Vincent therefore pulled back his forces so that if Harrison did try to reinforce his success, he would find the heights strongly held against him.

McClure's New York militia was prompt in following up the allied withdrawal, and during October and November there followed a spate of looting, burning and skirmishing in the peninsula. By mid-November, it was clear to Vincent that no American advance would in fact materialise, and he began therefore to push forward again. By early December, McClure had decided to abandon his foothold in Canada and re-cross the Niagara river, due largely to his militia refusing to serve longer, and on 10 December he gave orders for the evacuation of Fort George and the burning of the nearby small town of Newark.

The latter action is impossible to justify on military grounds, since there were no fortifications and Fort George was not being retained: the town, which had formerly been the provincial capital, was in many ways larger and more significant than York. It consisted of around 300 buildings including two churches, the registry office, and the library; burning it could only bring suffering to the 400 women and children evicted into bleak December weather – but McClure pressed on.

The relieving allied troops arrived just as the Americans had fled, too late either to prevent the destruction or to engage the Americans. Thus the American occupation of the Niagara peninsula ended, in the aftermath of the burning of both York and Niagara, on a note of great bitterness and resentment.

V. THE DESTRUCTION OF BUFFALO

The burning of Niagara was soon to be repaid with interest. On 13 December 1813 Lieutenant-General Gordon Drummond, a Canadian-born British officer, was appointed in succession to Rottenburg, president of the council and administrator of Upper Canada, as well as commander of all troops in the province. Drummond was well aware of the withdrawal of American regular troops from the Niagara frontier, and he was intent on revenge. On 17 December he arrived at the Right Division's headquarters in St David's and gave orders for an immediate attack on Fort Niagara. This was to be a surprise attack, mounted by night: boats were brought overland from Burlington heights, and a force of 550 British troops, mainly of the 100th Foot, with some militia and Indians was assembled under the command of Colonel John Murray. Murray's instructions were detailed:

> The troops must preserve the profoundest silence and the strictest discipline. They must on no account be suffered to load without the orders of their officers. It should be impressed on the mind of every man that the bayonet is the weapon on which the success of the attack must depend.[16]

Late on 18 December the troops embarked, slipped quietly across the river, and landed three miles from Fort Niagara. Surprise was complete, for the garrison's password was known to the attackers. The attack was made in three columns: the first column found the main gate left open; the second column stormed the north redoubt of the fort; the third column crossed the curtain wall. The most serious fighting took place in the south redoubt where, encouraged by their commander's cry of 'bayonet the whole!' the British troops fought hand to hand with the defenders.[17] The Americans however would not stand and by dawn the fort, along with 422 prisoners, 27 guns, 3,000 muskets and a great store of ammunition, tents and provisions, were in allied hands for only 8 casualties. Only 22 men escaped to carry the news to McClure.

Immediately after this success, another force of 500 British regulars and 500 Indians under Major-General Phineas Riall (replacing the sick Vincent) crossed the river and seized Lewiston. Here too more stores and guns were taken, but more importantly perhaps, the area of Queenston was at last freed from the threat of invasion. Riall burned the village of Youngstown and the Indian camp at Tuscarora, and then pressed on to Fort Schlosser and Manchester, both of which were put to the torch. Riall pressed on again, but finding that the bridges on the roads leading to Buffalo had been dropped, he retired to Queenston.

It was to Buffalo that McClure had gone after the evacuation of Fort George. Here he tried to raise troops, but found that his conduct across the frontier, which had already brought unwanted reprisal, had made him no friends: indeed the local militia commander, Brigadier General Timothy Hopkins, refused point blank to serve under McClure, citing his behaviour as the reason.[18] Indeed such was the feeling against McClure that Secretary of War Armstrong ordered him to be relieved of command and replaced by Major General Amos Hall of the New York militia. It was too late.

Drummond's intention was now to secure the Niagara river for the remainder of the winter, and if possible for the rest of the war. Aware of the attempts to raise troops in Buffalo, he was concerned that this might presage another invasion attempt. On 28 December therefore, he issued a general order for an attack which was to destroy both the naval base of Black Rock – which had been raided in July by a force of 200 British regulars under Lieutenant-Colonel Cecil Bisshop[19] – and the settlement of Buffalo, and in addition destroy three schooners of the Erie flotilla known to be drawn up below Buffalo. Command of the attack was given to Riall, with 1,100 British and Canadian troops and 400 Indians available.

Riall's initial assault wave crossed the river at night on 29 December and landed one and a half miles below Black Rock. The follow-up wave of 400 Royal Scots then crossed in daylight on the 30th, intending to land above Black Rock and turn the defenders' position. However the defenders' fire was so heavy that this second wave was effectively pinned down, despite covering fire from five guns on the Canadian shore, and the initial assault troops had to force the defenders out unaided from their entrenchments. This they did, and pressed on to Buffalo where the Americans mounted a second feeble resistance: Hall later attributed this partly to the lack of regulars but also, interestingly, to the defection of those Indians whom the Americans had cultivated during the preceding months.[20]

The American force of 2,000 men was rapidly driven out of the village, leaving eight guns and 130 prisoners behind them. Riall then turned his attention to the object of the attack. The three ships were burned to the waterline, and all stores which could not be carried off were likewise destroyed. Then both Black Rock and Buffalo were burned, so that the whole frontier had – literally – been reduced to ashes in reprisal for Newark.

Thus ended the campaign of 1813 on the northern front. After a promising start, it had cost the Americans dearly, and the allies had more than recovered their initial losses. In the process, the war had taken an ugly turn; the torch and the scalping knife would continue to characterise operations in Upper Canada for the rest of the war. But for now, a dangerous situation which might have seen the abandonment of all Upper Canada west of Kingston had been averted.

Feeble American leadership had thrown away the initial gains, and the naval stalemate on Lake Ontario seemed set to continue. Bold and resolute action by Vincent and Drummond had transformed the operational situation, which after Moraviantown had seemed hopeless, and success had brought the Canadian militia and the Indians back to the cause. Well might Hall write that 'The Niagara frontier now lies open and naked to our enemies.'[21]

NOTES

1. Stanley, p.169.
2. Chauncey to the Secretary of War, 28.iv.1813 in Fay, pp.85–6.
3. Dispatch dated 13.v.1813 in Stanley, p.179.
4. Fortescue, ix, pp.311–12.
5. Hitsman, p.131.
6. See Dearborn's dispatch dated 29.v.1813 in Fay, p.100.
7. Ibid.
8. Stanley, p.186.
9. Fortescue, ix, p.318.
10. Dispatch by Gen. Lewis in Fay, p.108. See also the account in Harman, *Stoney Creek*, pp.27–43.
11. Dispatch by Lewis to the Secretary of War, 14.vi.1813 in Fay, p.105.
12. Ibid.
13. Letter by FitzGibbon dated 30.iii.1818, cited in Stanley, p.197.
14. See Dearborn's Dispatch dated 25.vi.1813 in Fay, pp.112–13. See also Harman, *Beaver Dams*, pp.32–5 and 40–3, for maps and documents.
15. *Niagara Frontier*, ii, p.283.
16. Dispatch dated 17.xii.1813 in *Niagara Frontier*, xi, p.4.
17. See the account in Harman, *Niagara*, pp.22–7.
18. *Niagara Frontier*, ix, p.14.
19. See the account in Harman, *Black Rock*, pp.18–23.
20. Dispatch by Gen. Hall dated 6.i.1814 in *Niagara Frontier*, ix, pp.93–6.
21. Hall to Governor Tomkins of New York, dated 30.xii.1813 in Fay, p.168.

Chapter XXIII

Montreal and the St Lawrence

I. CHÂTEAUGUAY

C ONTROL OF THE city of Montreal was without doubt a decisive point on the road to success in any campaign in the Canadas. It dominated the St Lawrence, and controlled the access both to the Great Lakes, and to Quebec and the maritime provinces. Through the city passed large quantities of supplies for the allied army in the Canadas, supplies not just from Europe, but in large measure from New England as well. No wonder that the city had been a priority target captured in the campaigns of 1760 and 1775. Prevost clearly understood Montreal's importance, as his defensive plan showed by the placing of the military main effort in Lower Canada – if necessary at the cost of abandoning the Upper province.

But the Americans seemed less certain of the city's importance; during most of 1813 the frontier was quiet except for brief interludes, such as the Canadian raid on Ogdensburg in February and the attack on Sackett's Harbor. Even so, the military commander, Major-General Francis de Rottenburg, kept a close watch on military developments south of the frontier; he also did all he could to encourage the continuing trade from New England along the Lake Champlain route. As Prevost himself later pointed out, 'two thirds of the army in Canada are at this very moment eating beef provided by American contractors, drawn principally from the states of Vermont and New York . . . it is expected that Congress will take steps to deprive us of these resources.'[1]

Early in 1813 some attempts to stop this trade were indeed made by the Americans, principally by establishing a naval blockade on the northern end of Lake Champlain. This was ended by a bold stroke from the British garrison at Isle aux Noix, in which the two American armed schooners were seized on 3 June. This limited success encouraged a bolder move still, for by July, Wade Hampton's Lake Champlain army was assembling at Burlington in Vermont leaving the town of Plattsburg on the western side of the lake unguarded; moreover, the Americans could now only man two sloops of war. A force of 950 British and Canadian troops was therefore assembled under Lieutenant-Colonel John Murray, supported by Commander Thomas Everard's Royal Navy flotilla of two schooners and three gunboats. This force at the end of July sacked Plattsburg, bombarded Burlington in Vermont, and then went on to capture almost the whole of the American merchant fleet on Lake Champlain.

But it was not until after their repulse at Stoney Creek that the Americans formulated the plan designed to bring victory. The new commander in Niagara, Major General James Wilkinson, had decided to discontinue active operations in the north and north-west in order to concentrate all available naval and military forces at Sackett's Harbor. From there, an advance would be made down the St Lawrence to link up with Hampton's Lake Champlain army, after which the whole force would capture Montreal.

This plan, although promising, contained three significant flaws. First, it was left until late in the year, thus inviting disaster from the weather; second, Lake Ontario was left in allied hands so that Wilkinson's rear was always under threat; and third, although Wilkinson was placed in overall command, Hampton, who loathed him, never really accepted this arrangement and in effect conducted a separate campaign. Disagreements in the high command were not helped when Secretary of War Armstrong himself moved to Sackett's Harbor, encouraging the notion that Wilkinson was not trusted.

Arguments over whether Kingston or Montreal was the proper object of the attack went on for weeks, and it was not until 17 October that Wilkinson's army, 7,000 men of all arms formed in two divisions, embarked in a great fleet of 300 *bateaux* and sailed for the rendezvous with Hampton at the Isle Perrot. It was far too late in the year for such an attempt, and the autumn storms played havoc with the transports: 15 were sunk, others damaged, and all were dispersed, so that it was not until 5 November that the army was reassembled at Grenadier Island – a mere 15 miles from Sackett's Harbor.

Hampton meanwhile had been ordered to move from Burlington to Plattsburg, and this he did. In early September his 4,000 troops began to march northwards first to Chazy and then on 20 September to

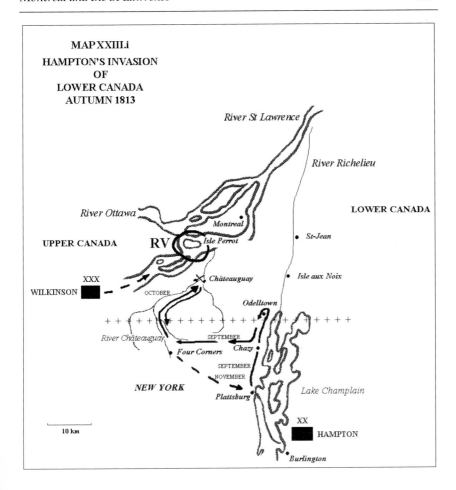

MAP XXIII.i

HAMPTON'S INVASION
OF
LOWER CANADA
AUTUMN 1813

River St Lawrence

River Richelieu

River Ottawa

LOWER CANADA

Montreal

UPPER CANADA

RV *Isle Perrot*

St-Jean

XXX
WILKINSON

OCTOBER

Châteauguay

Isle aux Noix

Odelltown

+ + + + + + + + + + + + + + + + + + + +

River Châteauguay

SEPTEMBER

Chazy

Four Corners

SEPTEMBER
NOVEMBER

NEW YORK

Lake Champlain

Plattsburg

XX
HAMPTON

10 km

Burlington

Odelltown in Lower Canada. From there onwards the road north passed through flat, swampy, and heavily forested country which was defended by a small force of embodied militia and Indians, supported by a larger number of sedentary militia, all under the command of Lieutenant Colonel Charles de Salaberry. This force had spent much time and effort erecting roadblocks and obstacles on the northward road, and it succeeded in inflicting so much delay on the advancing Americans that Hampton decided to go no further – probably he was also aware of the threat of a flank attack from the garrison of Isle aux Noix. Hampton gave his reason for turning back as a shortage of water, which was true, although this had not stopped the smuggling of at least 500 horses and 1,000 cattle up the same route that summer.[2]

Certainly Hampton missed the chance to establish a bridgehead in Lower Canada on the Richelieu river which might have forced the withdrawal of some of the outlying garrisons, and secured the route north. But now, unaware of thin the allied defence actually was, Hampton evacuated Odelltown and retired on Four Corners, New York. From there, although the route to Montreal was longer, water supplies were plentiful and an advancing force was out of reach of the Isle aux Noix garrison.

As he marched to Four Corners, Hampton received word from Armstrong that Wilkinson's army would not move for some time, but that Four Corners was to be secured as a base of operations, and further, that no invasion was to be undertaken until both armies were in a position to co-operate.[3] Apart from raiding, therefore, Hampton's army remained at Four Corners until 20 October.

On the allied side, Prevost was now well aware of the growing threat. As the American threat to Niagara receded, he removed his headquarters back to Montreal by 25 September, where he and Sheaffe, who had succeeded de Rottenburg in Lower Canada, began to muster their available forces. Along the frontier, Sheaffe deployed a covering force of Indians and militia which, with his civilian spies, was designed chiefly to gain information. The main defensive line was then formed by 3,000 militia manning the Châteauguay river, and another 5,000 manning a line from the river to the settlement of Hemmingford. These lines were stiffened by four battalions of Canadian regulars, two battalions of embodied militia, the regular garrisons at St Jean and Isle aux Noix, and some artillery.

Behind the main positions, Sheaffe created a reserve based on a field artillery brigade, a cavalry squadron, a company of guides, three battalions of regular troops, and a large force of sedentary militia. This force occupied a position south of Montreal, around La Prairie, L'Acadie, St Jean and St Pierre. Finally, the city of Montreal was itself fortified and garrisoned with militia and volunteers.

These defensive preparations were made possible by American delays which, by mid-October, had begun to raise serious doubts in Hampton's mind.[4] On 18 October he at last received word that Wilkinson's force was on the move and on the basis of this he decided that the time had come to march north once more. Although the New York militia was proving troublesome, Hampton had a force of 4,200 regular troops, 10 guns and plentiful supplies: Hampton felt confident that any opposition could be swept aside, and so on 21 October the army marched.

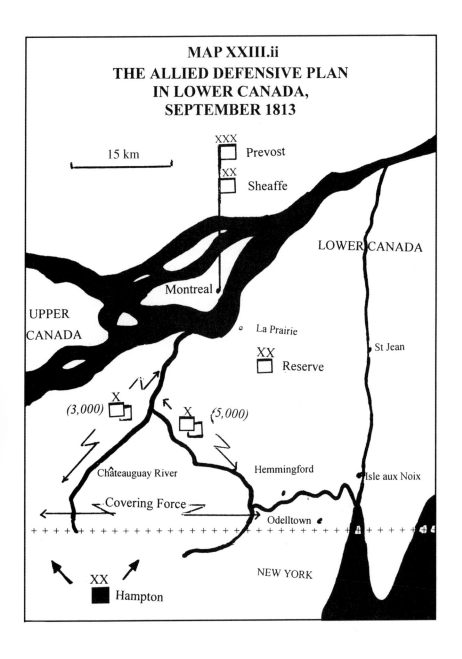

MAP XXIII.ii
THE ALLIED DEFENSIVE PLAN
IN LOWER CANADA,
SEPTEMBER 1813

The allied defenders were well aware of his movements and, although mostly Canadian and with few regular troops, were commanded personally by de Salaberry who had selected an ambush site with care. The position chosen was about 15 miles from the St Lawrence on the north side of the Châteauguay river, where the road ran close to the river bank on one flank and where the other flank was protected by a swamp in which a small force of Indians was concealed. The front of the position was secured by a gully and beyond this was an open area which would expose the Americans to the defenders' fire. The position was occupied by 350 Canadian troops, and was well fortified in depth with log barricades; finally, the river flank was secured by a small redoubt covering the one ford over the river. This force would have to hold on for some time, although reinforcements of regular troops were on their way under Major-General Louis de Watteville.

The Canadian position was scouted by the Americans on 25 October and Hampton was told that a strong frontal assault combined with a flank attack across the river ford, would certainly succeed. Hampton accordingly sent a brigade of 1,500 men south of the river during the night, whose task was to fall on the flank of the position; this would be the signal for the start of the main attack. After a thoroughly unpleasant night march, this flanking force finally emerged from the woods, but was promptly engaged by the 160-strong militia detachment guarding the river and thus no signal was sent to Hampton.

Hampton waited until 2.00 pm before deciding that he could delay no more, and gave the order to attack. As the Americans moved forward, de Salaberry himself stood up and shot a mounted American officer, an act which raised such loud hurrahs from the defenders that Hampton began to have second thoughts about the size of force opposing him. The result was that he did not press home the attack and after two hours of firing in which the combined loss was 75 casualties, the Americans broke off the attack just before dark.

The action at Châteauguay was certainly no more than a skirmish, but it was to prove highly significant in two respects: first, in terms of morale and Canadian folklore, it was a battle in which a small force of Canadian militia and Indians, only partially trained, had resisted a force of American regulars seven times as strong, and had won. Second as a tactical success, it led on to a greater success at the operational level, for the following day, Hampton decided to retire on Four Corners and go into winter quarters.[5] Hampton in fact did not stop at Four Corners, but went all the way back to Plattsburg, an action which, as Wilkinson rightly said, 'defeats the grand objects of the campaign'.[6] Hampton resigned in March 1814.

II. CRYSLER'S FARM

Once Wilkinson had collected his scattered army at Grenadier Island he determined to press on an effect a junction with Hampton as soon as possible, and this he communicated, with his proposed route, to Hampton,[7] not knowing that Hampton had already been halted at Châteauguay. On the night of 6–7 November he floated his 300 boats silently passed Fort Wellington at Prescott, having landed his troops on the American side of the St Lawrence. Next day, the army marched for Ogdensburg. Wilkinson was clearly worried at the lack of news from Hampton, and he was moreover being shadowed by a corps of observation sailed from Kingston under Lieutenant-Colonel Joseph Morrison, consisting of about 900 British and Canadian troops, including two regular battalions, about 30 Indians, and three gunboats.

For want of any ideas to the contrary Wilkinson decided to press on down the river, and on 8 November he reached the Long Sault rapids. If the boats were to go through, these rapids would take at least two days to traverse, and troops would have to be landed on the Canadian side to guard against any interference from the allies. On 9 November therefore, two brigades (3,700 men) under Brigadier General Jacob Brown landed on the north bank and pressed on to the village of Cornwall at the northern end of the rapids, pushing aside about 300 Canadian militia on their way. The bulk of the army was, however, held near the flotilla under the command of the senior brigadier, John Boyd. By dark on 10 November the flotilla had moored for the night at Crysler Island.

The next morning dawned bleak and cloudy after a night of rain. Wilkinson, who had taken to his bed with a fever, received news that Brown had reached Cornwall and that the boats should now be pushed down the rapids. As the Americans began their move, Morrison saw his chance. His three gunboats opened fire on the American flotilla and his small force advanced on Boyd's rear. His intention appears to have been to occupy a defensive position, inflict as much damage as possible on the American troops and their transport, and then retire.

His position was well chosen. His right flank rested on the river and was covered by the gunboats, and by 150 British and Canadian regulars,

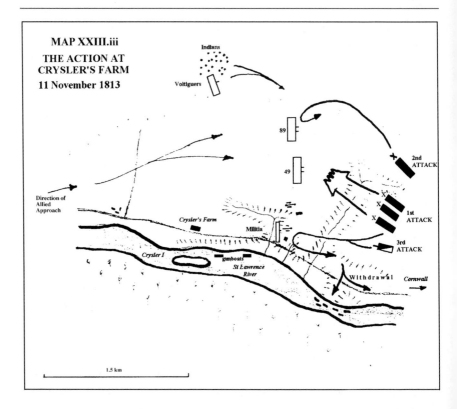

MAP XXIII.iii

THE ACTION AT
CRYSLER'S FARM

11 November 1813

Indians

Voltiguers

89

49

2nd ATTACK

1st ATTACK

Direction of
Allied
Approach

Crysler's Farm

Militia

3rd ATTACK

Crysler I

gumboats
St Lawrence
River

Withdrawal   Cornwall

1.5 km

with a field gun, which occupied the outbuildings of Crysler's Farm. The left was anchored on a swamp, which was occupied by his Indians and Canadian *Voltiguers*. The centre, about 500 yards in extent, was covered by two streams which although shallow as they emerged from the swamp, became sizeable gullies as they neared the river. In the centre were placed the two regular infantry battalions, with two field guns.

Boyd's available force was some 4,000 men and six guns, more than twice the strength of the allies, and as Morrison's troops came up on his rear, Boyd turned his force around. Seen from a distance, the allied force looked formidable, and Boyd decided that it must be destroyed. The Americans formed into three assault columns: Boyd's own brigade, and the two additional brigades of Leonard Covington and Robert Swartout.[8] These columns advanced initially around 2 p.m. on the British troops in the left and centre but as they crossed the streams, disciplined volley-fire and shrapnel from the 6-pounder guns brought them to a halt.

Having failed in the centre, Boyd ordered Covington to try to turn the allied left flank but this movement too was halted by a change of formation and a withering fire, which mortally wounded Covington himself, and the next two officers who took command of the brigade. As the American attack petered out and Boyd's artillery belatedly came into action, Morrison ordered a counter-attack which drove the Americans back in some disorder. Fearing a disaster, Boyd ordered a third attack, this time on the allied right, but this fared no better than the previous attempts.

His last throw was to order a charge by his 130-strong cavalry squadron towards the right flank, in an attempt to envelop the British rear. This almost succeeded, but as they crossed one gully, the cross-fire of the British regulars and Canadian infantry caused such heavy casualties that the cavalry turned tail and fled.

It was now 4.30 pm, and Morrison ordered a general advance which took the allied troops almost to the American boats, but from there, they were forced back by the covering fire of the 12 American gunboats. Boyd drew his brigades off as best he could, and the Americans passed on down the rapids having lost 450 casualties – or one-fifth of the force engaged – as well as a gun and quantities of stores.

Crysler's Farm, like.Châteaugay, was in itself only a minor tactical victory, but it too led on to operational success. In its aftermath, Wilkinson learned that Hampton had called off his advance and in these circumstances, he decided to cancel the whole invasion: 'the attack on Montreal should be abandoned for the present season, and the army near Cornwall should be immediately crossed to the American shore, for taking up winter quarters.'[9] This it duly did, with a speed and efficiency not previously seen in any of its operations. The great invasion was over, thwarted quite simply by determination and willingness to fight on one side, and by its absence on the other.

NOTES

1. Dispatch by Prevost to Lord Bathurst dated 27.viii.1814 in Stanley, p.240.
2. Cruikshank, p.71.
3. Ibid.
4. Cruikshank, p.76.
5. Dispatch to the Secretary of War dated 6.xi.1813 in Fay, p.155.
6. Cruikshank, p.90.
7. Dispatch dated 6.xi.1813 in Fay, p.152.
8. Dispatch to the Secretary of War dated 16.xi.1813 in Fay, pp.149–51.
9. Ibid.

Chapter XXIV

The Road to Ghent

❧❧❧

W HILE BRITAIN WAS fighting the United States in the Canadas, she remained allied with Spain in her war against Napoleon; but Spain and the USA continued to regard each other as neutrals. This situation is a particularly interesting complication in terms of coalition and world war, since quite apart from the whole Louisiana purchase affair discussed in Part One, Spain and the United States were in conflict over the Floridas. In 1812, Florida consisted of two provinces, East and West, and shortly before the outbreak of the Canadian war, Madison had ordered the annexation of West Florida, since the Spanish claim to this territory had lapsed in 1795.

Madison's action was driven in large measure by a continuing war against the Creek Indians, who had ceded much land in neighbouring Georgia in return for a guarantee of their remaining lands and a large measure of Creek self-government, to which the federal government had agreed. The Georgia state authorities, however, had objected to such a guarantee,[1] and encroachments by white settlers, with state backing, grew. Since 1811, a spiritual revival had been sweeping the Creek nation. By chance this co-incided with a visit from Tecumseh, himself the child of a Creek mother and therefore, to the matrilineal Creeks, one of themselves. Tecumseh's mission was to encourage the Creeks to join the north-western tribes in a confederation against further white expansion.[2] The Creeks listened attentively. Thus grew Major General Andrew Jackson's Creek war, which was in full spate from July 1813. Napoleon had at one time sought to encourage the Indians with gifts of weapons.[3] Under Jackson's Presidency in later years, the federal policy towards the now defeated Creeks changed to one of removal west of the Mississippi, where the Louisiana purchase had made land available.

The attitude of Spain, which continued to hold East Florida after

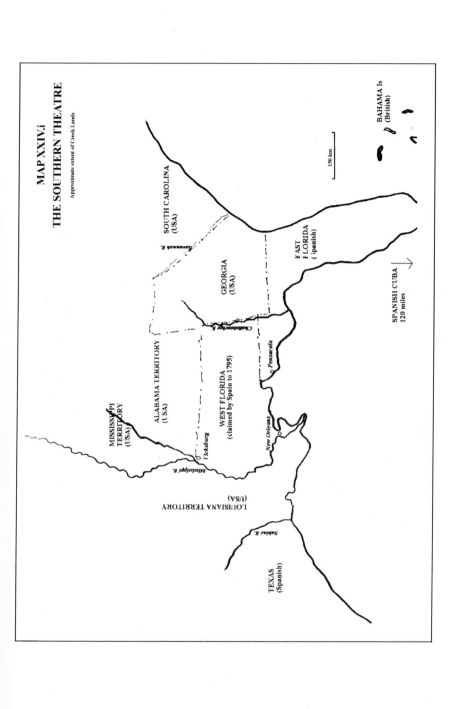

MAP XXIV.i

THE SOUTHERN THEATRE

Approximate extent of Creek Lands

BAHAMA Is
(British)

150 km

SOUTH CAROLINA
(USA)

Savannah R.

GEORGIA
(USA)

EAST
FLORIDA
(Spanish)

Chattahoochee R.

SPANISH CUBA
120 miles

ALABAMA TERRITORY
(USA)

Pensacola

MISSISSIPPI
TERRITORY
(USA)

WEST FLORIDA
(claimed by Spain to 1795)

Vicksburg

New Orleans

Mississippi R.

LOUISIANA TERRITORY
(USA)

Sabine R.

TEXAS
(Spanish)

Madison withdrew US troops from parts of it early in 1813, says much about the nature of coalitions in terms of the subordination of national interests in the short term in the face of external threat, and their re-emergence with the disappearance of that threat. Spanish proposals to divert troops from the war in the Peninsula to the Americas had caused no little tension between the *junta* and the British government which was effectively funding it. However it was equally clear by late 1813 that the Spanish authorities both in Cadiz and in exile were highly sensitive to any action by Britain to intervene on behalf of Spain in the Floridas, sensing perhaps a move to establish new British colonies both there and in the Louisiana territory. Quite simply, mindful of the old animosities between the colonial powers in the new world, Spain preferred to see West Florida in American hands than in British, and maintained neutrality even when Jackson, in defiance of his government's instructions, attacked and captured the port of Pensacola in Spanish East Florida.

So when also in 1814, Vice-Admiral Sir Alexander Cochrane contemplated an action in the Floridas and tried to raise the Creeks, he found them cowed by Jackson's successes. Moreover, he found himself with exactly the difficulty faced by Wellington with the Bourbon loyalists in southern France: he could make no promises either to the Spanish inhabitants or to the Creeks, that with the coming of peace they would not be handed back to American control. In this difficulty, and the search for its resolution, lay the seeds of the first and unsuccessful British attack on Fort Bowyer, and their disastrous attack on New Orleans.

The British interest in the southern war, as well as being an interesting glimpse into the political complexities of coalition war, also illustrates the essential truth of Wellington's remarks on the centre of gravity of the American war: maybe the USA 'had neither a heart to be pierced nor a head to be battered in',[4] but by late 1813 the British government was determined to turn the successful defensive operations of the year into an offensive – either military or diplomatic – especially as public opinion and the press were calling for more extreme measures against the USA. Leipzig and the battles in the Pyrenees had been fought and won, and there seemed a definite prospect that the American war could be settled on favourable terms. The interest in the south was one part of the British search for some vital, perhaps decisive, spot towards which their effort could be directed.

One of Britain's other allies, Russia, also had an interest in the American war. Russia still owned the territory of Alaska but quite apart

GREAT ENCOURAGEMENT.

AMERICAN WAR.

What a Brilliant Prospect does this Event hold out to every Lad of Spirit, who is inclined to try his Fortune in that highly renowned Corps,

The Royal Marines,

When every Thing that swims the Seas must be a

PRIZE!

Thousands are at this moment endeavouring to get on Board Privateers, where they serve without Pay or Reward of any kind whatsoever; so certain does their Chance appear of enriching themselves by PRIZE MONEY! What an enviable Station then must the *ROYAL MARINE* hold, -- who with far superior Advantages to these, has the additional benefit of liberal Pay, and plenty of the best Provisions, with a good and well appointed Ship under him, the Pride and Glory of Old England; surely every Man of Spirit must blush to remain at Home in Inactivity and Indolence, when his Country and the best of Kings needs his Assistance.

Where then can he have such a fair opportunity of reaping Glory and Riches, as in the Royal Marines, a Corps daily acquiring new Honours, and where, when once embarked in BRITISH FLEET, he finds himself in the midst of Honour and Glory, surrounded by a set of fine Fellows, Strangers to Fear, and who strike Terror through the Hearts of their Enemies wherever they go!

He has likewise the inspiring Idea to know, that while he scours the Ocean to protect the Liberty of OLD ENGLAND, that the Hearts and good Wishes of the whole BRITISH NATION, attend him; pray for his Success, and participate in its Glory!! Lose no Time then, my Fine Fellows, in embracing the glorious Opportunity that awaits you; YOU WILL RECEIVE

Sixteen Guineas Bounty,

And on your arrival at *Head Quarters*, be comfortably and genteely CLOTHED.--- And spirited Young BOYS of a promising Appearance, who are Five Feet high, WILL RECEIVE TWELVE POUNDS ONE SHILLING AND SIXPENCE BOUNTY, and equal Advantages of *PROVISIONS* and *CLOATHING* with the Men. And those who wish only to enlist for a limited Service, shall receive a Bounty of ELEVEN GUINEAS, and Boys EIGHT. In Fact, the Advantages which the *ROYAL MARINE* possesses, are too numerous to mention here, but among the many, it may not be amiss to state,—*That if he has a WIFE, or aged PARENT, he can make them an Allotment of half his PAY; which will be regularly paid without any Trouble to them, or to whomsoever he may direct: that being well Clothed and Fed on Board Ship, the Remainder of his PAY and PRIZE MONEY will be clear in Reserve for the Relief of his Family or his own private Purposes. The Single Young Man on his Return to Port, finds himself enabled to cut a Dash on Shore with his GIRL and his GLASS, that might be envied by a Nobleman. Take Courage then, seize the Fortune that awaits you, repair to the ROYAL MARINE RENDEZVOUS, where in a PLOWING BOWL of PUNCH, in Three Times Three, you shall drink*

Long live the King, and Success to his Royal Marines.

The Daily Allowance of a Marine when embarked, is—One Pound of BEEF or PORK.—One Pound of BREAD.—Flour, Raisins, Butter, Cheese, Oatmeal, Molasses, Tea, Sugar, &c. &c. And a Pint of the best WINE, or Half a Pint of the best RUM or BRANDY; together with a pint of LEMONADE. They have likewise in warm Countries, a plentiful allowance of the choicest FRUIT. And what can be more handsome than the Royal Marine's Proportion of PRIZE MONEY, when a Serjeant shares equal with the First Class of Petty Officers, such as Midshipmen, Assistant Surgeons, &c. which is Five Shares each; a Corporal with the Second Class, which is Three Shares each; and the Private with the Able Seamen, One Share and a Half each.

☞ *For further Particulars, and a more full Account of the many Advantages of this invaluable Corps, apply to SERJEANT FULCHER, at the EIGHT BELLS, where the Bringer of a Recruit will receive THREE GUINEAS.*

REPRINTED BY PARADE PRINTING WORKS, LTD., 19|11 SOUTHSIDE STREET, PLYMOUTH

THE ORIGINAL NOW HELD BY THE OFFICERS' MESS, R. M. BARRACKS, PLYMOUTH WAS PRINTED BY S. AND J. RIDGE, PRINTERS, MARKET PLACE, NEWARK

A British Royal Marine recruiting poster of 1813, originally published far inland at Newark-upon-Trent, Nottinghamshire. Marines served not only in Royal Navy ships but also on land in Canada and in many raids on the US eastern and southern coasts. Two battalions and two companies of Royal Marine Artillery (1,639 all ranks) arrived in the Chesapeake from Spain in June 1813.

from that, there had been a considerable amount of trade between Russia and the USA which the Tsar wished to see revived. More urgently, Alexander was unhappy with anything that distracted his ally and paymaster, Britain, from the business of defeating Bonaparte. As early as the autumn of 1812 the Tsar had suggested to John Quincy Adams, the American minister at St Petersburg, that he should act as mediator in the dispute. News of this offer reached Madison in March 1813, shortly after the none too welcome news that a Royal Navy squadron had entered the Chesapeake, and after the even more dreadful news of the 29th *Bulletin*.

At this point, neither Britain nor the USA was willing to yield on any point, but Madison did nominate two peace commissioners, Albert Gallatin and James A. Bayard, whom he sent to Russia. This was probably done out of a sense of duty, and the hope of inducing the British to accede to the American demands on impressment, rather than out of any genuine belief that a negotiated peace was yet possible or desirable. But what the nomination of commissioners did indicate quite clearly was that any thoughts either of the benefits which would follow a Napoleonic victory in Europe, or of the overthrow of colonial rule in Canada, had already been abandoned. To this extent, the allies had already achieved success.

Castlereagh obviously understood this position, as he politely declined the Tsar's offer of mediation, and in any case, it was late July before the US commissioners reached St Petersburg: by this time the Austrian mediation was in progress, and only two weeks later the autumn campaign opened in Central Europe. With such a titanic struggle reaching its climax, the Tsar could scarcely be expected to attend to American affairs – nor did he. The commissioners cooled their heels in St Petersburg for six months, and left when the allies were on the Rhine and the Bidassoa and the position of Britain had grown immeasurably stronger.

At about the same time as the Commissioners had departed for Russia, the Americans were also seeking to improve relations with France. In June 1813, word reached Madison of the death of the US Minister to Paris, Joel Barlow. In his place Madison turned to William H. Crawford, an influential senator from Georgia who had supported the war against the British and the acquisition of the Floridas. Crawford set sail on 18 June in USS *Argus*, a ship which was in August that year to be captured not far from Plymouth, Devon, by HMS *Pelican*. At the time of his arrival in Paris (late July), the Rambouillet decrees were still in force: his task was to gain removal of French restrictions on US trade, and indemnification for goods already confiscated, while also improving relations between the two countries.[5] This was a task which would have challenged the most experienced diplomat.

Although Crawford was reported to have gained an audience with a pre-occupied Napoleon at the end of 1813, details of the interview are impossible to ascertain. The US envoy did, however, warn Henry Clay at Ghent that 'My expectations of a happy result are not strong. The arrogance of the enemy was never greater than at the present moment.'[6] An interesting observation in that, despite the state of war with Britain, it is Napoleon who is referred to as 'the enemy'.

Crawford in fact got nowhere with Napoleon, and fared little better with the restored Bourbons in 1814. He therefore switched his attentions to gathering information, and warned the US authorities of the French defeat in Spain in late 1813 so that Madison had several months' warning of the likelihood of British veteran troops arriving in the Canadas. Thereafter he spent much time informing the US commissioners in Ghent about developments on the European political scene.

US engagement in Europe – in Paris, St Petersburg and Ghent – had achieved something, however, in that it had obliged the British government to revisit the whole question of its war aims and to consider diplomatic as well as military initiatives. For it could hardly condemn Bonaparte for rejecting the terms of the Congress of Prague and the Frankfurt proposals while themselves refusing to consider alternatives to war. Even so, ministers were inclined to take a harsh line with the US for the war had become '. . . a tiresome, pointless distraction for Britain; a nuisance, but not a serious threat . . . the British found it hard [at a time when resources were concentrated against the common enemy, Napoleon] to forgive their American cousins.'[7]

The question which clearly vexed the British government at the end of 1813 was, despite the continued need to confront and destroy Napoleon, how could naval and military power be exerted to end the American war as soon as possible? To find the answer, Lord Bathurst asked the advice of Wellington. Despite a lack of detailed knowledge, books or maps, Wellington wrote on 22 February 1814 one of the most telling appreciations of the situation in the Canadas which has ever appeared:

Any offensive operation founded upon Canada must be preceded by the establishment of a naval superiority on the Lakes . . . the defence of Canada and the co-operation of the Indians depends on the navigation of the Lakes . . .

Then in direct answer to the question, he wrote that

In such countries as Canada, very extensive, thinly peopled, and producing but little food in proportion to their extent, military operations are impracticable without river or land transport. Coastal amphibious operations are liable to the same objections, though to a greater degree, than an operation founded in Canada . . . But I do not know where you could carry on such an operation which would be so injurious to the Americans as to force them to sue for peace.[8]

So perhaps, with no identifiable centre of gravity, the American war was unwinnable by either side.

On 30 December 1813, a dispatch reached Madison informing him that British negotiators would meet the Americans: thus the mere setting up of peace-making machinery was in itself a factor in achieving a political settlement. And in spite of Cochrane's expeditions there was, perhaps, an unspoken belief that after all, Wellington might be right. Even so it was another year before peace was agreed at Ghent, and longer still until hostilities ceased. In that time, Washington had been burned and a British expedition defeated in the Gulf of Mexico.

When peace did come, the world had changed in America just as it had in Europe. The war certainly cemented the bonds between Britain and Canada, which still endure. But by encouraging the self-reliance of the Canadians it also strengthened the links between French and English Canadians by dispelling mutual doubts. After the war, therefore, the unity which had defied the Americans extended to the beginnings of the desire for Canadian self-government, while underwriting the rights of both communities to the maintenance of their distinct language and cultural identity.

The real losers were the Indians. The alliance of 1812 is understandable only when seen in the continuum of the pursuit by the Indians of their own interests, but the war marked the end of an age: the age in which the Indians were a military force in European wars in North America. After the Rush-Bagot Convention of 1817, the Great Lakes were demilitarised and warfare ceased to be an issue between the USA and Canada; so the Indians' utility as allies and trading partners was destroyed.

As they ceased to be allies, they became an obstacle to the new wave of immigration from Europe, which thus marked the start of a new round of red *versus* white racial conflict resulting from westward expansion of the USA – and to a lesser extent Canada. Co-operation rapidly turned to coercion, and from this, the Indians emerged with few guarantees of the territorial and cultural rights for which Tecumseh had fought. It is a sobering thought that, since the end of the Second World War, these issues relating to the cultural and territorial claims of all three racial groups in Canada have re-emerged once more.

NOTES

1. See especially Berger, p.63.
2. Heidler, p.132.
3. Fregosi, p.231.
4. Forester, p.172.
5. Heidler, p.131.
6. Shipp, p.120.
7. Muir, p.240.
8. *Dispatches*, ix, pp.525–6.

CONCLUSION

Chapter XXV

The Partnership of Unequals

❧

I. THE POLITICS OF COALITION

THE BRITISH DIPLOMAT and writer Harold Nicolson remarked that 'The basis of any alliance, or coalition, is an agreement between two or more sovereign states to subordinate their separate interests to a single purpose.'[1] The campaigns of 1813 are as good an illustration of the truth of this assertion as can be found anywhere in the pages of history. That single purpose in central and southern Europe, and in Canada, was the defeat of a common enemy. In Canada that enemy was American territorial ambition; in Europe it was in the beginning the export of revolutionary chaos from France, and later the great, towering figure of Napoleon.

It would be hard to find another time in the last 200 years which is as full of dramatic crises as the spring and summer of 1813, which led up to the breaking of Napoleon's strength and reputation at Leipzig. But because of the gulf of time which now lies between us and 1813, it is difficult for us to grasp the mixture of emotions with which Napoleon was beheld. On the one hand, an adulation verging on deification; on the other fear and loathing. As Michael Broers has said: 'Napoleon Bonaparte is synonymous with power, so much so that the myth he spun around himself in exile sought to soften, even to obscure, that uncomfortable truth.'[2]

In our own time perhaps only Hitler can be compared with him – as Clarendon said of Cromwell, 'a great, bad, man', – who in pursuit of universal power, eventually brought on himself universal enmity. But Britain and America have fought two world wars this century, and taken part in operations in Korea, the Gulf, and the Balkans, all in coalition. Both countries, too, were founder members of the greatest peacetime alliance that the world has ever known – NATO.

So however great a bogeyman Napoleon was then, he continues to arouse interest not just because of his military genius, but because in the situation of his opponents, the allies of 1813, can be seen problems which mirror those which continue to be experienced today. In particular, their incomplete success in agreeing war aims, and the effect this had on operational effectiveness, has for example been seen among the members of NATO in Bosnia before the Dayton Agreement of 1995.

Again, problems in the alliance of 1813 were caused by the ability of heads of government directly to influence the tactical battle by their physical presence were experienced again in the 1991 Gulf War as a result of real-time, direct communications between heads of government and field commanders. But Napoleon does show that the unity of purpose which such an enemy can inspire among a diversity of opponents is remarkable: Britain and Spain, enemies since the time of Elizabeth I; and across the Atlantic, the alliance of British, French Canadians and Indians formed to oppose America.

But it also seems to be true that coalitions, formed for adversity, seldom survive strategic success. With victory in sight, national interests tend to re-emerge as each partner looks to reward its own people for their share in the struggle. This tendency brings tensions which may already have begun to emerge in the form of rivalries, suspicions and jealousies. The coalitions of 1813 again provide excellent examples of these processes in action: the divergence between Britain and Austria over a continental versus a maritime peace; the re-emergence of Spanish–Portuguese hostility; and the abandonment of the Indian cause are all examples.

And if coalitions tend to drift apart at the conclusion of war, they tend also to drift together, forming around a nucleus of opposition and increasing with the spur of success. This is well illustrated by the gradual formation of the central European alliance of 1813. Such a process of gradual development can bring its own tensions, which may later contribute to the processes of disintegration. The original coalition members, who have faced the enemy longest, may tend to feel that their war aims must overshadow those of the later comers no matter how decisive the later interventions – hence the absolute insistence by Britain on the question of maritime rights.

The reverse may also be true, that later comers feel that their intervention tipped the scales and must therefore attract a large share of the spoils of victory. The enlargement of the Austrian empire at the expense of France and her clients after 1814 can be seen in this light. Also, while the reconciliation of war aims between two partners may prove fairly simple in the face of a common danger, the more partners who join, the wider the spread of interests and the more difficult becomes the achievement of unity. The coalition of 1813 illustrates this in the arguments of the late summer over war aims and by the friction which emotional territorial disputes over Poland and Saxony brought between Prussia, Russia and Austria.

The diplomats and politicians of 1813 were well aware of these difficulties, and as well aware as anyone in the present era of the needs of preserving coalition unity. That it was not until 1814 that open disagreements began to emerge only underlines the nature of the threat – that no one partner wished to imperil the alliance while Napoleon remained at large. Henry Kissinger summed this up when he wrote that

> As long as the enemy is more powerful than any single member of the coalition, the need for unity outweighs all considerations of individual gain . . . But when the enemy has been so weakened that each ally has the power to achieve its ends alone, a coalition is at the mercy of its most determined member. Confronted with the complete collapse of one of the elements of equilibrium, all other powers will tend to raise their claims in order to keep pace.[3]

The pressures of public opinion are also a factor in preserving allied unity even though in 1813, the press was not in the position it occupies today, able immediately to force a political reaction to circumstances. It was certainly pressure of public opinion which forced Frederick William of Prussia to accede to the Treaty of Kalisch; which brought about the alignment of Spain with Portugal and Britain; and which threw the large French-speaking population of Canada into arms against America.

The achievement of this unity of purpose at the grand strategic level has to be seen as a vital ingredient in the success of coalition war in 1813. It was not easily achieved, but when one compares the results of the enforced alignment of Prussia and Austria with the French invasion of Russia in 1812 to the combination of nations exercising free will in 1813, one significant factor emerges – that of military resilience. In 1812, Prussia and Austria were quite unprepared to suffer for the French cause, and yet in 1813, both were willing to endure enormous casualties. Conversely as 1813 progressed, Napoleon's coalition gradually fell apart as his German partners realised that he was losing – hence the defections during and after Leipzig.

Once achieved, however, unity of purpose at the political level translates into effective military structures. This can be seen in the multinational allied armies formed in Central Europe,[4] in Bonaparte's use of client troops in his *Grande Armée*,[5] and in the integration of regular and irregular forces in Spain and Canada. In this respect Wellington's army in the Peninsula provides an interesting example. His integration of Portuguese brigades into British framework divisions is usually quoted as being necessary for efficiency – stiffening the initially unreliable Portuguese with the rock-steady British regulars – and this is certainly partly true.

But such integration can also be seen in exactly the same way as Napoleon's integration of client contingents into his corps structure, and the mixture of Russian, Prussian and Swedish corps in the armies of central Europe. After five years' campaigning, the Portuguese needed no stiffening whatever: their integration was a clear statement of coalition unity, of indivisible purpose.

But even when unity of purpose is achieved, coalitions remain a partnership of unequals. The Napoleonic coalitions are an excellent illustration of this characteristic since all were absolutely dominated by the French. Strategic and operational plans were directed entirely towards the furtherance of French national interest and the other partners – German and Italian states, along with clients like Denmark and Switzerland, or annexed territories like Holland – became more and more merely a source of troops and money.[6]

Thus power in coalition warfare lies with the strongest member and the effectiveness of the coalition will be determined by that member. This is also illustrated by the coalitions in Spain and Canada, and in an oblique way by the central European coalition where a clear dichotomy of interest arose between Britain and Austria. It might be supposed that Austria as the dominant military power might have held sway, but in the end, dominance was achieved through economic factors.

We may conclude therefore that since coalitions mean different things to different partners, it is much harder for a partnership of near-equals to formulate an effective strategy, hence the long-drawn out processes by which the 6th Coalition eventually arrived at a unified plan.[7]

The stresses that such a partnership of unequals brings are partly offset by burden-sharing, particularly in combat. At one extreme, weaker partners may push themselves forward, so as to demand a greater share in the eventual spoils; at the other, there are 'nations who want the credibility of participating, but are loath to risk any action'.[8]

Bernadotte's handling of the Army of the North is an example of this tendency, which can only be corrected by diplomacy, in order that coalition field commanders like Schwarzenberg are not placed in an impossible position. Bernadotte clearly understood however that the smaller the input to a coalition force, the less influence on policy and the appointment of the Commander-in-Chief – hence the appointments of Schwarzenberg, Wellington and Prevost.

Following this logic to its rather brutal conclusion, it seems that smaller partners will generally have to accept a coalition plan dictated by the more powerful members, or leave, and thus for those small partners – like Portugal in 1813 – there is seldom any such thing as independent command. NATO with its unvaryingly American Supreme Allied Commander Europe shows that this logic still holds good.

The strategic direction of coalition war has been referred to somewhat obliquely several times. It is a thorny subject which is often bypassed, but the coalitions of 1813 do offer some important lessons. These lessons were reflected upon by that veteran of 1813, Karl-Maria von Clausewitz. Clausewitz believed that although states might combine in coalition, the result of their combination would still be a single war; therefore the greater the subordination of lesser partners to the will of the dominant member, the easier on one hand for a coalition to be given strategic direction, and on the other, for the coalition to be regarded as a single entity.

Logically therefore, in a partnership of unequals, the dominant member becomes the centre of gravity, especially since 'War is thus an act of force to compel our enemy to do our will.'[9] So that compliance by weaker members of a coalition will naturally follow the subjugation of the strongest.

For their part the British government understood this very well. Campaigns against Napoleon and his clients (including America) might be useful for colonial expansion in the West Indies and the Americas, the Mediterranean, or the Far East, but Napoleon could only be decisively defeated in Europe. His invasion of Portugal and annexation of Spain gave an opportunity for this both directly in terms of military intervention, and indirectly through the maintenance of core of allies upon whom future coalitions could be built.[10]

Clausewitz also addressed the mechanics of strategic direction:

The first, the supreme, the most far-reaching act of judgement that the statesman and commander have to make is to establish . . . the kind of war on which they are embarking; neither mistaking it for, nor trying to turn it into, something which is alien to its nature. This is the first of all strategic questions and the most comprehensive.[11]

Clausewitz believed this to be true of all war, but in coalition war he implies that it is vital that the political nature of the coalition is set out at the strategic level and its aims communicated to the military. Equally, military commanders have a duty to represent the changing realities of the military situation to their political masters to maintain the causal relationship. For military objectives may not be identical with political aims, although the one leads directly or indirectly to the other; and the constraints imposed by the partnership of unequals may severely limit military freedom of action: the six British infantry battalions sent to Stralsund[12] might, for example, have formed the basis of another division in Wellington's army had they not been required to make a statement of political solidarity.

In 1813, this political/military interface was rather artificially compressed. In the Empire, Napoleon represented the supreme authority in both civil and military affairs. In the case of the allies, things were different. Prevost, in Canada, was perhaps in the happiest situation in that he received initial guidance from his distant political masters and was then left alone. Wellington was less well off, having to contend with interference from London, Lisbon and Cadiz which usually required his personal attention. In Central Europe, although first Wittgenstein, then Barclay de Tolly and finally Schwarzenberg were appointed to the supreme military command, the personal presence of the allied monarchs – especially the Tsar – inevitably led to a blurring of responsibilities and an interference in operational detail which with the advent of instant communications has become familiar to modern commanders.

In the case of Bernadotte, his personal presence also allowed him to pursue his hidden national agenda of wresting Norway from Denmark under the cloak of contributing to the coalition. His methods were clearly understood by his allies, but his personal presence greatly outweighed, in politico-military terms, the inconvenience of his avoidance of battle: 'The political object – the original motive for the war – will thus determine both the military objective to be reached and the amount of effort it requires.'[13]

II. ALLIED COMMAND

Armies are bodies which meet and endeavour to frighten one another.

Napoleon

When he made his celebrated remark, Napoleon was probably thinking of opposing, rather than allied, armies. But although coalition war may be dictated at the political level, there comes a time when functional command at the operational level has to be established so that the political resolve to fight in a common cause can be linked to the actual business of campaigning. Until 1813 it can be argued that one reason for French success and allied failure was that of supreme command. Napoleon exercised supreme military as well as political control and delegated only limited command functions to deputies.

In Central Europe, the early coalitions made no attempt to establish a unified command and even Wellington had no authority over the Spanish armies until after Salamanca. In 1813 things began to change. In Canada, Prevost held the undisputed allied command and in Spain, Wellington was able at last to direct and integrate the activities of all forces, both regular and irregular, in the Peninsula.

Things took longer to resolve in Central Europe: Wittgenstein was first appointed to the allied command but resigned in the face of continual interference by the Tsar in his operational plans. Once Austria had acceded to the coalition it was clear that the supreme command would go to an Austrian general, chiefly because theirs would would be the largest contribution. Neither the Russians nor the Prussians had shown great talent for operational or strategic direction in the spring campaign, and the reverses of Lützen and Bautzen can be put down to Prussian impetuosity on one hand, and the Tsar's interference on the other.[14] Even though Bernadotte was held in great esteem by the Emperor of Austria, who thought Bernadotte was privy to Napoleon's secrets in the art of war and would turn them on his old master,[15] he had not, as we have seen, committed enough troops to qualify for the post. Metternich was therefore determined that the huge contribution which Austria was making[16] would be acknowledged.

The eventual appointee, Schwarzenberg, was clearly a political choice. Schwarzenberg had no previous stature as a battlefield commander and thus did little to resolve lack of unity and divided counsels among the allies, since he was held in the lowest esteem by Prussia and Russia. This can be attributed directly to Metternich who although stating that 'we need a commander who makes war and not one who is a politician',[17] clearly wanted a general who would be amenable to his direction.

In the end Schwarzenberg must be given some credit. While he never showed the bold, ruthless and enterprising qualities which brought success to Wellington, he did succeed in holding the coalition together by tact and conciliation – and in this, paradoxically, he was at times assisted by the close presence of the allied monarchs – so that the defeat of Napoleon was eventually achieved.

In this respect the designs of the British government to shift Wellington and his Peninsular army to Central Europe after the expulsion of the French from Spain are significant, both in terms of the sort of direction Wellington could have given, and as an illustration of economic power rather than size of forces as a political lever on operational command.[18]

An important aspect of allied command is the framing and orchestration of a plan – and a plan which will bring success. The Trachenberg-Reichenbach[19] plan is an excellent example of such orchestration, avoiding a decisive engagement until success could be guaranteed, while manoeuvring three armies against Napoleon's flanks and rear. This plan also demonstrates the necessity for some tactical success in coalition operations, no matter how limited, as vital in maintaining allied unity. Co-operation between the Anglo-Portuguese and Spanish armies illustrates this well.[20]

Operational plans may, however, be subject to political interference and it seems that allied field commanders must be prepared to fend this off. Wellington's almost daily exchanges with London, some of which are described in Part Three, show this. Schwarzenberg's difficulties with allied monarchs were more immediate: the Tsar's insistence on an attack at Dresden led to a defeat which was only counterbalanced by the successes of Kulm, Dennewitz and the Katzbach. On the other hand, the Tsar's intervention at Leipzig undoubtedly saved the day. Many a modern commander faced with instant communications out of theatre would recognise Schwarzenberg's situation at once.

Political intervention may also manifest itself in the maintenance of multinational formations, although these may also be a necessity born of differences in the capabilities of various contingents. Such formations may be highly desirable in terms of solidarity but they can bring some significant practical problems to the field commander. Among these is likely to be language: most of the allies' business in

Central Europe seems to have been conducted in the language of the enemy; French was also widely spoken in the Peninsula, and in Canada too.

Logistical difficulties are also likely to be high on any commander's list although in 1813, guns and muskets changed hands so frequently that a degree of commonality in ammunition seems to have been present which any modern commander would envy. Not that such commonality resulted from deliberate policy, but rather from the relatively slow development of military knowledge throughout Europe. Clausewitz commented on this at the time, saying that '. . . armies are so much alike in weapons, training and equipment that there is little difference between the best and the worst of them'.[21]

Logistical difficulties certainly took up much of both Wellington's and Prevost's time in view of the large distances involved. Added to this, Wellington found himself having to divert food and ammunition meant for his British, German and Portuguese troops to the Spanish who because of the difficulties of their own government were often close to actual starvation.

Some of these difficulties can be overcome by an integrated functional staff system to support the commander. This was fully developed by 1813 in the French Army and accounts for much of Napoleon's success in raising his new armies. It was present to a degree in the Peninsula, and again contributed greatly to Wellington's ability to field his largest-ever army for the campaign of Vitoria. It was never developed in Central Europe where Schwarzenberg often found that his own orders were being contradicted by other orders from national commanders, and which the system of liaison officers instituted by the British only partially solved since it was designed chiefly to provide information to London: 'Schwarzenberg says that in the disagreeable Command he has over the Russians and Prussians, if it were not for Wilson there are many things which he would never venture to propose.'[22]

At the end of the day, the personal qualities of the allied field commander may well be the major factor in determining the success or failure of a coalition force at the operational level. It is likely to be a hugely stressful business, both physically and psycologically, in which only the strongest will can triumph.[23] In this respect, Wellington stands head and shoulders above all others in 1813, Napoleon himself not excepted. As John Terraine concludes:

We must give all . . . credit to the infinite patience, far-sighted sagacity and iron nerve of the 'Sepoy General'. Beating the French in the field never presented half the difficulties of dealing with his perplexing, exasperating, but always essential allies.[24]

III. FIGHTING COALITION WAR

Already the subject of the operational level of command has been raised. The operational commander directs and commands all allied forces in a particular theatre of operations, and his plan is the means by which strategic goals will be achieved. In terms of the sort of war-fighting in progress in 1813, operational plans have to address the physical defeat of the enemy through the destruction of his centre of gravity.

Jomini, a participant on both sides of the campaign of 1813 in Central Europe, laid down four principles by which this could be achieved.[25] However Jomini was far from being infallible as his rather inconsistent practical performance in the field showed. Moreover Jomini tended to treat military activity as an action on an inanimate target rather than a situation in which the enemy, however inferior, will seek constantly to frustrate the design of his opponent. Jomini's principles are however an enlightening insight into the thinking of the time. First, Jomini believed in 'directing the mass of one's own forces successively on to the decisive points in the theatre of war – as far as possible against the communications of the enemy without disrupting one's own'. Clearly, Jomini had before him the example of the allied autumn campaign in which he had played a part, although Wellington's march to Vitoria is also an illustration of this principle.

Second, Jomini believed 'in manoeuvring so as to engage this concentration of forces only against fractions of the enemy's strength'. This was without doubt the aim of the Trachenberg-Reichenbach plan.

Third, Jomini believed that a commander must concentrate on the battlefield

> the bulk of [his] force at the decisive point or against the section of the enemy line which one wishes to overwhelm, and ensuring that these forces are sent forward with vigour and concentration so as to produce a simultaneous result.

The idea of simultaneity in early nineteenth century warfare will be expanded further, but the notion of opposing enemy weakness with strength can be seen played out time after time in Napoleon's battles. The allies, however, never quite grasped this: even the successful Trachenberg-Reichenbach plan was essentially attritional. With the exception of Wellington, Napoleon had a far greater understanding of how and where to place and form his main effort, as the battles of Lützen, Bautzen, Dresden and even Leipzig show.

Last, Jomini believed that 'the objective is always the destruction of the enemy army in battle'. An idea derived entirely from Napoleon and in direct contrast to the elegant notions of manoeuvre of the eighteenth century.

Napoleon clearly believed that the centre of gravity of an enemy force is always his army, and this belief had characterised his conduct of all his campaigns up to 1813. When destroyed, the enemy's means to resist was gone and compliance with the will of the conqueror would follow. All other objectives could then be pursued at leisure.[26] Napoleon also believed, as Clausewitz later stated,[27] that when faced with a coalition, several centres of gravity can be reduced to one by striking at the principal coalition partner. By this mean, the vital concept of allied unity – which in a coalition may actually be the centre of gravity rather than any physical aspect – may be shattered.

This explains his determination over the years to destroy Britain by the Continental System. It may also partly explain his defeat in 1813 since on several occasions Napoleon set his sights on particular pieces of territory rather than on the business of delivering a knockout blow against either the Russian or Austrian armies. His enemies clearly profited by this mistake. The Americans too had some notion of shattering coalition unity through military defeat, as their victory on the Thames proved, although they were never able to pursue this process to its conclusion.

The idea of simultaneous effect is worthy of mention in this context. Napoleon understood this well and would achieve it through dispersed moves and battlefield concentration; through pinning an enemy force by attritional attack, drawing off reserves by moving other forces into a position from where an attack could be threatened; and then exploiting the weakness produced by a massive combination of artillery fire, infantry attack, and cavalry exploitation. Wellington's handling of the Battle of Vitoria and the attack across the Bidassoa show his mastery of this concept at the tactical level.

But the campaigns of 1813 also provide an illustration of simultaneity by the allies at the operational level through the complementary use of regular and irregular forces. In Central Europe this involved the

Freikorps, Cossacks, Bashkirs and Kalmacks; in Spain the guerrillas; and in North America, the Indians. More has been said about each particular example, but clearly an enemy who disperses to counter irregular forces lays himself open to destruction by a concentrated regular force; while if the same enemy then concentrates himself, he becomes vulnerable to irregular activity. By these means, the enemy is faced, quite simply, with a dilemma which he cannot solve.

The notion of the centre of gravity is clearly applicable when viewed from the reverse angle. The Central European allies were in no doubt that Napoleon himself represented the centre of gravity and indeed, once he himself had been defeated at Leipzig, the bulk of his allies began to fall away. In America, the situation was more complex, providing an illustration of the difficulties of identifying the centre of gravity in a relatively undeveloped nation. Parts Two, Three and Four of this book have attempted to show how the various commanders in 1813 tried to approach the perceived centre of gravity of their enemies through a series of decisive points: usually these were sieges of major towns and fortresses, battles, and major engagements; and how other lines of operation – economic, political and diplomatic – contributed to the same process.

The final word belongs with the common enemy, Napoleon. Even at the end of 1813, Napoleon could have preserved his empire, albeit within the limits of the natural frontiers, through diplomatic compromise, but he made the fatal mistake of holding out too long. He had already driven Portugal and Spain into alliance with Britain, in 1813, he drove first Sweden, then Russia and Prussia, and then Austria into the same alliance: in the final analysis he misunderstood when the ultimate in peace terms had been offered and by not accepting, lost everything.

It was therefore a waste of that military genius by which, time and again until Leipzig, Napoleon had outmanoeuvred the allies at the operational level of war, and outfought them at the tactical level. For even as he did so the coalition against him continued to grow, while his own allies dropped away. He failed to compromise because he underestimated the alliance. He never appreciated that the unifying purpose behind the 6th Coalition was stronger than the forces which divided its members, and far stronger than that holding his empire together.

Despite his experiences in Russia, and because he despised their commanders, he underestimated too the fighting qualities of the new allied levies and the nature of the nationalism which was the force which drove them on:

The common people of Europe, in their millions, hated Napoleon exactly because he espoused the Enlightenment, just as they had detested the enlightened absolutists who preceded him . . .

This is the major problem besetting those who attempt to set Napoleon in a genuinely European, rather than Francocentric, context.[28]

He underestimated the drain of the Spanish war, the effects of his Continental System, and the British blockade. And last, he never understood the intense personal loathing he inspired in so many of his enemies and hence their determination to sink their personal differences in order to beat him. 'Dry your tears', Tsar Alexander had said to King Frederick William when they had met as allies at the beginning of the year, 'they are the last that Napoleon will cause you to shed.'

NOTES

1. Nicolson, p.49.
2. Broers, p.1.
3. Kissinger, pp.9–10.
4. See Part Two.
5. See Part One, Chapter III.
6. See Part One, Chapter III.
7. See Part One, Chapter II; Part Two; and Drage, p.8.
8. Ibid. p.16.
9. Clausewitz, p.16.
10. Muir, p.32.
11. Clausewitz, p.118.
12. See Part One, Chapter II.
13. Clausewitz, p.81.
14. Muffling, pp. 36 ff.
15. Rösling, p.148.
16. Ibid. p.132.
17. Regele, p.118.
18. See Part Three.
19. See Part Two.
20. Muir, p.156.
21. Clausewitz, p.282.
22. Aberdeen to Castlereagh, cited in *Journal*, p.219.
23. See Breakwell and Spacie, pp.10, 11, 13, although no examples or case studies are offered in support of their thesis.
24. John Terraine in Griffith, p.87.
25. *Précis*, Part 3.
26. An idea taken up by Clausewitz, see esp. p.77.
27. Clausewitz, pp.596–7.
28. Broers, p.3.

Chronology of 1813

(Roman numerals in brackets refer to chapters and sections)

	CENTRAL EUROPE (PART TWO)	SPAIN (PART THREE)	MEDITER-RANEAN (PART THREE)	AMERICA (PART FOUR)
January	Revolts against French rule in the Confederation of the Rhine	About 53 major guerrilla actions v. French N. of the Tagus (– April)		
10				Harrison begins US invasion of the North-West (XXI)
16	Eugène de Beauharnais appointed to command French Armies in Germany (VI)			
18				Americans reach Frenchtown
22	Frederick William leaves Berlin for Breslau			Proctor's attack – Battle of the Raisin River (XXI.i)
29		29th Bulletin reaches Joseph Bonaparte		
February		Clausel replaces Caffarelli in command of the Army of the North		US troops withdraw from Spanish E. Florida (– March)
				RN squadron in the Chesapeake (– Sept.)
3–4	Prussian mobilisation begins (V.ii)			

February to April	CENTRAL EUROPE (PART TWO)	SPAIN (PART THREE)	MEDITER-RANEAN (PART THREE)	AMERICA (PART FOUR)
14		Joseph receives news of Napoleon's return to Paris (X.iii)		
28	Treaty of Kalisch between Russia and Prussia (V.ii)			
March				Tsar's mediation
11	Napoleon's plan for the reconquest of Germany outlined. (VI.ii)			
	Russo-Swedish Treaty of Stockholm endorsed by Britain			
17	Frederick William's Proclamation *An Mein Volk*			
27	Blücher occupies Dresden (VI.ii)			
31	Eugène moves E. of the Elbe (V.ii)			
April			Bentinck detaches 2,000 men to Sicily from Anglo-Sicilian Army (XVIII)	Naval operations feasible on Great Lakes (– Nov.)
1	Prussia accedes to Stockholm Treaty			
3–5	BATTLE OF MÖCKERN (VI.ii)			
6	Eugène withdraws W. of the Elbe			
11			Suchet advances in Catalonia (XVIII.ii)	
12			Combat of Biar	
13			Battle of Castalla (XVIII.ii)	

April to May	CENTRAL EUROPE (PART TWO)	SPAIN (PART THREE)	MEDITER-RANEAN (PART THREE)	AMERICA (PART FOUR)
15	NAPOLEON LEAVES PARIS			US troops occupy Mobile, Spanish W. Florida
23				Proctor's counter-move against Harrison (XXI.ii)
25	Napoleon reaches Erfurt and takes command (VII)			
27				Pike's attack on York: burned (XXII.i)
28				Proctor's first siege of Fort Meigs begins. RN raids in the Chesapeake (– Sept.)
May				
1	Napoleon begins advance towards Leipzig. Battle of Poserna and death of Bessières (VII.i)			Proctor begins bombardment of Fort Meigs (XXI.ii)
2	BATTLE OF LÜTZEN (VII.ii)			
5	Battle of Colditz (VII.iii)			Attempt to lift siege of Ft Meigs fails
7–8	Napoleon crosses the Elbe at Dresden			
9				Proctor lifts siege of Ft Meigs and retires. Madison sends Gallatin on peace mission to Russia
18	Bernadotte's Swedish Army lands at Stralsund		Murray embarks for Tarragona (XVIII.iii)	

May to June	CENTRAL EUROPE (PART TWO)	SPAIN (PART THREE)	MEDITER-RANEAN (PART THREE)	AMERICA (PART FOUR)
20	BATTLE OF BAUTZEN (VII.4)	Joseph learns of Wellington's intentions, but takes no action		
21	Bautzen: 2nd day			
22	Pursuit and Battle of Reichenbach: Death of Duroc	WELLINGTON'S MARCH TO VITORIA BEGINS (XIV)		
23	Davout captures Hamburg			
27				Allies abandon Fort George (Niagara) (XXII.ii)
28				Allied attack on Sackett's Harbour (XXII.iii)
31			Spanish attack towards Xucar begins (XVIII)	
June				
1	Napoleon occupies Breslau			HMS *Shannon* captures USS *Chesapeake* off Boston
2	Ceasefire (VIII.i)	French evacuate Toro (XVIII)		
4	TEN WEEKS' TRUCE begins (VIII)	Allies cross the Douro, French evacuate Valladolid (XIV.ii)		
6			Allies besiege and bombard Tarragona	ALLIED NIGHT VICTORY AT STONEY CREEK (XXII.iv)
7		French evacuate Palencia		
12		French evacuate Madrid, blow up Burgos fortress	Allies lift siege of Tarragona	
14	British alliance with Prussia signed			

June	CENTRAL EUROPE (PART TWO)	SPAIN (PART THREE)	MEDITER- RANEAN (PART THREE)	AMERICA (PART FOUR)
15	British alliance with Russia signed (Treaties of Reichenbach)		Allies again disembark near Tarragona	
17		Allies reach Punte Arenas having advanced 300 miles	Allies finally abandon Tarragona (XVIII.iii)	
18		Allies meet Reille at San Millan		
19		French Armies of Portugal, the South and the Centre assemble at Vitoria		Rottenburg relieves Sheaffe in Upper Canada
20		Allies begin the final approach to Vitoria		
21		BATTLE OF VITORIA (XIV)		
22		Allied pursuit to the frontier begins (XV) Siege of Pamplona begins		
23			Action at Palamos. Bentinck repulsed	Allies besiege Fort George
24				Indian victory at Beaver Dams
25		Allied victory at Tolosa		British capture and sack Hampton, Virginia
26	Congress of Prague (– 7 Aug)			
27	Austria signs Treaty of Reichenbach	SAN SEBASTIAN BESIEGED		
29		Allied siege train at Santander		

June to July	CENTRAL EUROPE (PART TWO)	SPAIN (PART THREE)	MEDITER-RANEAN (PART THREE)	AMERICA (PART FOUR)
30		French retreat across the frontier complete		
		Spanish Regency removes Castaños and Giron. Reinstated later		
July				US–Creek Indian War begins
1	Napoleon receives news of Vitoria. Appoints Soult as his Lieutenant in Spain (XV.iii)			
	Truce and Congress of Prague continue			
3		RN blockade of St Sebastian begins		
4			SUCHET hears of Vitoria and ABANDONS VALENCIA (XVIII.iv)	
6				Dearborn relieved of command
7		Allied siege train landed at Passages		
9			Bentinck occupies Valencia	
25		SOULT ATTACKS THROUGH THE PYRENEES. Battles of Maya and Roncesvalles (XVI.i)		
		First Allied storming of St Sebastian repulsed		
26	Napoleon at Mainz (– 1 Aug.)		Bentinck marches on Tarragona	

July to August	CENTRAL EUROPE (PART TWO)	SPAIN (PART THREE)	MEDITER-RANEAN (PART THREE)	AMERICA (PART FOUR)
28–30		BATTLE OF SORAUREN (XVI.iii)		Proctor lifts second siege of Ft Meigs
August				
1	Napoleon receives news of Maya, Roncesvalles and St Sebastian	Soult retreats to the frontier pursued by the Allies		
2		Battle of Echalar. (XVI.iv) FRENCH BACK ACROSS THE FRONTIER		Proctor repulsed from Fort Stephenson (XXII.ii)
7	End of the Congress of Prague. Austria accedes to the coalition and the Allied armies begin to march (IX.i)			
12	Treaty of Teplitz			
14			Suchet's counter move in Catalonia	
17	HOSTILITIES RESUME			
18	Napoleon at Görlitz			
20				Wilkinson arrives at Sackett's Harbor for autumn Montreal campaign
22	Allies advance on Dresden (IX.i)			
23	Battle of Grossbeeren			
25		Bombardment of San Sebastian restarts		
26	BATTLE OF DRESDEN (IX.iii,iv)			
	Battle of the Katzbach			

August to October	CENTRAL EUROPE (PART TWO)	SPAIN (PART THREE)	MEDITER-RANEAN (PART THREE)	AMERICA (PART FOUR)
27	Dresden: 2nd day			
28	Allied withdrawal into Bohemia			
29	Allied withdrawal			
30	Battle of Kulm		Bentinck reaches Tarragona (XVIII.vii)	Fort Mims Massacre by the Creeks
31		Assault on SAN SEBASTIAN. Town captured and sacked (XVII.i) Battle of San Marcial (XVII.ii)		
September				
6	BATTLE OF DENNEWITZ (X.i)			
9		Citadel of San Sebastian surrenders		
10				US NAVAL VICTORY ON LAKE ERIE
13		Wellington meets Adm. Martin	Combat of Ordal (XVI.vii)	
20				Wade Hampton advances to Odelltown
22				Proctor retreats from the Detroit frontier
27			Monzon besieged	US troops occupy Amherstburg
October				
3	Blücher crosses the Elbe at Wartenburg			
5				US VICTORY AT MORAVIANTOWN. DEATH OF TECUMSEH (XXI.iii)

October to November	CENTRAL EUROPE (PART TWO)	SPAIN (PART THREE)	MEDITER-RANEAN (PART THREE)	AMERICA (PART FOUR)
7		ALLIES CROSS THE BIDASSOA INTO FRANCE. COMBAT OF HENDAYE (XVII.iii)		
14	Action of Liebert-wolkwitz: Leipzig (XI) Bavaria declares war v. Napoleon			Harrison retreats to Detroit
16	BATTLE OF LEIPZIG (XI.ii)			
17	Leipzig: 2nd day			Harrison relieved of command Wilkinson begins advance on Montreal
18	Leipzig: 3rd day			
19	Fall of Leipzig. FRENCH RETREAT towards the Rhine			
25				Allied victory at Châteauguay (XXIII.i)
28	Napoleon keeps Polish officers loyal			
29	Allied conference at Meiningen			
30	Battle of Hanau (XI.v)			
31	Napoleon reaches Frankfurt-Main	Pamplona surrenders to the Allies		
November			Suchet made Governor of Catalonia	
2	Napoleon reaches Mainz			
4				Castlereagh agrees to meet US for negotiations (XXIV.)
6				

November to December	CENTRAL EUROPE (PART TWO)	SPAIN (PART THREE)	MEDITER-RANEAN (PART THREE)	AMERICA (PART FOUR)
8	Allied cavalry enters Holland			
9	Allied initial moves to invade France, halted by Frederick William. Preparation of the Allied manifesto to the French people.			Jackson defeats the Creeks at Talledega, Alabama. RN blockade takes in Long Island Sound.
10	NAPOLEON BACK IN PARIS	Battle of the Nivelle (XIX)		
11	Dresden surrenders to the Allies			ALLIED VICTORY AT CRYSLER'S FARM (XXIII.ii)
December				
9		Battle and crossing of the Nive (XIX)		
10		Nive: 2nd day		US troops burn Newark and retreat from the Niagara frontier
11		Napoleon releases Ferdinand VII. Treaty of Valençay, later repudiated by the *Cortes* (XIX)		
13		Battle of St Pierre-d'Irrube		
18				ALLIES CAPTURE FORT NIAGARA (XXII.v)
21	ALLIES ATTACK ACROSS THE RHINE (XII)			
28	Castlereagh arrives at Allied HQ			
30	Danzig surrenders to the Allies			ALLIES attack across the Niagara, BURN Black Rock and BUFFALO (XXII.v)

Bibliography and List of Abbreviations used in Endnotes

ℰⱷⱺᏔ

Archives	*Archives de la Ministère des Affaires étrangères* (Paris).
Aubert	Le Chambellan Aubert *Mémoires sur les Événements qui se Rapportent a la Réoccupation de Hambourg par les Français* (Paris, 1825).
Bardenfleth	Lieutenant Colonel Charles de Bardenfleth *Mémoire à l'Armée Danoise et au 13ème Corps Français 1813* (Paris, 1825).
Beardsley	E.M. Beardsley *Napoleon: The Fall* (London, 1918).
Berger	Thomas R. Berger *A Long and Terrible Shadow. White Values, Native Rights in the Americas 1492–1992* (Washington, 1991).
von Berhardi	Felix Theodor von Berhardi *Denkwürdigkeiten aus dem Leben des Kaiserlichtes russiches Generals von der Infanterie Carl Friederich Grafen Toll* (4 vols, Leipzig, 1856–58).
di Borgo	Pozzo di Borgo *Correspondance Diplomatique* (2 vols, Paris, 1890).
Bragge	W. Bragge ed. A.C. Cassels *Peninsular Portraits: Letters of Captain William Bragge* (London, 1963).
Breakwell and Spacie	Glynis Breakwell and Keith Spacie 'Pressures Facing Commanders'. *Strategic and Combat Studies Institute Occasional Paper Number 29,* 1997.
Brialmont & Gleig	M. Brialmont and G.R. Gleig *History of the Life*

	of Arthur, Duke of Wellington (2 vols, London, 1858)
Brinton	Crane Brinton in *Makers of Modern Strategy: Military Thought from Machiavelli to Hitler,* ed. E.M. Earle, G.A. Craig and F. Gilbert (Princeton, 1943).
Broers	Michael Broers *Europe Under Napoleon 1799–1815* (New York, 1996).
Browne	*The Napoleonic War Journal of Captain Thomas Henry Browne 1807–1816* ed. R.N. Buckley (Army Records Society, 1987).
Browning	Oscar Browning *The Fall of Napoleon* (London, 1907).
Bryant	Arthur Bryant *The Age of Elegance 1812–1822* (London, 1950 repr. 1975).
Bulletins	*Bulletins de la Grande Armée* (ed. Alexandre Goujon, 2 vols, Paris, 1822).
Byrd and Dunn	Melanie Byrd and John Dunn 'A Document on Napoleon and his Polish Allies in 1813', *Journal of Slavic Military Studies,* Vol 10, no. 1 (March 1997) pp.196–199.
von Caemmerer	General R. von Caemmerer *Die Befreiungskriege 1813–1815* (Berlin, 1866).
Caffrey	Kate Caffrey *The Lion and the Union. The Anglo-American War 1812–1815* (London, 1977).
Cameron-Mowat	I. Cameron Mowat Staff College Commandant's Research Papers (Unpublished, 1993).
Cary	A.D.L. Cary and Stouppe McCance *Regimental Records of The Royal Welch Fusiliers, Vol. I, 1689–1816* (London, 1921).
Caulaincourt	General A.A.L. de Caulaincourt *Mémoires du Général de Caulaincourt, Duc de Vincenza* (3 vols, English pocket edition, London, 1950).
Chandler	David Chandler *The Campaigns of Napoleon* (London, 1966).
Chandler *Marshals*	David Chandler *Napoleon's Marshals* (London, 1987 repr. 1998).
Chandler *DNW*	David Chandler *Dictionary of the Napoleonic Wars* (London, 1979).

Chandler *Essays*	David Chandler *On the Napoleonic Wars. Collected Essays* (London, 1994).
Charras	Lieutenant Colonel Charras *Histoire de la Guerre de 1813 en Allemagne* (Leipzig, 1866).
Clausewitz	Carl-Maria von Clausewitz *On War* (Ed. and tr. Michael Howard and Peter Paret, Princeton, 1989).
Coles	Harry L. Coles *The War of 1812* (Chicago, 1965).
Colville	John Colville (ed.) *The Portrait of a General* (London, 1980).
Command	Martin Blumenson and James L Stokesbury *Masters of the Art of Command* (New York, 1975).
Connelly	Owen Connelly *Napoleon's Satellite Kingdoms* (London, 1965).
Correspondance	*Correspondance de Napoleon Ier, Publiée par Ordre de l'Empereur Napoleon III*, Volumes xxv and xxvi (Paris, 1870).
Costa de Serda	E. Costa de Serda *Opérations des Troupes Allemandes en Espagne de 1808 à 1813* (Paris, 1874).
Crackell	Theodore J Crackell 'The Battle of Queenston Heights, 13 October 1812' in *America's First Battles, 1776–1965*, ed. Charles E. Heller and William A. Stofft (Kansas, 1986).
Craig	Gordon A Craig 'Command and Staff Problems in the Austrian Army, 1740–1866' in *The Theory and Practice of War*, ed. Michael Howard (London, 1965).
Craig's *Strategy*	Gordon A. Craig 'Delbrück: The Military Historian' in *Makers of Modern Strategy* (Princeton, 1943).
Cruikshank	E.A. Cruikshank 'From Isle aux Noix to Châteauguay. A Study of Military Operations on the Frontier of Lower Canada in 1812 and 1813', *Transactions of the Royal Society of Canada*, Vol viii, no. 3 (June 1941).
Danilewski	Lieutenant General Mikhailovski-Danilewski *Military Operations of the Emperor Alexander against Napoleon from 1805* (St Petersburg, 1886).

Davis	Colonel John Davis *The History of the 2nd Queen's Royal Regiment, Vol. iv, 1800–1837* (London, 1902).
Delbrück	Hans Delbrück *Geschichte der Kriegskunst, Vol. iv* (new ed. Berlin, 1962).
Dispatches	J. Gurwood, ed. *The Dispatches of the Field Marshal the Duke of Wellington* (12 vols, London, 1834–39).
Drage	J.W. Drage Staff College Commandant's Research Paper (Unpublished, 1993).
Duane	W. Duane *Hand Book for Infantry* (5th edn, Philadelphia, 1814).
Dunnigan	James F. Dunnigan *Leipzig* (Simultaneous Publications Wargame, 2nd edn, 1971).
Ellis	Geoffrey Ellis *The Napoleonic Empire* (London, 1990).
Elting	Colonel John R. Elting *Swords Around the Throne: Napoleon's Grande Armée* (New York, 1989)
Emsley	C. Emsley *The Longman Companion to Napoleonic Europe* (London, 1993).
Esdaile	C.J. Esdaile *The Duke of Wellington and the Command of the Spanish Army 1812–14* (London, 1990).
Fain	Le Baron Fain *Manuscript de 1813* (2 vols, Paris, 1825).
Fay	H.A. Fay *Battles of the War of 1812* (New York, 1817).
Forester	C.S. Forester *The Naval War of 1812* (London, 1957).
Fortescue	Sir J.W. Fortescue *History of the British Army* (13 vols, London, 1899–1930).
Foy	Girod de l'Ain, ed. *Vie Militaire du Général Foy* (Paris, 1900).
Foy's History	Maximilien Foy *History of the Peninsula War, Vol ii* (English edn, London, 1827).
Fregosi	Paul Fregosi *Dreams of Empire. Napoleon and the First World War 1792–1815* (London, 1978).
Freytag	Freiherr von Freytag-Loringhoven *Kriegslehren*

nach Clausewitz aus dem Feldzügen 1813 und 1814 (Berlin, 1908).

Friederich — Rudolf Friederich *Die Befreiungskriege 1813–1815, Vol. ii* (Berlin, 1912).

Friederich *Geschichte* — Rudolf Friederich *Geschichte des Herbstfeldzuges 1813, Vol. ii* (Berlin, 1904)

Fuller — J.F.C. Fuller *Decisive Battles of the Western World, Vol. ii* (London, 1956).

Glover — Michael Glover *Wellington's Peninsular Victories* (London, 1963).

Gregory — Desmond Gregory *Sicily: The Insecure Base. A History of the British Occupation of Sicily 1806–1815* (Farleigh Dickinson UP USA, 1988).

Griffith — Paddy Griffith, ed. *Wellington Commander. The Iron Duke's Generalship* (Chichester, 1985).

Hall — Christopher D. Hall *British Strategy in the Napoleonic Wars* (Manchester UP, 1992).

Hall's *Royal Navy* — Christopher D. Hall 'The Royal Navy and the Peninsular War', *The Mariner's Mirror*, vol. 79 no. 4 (November 1993) pp.403–18.

Hamilton — Sir R.V. Hamilton *Letters and Papers of Admiral of the Fleet Sir T. Byam Martin* (Navy Records Society, 1898)

Hansard — Hansard *Parliamentary Debates, Vols vi–xii* (London, 1805–1814).

Harman *Beaver Dams* — Arthur Harman 'The Battle of Beaver Dams, 24th June 1813', *Miniature Wargames nos. 175 and 176* (December 1997 and January 1998) pp.32–5 and 39; pp.32–5 and 40–3.

Harman *Catalonia* — Arthur Harman 'Lord William Bentinck's Campaign in Catalonia 1813', *Miniature Wargames no. 74* (July 1989) p.22–7.

Harman *Niagara* — Arthur Harman 'Bayonet the Whole! The Storm of Fort Niagara, 18th/19th December 1813', *Miniature Wargames no. 137* (October 1994) pp.22–7.

Harman *Raisin River* — Arthur Harman 'Remember the Raisin! The Engagements at Frenchtown, 18th and 22nd January 1813', *Miniature Wargames no. 139* (December 1994) pp.22–5.

Harman *Roncesvalles*   Arthur Harman 'Bayonet Away! The Combats of Roncesvalles, 25th July 1813', *Miniature Wargames, no. 150* (November 1995) pp.20–7.

Harman *San Marcial*   Arthur Harman 'You May As Well It for Yourselves', San Marcial, 31st August 1813', *Miniature Wargames, nos. 145 and 146* (June and July 1995) pp. 46–53; pp. 27–31.

Harman *Stoney Creek*   Arthur Harman 'Where is the Line? Where is the Line? Stoney Creek, 6th June 1813', *Miniature Wargames, no. 149* (October 1995) pp. 27–43.

Haycock   F.W.O. Haycock *Napoleon's European Campaigns 1796–1815* (London, 1910).

Hayman   Sir Peter Hayman *Soult – Napoleon's Maligned Marshal* (Arms & Armour, 1989)

Henderson   E.F. Henderson *Blücher and the Uprising of Prussia against Napoleon, 1806 – 1815* (London, 1911).

Henegan   *Seven Years Campaigning in the Peninsula and the Netherlands from 1808 to 1815* (London, 1846).

Herrold   J. Christopher Herold *The Age of Napoleon* (London, 1970).

Hitsman   J.M. Hitsman *The Incredible War of 1812* (Toronto, 1965, new edn 2000).

von Holleben   A. von Holleben, *Geschichte des Fruhjarsfeldzüges 1813 und sein Vorgeschichte* (Berlin, 1813).

Holzhausen   Paul Holzhausen *Die Deutschen in Russland 1812* (Berlin, 1912).

James   Walter H. James *The Vitoria Campaign* (London, 1899).

Janson   Generalleutnant von Janson *Geschichte des Feldzüges 1814 in Frankreich* (Berlin, 1903–5).

Jedlika   Ludwig Jedlika 'Erzherzog Karl, der Sieger von Aspern', in *Gestalter der Geschiche Österreichs* ed. Hugo Hantsch (Vienna, 1962).

Jomini   Baron Jomini *Campagnes de 1812–1814* (2 vols, Paris, 1886).

Josselson   Michael and Diana Josselson *The Commander: A Life of Barclay de Tolly* (OUP, 1980).

Jourdan   Marshal Jourdan *Mémoires Militaires* (Paris, 1899).

Journal	A. Brett-James, ed. *General Wilson's Journal 1812–1814* (London, 1964).
Kerchnawe	Hugo Kerchnawe *Feldmarschall Karl Fürst zu Schwarzenberg* (Vienna, 1913).
Kissinger	Henry A. Kissinger *A World Restored* (New York, 1964).
Kraehe	Enno E. Kraehe *Metternich's German Policy: I. The Contest with Napoleon, 1799–1814* (Princeton, 1963).
Lanctôt	G. Lanctôt *L'Administration de la Nouvelle-France* (Paris, 1929).
Lanctôt's *Quebec*	G. Lanctôt 'Le Quebec et les Colonies Américaines 1760–1820' in *Les Canadiens Français et leurs Voisins du Sud* (Montreal, 1941).
Lanrezac	C.C.M. Lanrezac *Mémoires – La Manoeuvre de Lützen* (Paris, 1904).
Larpent	G. Larpent, ed. *Private Journal of Judge Advocate Larpent* (3rd edn, London, 1854).
Lefebvre	Georges Lefebvre, tr. J.R. Anderson *Napoleon from Tilsit to Waterloo* (London, 1969).
Lehmann	Max Lehmann, *Scharnhorst* (Leipzig, 1886).
Lettres	*Lettres de Napoleon non Insérées dans les Correspondances, Aug.–Sep.–Oct. 1813* (Paris, 1907).
Liddell Hart	B.H. Liddell Hart *The Ghost of Napoleon* (London, 1933).
Lloyd	Alan Lloyd *The Scorching of Washington. The War of 1812* (Vancouver, 1974).
Lobanov	A.A. Lobanov-Rostovsky *Russia and Europe, 1789–1825* (Durham NC, USA, 1947).
Longford	Elizabeth Longford, *Wellington. The Years of the Sword* (London, 1969).
Lorenz	R. Lorenz 'Erzherzog Karl als Denker' in *Das Bild des Krieges im Deutschen Denken Vol. I* ed. August Faust (Berlin, 1941).
Luttwak	Edward N. Luttwak *Strategy. The Logic of War and Peace* (Cambridge, Massachusetts, 1992).
McDonald	Felix McDonald 'Exeunt Omnes. Sir John Murray at Tarragona, 1813', *Miniature Wargames no. 122* (July 1993) pp.10–15, 43–5.
Markham	Felix Markham *Napoleon* (London, 1963).

Marmont	Marshal A.F.L.V. Marmont *Mémoires* (Paris, 1857).
Martens	M. Martens *Receuil des Traités Conclus par la Russie* (4 vols, Paris, 1864).
Maude	Colonel F.N. Maude *The Leipzig Campaign 1813* (London, 1908).
Metternich	Prince C.W.L. Metternich-Winneburg *Mémoires* (French edn, Paris, 1886).
Mil Occurrences	William James *Military Occurrences of the Late War between Great Britain and the United States of America* (2 vols, London, 1818).
Miller	J.R. Miller *Skyscrapers Touch the Heavens* (Toronto, 1989).
Miot de Melito	A.F. Comte Miot de Melito, ed. General Hector Fleischmann *Mémoires du Comte Miot de Molito* (2 vols, New York, 1858).
Mollison	K. Mollison Staff College Commandant's Research Paper (Unpublished, 1993).
Moniteur	*Le Moniteur Universel* (Paris, 1813).
Montholon	C.J.F.T. de Montholon *Mémoires de Napoleon* (Paris, 1823).
Mowat	R.B. Mowat *The Diplomacy of Napoleon* (London, 1924).
Müffling	Friedrich Carl Ferdinand Freiherr von Müffling *Aus Meinem Leben* (Berlin, 1851).
Muir	Rory Muir *Britain and the Defeat of Napoleon 1807–1815* (London, 1996).
Nafziger	George Nafziger *Napoleon's Spring Campaign of 1813* (Chicago, 1993).
Nafziger's *Dresden*	George Nafziger *Napoleon at Dresden – the Battle of 1813* (Chicago, 1995).
Nafziger *et al.*	George Nafziger, M.T. Wesolowski, and T. Devoe *Poles and Saxons of the Napoleonic Wars* (Chicago, 1995).
Napier	W.F.P. Napier *History of the War in the Peninsula* (6 vols, London, 1862 [orig. 1834–40]).
Napoleonic Wars	David Chandler *On the Napoleonic Wars* (London, 1994, in paperback 1999).
Niagara Frontier	E.A. Cruikshank, ed. *The Documentary History of*

	the Campaigns upon the Niagara Frontier 1813 (Welland, Ontario, 1902).
Nicolson	Harold Nicolson *The Congress of Vienna 1812–1817: A Study in Allied Unity* (London, 1946).
D'Odeleben	le Baron E. d'Odeleben, ed. M.A. de Vitry *Relation Circonstanciée de la Campagne de 1813 en Saxe* (Paris, 1817).
Oman	Sir Charles Oman *A History of the Peninsular War* (7 vols, Oxford, 1902–30).
Oncken	W. Oncken *Österreich und Preussen im Befreiungskriege 1813* (2 vols, Berlin, 1876–79).
Palmer	Alan Palmer *Metternich. Councillor of Europe* (London, 1972).
Parkinson	Roger Parkinson *Clausewitz* (London, 1970).
Paret	Peter Paret *Yorck and the Era of Prussian Military Reform 1807–1815* (Princeton, NJ, 1966).
Pasquier	E.D. le Duc de Pasquier *Histoire de Mon Temps* (2 vols, Paris, 1893).
Petre	F. Lorraine Petre *Napoleon's Last Campaign in Germany 1813* (London and New York, 1974).
Pflugk-Hartung	J.A.C. Pflugk-Hartung *Das Befreiungsjahr, 1813* (Berlin, 1893).
Plotho	Charles de Plotho, tr. M. Philippe Himly *Relation de la Bataille de Leipzig* (Paris, 1840). The original is in German, Himly's translation is in French.
Précis	Baron Jomini *Précis de l'Art de la Guerre* (St Petersburg, 1837).
von Prokesch	A. von Prokesch-Ostens *Denkwürdigkeiten aus dem Leben des Feldmarschalls Fürst zu Schwarzenberg* (Vienna, 1871).
Regele	Oskar Regele *Feldmarschall Radetsky, Leben, Leistung, Erbe* (Vienna, 1957).
Ritter	Gerhard Ritter *Staatskunst und Kriegshandwerk, Vol. iii* (Munich, 1954).
Robinson	Major-General C.W. Robinson CB *Canada and Canadian Defence* (London, 1910).
Rosselli	John Rosselli *Lord William Bentinck and the British Occupation of Sicily 1811–1814* (CUP, 1956).
Rössler	Helmuth Rössler *Österreichs Kampf um Deutschlands Befreiung* (Hamburg, 1940).

Rousset	Camille Rousset *Recollections of Marshal Macdonald, Duke of Tarentum* (London, 1893).
St Cyr	Marshal G. St Cyr *Mémoires* (Paris, 1834).
Scott	Franklin D. Scott *Bernadotte and the Fall of Napoleon* (Cambridge, Mass, USA, 1935).
Seeley	J.R. Seeley *The Life and Times of Stein* (3 vols, Cambridge, 1878).
Shanahan	William O. Shanahan *Prussian Military Reforms 1786–1813* (New York, 1945).
Simmons	G. Simmons, ed. W. Verner *A British Rifleman* (London, 1899).
Smith	ed. G.C. Moore-Smith *The Autobiography of Sir Harry Smith* (London, 1901).
Sorel	A. Sorel *L'Europe et la Révolution Française, vol. viii* (Paris, 1904).
Soult	Marshal Soult, Duc de Dalmatie *Mémoires: Espagne et Portugal* (Paris, 1955).
Stanley	George F.G. Stanley *The War of 1812. Land Operations* (Toronto, 1983).
Suchet	Marshal Suchet *Memoirs of the War in Spain 1808–1814* (English edn, London, 1829).
Sup Dispatches	2nd Duke of Wellington, ed. *Supplementary Dispatches and Memoranda of the Duke of Wellington* (14 vols, London, 1858–72).
Teffeteller	Gordon L. Teffeteller *The Surpriser: The Life of Rowland, Lord Hill* (Associated UP, 1983).
Vidal de la Blanche	*L'Évacuation de l'Espagne et l'Invasion dans le Midi* (2 vols, Paris, 1914).
Wade	Mason Wade *The French Canadians 1760–1945* (London, 1955).
Ward	S.G.P. Ward *Wellington* (London, 1963).
Webster	C.K. Webster *The Foreign Policy of Castlereagh, 1812–1815* (London, 1931).
West Point	Albert Sidney Britt III *Wars of Napoleon* (West Point and Wayne, New Jersey, USA, 1985).
Wood	William Wood, ed. *Select British Documents of the Canadian War of 1812, Vol. ii* (Toronto, 1920).
Woolf	Stuart Woolf *Napoleon's Integration of Europe* (London, 1991).

INDEX OF PERSONS

[For places and events the reader should use the table of contents and the chronology of 1813. Page references in bold type refer to illustrations.]